A
LITERARY
HISTORY
OF
SPAIN

A LITERARY HISTORY OF SPAIN

General Editor: R. O. JONES
Cervantes Professor of Spanish, King's College, University of London

THE MIDDLE AGES
by A. D. DEYERMOND
Professor of Spanish, Westfield College, University of London

THE GOLDEN AGE: PROSE AND POETRY
by R. O. JONES

THE GOLDEN AGE: DRAMA
by EDWARD M. WILSON
Professor of Spanish, University of Cambridge
and DUNCAN MOIR
Lecturer in Spanish, University of Southampton

THE EIGHTEENTH CENTURY
by NIGEL GLENDINNING
Professor of Spanish, Trinity College, University of Dublin

THE NINETEENTH CENTURY
by DONALD L. SHAW
Senior Lecturer in Hispanic Studies, University of Edinburgh

THE TWENTIETH CENTURY
by G. G. BROWN
Lecturer in Spanish, Queen Mary College, University of London

SPANISH AMERICAN LITERATURE
SINCE INDEPENDENCE
by JEAN FRANCO
Professor of Latin American Literature, University of Essex

CATALAN LITERATURE
by ARTHUR TERRY
Professor of Spanish, The Queen's University, Belfast

A LITERARY HISTORY OF SPAIN

THE MIDDLE AGES

A LITERARY
HISTORY OF SPAIN

THE MIDDLE AGES

A. D. DEYERMOND

Professor of Spanish, Westfield College,
University of London

LONDON · ERNEST BENN LIMITED

NEW YORK · BARNES & NOBLE INC

First published 1971 by Ernest Benn Limited
Bouverie House · Fleet Street · London · EC4A 2DL
and Barnes & Noble Inc. · 105 Fifth Avenue · New York 10003

Distributed in Canada by
The General Publishing Company Limited · Toronto

© A. D. Deyermond 1971

Printed in Great Britain

ISBN 0 510-32251-4

ISBN 0-389-04183 (U.S.A.)

Paperback 0 510-32252-2

Paperback 0-389-04184-X (U.S.A.)

To the Memory of
GEORGE DEYERMOND

CONTENTS

xi

FOREWORD BY THE GENERAL EDITOR

SPANISH, the language of what was in its day the greatest of European powers, became the common tongue of the most far-flung Empire the world had until then seen. Today, in number of speakers, Spanish is one of the world's major languages. The literature written in Spanish is correspondingly rich. The earliest European lyrics in a post-classical vernacular that we know of (if we except Welsh and Irish) were written in Spain; the modern novel was born there; there too was written some of the greatest European poetry and drama; and some of the most interesting works of our time are being written in Spanish.

Nevertheless, this new history may require some explanation and even justification. Our justification is that a new and up-to-date English-language history seemed called for to serve the increasing interest now being taken in Spanish. There have been other English-language histories in the past, some of them very good, but none on this scale.

Every history is a compromise between aims difficult or even impossible to reconcile. This one is no exception. While imaginative literature is our main concern, we have tried to relate that literature to the society in and for which it was written, but without subordinating criticism to amateur sociology. Since not everything could be given equal attention (even if it were desirable to do so) we have concentrated on those writers and works of manifestly outstanding artistic importance to us their modern readers, with the inevitable consequence that many interesting minor writers are reduced to names and dates, and the even lesser are often not mentioned at all. Though we have tried also to provide a usable work of general reference, we offer the history primarily as a guide to the understanding and appreciation of what we consider of greatest value in the literatures of Spain and Spanish America.

Beyond a necessary minimum, no attempt has been made to arrive at uniform criteria; the history displays therefore the variety of approach and opinion that is to be found in a good university department of literature, a variety which we hope will prove stimulating. Each section takes account of the accepted works of scholarship in its field, but we do not offer our history as a grey consensus of received opinion; each contributor has imposed his own interpretation to the extent that this could be supported with solid scholarship and argument.

Though the literature of Spanish America is not to be regarded simply as an offshoot of the literature of Spain, it seemed natural to link the two in our history since Spanish civilisation has left an indelible stamp on the Americas. Since Catalonia has been so long a part of Spain it seemed equally justified to include Catalan literature, an important influence on Spanish literature at certain times, and a highly interesting literature in its own right.

The bibliographies are not meant to be exhaustive. They are intended only as a guide to further reading. For more exhaustive inquiry recourse should be had to general bibliographies such as that by J. Simón Díaz.

R.O.J.

PREFACE

THE COMMON AIMS of this series are set out in the Editor's Foreword, but each period of literature imposes its own requirements, and some additional words of explanation for the present volume may be helpful. The works of greatest literary merit in the period have been given the greatest amount of space, but historical importance has also been a criterion. The earliest vernacular prose-works, for example, have little claim to attention on their aesthetic merits, but if the development of Spanish prose is to be understood, these books, written before Alfonso X came to the throne, must be described and evaluated. At the end of the Middle Ages, an arbitrary line has to be drawn: the plays of Juan del Encina and Lucas Fernández, the printed version of *Amadís de Gaula*, and the prose-works of the early humanists belong both to medieval and to Golden Age literature, and to avoid repetition they are treated not here but in the next volumes.

Some parts of this volume are based on existing or future publications of my own. I have not thought it necessary to call attention to such cases, nor have I made explicit acknowledgment when incorporating the results of published research by other scholars, though their work is, of course, cited in notes or in the Bibliography at the appropriate point. On some occasions, however, I have made use of forthcoming studies which the authors have kindly allowed me to consult, and I have drawn attention to all these cases.

In accordance with the general practice of this series, the Bibliography contains editions of the main texts discussed (where more than one edition is listed, an asterisk indicates the one from which quotations are taken), and the most important books on the subject; articles and other books are cited at the ends of chapters in the notes. Bibliography and notes should therefore be consulted as a single unit. Recent works (including those whose publication is imminent as this volume goes to press) play the largest part, since they are generally not to be found in other works of reference. Utility to the reader has taken precedence over theoretical consistency: translations of medieval works into English or modern Spanish are generally excluded, but I have cited a few which contain valuable critical matter; if an article in a learned journal has been reprinted in a book, I have cited the version most likely to be accessible to readers; studies written in English or Spanish have, where there is a choice, been preferred to those in other languages, those in any Romance tongue have been cited where necessary, but I have assumed—perhaps unreasonably—that studies in German would present severe linguistic difficulties to most readers. The abbreviations used are generally those of *The Year's Work in Modern Language Studies*, whose critical bibliography is an indispensable annual guide to research in this field.

In the quotations, accents and punctuation follow modern usage (specialists will notice that where the accentuation is in dispute I have not committed myself). The use of *u* and *v*, *i* and *j*, chaotic in medieval Spanish orthography, has been regularised, but there has been no other attempt to modernise the spelling.

I have been greatly helped by a number of scholars who have read and commented on drafts of this volume, thereby saving me from many errors, omissions and obscurities. Mrs Margaret Chaplin, Mr A. J. Foreman, Dr J. Gibbs, Dr R. Hitchcock, and Dr Dorothy S. Severin read one or more chapters; Professor I. D. L. Michael, Mr J. C. Musgrave, and Dr R. M. Walker read the whole book. I am even more deeply indebted to the editor of the series, Professor R. O. Jones, for his meticulous reading of an excessively long penultimate version and his invaluable suggestions for compression. Miss Kate Midgley and Mrs Brenda Stroud transformed my original and mangled typescript into a neat version for the printers. I am most grateful for all this assistance.

Westfield College, London   A.D.D.
February 1971

LIST OF ABBREVIATIONS

ACLLS	*Annali del Corso di Lingue e Letterature Straniere* (Bari)
AEM	*Anuario de Estudios Medievales*
AFA	*Archivo de Filología Aragonesa*
AHDE	*Anuario de Historia del Derecho Español*
AION, Sez. Rom.	*Annali dell'Istituto Universitario Orientale di Napoli, Sezione Romanza*
Al-An	*Al-Andalus*
Arch	*Archivum*
BAE	Biblioteca de Autores Españoles
BBMP	*Boletín de la Biblioteca Menéndez y Pelayo*
BF	*Boletim de Filologia*
BFC	*Boletín de Filología* (Chile)
BFE	*Boletín de Filología Española*
BFPLUL	Bibliothèque de la Faculté de Philosophie et Lettres de l'Université de Liège
BH	*Bulletin Hispanique*
BHS	*Bulletin of Hispanic Studies*
BJR	*Bulletin of the John Rylands Library*
BRABLB	*Boletín de la Real Academia de Buenas Letras de Barcelona*
BRAE	*Boletín de la Real Academia Española*
BRAH	*Boletín de la Real Academia de la Historia*
BRH	Biblioteca Románica Hispánica (Gredos)
Brot	*Brotéria*
BSS	*Bulletin of Spanish Studies*
CC	Clásicos Castellanos
CCMe	*Cahiers de Civilisation Médiévale*
CH	Clásicos Hispánicos
CHE	*Cuadernos de Historia de España*
CHM	*Cahiers d'Histoire Mondiale*
CL	*Comparative Literature*
CN	*Cultura Neolatina*
CODOIN	Colección de Documentos Inéditos para la Historia de España
ELH	*English Literary History*
ELu	*Estudios Lulianos*

EMP	*Estudios dedicados a Menéndez Pidal* (Madrid)
EMRLL	Elliott Monographs in the Romance Languages and Literatures
EstE	*Estudios Escénicos*
Fi	*Filología*
FiR	*Filologia Romanza*
FMLS	*Forum for Modern Language Studies*
FS	*French Studies*
GAKS	*Gesammelte Aufsätze zur Kulturgeschichte Spaniens*
HBalt	*Hispania* (U.S.A.)
His	*Hispania* (Madrid)
HispI	*Hispanófila*
HR	*Hispanic Review*
HSCL	Harvard Studies in Comparative Literature
HumT	*Humanitas* (Tucumán)
IR	*Iberoromania*
ISt	*Italian Studies*
It	*Italica*
IUHS	Indiana University Humanities Series
JJS	*Journal of Jewish Studies*
JWCI	*Journal of the Warburg and Courtauld Institutes*
KFLQ	*Kentucky Foreign Language Quarterly*
KRQ	*Kentucky Romance Quarterly*
LR	*Les Lettres Romanes*
MA	*Le Moyen Age*
MAe	*Medium Aevum*
MH	*Medievalia et Humanistica*
MHRA	*Annual Bulletin of the Modern Humanities Research Association*
MLN	*Modern Language Notes*
MLR	*Modern Language Review*
MP	*Modern Philology*
MRo	*Marche Romane*
N	*Neophilologus*
NBAE	Nueva Biblioteca de Autores Españoles
NMi	*Neuphilologische Mitteilungen*
NMS	*Nottingham Medieval Studies*
NRFH	*Nueva Revista de Filología Hispánica*
Ocid	*Ocidente*
PBA	*Proceedings of the British Academy*
PMLA	*Publications of the Modern Language Association of America*
PQ	*Philological Quarterly*
PSA	*Papeles de Son Armadans*
QIA	*Quaderni Ibero-Americani*

R	*Romania*
RABM	*Revista de Archivos, Bibliotecas y Museos*
RBAM	*Revista de la Biblioteca, Archivo y Museo de Madrid*
RF	*Romanische Forschungen*
RFE	*Revista de Filología Española*
RFH	*Revista de Filología Hispánica*
RFL	*Revista da Faculdade de Letras* (Lisbon)
RH	*Revue Hispanique*
RHel	Romanica Helvetica
RHM	*Revista Hispánica Moderna*
RJ	*Romanistisches Jahrbuch*
RLC	*Revue de Littérature Comparée*
RLit	*Revista de Literatura*
RO	*Revista de Occidente*
RoN	*Romance Notes*
RPh	*Romance Philology*
RR	*Romanic Review*
RVF	*Revista Valenciana de Filología*
S	*Symposium*
SBE	Sociedad de Bibliófilos Españoles
Sc	*Scriptorium*
Sef	*Sefarad*
SM	*Studi Medievali*
SMV	*Studi Mediolatini e Volgari*
SN	*Studia Neophilologica*
SP	*Studies in Philology*
Sp	*Speculum*
TLS	*Times Literary Supplement*
UCPMP	University of California Publications in Modern Philology
UNCSRLL	University of North Carolina Studies in Romance Languages and Literatures
VR	*Vox Romanica*
YCGL	*Yearbook of Comparative and General Literature*
YRS	Yale Romanic Studies
ZRP	*Zeitschrift für Romanische Philologie*

Chapter 1

THE EARLIEST LYRIC AND ITS DESCENDANTS

I. THE BEGINNINGS OF SPAIN

THE MOST DISTANT ORIGINS OF SPANISH LITERATURE, like those of any other literature, are unknowable: they belong to the beginnings of human speech, of human emotions, and of social organisation. Yet the earliest surviving Spanish poem is less than a thousand years old, and the earliest prose-work less than eight hundred, and if we look for the causes that have produced a recognisably distinct *Spanish* literature, we shall find them all within the past two thousand years. The most important of these causes are three events in the life of the Roman Empire: first, the Roman conquest of the Iberian Peninsula, begun in the late third century B.C. and substantially completed by 19 B.C. (some mountainous areas, especially the Basque country, held out longer); secondly, the conversion of the Empire to Christianity; and thirdly, the breaking up of the Empire by the barbarian invasions. The first of these events meant that the peoples of the Peninsula spoke, on the whole, a form of Latin, though most men and women used a simplified popular form of the language; the second made the Latin-speaking peoples Christian. Thus by language and religion the Hispanic peoples were linked to their neighbours beyond the Pyrenees. The third event, however—the barbarian invasions—was the cause not of similarities but of differences: as the frontiers were breached, each part of the Empire was overrun by a different barbarian nation, communications and trade broke down, and the once united areas drifted inexorably apart in their speech, their culture, and their institutions. But the European similarities remained greater than the national differences, and among learned men, among poets and prosewriters, the sense of a common inheritance was strong.

The first of the Germanic tribes to invade the Peninsula—the Suevi, Alani, and Vandali in the early fifth century A.D.—came to plunder and destroy, but they were quickly followed by the Visigoths, who were, when they crossed the Pyrenees, already Latin-speaking and believers in a form of Christianity. For this reason the direct influence of the Visigoths on the language of Spain is small, and the influence

I

on literature very small indeed.[1] In this respect Spain contrasts sharply with France, since the Franks who conquered Gaul were still strongly Germanic in language, culture, and religion. The Visigoths swiftly established, from the mid-fifth century, a united Hispanic kingdom which possessed social, though not political, stability, and which provided an opportunity for cultural development. One of the leading literary figures of the Visigothic period was St Isidore of Seville (died 636), whose *Etymologiae* was to remain one of the most influential books in Europe for a thousand years. Isidore, like all his learned contemporaries in the West, wrote in a form of Classical Latin, but the Vulgar Latin spoken by the people was already evolving into early Spanish. It may well be that, even in Isidore's time, love-songs were composed in the common speech of the people, but conclusive evidence and extant texts are not found until the period of the Moorish occupation.

In the Arabian city of Mecca, in the year A.D. 610, Mohammed had a vision which led him to found Islam, the third great monotheistic religion of the Mediterranean world, a powerful rival to Judaism and Christianity. Within a hundred years, Islamic armies conquered North Africa, much of western Asia, and even part of Europe. The Visigothic kingdom of Spain was overthrown, and almost all of the Peninsula occupied, with astonishing speed: the invaders crossed the Straits of Gibraltar in 711, and by 718 the Peninsula was under well-established Islamic rule. Most of it was to remain so for three centuries, much for five, and some for nearly eight. The Moorish (predominantly Berber rather than Arab) occupiers developed a society that was militarily powerful, technologically advanced, culturally brilliant, bilingual, and tolerant. Not only did this society contain, in comparative harmony, Spanish-speaking Christian Ibero-Romano-Visigoths and Arabic-speaking Muslim Moors, but it also attracted large and prosperous Jewish communities. The aggressive proselytising nature of Islam was tempered in Spain by economic realism (Christians and Jews paid taxes from which Muslims were exempt) and by the extent to which the occupying Moors adapted to their new surroundings. In this atmosphere, Hispanic Jews were able to create the most flourishing centre of medieval Jewish civilisation. Thus, one of the culminating points of Judaic theological writing, *The Guide for the Perplexed*, was composed by a Hispanic Jew, Maimonides (1135-1204). This has justly been compared with the *Summa theologica* of St Thomas Aquinas, which it may have influenced.

While this brilliant and complex society developed in Moorish Spain, small Christian kingdoms arose in the north and, slowly and fitfully, began the Reconquest. In mountainous regions that were scarcely worth the effort of strict occupation by the Moors, Basques and Asturians organised themselves into raiding bands that grew into the armies of states able to maintain a precarious independence. Tradition tells of a battle of Covadonga which, in the year that the Moorish conquest was completed, began the Reconquest and founded the kingdom of Asturias. The reality was less clear-cut and less dramatic, but in the end no less effective: by the end of the eighth century there were independent kingdoms of Asturias and Navarre, and Charlemagne's campaigns had established Christian control over Catalonia, the 'Spanish March' of his empire. The Basque kingdom of Navarre maintained its separate existence until 1512, when it was incorporated into a united Spain; for a short time, just after A.D. 1000, it dominated the Christian north, but having established itself, it took little part in the Reconquest.

The kingdom of Asturias was a more important point of growth. As it expanded southwards, it became the kingdom of León, claiming all the time to be the rightful heir to Visigothic Spain, and carefully restoring, as far as it understood them, the political, legal, and ecclesiastical institutions of the Visigoths. This archaising but increasingly powerful kingdom controlled two areas that passed through nebulous autonomy into independence: Galicia to the west, and Castile to the east. These were alternately reunited with León by the conquests of able and ambitious monarchs, and separated again by the desire of monarchs to divide their territories among their heirs. The main political importance of Galicia was that, at the end of the eleventh century, a region on its southern frontier became the county, and within fifty years the kingdom, of Portugal. Castile's influence was more fundamental, partly because of her central position in the Christian north, but chiefly because of the vigour and the innovating zeal of the Castilians, which showed itself in law and language as well as politics and warfare. Castile, originally subservient to León, became an equal, and eventually a dominant, partner. Meanwhile, in the east of the Peninsula, a number of counties between Catalonia and Navarre coalesced into the kingdom of Aragon, and in due course Catalonia joined the kingdom, so that the Peninsula contained six Christian states: Portugal, Galicia, León, Castile, Navarre, and Aragon.

As the Reconquest advanced, the Christian kingdoms contained growing numbers of Moors, Jews, and Spaniards who were accustomed to Moorish rule. The multiracial nature of Moorish Spain thus came to characterise the northern kingdoms also, and particularly the three most active in the Reconquest, Portugal, Castile, and Aragon.

II. POPULAR SONG

The coexistence of Spaniard, Moor, and Jew has been claimed by Américo Castro as the decisive factor in the growth of Spanish culture, and Castro and others have tried to explain the special qualities of a number of medieval Spanish literary works in terms of this cultural mixture (*mudejarismo*).[2] Such claims are almost certainly exaggerated, but this coexistence, or *convivencia*, was undoubtedly responsible for the preservation of the earliest extant Spanish lyrics.

It is likely that almost all communities develop songs for various purposes, usually ritual ones, but when such communities are illiterate (as they are in the initial stages), songs can only be composed and transmitted orally. Even when some members of the community are literate, the songs are not written down unless there is some practical reason for doing so. Thus no direct evidence can be obtained of the early stages of Spanish song, and we have to rely on the comparative method; that is, on a study of primitive societies in other parts of the world, whose songs may give us valuable hints as to the nature of the earliest Spanish developments, now irrecoverably lost. Songs may well go back to the late Paleolithic period (30,000-15,000 B.C.), thus being of the same antiquity as the cave paintings, being normally preceded by dance (this point, as we shall see, may well be important for an understanding of the forms of Hispanic popular lyric). The earliest songs seem to be for ritual occasions such as hunting, fertility, or farewell, and are thought to have magical properties; love-songs are frequent only when a settled agricultural stage is reached.[3]

III. THE 'KHARJAS': NATURE AND ORIGIN

For a later stage, we now have direct evidence. The earliest surviving lyrics in Provençal date from *c.* 1100 (the poems of Guilhem IX, 1071-1126, duke of Aquitaine and count of Poitou). In Galician-Portuguese, the earliest poems that we possess were probably composed in the last decade of the twelfth century. For Castilian, the date is later still. It was long believed that all lyric poetry in the Romance languages derived from Provençal, but this theory was demolished by S. M. Stern's discovery in 1948 of short fragmentary poems in Mozarabic, the archaic dialect of Spanish spoken in the areas under Moorish rule.[4] That previous investigators had missed the significance of the material is hardly surprising: even when the earliest of these poems is transcribed from Hebrew into Roman characters, it is not easily recognisable as a Spanish poem:

> tnt'm'ry tnt 'm'ry   ḥbyb tnt 'm'ry
> 'nfrmyrwn wlywš gydš [?]   ydwln tn m'ly

It is only when we insert the vowels (normally omitted in Hebrew, as in Arabic, script) that all but two of the words become obviously Spanish:

> Tant' amare, tant' amare,
> ḥabib, tant' amare,

enfermiron welyos nidioš
e dolen tan male.[5]

The four lines just quoted come at the end of a panegyric addressed by Yosef the Scribe to two brothers; one of them died in 1042, and since the rules of Hebrew poetry at that time made it impossible to address a panegyric to the dead, it is clear that Yosef the Scribe's poem cannot be later than 1042. If the four lines in Spanish are not Yosef the Scribe's work but a popular fragment borrowed by him (the evidence for this is strong, as we shall see), then the four lines are unlikely to have been composed much after A.D. 1000, and they may well be older still.

The panegyric in which they occur is a *muwaššaḥa*, a Hispano-Arabic verse-form taken over by Hispano-Hebraic poets (the Hebrew poetry of medieval Spain draws its technical inspiration from Arabic). The *muwaššaḥa* usually consists of five stanzas, each made up of two parts: one with a rhyme of its own, and the other with a rhyme common to all the stanzas; this common rhyme may sometimes be found at the beginning of the poem also. Thus, a typical form would be: (AA) BBBAA CCCAA DDDAA EEEAA FFFAA. The *muwaššaḥa* is in Classical Arabic or Hebrew, except for the common-rhyme lines of the final stanza (these are known as the *kharja*), which are in Vulgar Arabic or in Spanish. Here, in other words, are to be found the Spanish poems or fragments whose existence and significance was discovered by Stern. Another verse-form, the *zajal*, is metrically very similar to the *muwaššaḥa*, the chief difference being that the *zajal* always begins with common-rhyme lines; there is also an important linguistic difference, since the Arabic *zajal* is always in Vulgar, not in Classical, Arabic, and although it incorporates isolated Spanish words (this was a feature of the Vulgar Arabic of Spain), it never has a Spanish *kharja*. These two forms differ radically from the standard form of Arabic poetry, the *qaṣīda*: whereas the *qaṣīda* has only one rhyme, is not divided into stanzas, and allows only full rhyme (consonants as well as vowels rhyming), the *zajal* and *muwaššaḥa* are multi-rhymed and stanzaic, and they tolerate assonance (vowels but not consonants rhyming). These two forms grew up in Spain, and attempts to find a convincing ancestry for them in Arabic poetry outside the Peninsula have been singularly unsuccessful. On the other hand, the features which distinguish them so sharply from the *qaṣīda* are shared with the popular lyrics of other parts of the Peninsula and much of Europe. There is thus a strong case for believing that the *zajal* and the *muwaššaḥa* represent the adoption into Arabic (and thence, with the *muwaššaḥa*, into Hebrew) of a widespread form of popular European verse.

This case is greatly strengthened by the testimony of Arabic literary historians, and by a consideration of the social background. We are told by two literary historians of the twelfth century that the *muwaššaḥa* was invented about A.D. 900 by one Muqaddam (or Muhammad), who took verses in the language of the people and built his poem upon them. The Arabic (and later the Hebrew) poet would thus start with the *kharja* and would use it as the metrical basis for his own *muwaššaḥa*. A number of *kharjas* are used by two poets, and nearly always in slightly different versions, which again suggests a borrowing from a popular tradition. Indeed, poets disagree about the meaning of one *kharja*:

> Vay-se meu corazón de mib,
> ¡Ya Rabb, si me tornarád!   (*Rabb*: Lord)
> ¡Tan mal me dóled li-l-ḥabib!   (*li*: for)
> Enfermo yed: ¿cuánd sanarád?   (*yed*: is)
> (Stern 9; GG appx. 9)

One of the Hebrew poets who uses this *kharja* takes the last line to refer to the girl's heart, while the other assumes that it refers to her lover.[6]

Almost all of the *kharjas* are woman's love-poetry: they express a girl's longing for her absent lover, her grief at his departure or his infidelity, or—less often—her joy in his presence. However, although the emotions expressed in the *kharjas* are those of women, no extant *muwaššaḥa* is a love-poem addressed by a woman to a man, and relatively few are heterosexual love-poems. The majority are panegyrics and other poems addressed to a patron, or are the expression of homosexual love. Thus the *kharja* becomes a kind of extended simile: the poet deprived of his patron's support is like a girl without her lover; and when this connection has been established in the transitional lines of the last stanza, the girl's song follows as an emotional climax to the poem. The weaker poets have an awkward transition to the *kharja*, but all accept that a girl's love-song is the appropriate ending for a *muwaššaḥa*.

Only very rarely does a poet compose his own *kharja* to fit the occasion of the poem, so that it comes almost as a shock to find, at the end of a *muwaššaḥa* by Yehuda Halewi celebrating the visit of a patron of Spain's Jewish communities, the appropriateness of:

> Des cand meu Cidiello vénid
> —¡tan bona l-bišara!—   (*bišara*: news)
> como rayo de sol éxid   (*éxid*: comes out)
> en Wad al-ḥaŷara.   (Guadalajara)
> (Stern 3; GG appx. 3)

The customary discrepancy in subject-matter between *muwaššaḥa* and *kharja* suggests strongly that the Hebrew and Arabic poets are drawing on an established tradition of popular song. Of course it is possible, once the practice of using popular poems or fragments in this way has become well-established, for a skilled poet to compose his own *kharja* in the popular style, and we can seldom decide whether or not this has been done in a particular case. Again, we cannot tell how much cultured poets have contributed to those reworkings of the Galician-Portuguese popular tradition that are known as *cantigas de amigo*. Yet in one way the difficulty is unimportant, since if a cultured poet is capable of writing in the traditional way, he is himself part of the tradition.

We are here confronted with the wider problem of what is meant by a popular tradition. The nineteenth-century Romantic belief that lyrics and epics were composed 'by the people' stands at one extreme; at the other is the theory that all supposedly popular poetry was composed by learned men. Certainty is impossible here, but the most satisfactory hypothesis is that, at an early stage, lyrical and narrative songs were composed by ordinary people who possessed a specialised talent; that, later, learned poets arose who composed a more sophisticated and elaborate poetry; that popular and cultured poetry influenced each other, with learned elements being incorporated into popular tradition, and popular techniques and narrative material being adopted by learned writers (we shall see some of the effects of this in Chapter 3); that some learned poets were simultaneously popular, in the sense that they were able to compose songs indistinguishable from any others in the popular tradition; and that once a song entered the popular tradition, from whatever source, it was accepted by performers and audiences, and was transmitted in the traditional way.[7]

It is in the transmission of songs, not in their composition, that 'the people' have an important part to play. Menéndez Pidal's *Poesía juglaresca* gives us a vivid picture of the *juglares* (minstrels) and their methods of operation, and contributes to the formulation of his statement that traditional poetry 'vive en variantes y refundiciones'. One of his major contributions to the study of medieval literature is his substitution of the concept of traditional poetry for that of popular poetry, though we must bear in mind a fact often overlooked by Menéndez Pidal: the learned origin of much traditional verse. This is perhaps the best point at which to emphasise that some of the widely accepted divisions established by nineteenth-century medievalists are far from watertight. It is impossible to separate rigorously popular and learned verse, oral and written transmission, sacred and profane love-poetry, ecclesiastical and secular life, fact and fiction. This complicating factor will meet us at almost every stage in the study of medieval literature.

To return to the *kharjas*: consideration of their social setting strengthens the case for believing that popular Spanish love-songs preceded and gave rise to the typical poetic forms of Moorish Spain, the *muwaššaha* and the *zajal*. The conquering Islamic armies brought very few women with them, with the result that racially mixed families (Moorish father, Spanish mother) were rapidly established. The children of such unions were bilingual, and it would be natural for them to regard Spanish as the language of the home, and Arabic as the language of official and commercial life. In such a situation, Spanish, the maternal tongue, would be the language of emotional life, and women's love-songs in that language would naturally become known to, and accepted by, a large part of the Arabic-speaking community. Some of the technical terms for parts of the *muwaššaha* bear a close relation in form or meaning, or both, to Spanish words for parts of a poem. Moreover, the Muqaddam ibn Mu'āfā whom one Arabic writer names as the inventor of the *muwaššaha* may well have been an Arabic-speaking Mozarab (i.e. a man of Spanish Christian origin).[8] If this is so, it means that the characteristic forms of Hispano-Arabic (and therefore of Hispano-Hebraic) poetry have their origin in the racial and linguistic mixture of Andalusian society.

The *kharjas*, as we have already seen, form the climax of the *muwaššahas* which are built on them. Some, including the three previously quoted, might at one time have been independent poems, and a very few stand even more easily on their own.

On the other hand, some are in themselves so slight that it is natural to think of them as fragments of a longer poem, for example:

¡Que tuelle me ma alma!
¡Que quita me [? *or* quiere] ma alma!
(GG 16)

Como si filyolo alyeno,
non mas adormes a meu seno.[9]
(Stern 7; GG 18)

This may explain why verse-forms of the *kharjas* often bear a strong resemblance to the refrains of traditional poems elsewhere in the Peninsula.[10] On the whole, it seems likely that the *muwaššaha* imitates the stanza-plus-refrain form of early Spanish love-song, and also incorporates the climactic and most concentrated part of the Spanish song as a *kharja*.[11] This would help to explain the inward-looking nature of most *kharjas*, the absence of concrete setting. Most *kharjas* are not as strongly internalised as

¡Ya corazoni, que queres bon amar!
¡A liyorar
laita-ni oviese welyos de mar! (*Laita-ni*: O that)
(GG 29)

but they contain astonishingly few references to houses, clothing, or natural scenery; almost all of the concrete objects mentioned are similes or metaphors. By contrast, references to the girl's heart or to the pains of love abound. One of the most striking results of this internalisation is to be seen in the *kharjas*' use of an almost universal type of love-poem, the dawn-song. The two varieties—the *alba*, in which lovers who have spent the night together have to part at dawn, and the *alborada*, in which lovers are joyfully reunited at dawn—are represented in many languages. The *alborada* is found in Galician-Portuguese, and both varieties in Castilian, yet the four *kharjas* that refer to dawn prove to be, not actual dawn-songs, but poems in which dawn is used as a metaphor for the lover.[12] This metaphorical use implies a previous tradition of *alboradas* (not of *albas*, since the metaphor is favourable in each case), and it emphasises the extent to which, in the climactic lines that are used as *kharjas*, external description is subordinated to intro-spection.

The *kharjas* do not, because of their internalisation and also because of their scarcity,[13] include all the types of love-poem or all the themes found elsewhere in the medieval Hispanic lyric, but they include enough types and enough themes to show beyond any doubt that—although they have some themes peculiar to Hispano-Arabic society, such as the presence of the *raqibe* (guard)—they are part of the same tradition. The *kharjas* already quoted provide some support for this statement, and the point will become even clearer with three more examples. The mixture of religion and sexual love in

> Vénid la Pasca, ay, aun sin elle,
> lazrando [?] meu corazón por elle.
> (Stern 5; GG 12)

is found again in the pilgrimage-songs of Galicia and in a number of Castilian *villancicos* (see below, p. 17); the mixture here takes the form of Easter as the occasion for a spring love-song, and the spring-song too is a continuing part of the tradition. Sensuality is rare in the *kharjas*, as in the traditional lyric in general, but is undeniably present in all areas, being represented here by:

> ¡Non me mordas, ya ḥabibi! ¡La,
> no quero daniyoso!
> Al-gilala rajisa. ¡Basta!   (my bodice is fragile)
> A toto me rifyuso.
> (GG 22)[14]

Most noteworthy of all, perhaps, is the theme of sleeplessness as part of the deserted girl's sufferings:

> No se quedó ni me quiéred garire   (*garire*: speak)
> kelma.
> No sey con seno mašuto dormire
> mamma.
> (GG 15)[15]

This theme is found also in a Galician-Portuguese *cantiga de amigo* and a Castilian *villancico*, and other Castilian versions are used in cultured poems of the fifteenth and sixteenth centuries.

The similarities of content and form between the *kharjas* and the love-lyric of other parts of the Peninsula are also, to some extent, similarities between Hispanic love-lyric and that of other parts of medieval Europe, and even of other continents. There are two reasons for this: any group of heterosexual love-poems will inevitably resemble any other group to some extent, simply because of the resemblances in the basic emotions; and there are grounds for believing that south-western Europe had, in the Middle Ages, a common tradition of popular love-song which was born of similar social and cultural conditions. It is this, and not the influence of one group of lyrics on the other, that explains such remarkable parallels as those between the *kharjas* and northern French popular lyric. Direct influences do occur, but they occur in cultured love-poetry and not in the popular tradition. One of the most important of these influences now claims our attention.

IV. GALICIAN-PORTUGUESE

Although the love-poetry of twelfth-century Provence can no longer be regarded as the source from which all other Romance lyrics derive, its influence on the cultured love-poetry of other countries remains fundamental, and it is impossible to understand the poetic history of Europe without taking account of it. The earliest extant poems written by Catalans are in Provençal (the political, economic, ecclesiastical, and linguistic connections between Catalonia and Provence were very close). When Catalan poets began to write in their own language, they continued for some time to base themselves on Provençal models. In Galicia, there was also a flourishing Provençal-based poetry, though in this case the links with Provence were not strong enough to make the local poets write in another language.

The principal reason for the powerful Provençal influence on Galician culture, and for the prosperity and self-confidence that favoured literary growth, was the pilgrim-road to Santiago de Compostela. The supposed tomb of St James, discovered in the ninth century, rapidly became the centre of a cult which had not only the economic importance of any major tomb-cult in the Middle Ages, but also great political and even military significance. St James, the patron saint of Spain, became a rallying-point for the reconquest of Moorish-occupied terri-tory, and the power of the bishops of Santiago grew to such an extent that their claim to be archbishops was conceded not long before the first flowering of Galician poetry. The pilgrim-road to Compostela began in southern France, crossed the Pyrenees, and ran through Navarre, Castile, and León before entering Galicia. Not all of the foreign pilgrims (and the poets and minstrels who joined the pilgrimages) were French or Provençal, but very many were, and this fact, the starting-point of the road, and the French commercial settlements in cities along the route, combined to give it the name of *camino francés*.

Galician-Portuguese secular verse (there are also religious poems) may be divided into three categories, two of which are obviously Provençal in inspiration, while the third owes something to Provençal technique. This division originates in a theoretical treatise contained in one of the three great *cancioneiros*, or anthologies, which preserve the poems for us. Since, with the exception of poems by Martin Codax and the religious poems of Alfonso X, the work of the Galician-Portuguese poets is known to us only through the three *cancioneiros*, we should first of all consider these.

The earliest known poet from this region is João Soares de Paiva (born 1141), and the last to be recognised as a truly Galician-Portuguese poet is Pedro, conde de Barcelos (died 1354). The *cancioneiros*, however, date from the fifteenth century, a time-lag which at once presents us with the question of whether the texts so transmitted are reliable. It is likely that collections of the work of individual poets served as the basis for larger collections prepared at the Castilian Court of Alfonso X, and that the three extant manuscript *cancioneiros* derive ultimately from the Alfonsine compilations, thus being at a considerable distance from the individual collections which alone had any authority, and all but one of which are now lost. Moreover, some material hitherto accepted as authentic may well be the product of fifteenth-century interpolations: the stanza

> Na serra de Sintra
> a par desta terra,
> vi uma serrana
> que braamava guerra,

which has been accepted as the only specimen of poetry about *serranas* (wild hill-women) earlier than the fourteenth-century *Libro de Buen Amor*, and therefore as evidence for a Peninsular tradition of such poems, seems to date only from the fifteenth century and to be influenced by the *serrana*-poems of the *Libro de Buen Amor* (see below, pp. 112-13).[16]

The one extant manuscript of an individual poet, that of Martin Codax, has a special interest even apart from its status as a survivor, since it contains not only the texts of Codax's poems but also their music. Here alone are we able to obtain some idea of the kind of music to which the love-poems of medieval Galicia were sung. Of the three *cancioneiros*, each has a strong claim on our attention: the *Cancioneiro da Ajuda* includes miniatures of poets (though the problem of their authenticity will now have to be faced); the *Canc. Colocci-Brancuti* (now owned by the National Library in Lisbon and renamed *Canc. da Biblioteca Nacional*) contains the theoretical treatise already referred to; and the *Canc. da Vaticana* appeals most strongly to our modern taste by its plentiful representation of the semi-traditional *cantigas de amigo*.

The *cantigas de amigo* express women's love, whereas *cantigas de amor* express the emotions of men. The difference is stated technically in *Colocci-Brancuti*: in *cantigas de amigo* the woman alone speaks, or speaks first; in *cantigas de amor*, the sole or first speaker is the man. This classification is, of course, arbitrary, and can sometimes be misleading, since occasionally a poem whose main point is the expression of a woman's love in the traditional style begins with words spoken by her lover, whereas another poem which expresses the courtly attitude of men's love-poetry may be spoken entirely by a woman who is merely the man's mouthpiece. The existence of borderline cases is inevitable, but the great majority of poems in the two categories are immediately recognisable, and there is no continuous spectrum of the kind that defeats some other attempts at literary classification.[17]

The *cantigas de amor* are, broadly speaking, poems of courtly love. This is a controversial term, for there has been a violent reaction against earlier attempts at definition. The love-poems of the Provençal troubadours express a range of attitudes, but they have enough in common to make them a clearly-defined group. When, in due course, these poems were collected in manuscript anthologies, Lives of the poets were added to them, but the Lives were in general based not on independent biographical evidence but on the information that could be reconstructed from the poems themselves. This process sometimes gave strange results, both in what was said of the poets' lives (for example, the famous story of Jaufré Rudel's love for the countess of Tripoli, and his fatal sea-voyage), and in the impression given of the poets' attitudes to love. A third stage in the formulation of the Provençal view of love was the composition in the late twelfth century by Andreas Capellanus of *De amore* (or *De arte honeste amandi*). This work, written in northern France, purports to be the handbook of courtly love, with a final section in which love is denounced as sinful. Andreas bases himself on the Provençal writings, but includes idiosyncratic views of his own; in particular, he insists that marriage cannot be the aim of the courtly lover, and he invents a distinction between *amor purus* (unconsummated love, though any degree of intimacy short of sexual intercourse is not merely permissible but praiseworthy) and *amor mixtus* (*amor purus* which then proceeds to intercourse); if consummation is intended from the beginning, and is achieved, then Andreas believes that true love is absent.[18]

It is clear that Andreas's *De amore* does not give an accurate picture of the Provençal troubadours' attitudes to love, and interpretations of courtly love based on Andreas have been replaced by an insistence on the troubadours themselves as the only reliable basis. This has been accompanied by the discovery of courtly elements in poems widely separated from each other in time, space, and social background.[19] Two points should, however, be borne in mind. First, although individual features of courtly love are to be found in many literatures, they are not found together until twelfth-century Provençal; from then onwards, they are found together in many works whose authors are clearly aware of writing in a tradition that can reasonably be called courtly. Secondly, although Andreas Capellanus's view of love is different from that of the troubadours, it remains important to us because De amore was widely read and translated for more than three hundred years, and had a considerable influence on later medieval literature, in Spain as elsewhere.[20]

A study of medieval Hispanic works reveals ten main features of courtly love. First of all, the love is of course courtly: it implies some degree of nobility, both of descent and of conduct, in the man and in the woman; the lover possesses a number of admirable qualities, or feels that he should possess them. Secondly, love not only makes the beloved seem admirable, but also produces virtue in the lover. Thirdly, although marriage is not excluded, it is not often referred to (but this does not mean that the love is necessarily adulterous). Fourthly, the aim of the lover is usually sexual intercourse, whether within or outside marriage. Fifthly, courtly love is a frustrated love, either because consummation is impossible (this situation occurs with surprising frequency, perhaps because of Andreas's influence—though it must be added that Andreas's prescription of physical intimacy falling short of intercourse finds little support in Spanish literature), or because disaster follows quickly upon consummation. Sixthly, because of this and also because of prevailing medical theories,[21] courtly love is tragic not comic, though it hardly needs to be said that there is plenty of comic treatment of sexual matters in medieval Spanish literature. Seventhly, there is often a transfer of religious emotion and religious imagery to sexual love. Eighthly, the lover proclaims, quite sincerely, his inferiority to his lady, whether or not he is objectively inferior. Ninthly, the lover's passion may be fully reciprocated by his lady: the belle dame sans merci does exist in medieval literature, but is a comparative rarity. Tenthly, the lovers usually try to keep their love secret.[22] When we find a medieval Hispanic work that has most or all of these features, it can usefully be described as courtly. Judged by this test, the cantigas de amor are poems of courtly love.

The cantigas de amor are not merely replicas of the Provençal love-poems. Although these poems have substantially the same kinds of verse-form as those of the Provençal troubadours, the Galician poets attach less importance to technical virtuosity and complexity of form; furthermore, they sometimes write *cantigas de amor* that are affected by the parallelistic verse-form of the *cantigas de amigo*. Thus, in form, the *cantigas de amor* are simplified versions of their Provençal models. In content, they are frequently more abstract than their models, with much less description of the lady, and open sensuality is much rarer. On the other hand, the fundamental courtly attitude remains.[23] A fairly typical example is a poem by King Dinis:

> Senhor, que de grad'oj' eu querria,
> se a Deus e a vos prouguesse,
> que hu vos estades estevesse
> con vosqu'e por esto me terria
>   por tan ben andante
>   que por rey, nen iffante
>   des ali adiante
>   non me cambharia . . .[24]

Dinis (1261-1325) is the most prolific, and may well be the best, of the Galician-Portuguese poets. He wrote in each of the three categories of secular verse, and was also a patron of poets, making his Court a major literary centre.

It is possible that we do not yet fully understand the *cantigas de amor*. There has been no systematic study of their vocabulary, though the meaning of some words has been discussed. One example may be given: it has been shown that *fazer bem*, literally 'to do good to someone', sometimes implies sexual possession, but there are other cases where such a meaning is improbable, and scholars disagree about the extent to which the meaning is present.[25] An analogous problem is that of *falar*, 'to talk to'. There are cases, in both *cantigas de amigo* and *cantigas de amor*, where it is clearly a euphemism, and other cases where it is equally clearly innocent.

The *cantigas de amor* and the satirical *cantigas d'escarnho e de maldizer* have little in common with the other Hispanic lyrics discussed in this chapter; their connections are rather with the court lyrics of fifteenth-century Castile, to be considered in Chapter 7. Yet they cannot easily be separated from the history of early lyric forms in the Peninsula, and it is therefore best to complete the picture by dealing with the satirical poems. The *cantigas d'escarnho e de maldizer* are, like the *cantigas de amor*, very obviously based on the Provençal tradition. They are elaborately, ingeniously, and comically scurrilous, and are, typically, directed against a named victim. As in Provence, the same men often wrote idealistic love-poems and obscene satire. Indeed, King Alfonso X of Castile, author of the devout *Cantigas de Santa Maria*, also wrote secular poems of which only a few *cantigas d'escarnho* survive; these are at least as scurrilous as those of other poets. There is no need to assume insincerity in the love- or religious poems of such men; they are simply writing in more than one convention, and doubtless in more than one mood. Nor is such a practice confined to thirteenth-century Galician-Portuguese; at the end of the fifteenth century, Diego de San Pedro wrote idealistic courtly-love fiction, a long poem on the Crucifixion, and a short poem so obscene that a modern editor suppresses it.[26]

The *cantigas d'escarnho* use the same verse-form as the *cantigas de amor*, and there is even, in a few cases, overlap of content between the two types of poem: satirical elements have been found in some *cantigas de amor*, though there are very few or none in the *cantigas de amigo*.[27]

Many *cantigas de amigo* are written in the same kind of verse as the *cantigas de amor* and *d'escarnho*; that is, in stanzas of four or more lines, with a refrain after each stanza. Many, on the other hand, use a quite different form, as in the thirteenth-century poem by Meendinho:

Sedia-m'eu na ermida de San Simion
e cercaron-mi as ondas, que grandes son:
eu atendend' o meu amigo.

Estando na ermida ant'o altar,
e cercaron-mi as ondas grandes do mar:
eu atendend'o meu amigo.

E cercaron-mi as ondas, que grandes son,
non ei i barqueiro, nen remador:
eu atendend'o meu amigo.

E cercaron-mi as ondas do alto mar,
non ei i barqueiro, nen sei remar:
eu atendend'o meu amigo.

Non ei i barqueiro, nen remador,
morrerei fremosa no mar maior:
eu atendend'o meu amigo.

Non ei i barqueiro, nen sei remar,
morrerei fremosa no alto mar:
eu atendend'o meu amigo.

The verse-form used here has two distinctive features. First, the lines are grouped in pairs, with two assonance-patterns running through the poem (the first, third, and fifth pairs assonate in *o*, and the second, fourth, and sixth in *a*), and a different assonance for the refrain, so that the poem follows the scheme AAC, BBC, AAC . . .; the second pair of lines repeats the content of the first, and the fourth repeats the content of the third, with hardly any changes except those needed to change the assonance. Secondly, a device known as *leixa-pren* ('put down and take up again') ensures continuity of content: the first line of the first two pairs is abandoned, the second line becomes the first line of the next two pairs, a new second line is introduced, and so on; thus each pair has one familiar line and one new one, so that the content is carried forward but without a break at any point. By this combination of alternating assonance with *leixa-pren*, the poem is given a tight parallelistic structure.[28] It is, of course, possible to have parallelism with alternating assonance but without *leixa-pren*, and a substantial number of *cantigas de amigo* do not use parallelism at all, as we have already noted, but this is the characteristic form, and one of the clearest indications of the popular origin of the *cantigas de amigo*. All the poems of this type that survive are the work of cultured poets, or reworkings by such poets, so we find that the form can be modified for artistic purposes, as when King Dinis breaks the pattern of *leixa-pren* in order to emphasise that an answer is being given to the girl's question:

> Ai flores, ai flores do verde pino,
> se sabedes novas do meu amigo?
> ai Deus, e u é?
>
> Ai flores, ai flores do verde ramo,
> se sabedes novas do meu amado?
> ai Deus, e u é?
>
> Se sabedes novas do meu amigo,
> aquel que mentiu do que pôs comigo?
> ai Deus, e u é?
>
> Se sabedes novas do meu amado,
> aquel que mentiu do que mi á jurado?
> ai Deus, e u é?
>
> Vós me preguntades polo voss'amigo?
> E eu ben vos digo que é san'e vivo;
> ai Deus, e u é?
>
> Vós me preguntades polo voss'amado?
> E eu ben vos digo que é viv'e sano;
> ai Deus, e u é?
>
> E eu ben vos digo que é san'e vivo,
> e será vosc'ant'o prazo saido;
> ai Deus, e u é?

> E eu ben vos digo que é viv'e sano,
> e será vosc'ant'o prazo passado;
> ai Deus, e u é?

Critics have grouped the *cantigas de amigo* into several sub-categories. One of these is represented by Meendinho's poem, quoted above: the *cantigas de romaria*, or pilgrimage-songs, in which the girl's pilgrimage to a local shrine is a pretext for meeting her lover. The outcome is sometimes happy, sometimes unhappy; in Meendinho's poem, the girl feels herself deserted and frightened, with the fierce waves of the sea being both a real setting which presents physical danger, and an image for the passion which she cannot control. The *cantigas de romaria* may even hint at a pagan tradition of fertility rituals in connection with pilgrimages, as in Pedro Viviaez's poem, where the pilgrimage is for the mothers an occasion for worship, and for the daughters an opportunity to dance before their lovers:

> Pois nossas madres vam a San Simon
> de Val de Prados candeas queimar,
> nós, as meninhas, punhemos d'andar
> con nossas madres, e elas enton
>   queimen candeas por nós e por si
>   e nós, meninhas, bailaremos i.

> Nossos amigos todos lá iram
> por nos veer e andaremos nós
> bailand'ant'eles, fremosas, en cós,
> e nossas madres, pois que alá van,
>   queimen candeas por nós e por si
>   e nós, meninhas, bailaremos i.

> Nossos amigos iran por cousir
> como bailamos e poden veer
> bailar moças de [mui] bon parecer,
> e nossas madres, pois lá queren ir,
>   queimen candeas por nós e por si
>   e nós, meninhas, bailaremos i.

There is a firm foundation in social reality for the poets' association of pilgrimages with love, and the reality was European rather than merely Galician; there are, for example, documents forbidding nuns to go on pilgrimages because their reputations would be sullied.

The maritime interests of Galicia and Portugal are reflected in *barcarolas*, poems which are at once boat-songs and love-songs; some of the best are by Joan Zorro. A poem may belong to more than one sub-category, so that Meendinho's *cantiga de romaria* also has features

of the *barcarola*. *Bailadas*, dance-songs, are based on the association,
familiar to almost all cultures, of dancing with love. There are, as we
shall see, strong grounds for believing that the two main verse-forms
used for the traditional love-song are based on the dance, but the
bailadas actually take dancing as their subject. Here, too, it is possible to
find overlap with other types of *cantigas de amigo*: the poem quoted
above combines *bailada* and *cantiga de romaria*.

The *alborada*, or poem of dawn greeting, does not have many
representatives in Galician-Portuguese, but one of them makes an individual and subtle contribution to the genre:

> Levad', amigo que dormides as manhãas frias;
> todalas aves do mundo d'amor dizian;
> leda m'and'eu.

> Levad', amigo, que dormide'-las frias manhãas;
> todalas aves do mundo d'amor cantavan;
> leda m'and'eu.

> Todalas aves do mundo d'amor dizian;
> do meu amor e do voss'en ment'avian;
> leda m'and'eu.

> Todalas aves do mundo d'amor cantavan;
> do meu amor e do voss'i enmentavan;
> leda m'and'eu.

> Do meu amor e do voss'en ment'avian;
> vós lhi tolhestes os ramos en que siian;
> leda m'and'eu.

> Do meu amor e do voss'i enmentavan;
> vós lhi tolhestes os ramos en que pousavan;
> leda m'and'eu.

> Vos lhi tolhestes os ramos en que siian
> e lhis secastes as fontes en que bevian;
> leda m'and'eu.

> Vos lhi tolhestes os ramos en que pousavan
> e lhis secastes as fontes u se banhavan;
> leda m'and'eu.

Here the thirteenth-century poet Nuno Fernandes Torneol uses the
convention of the *alborada* to show that the girl's lover has abandoned

her, and has destroyed the symbolic landscape of love (the singing birds are banished, the waters of fertility dried up); thus the assertion of happiness in the refrain becomes ironic.[29]

One sub-category, the *pastorela*, should strictly be classed as a *cantiga de amor*, since a man is the first speaker in most of the poems, but there can be little doubt that the poets themselves regarded this as a type of *cantiga de amigo*. Whereas the pastourelle in most of Europe presents the attempted seduction of a shepherdess by a knight, the Galician-Portuguese *pastorela* uses the encounter chiefly as a pretext for the shepherdess's song about her love:

> Oi oj'eu ũa pastor cantar,
> du cavalgava per ũa ribeira,
> e a pastor estava i senlheira,
> e ascondi-me pola ascuitar
> e dizia mui bem este cantar:
> 'So lo ramo verde frolido
> vodas fazen a meu amigo
> e choran olhos d'amor' ...
> (Airas Nunes; *V* 454/*CB* 869)

Other *cantigas de amigo* do not belong to any of the special sub-categories discussed above, but it is possible to classify them in other ways. The poems with a rural setting (represented by King Dinis's 'Ai flores ...') are generally simple in content, with the girl's attitude fairly lightly sketched; parallelistic structure is most frequent in such poems. Outstanding among these are the poems of Pero Meogo, in all of which stags or does appear, usually accompanied by a fountain or a stream; for example,

> —Digades, filha, mia filha velida:
> porque tardastes na fontana fria?
> os amores ei.
>
> Digades, filha, mia filha louçana:
> porque tardastes na fria fontana?
> os amores ei.
>
> —Tardei, mia madre, na fontana fria,
> cervos do monte a augua volvian:
> os amores ei.
>
> Tardei, mia madre, na fria fontana,
> cervos do monte volvian a augua:
> os amores ei.

—Mentir, mia filha, mentir por amigo;
nunca vi cervo que volvess'o rio:
  os amores ei.

Mentir, mia filha, mentir por amado;
nunca vi cervo que volvess'o alto:
  os amores ei.

(*V* 797/*CB* 1192)

The folklore connections of these poems are unmistakable, and the stags have a symbolic and probably a ritual value; in the fourth century, a bishop of Barcelona condemned folk-rituals which included a stag-dance, and forbade the faithful to *cervulum facere*. It would be extremely rash to suggest that all features of the landscape in the *cantigas de amigo* derive from ritual, but it is certainly true that in these poems landscape is never described for its own sake, that it is made significant by its connection with love, and that all its features have a symbolic value.[30]

Cantigas de amigo with an urban setting usually have a more substantial content, with more psychological detail; they often present a three-sided relationship (most frequently the girl, her lover, and her mother); and fewer of them have a parallelistic verse-form. A still higher level of sophistication is reached in the poems which show courtly love from the woman's point of view. Yet we must not take too limited a view of sophistication: although the basic situation of Nuno Fernandes Torneol's *alborada* is simple enough, the use made of it by the poet is far from simple.

The poets who wrote in Galician-Portuguese came from all social levels: Meendinho, like a few others, was a *jogral* (minstrel); Airas Nunes was a priest; Pai Gomes Charinho was High Admiral of Castile; and two of the most prolific poets were kings, Dinis of Portugal and Alfonso X of Castile (for his religious poems, see below, p. 93). For many of the poets, including some of the best, we lack accurate biographical details. By no means all of these poets came from the western part of the Peninsula: they included Castilians and Andalusians, as well as Galicians and Portuguese; for educated medieval Europeans, genre rather than the writer's nationality often determined which language was used.[31] The widely accepted use of Galician-Portuguese for the cultured lyric is referred to by the fifteenth-century Castilian, the marqués de Santillana: 'que non ha mucho tienpo qualesquier dezidores e trobadores destas partes, agora fuessen castellanos, andaluzes o de la Estremadura, todas sus obras conponían en lengua gallega o portuguesa'. Indeed, one of Santillana's own poems is in this language. Although there are isolated cases of cultured lyrics in Castilian in the fourteenth century (those contained in the *Libro de Buen Amor* are the most notable), it is not until about 1400 that Castilian is regularly used for this kind of poetry. It is at about the same time that popular Castilian lyrics, *villancicos*, begin to be written down.

V. 'VILLANCICOS'

Most *villancicos* do not appear in manuscript or print until the sixteenth century, even though they are almost certainly much older than this late appearance would suggest. They have survived in greater numbers than the *cantigas de amigo*, and in far greater numbers than the *kharjas*, and they display greater variety. Until the early seventeenth century, when the *villancico* was replaced by the *seguidilla*, it was one of the dominant forms of Castilian poetry,[32] and it is not easy to see differences between those first recorded in the fifteenth century and those which first appear in the sixteenth. Thus the *villancico*, like the ballad, belongs to the literary history both of medieval Spain and of the Golden Age.

The *villancico* consists of two parts: the *estribillo*, two, three, or four lines at the beginning, which are repeated at the end of each stanza; and the *glosa*, stanzas which develop the theme of the *estribillo*. Most extant *glosas* are cultured, though a few popular ones survive.[33] As with the *kharjas*, cultured poets may compose *estribillos* in the traditional style.

Villancicos are love-poems, and the speaker is a girl, though at a later and more sophisticated stage of the tradition a man's love may be the subject:

> Los cabellos de mi amiga
> d'oro son;
> para mí, lanzadas son.
> (Alonso and Blecua no. 17)

As with the *kharjas* and the *cantigas de amigo*, unhappy love is the most frequent subject, and it very often takes the form of a girl's lament for her lover's absence:

> Aquel pastorcico, madre,
> que no viene,
> algo tiene en el campo
> que le duele.
> (Frenk Alatorre no. 223)[34]

> Estas noches atán largas
> para mí
> no solían ser así.

Solía que reposaba
las noches con alegría,
y el rato que no dormía
en sospiros lo pasaba:
mas peor está que estaba;
para mí
no solían ser así.
(Alonso and Blecua no. 46)

The thematic resemblances of these two poems to the traditional lyrics of Andalusia and Galicia scarcely need to be pointed out. Resemblances may also be found in the symbolic use of landscape:

Dentro en el vergel
moriré.
Dentro en el rosal
matarm'han.

Yo m'iba, mi madre,
las rosas coger;
hallé mis amores
dentro en el vergel.
Dentro del rosal
matarm'han.
(Alonso and Blecua no. 44)

Here we have the *locus amoenus* as a setting, the plucking of roses as an image for the enjoyment of love (an image whose meaning the girl does not recognise until it is too late, or so at least she tells her mother), and death as a hyperbolic expression of the anguish of love (or possibly as a euphemism for sexual fulfilment).

Thematic resemblances between the *villancicos* and the other types of traditional lyric are plentiful, but the *villancicos* are wider-ranging. They include, for instance, counterparts of the French *chanson de mal-mariée*:

Soy garridica
y vivo penada
por ser mal casada.
(Frenk Alatorre no. 289)

They also include two types arising out of particular Spanish social conditions. One is the protest of the girl whose parents insist on her becoming a nun:

¿Agora que sé de amor
me metéis monja?
¡Ay Dios, qué grave cosa!

> Agora que sé de amor
> de caballero,
> ¿agora me metéis monja
> en el monesterio?
> ¡Ay Dios, qué grave cosa!
> (Frenk Alatorre no. 120)[35]

and the other reflects the problems facing the girl whose dark skin suggests, whether rightly or wrongly, that she has Moorish blood:

> Aunque soy morena
> no soy de olvidar,
> que la tierra negra
> pan blanco suele dar.
> (Frenk Alatorre no. 202)[36]

Finally, broad humour—absent from the *cantigas de amigo* and rare in the *kharjas*—is more frequent in *villancicos*:

> —Tú la tienes, Pedro,
> la tu mujer preñada.
> —Juro a tal, no tengo,
> que vengo del arada.

> —¿Quién la ha empreñado,
> dilo tú, amigo?
> —Yo no sé quién:
> Dios me es testigo.
> (Frenk Alatorre no. 561)

VI. THE PENINSULAR LYRIC— GENERAL PROBLEMS

The general impression given by the content of the *villancicos* is that they belong to the same tradition of love-poetry as the *kharjas* and the *cantigas de amigo*, but that they give a fuller picture of the tradition.[37] Their form also indicates that they are part of a Peninsular tradition. They consist of stanza and refrain, with refrain as the dominant partner, as do the *muwaššaḥa*, the *zajal*, the popular Spanish lyric of Andalusia (in so far as we can deduce its form), and, with modifications, the Provençal model borrowed by the Galician-Portuguese poets for *cantigas de amor* and *cantigas d'escarnho*. This is also the form of some *cantigas de amigo*, but it is impossible to say whether they have adopted the Provençal model or whether the popular poems of Galicia used this type of verse as well as the parallelistic type. The refrain-based form is widespread outside the Peninsula; it is, for example, characteristic of the northern French popular lyric and of the *laude* which are thought to be a Christianised version of the popular lyric of Italy.

The refrain-based form is, then, the main form taken by the popular lyric tradition of south-western Europe, but parallelistic poems are not confined to Galicia. They are found in Castilian, as in the *alborada*:

Al alba venid, buen amigo,
al alba venid.

Amigo el que yo más quería,
venid al alba del día.

Amigo el que yo más amaba,
venid a la luz del alba.

Venid a la luz del día,
non trayáis compañía.

Venid a la luz del alba,
non trayáis gran compaña.
(Frenk Alatorre no. 110)[38]

They occur also in Catalan and in Judeo-Spanish. The Jewish communities of Spain were persecuted from 1391 onwards, and in 1492 all Spanish Jews were given the choice of conversion to Christianity or immediate expulsion (see below, p. 141). Spanish-speaking Jews were thus dispersed throughout the Mediterranean and in other parts of Europe, and they carried with them their traditional songs as well as their language. These songs, both lyrics and ballads, have in recent years been collected from oral tradition, and have provided valuable evidence which had been lost in the Peninsular tradition. The occurrence of parallelistic lyrics in Judeo-Spanish as well as in Castilian and Catalan shows that the Hispanic love-lyric throughout most of the Peninsula (perhaps all—the evidence of the *kharjas* is too scanty for us to know whether parallelistic poems existed in Andalusia) had two forms, with parallelism dominant in the north-west, and the refrain-based poem dominant elsewhere.

It is likely—though proof is impossible—that these two verse-forms originate in the dance. Two widespread forms of popular dance are the double ring of dancers, with one ring moving clockwise and one anti-clockwise (as in the modern Paul Jones), and the single ring moving round a central figure who directs the dance (as in some types of Highland dancing). The parallelistic lyric may well have been associated with the first type of dance (one ring singing the first, third, and fifth pairs of lines, the other ring singing the second, fourth, and sixth pairs, and both rings joining in the brief refrain), and the refrain-based lyric associated with the second type (the directing central figure singing the stanzas—perhaps even improvising them—and the circle of dancers singing the refrain).

Such an explanation assumes the fundamental correctness of the popular theory of lyric origins. The theories that seek to explain the origin of the Romance lyric fall into three groups: those that postulate a popular or folkloric origin, those that derive the lyric from liturgical Latin, and those that account for it by Arabic influence. Any variant of each theory has some evidence to support it, and until Stern's discovery of the Romance *kharjas* it was impossible to say that any one theory had established a definite advantage over its rivals.[39] The picture is now much clearer. We know that soon after A.D. 1000 cultured poets were making use of poems that are to all appearances popular, and we have good evidence (the medieval Arabic literary historians) for the belief that such use began about 900. Therefore an apparently popular tradition must have existed for some time before 900, and it would be very surprising indeed if Latin liturgical influence had been responsible for so early a tradition. It is very nearly certain that the *kharjas* represent a genuine and early popular tradition, and that they gave rise to two types of cultured Hispano-Arabic poetry. The striking resemblances of form and content between these early Andalusian poems and the apparently popular love-poetry of other parts of south-western Europe confirm that the *villancicos*, the *cantigas de amigo*, the northern French *refrains*, and the Italian *laude* really are of popular origin (though of course they have undergone varying degrees of learned reworking). Further, the fundamental similarity in form between the Provençal cultured poems and the refrain-based popular lyric suggests strongly that the Provençal poets, like their Hispano-Arabic counterparts, took a popular form as their model.

A cultured poet using a tradition of popular verse can adopt the verse-form and write his own poems in it (Hispano-Arabic, and probably Provençal); or embody a popular fragment in his own poem (Hispano-Arabic and sixteenth-century Castilian); or rework a popular poem, preserving the form, the theme, and some of the techniques, but filtering the poem through a cultured sensibility (Galician-Portuguese). All of these methods seem to have contributed to the rise of a cultured love-lyric from a popular, and now largely lost, basis. Once the tradition of cultured poetry was established in one area, it could influence that of another area, or even stimulate the growth of cultured poetry in an area that previously lacked it, as Provençal influence did in Galicia. Moreover, cultured vernacular poets of Christian Europe could scarcely escape the influence of medieval Latin; some of them, indeed, wrote both in Latin and in the vernacular. The remarkable similarities that Peter Dronke has established between Latin and vernacular verse thus take their place in the total picture: some may be mere coincidence, but many must represent the influence of Latin on the vernacular poets. Again, it would be wrong to ignore the detailed similarities in verse technique between the *zajal* and the Provençal poems.[40] Yet it seems safe to say that the Latin and Arabic influences are in points of detail, whereas the popular tradition is not an influence but a fundamental cause.

One question remains to be considered: the relationship between *kharjas, cantigas de amigo,* and *villancicos.* In the excitement generated by the discovery of the *kharjas,* some critics took the view that these were the earliest Romance lyrics (not just the earliest extant), and that similarities between them and other popular lyrics of the Peninsula were the result of direct influence.[41] It would on general grounds be surprising if one popular lyric tradition influenced another in this way, especially when the supposed source was to be found in Moslem Spain, and would have had to influence Italy and northern France also. In fact, a brief consideration of chronology may help us to solve the problem. The popular lyric of Andalusia appears in writing (as the *kharjas*) when there are cultured poets in the region who can make use of it; no one wrote down a lyric from oral tradition in the Middle Ages unless it could serve some useful purpose. The popular lyric of Galicia appears in writing, in a reworked form, as soon as cultured poets begin to write under Provençal influence. Cultured lyric appears late in Castilian as an established tradition, but very soon after cultured poets form the habit of composing their lyrics in the language, *villancicos* are written down. It can hardly be a coincidence that in each region the written appearance of the popular poems follows so closely upon the emergence of cultured poets who could make use of them. If the arguments outlined above are accepted, the conclusion must surely be that the three areas of the Peninsula had popular lyric traditions of equal antiquity (and, no doubt, that Provence, northern France, and Italy had them also), that the *kharjas* are not the earliest Romance lyrics to be composed but simply the first to be written down, and that the similarities between *kharjas, cantigas de amigo,* and *villancicos* are the result not of influence but of origin in a common tradition.

NOTES

1. Many Spanish scholars would rate the Visigothic contribution far more highly, especially in the epic (see below, p. 32). For the history of this period, see E. A. Thompson, *The Goths in Spain* (Oxford, 1969).

2. Castro's views, first stated fully in *España en su historia* (1948), have since been elaborated in *La realidad* and other works. For a comprehensive attack on Castro's theories, see Claudio Sánchez-Albornoz, *España, un enigma*; see also Eugenio Asensio, 'Américo Castro historiador: reflexiones sobre *La realidad*

THE EARLIEST LYRIC 27

histórica de España', *MLN*, LXXXI (1966), 595-637, and 'La peculiaridad literaria de los conversos', *AEM*, IV (1967), 327-51.

    3. See Bowra, *Primitive Song*.

    4. Stern, 'Les vers finaux en espagnol dans les *muwaššaḥ* hispano-hébraïques', *Al-An*, XIII (1948), 299-346. The findings of Stern and of Emilio García Gómez, published in articles, are consolidated in *Les Chansons* and *Las jarchas romances*. See also Dámaso Alonso, 'Cancioncillas "de amigo" mozárabes. Primavera temprana de la lírica europea', *RFE*, XXXIII (1949), 297-349; R. Menéndez Pidal, 'Cantos románicos andalusíes (Continuadores de una lírica latina vulgar)', *BRAE*, XXXI (1951), 187-270, reprinted in *España, eslabón entre la Cristiandad y el Islam* (Madrid, Austral, 1956); Leo Spitzer, 'The Mozarabic Lyric and Theodor Frings' Theories', *CL*, IV (1952), 1-22, translated in *Lingüística e historia literaria* (2nd ed., Madrid, 1961); G. E. von Grunebaum, ' "Lírica románica" before the Arab Conquest', *Al-An*, XXI (1956), 403-5; and Francisco Cantera, *La canción mozárabe* (Santander, 1957). For the literary connections of the *kharjas*, see also Margit Frenk Alatorre, 'Jarŷas mozárabes y estribillos franceses', *NRFH*, VI (1952), 281-4; I.-M. Cluzel, 'Les jarŷas et l' "amour courtois" ', *CN*, XX (1960), 233-50; and cf. James T. Monroe, 'The Muwashshahât', *Collected Studies in Honour of Américo Castro's 80th Year* (Oxford, 1965), pp. 335-71, and Vincent Cantarino, 'Lyrical Traditions in Andalusian Muwashshahas', *CL*, XXI (1969), 213-31.

    5. *Nidioš*, 'healthy', is Rafael Lapesa's suggested reading of an obscure word. (The texts of *kharjas*, especially those preserved in Arabic script, present great difficulties, and those quoted here are sometimes tentative and disputed reconstructions.) *Ḥabib*, the Arabic word for lover, was used in both Hebrew and Spanish love-poems of this region. This *kharja* is no. 18 in Stern, *Les Chansons*, and in the appendix to García Gómez, *Las jarchas*.

    6. The poets are Yehuda Halewi (c. 1080-after 1145) and Todros Abulafia (1247-c. 1300). Their interpretations are clear from the lines that serve as transition between the main part of the *muwaššaḥa* and the *kharja*. For another view, see Dronke, *Medieval Latin*, I, 31-2.

    7. The position is in fact more complex than this, since Latin literature has a continuous and flourishing existence in medieval Europe, and precedes not only cultured vernacular literature but also popular traditional verse. Nevertheless, I believe that the hypothesis stated here is fairly close to the reality of medieval Spain.

    8. Brian Dutton, 'Some New Evidence for the Romance Origins of the *Muwashshahas*', *BHS*, XLII (1965), 73-81.

    9. This *kharja* is used by three poets, one Arabic and two Hebrew.

    10. For details, see García Gómez, *Las jarchas*.

    11. A problem raised by the discovery of the *kharjas* is the relative chronology of *muwaššaha* and *zajal*. Did Arabic poets compose a Vulgar Arabic equivalent of the popular Spanish love-song, and later refine this to produce a Classical Arabic genre in the same verse-form which incorporated a fragment of the Spanish song? Or did the *muwaššaha* come first, with the *zajal* later spreading to the whole poem the popular speech that had at first been confined to the *kharja*?

    12. In one case (Stern 28; GG 7) it is possible that a literal dawn-situation is involved. For the dawn-song in general, see *Eos. An enquiry into the theme of lovers' meetings and partings at dawn in poetry*, ed. Arthur T. Hatto (The Hague, 1965); the Iberian chapter is by S. M. Stern and E. M. Wilson.

    13. About fifty Spanish or mainly Spanish *kharjas* have been discovered, and some of these are too fragmentary to study usefully. Most of them contain some Arabic or Hebrew words, and some *kharjas* mainly in Vulgar Arabic have

a few words of Spanish. This linguistic mixture seems to have been typical of the popular speech of Andalusia, but it would be possible to go further and conclude that the distinction between Spanish and Vulgar Arabic *kharjas* is unreal.

14. Another version of the *kharja* (both are used by Arabic poets) has *tanqas*, 'touch', instead of *mordas*, 'bite'.

15. The third line of the *kharja* is very hard to decipher. In his speculative reconstruction, García Gómez prefers *mašuto*, 'burnt', but suggests *exuto*, 'dry', as an alternative. On the theme, see Bruce W. Wardropper, 'La más bella niña', *SP*, LXIII (1966), 661-76.

16. Giuseppe Tavani, *Poesia del duecento nella penisola iberica. Problemi della lirica galego-portoghese* (Officina Romanica 12, Roma, 1969); Luciana Stegagno Picchio, 'Per una storia della *serrana* peninsulare: la *serrana* di Sintra', *CN*, XXVI (1966), 105-28. *O Cancioneiro de Martin Codax*, ed. C. F. da Cunha (Rio de Janeiro, 1956).

17. W. J. Entwistle, 'From *Cantigas de amigo* to *Cantigas de amor*', *RLC*, XVIII (1938), 137-52; M. Rodrigues Lapa, *Lições*. For a contrary view: C. P. Bagley, '*Cantigas de amigo* and *Cantigas de amor*', *BHS*, XLIII (1966), 241-52.

18. *De amore libri tres* (with fragmentary medieval Catalan translation), ed. Amadeu Pagès (Castelló de la Plana, 1930); *The Art of Courtly Love*, trans. J. J. Parry (New York, 1941).

19. For the earlier view, see C. S. Lewis, *The Allegory of Love* (Oxford, 1936), and A. J. Denomy, *The Heresy of Courtly Love* (New York, 1947). This is attacked by Dronke, *Med. Latin*, I, and by Moshé Lazar, *Amour courtois et fin'amors dans la littérature du XIIe siècle* (Paris, 1964). Other important studies are D. R. Sutherland, 'The Language of the Troubadours and the Problem of Origins', *FS*, X (1956), 199-215; Maurice Valency, *In Praise of Love. An introduction to the love-poetry of the Renaissance* (New York, 1958); Kenelm Foster, *Courtly Love and Christianity* (Aquinas Paper 39, London, 1963); and *The Meaning of Courtly Love*, ed. F. X. Newman (Albany, N.Y., 1968).

20. A. D. Deyermond, 'The Text-Book Mishandled: Andreas Capellanus and the opening scene of *La Celestina*', *N*, XLV (1961), 218-21.

21. J. Livingston Lowes, 'The Loveres Maladye of Hereos', *MP*, XI (1913-14), 491-546; *La comedia Thebaida*, ed. G. D. Trotter and Keith Whinnom (London, Tamesis, 1969), p. xxxvi.

22. Several attempts have been made to establish the origins of courtly love, but none has succeeded. The different features have separate origins, and the particular circumstances of twelfth-century Provence seem to have favoured their combination.

23. C. P. Bagley, 'Courtly Love-Songs in Galicia and Provence', *FMLS*, II (1966), 74-88.

24. Full text and translation in Bernárdez, *Florilegio*, no. 5. *Senhor* meant 'lady' as well as 'lord' at this stage of the language, but we cannot entirely rule out influence of the Provençal convention of using *midons*, 'my lord', for the courtly lady.

25. A. J. Saraiva, *História da cultura em Portugal*, I (Lisboa, 1950), 279-356; Segismundo Spina, *Do formalismo estético trovadoresco* (São Paulo, 1966), pp. 176-85.

26. See Whinnom, *Spanish Literary Historiography*, p. 19. It would be an error to draw conclusions about the Hispanic (or even the medieval European) character from these facts. To take just one example from the centre of

Victorian respectability, W. S. Gilbert wrote an obscene comic opera which has not been published: see N. St John Stevas, *Obscenity and the Law* (London, 1956), p. 189n.

27. Frank R. Holliday, 'The Frontiers of Love and Satire in the Galician-Portuguese Mediaeval Lyric', *BHS*, XXXIX (1962), 34-42, and 'Extraneous Elements in the *Cantiga de amigo*', *RFL*, 3rd ser., VIII (1964), 151-60. For a possible trace of satire in a *cantiga de amigo*, see Brian Dutton, '*Lelia doura, edoy lelia doura*, an Arabic Refrain in a Thirteenth-Century Galician Poem?', *BHS*, XLI (1964), 1-9.

28. Dorothy M. Atkinson, 'Parallelism in the Medieval Portuguese Lyric', *MLR*, L (1955), 281-7; Asensio, *Poética y realidad*.

29. Tavani, *Poesia del duecento*, pp. 265-74.

30. Asensio, *Poética y realidad*; Hatto, *Eos*, pp. 771-819; Reckert, *Lyra Minima*. For comparisons with the visual arts, see Kenneth Clark, *Landscape into Art* (London, 1949). *O Cancioneiro de Pero Meogo*, ed. X. L. Méndez Ferrín (Vigo, 1966). I draw also on a forthcoming study by Jane Hawking.

31. H. J. Chaytor, *From Script to Print*, Ch. 3. On the reasons for the use of Galician-Portuguese by Castilian poets, see Castro, *La realidad*; Rafael Lapesa, *De la Edad Media a nuestros días. Estudios de historia literaria* (Madrid, BRH, 1967), pp. 48-52; and Tavani, *Poesia del duecento*, pp. 9-76.

32. Margit Frenk Alatorre, *Lírica hispánica*, and paper in *Actas del III Congreso Internacional de Hispanistas* (México, 1970).

33. Margit Frenk Alatorre, 'Glosas de tipo popular en la antigua lírica', *NRFH*, XII (1958), 301-34.

34. This shows the interchange between religious and sexual emotion from the other side (we have already seen how religious material is borrowed by love-poems): San Juan de la Cruz produces a Christianised version in which the *pastorcico* is Christ, and the pain the Crucifixion. See Bruce W. Wardropper, *Historia de la poesía lírica a lo divino en la Cristiandad occidental* (Madrid, 1958).

35. See Wardropper, 'The Reluctant Novice: a critical approach to Spanish traditional song', *RR*, LV (1964), 241-7.

36. Two views of this theme are given by Wardropper, 'The Color Problem in Spanish Traditional Poetry', *MLN*, LXXV (1969), 415-21; and J. M. Aguirre, *Ensayo para un estudio del tema amoroso en la primitiva lírica castellana* (Zaragoza, 1965), pp. 8-14.

37. The traditional Castilian lyric is of even wider scope than this would suggest, since it includes, in addition to *villancicos*, songs of lament known as *endechas*. The earliest extant mourn the deaths of Fernando III in 1252 (R. Menéndez Pidal, *Crestomatía del español medieval*, I, Madrid, 1965, 184-5), and of Guillén Peraza in the conquest of the Canaries in 1443 (Frenk Alatorre no. 61). The Judeo-Spanish tradition has preserved a large number of these laments; see Manuel Alvar, *Endechas judeoespañolas* (Granada, 1953).

38. This poem has an *estribillo* as well as parallelistic structure, but there are others which do not.

39. A clear and thorough survey is given by Gerald Gillespie, 'Origins of Romance Lyrics: a review of research', *YCGL*, XVI (1967), 16-32. See also Pierre Bec, 'Quelques réflexions sur la poésie lyrique médiévale. Problèmes et essai de caractérisation', *Mélanges offerts à Rita Lejeune* (Gembloux, 1969), II, 1309-29; Maurice Delbouille, 'A propos des origines de la lyrique romane: tradition "populaire" ou tradition "cléricale" ', *MRo*, XX (1970), 13-27.

40. R. Menéndez Pidal, 'La primitiva lírica europea. Estado actual del

problema', *RFE*, XLIII (1960), 279-354. For Menéndez Pidal's earlier views on problems of the lyric, see his studies of 1919, 1937, and 1943 in *Estudios literarios* (Buenos Aires, Austral, 1938), *Poesía árabe y poesía europea* (Madrid, Austral, 1941), and *De primitiva lírica española y antigua épica* (Buenos Aires, Austral, 1951).

41. It is significant that neither of the scholars who could speak with most authority on the *kharjas*, Stern and García Gómez, took this view.

Chapter 2

THE EPIC

I. CHARACTERISTICS OF EPIC

NARRATIVE POETRY USUALLY DEVELOPS LATER than the lyric; because its objective character implies some degree of sophistication, it is rare among the most primitive people.[1] Nevertheless, it seems in most areas to occur long before the spread of literacy, and an orally-composed and orally-diffused narrative poetry is thus common. It is especially common in the form of the epic, and there is ample evidence to suggest that, even when epic poets began to compose in writing, they intended their work to be orally diffused.

Epic is heroic narrative in verse (saga is its prose equivalent), and its essential subject has been well defined as 'the pursuit of honour through risk'.[2] It deals with the exploits of a hero or a group of heroes, who are in most cases firmly set in the context of their community. All oral narrative is likely to have some features in common, and the oral epics of widely differing peoples display a high degree of similarity. It would be tempting to conclude that such resemblances are caused by descent from a common ancestor, but a more likely explanation is that the basic circumstances of oral composition and of diffusion to a popular audience tend to produce similar results wherever they occur.

One important distinction must be made at this point: the distinction between heroic epic (a convenient term which covers the poems aimed at a popular audience, whether they were composed orally or in writing) and literary epic, which in medieval and Renaissance Europe descends chiefly from Virgil's *Aeneid*. The literary epic of the Middle Ages is usually in Latin, though there are some impressive vernacular poems such as the Spanish *Libro de Alexandre*; in the Renaissance, the vernacular predominates. Literary epics share some of the heroic epic's narrative characteristics, but few of its stylistic features, and their conscious dependence on a literary tradition, together with the sophistication of their audience, sets them apart from the poems which tell the people of the deeds of their real or imaginary heroes.[3] However, learned men could—and in Spain certainly did—compose heroic epics which were performed by the minstrels and eagerly received by the ordinary people; we shall see the importance of this point later in the chapter.

The essential difference between heroic and literary epic is, then, not a difference of authorship or subject-matter (though these may well be different in particular cases), but of audience and of the tradition in which the poets are working.

Among many peoples, the best-known and best-loved epics tell of a heroic age, of a time, perhaps far distant, when heroes were larger than life; a time which may inspire the lesser men of the present to emulate the deeds of their ancestors.[4] The epics may themselves descend from poems composed in the heroic age, though they need not do so. When, if at all, was the heroic age of medieval Spain? There are four obvious possibilities, ranging from the fifth to the eleventh century: the Visigothic conquest; the beginnings of resistance to the Moorish conquerors; the period in which Castile struggled for independence from León; and the lifetime of the Cid. No serious case has been made out for the first of these as the originating point of Spanish epic: it has often been asserted that the Germanic epics of the Visigoths gave rise to a Spanish tradition,[5] but the Visigoths were already Latinised when they crossed the Pyrenees, and no evidence has been produced for epics of their conquest of Spain. There is some evidence that the Moorish invasion and the first steps in the Reconquest inspired contemporary epics, but it is unconvincing. Only when we turn to the beginnings of Castilian independence do we find adequate evidence of a heroic age.

II. LOST SPANISH TEXTS: THEIR RECOVERY FROM CHRONICLES

The student of French epic has roughly one hundred poems at his disposal, some of them in several manuscripts with important variations; about a million lines of verse survive, and even this total excludes some late reworkings of earlier poems. Spain presents a striking and puzzling contrast: there are three texts in the traditional epic metre (assonanced lines of irregular length but averaging fourteen to sixteen syllables). Two of these texts, the *Cantar de Mio Cid* and the *Mocedades de Rodrigo*, are incomplete, and the third, *Roncesvalles*, is a mere fragment; there is also the *Poema de Fernán González*, a reworking in a different verse-form. The total number of lines is only some five thousand, or, including the reworking, eight thousand. The usual explanation offered for the scarcity of extant texts is that manuscripts have been lost, either because a change in the style of handwriting favoured by scribes made them obsolete, or because the Spanish manuscripts were intended as prompt-copies for minstrels, whereas French epic manuscripts were destined for the private reader and the library.[6] The latter theory raises another problem—why did epic manuscripts in the two countries have such markedly different purposes?—but it may nevertheless be true. It may be that in Spain additional written copies of epic poems, even epics originally composed in writing, were not made unless they could serve some immediately practical purpose (the same appears to have been true of the popular lyric, as we saw in the last chapter). The two most obvious purposes for epics would be political or economic propaganda for a monastery or a church, and the provision of material for chroniclers. Spanish epics were used for both of these ends, as well as for the almost universal purpose of informing, entertaining, and inspiring the people as a whole. Thus written copies would have a practical use for learned men under some circumstances, but oral diffusion would be the best way of reaching a mass audience. Admitting, then, that we cannot account fully for the difference between France and Spain in this respect, and that Spanish epics were less plentiful than French, let us consider the ways in which we can gather some knowledge of the lost poems.

Medieval chroniclers relied heavily on epic poems. It is difficult to say with any certainty when this practice began,[7] but the *Estoria de España* (or *Primera crónica general*), compiled in the second half of the thirteenth century under the direction of Alfonso el Sabio, makes very extensive use of epics and acknowledges the fact openly. Some of this chronicle's references to epic sources are ambiguous, but there is little room for doubt when we read that 'algunos dizen en sus cantares et en sus fablas de gesta'.[8] *Fablas* may well refer to oral tradition that need not take the form of an epic poem, but *cantares* can only in this context mean heroic poetry. In one case, we are even given the title of the poem, whose account is contrasted with that of the Hispano-Latin historians:

Mas pero que assí fue como el arçobispo et don Lucas de Túy lo cuentan en su latín, dize aquí en el castellano la estoria del Romanz dell inffant García dotra manera, et cuéntalo en esta guisa . . .
(II, 471)

The *Estoria de España* uses epics in two ways: it gives a fairly full summary of the plots of several poems, and it incorporates prosified versions of long sections from a few epics. It is dangerously easy to read too much into the evidence, but some stories are told at such length, and with such frequent use of traditional epic motifs, or narrative elements, that no other explanation meets the case. Moreover, a comparison of the extant text of the *Cantar de Mio Cid* with the corresponding section of *EE* shows that the prose account of the hero's later career follows the poem for much of its length. Evidence for the actual prosification of an epic text is provided when a series of words, distributed at fairly regular intervals through a section of the chroniclers' prose, has the same assonance (vowel-rhyme). While this evidence also must be cautiously interpreted,[9] several long series of assonating words within a story rich in epic motifs show that the chroniclers incorporated many epic lines in more or less their original form. The classic case of this is the lost epic of the *Siete Infantes de Lara* (or *de Salas*), where the preservation of assonance enabled Menéndez Pidal, in his first major work of scholarship, to reconstruct some 550 lines of verse from the prose of the chronicles.[10]

To this evidence may be added that of ballads. The relations between ballad and epic in Spain will be discussed later (see below, pp. 124-7); at present we need note only that some ballads take their content, and sometimes their words, from extant epic poems and from others now lost.[11] As with the chronicles, comparisons between ballads and extant epics validate the cautious use of ballads to establish the content of lost poems; this method gains in reliability if ballad and chronicle coincide (unless, of course, one derives from the other, as in the case of King Rodrigo and the Moorish conquest). A notably successful example of this approach is the use of a ballad and of the French *Chanson de Roland* in order to discover the content, though not the words, of a lost section of *Roncesvalles*.[12]

III. SUPPOSED EPICS OF THE MOORISH CONQUEST

Taking the surviving texts together with the lost epics attested by the chroniclers and ballads, we may now consider the main subjects on which Spanish epics were, or are thought to have been, composed. First come the fall of Spain to the Moors and the beginnings of the Reconquest. The real cause of Visigothic Spain's weakness in the early eighth century was a dynastic feud, but this became obscured in popular tradition by a story of sexual intrigue and the avenging of family honour by calling in the Moors. This story appears first among the Hispano-Arabic historians, and assumes its final form in the *Crónica sarracina* of Pedro del Corral (*c.* 1430), from which derive the Spanish ballads of King Rodrigo's sin and its punishment. There is no evidence whatsoever that an epic poem on the subject was composed in medieval Spain, whether at the time of the Moorish conquest or later; there is, however, plentiful evidence that the story is one branch of a widespread European, and especially Germanic, folk-tradition.[13] Another supposed epic of this period proves equally illusory: that of Covadonga, the possibly legendary first battle of the Reconquest, which is recorded in two versions of the late ninth-century *Chronica Visegothorum*.[14] There is, again, no evidence of an epic; the story in the Latin chronicle reads very much like an ecclesiastical legend, with interest concentrated on a bishop who went over to the enemy, and on a miracle performed

by the Virgin Mary. There are no grounds for believing that the
events of the early eighth century, important though they were, formed
the subject of epic poems whether at the time or later in the Middle
Ages. The Moorish invasion was not Spain's heroic age.

IV. CAROLINGIAN EPICS

Spanish poems were undoubtedly composed about the struggles of
the late eighth century, but they were composed long afterwards, as
the result of French influence. The Emperor Charlemagne's invasion
of Moorish Spain, and the defeat of the French rearguard at Roncesvalles, are given artistic form in the most famous of French epics, the
Chanson de Roland. The dating of the *Roland* is disputed: some
scholars have argued that the first version was composed at the time of
the events, and that successive versions showed increased length and
a diminishing fidelity to the historical facts; others believe that the
poem originated in the late eleventh century, in a form very similar to
that in which we know it. The *Roland* exercised a strong influence in
France and in other countries, and it probably had more than one
Spanish descendant.[15] All that now remains of these is a hundred-line
fragment of *Roncesvalles*,[16] containing Charlemagne's lament over the
bodies of his dead warriors, which is presented economically and
powerfully. The manuscript is of the early fourteenth century, and the
poem seems to have been composed in the late thirteenth, probably in
the Navarro-Aragonese dialect. *Roncesvalles*, like its French source,
deals with real events, even if they have been heavily fictionalised, but
two other Spanish epics of this group, both now lost, are wholly
fictional. *Mainete*, which is summarised in *EE*, gives a romanticised
account of Charlemagne's youth. The immediate source is the French
Mainet, but this in turn is of Spanish inspiration, since the exile of
Alfonso VI of León in the Moorish city of Toledo has been transferred
from the eleventh to the eighth century, a romantic interest has been
added, and Alfonso changed into Charlemagne.[17] *Bernardo del Carpio*,
on the other hand, represents a nationalist reaction against the Carolingian poems, and tells of a Leonese noble's revolt against his king's
collaboration with Charlemagne; it thus falls into the well-known category of epics about rebel vassals. It cannot have been composed until the
French epics had been circulating in Spain for some time, and 1200
seems to be the best approximate date, since the poem is first summarised in the *Chronicon mundi* of Lucas, bishop of Túy (1236). It is
also found in Archbishop Rodrigo Ximénez de Rada's *De rebus
Hispaniae* (1243), and in *EE*.[18] The Spanish Carolingian and anti-
Carolingian poems are much later than the events they describe; in

any case, the wars of Charlemagne against the Moors would scarcely have constituted the heroic age of Spain, and it is clear that these poems were adapted to an already established pattern of Spanish epic.

v. 'POEMA DE FERNÁN GONZÁLEZ'

We come now to a group of poems which deal with the first counts of autonomous Castile, and with events said to have occurred under their rule. Only one is extant, but the chronicles give us a full and clear account of the content of several others. The extant poem is not in the traditional epic metre, but in the learned *cuaderna via* (see below, pp. 58-9). This is the *Poema de Fernán González*, composed *c.* 1250 at the monastery of San Pedro de Arlanza. Fernán González was born about 915, became count of Castile in 932, and immediately joined his overlord, the king of León, in warfare against the Moors. Soon he was involved in military struggles against the kingdom of Navarre, on his eastern flank, and in the political struggle to win autonomy from León, which lay to the west. In a chequered career, he may have been imprisoned by both the Navarrese and the Leonese monarchs, but before his death in 970 Castile was well on the way to autonomy. The poem reflects these events, while reshaping them. The threefold struggle against Moors, Navarrese, and Leonese is preserved, but the order of events seems to have been changed, and the poem owes more to folklore than to the historical facts, as in the story of the hero's escape from a Navarrese prison with the help of his captor's sister.[19] The narrative is introduced by a summary of Spanish history which stresses religious aspects, and which includes the poet's praise of his native country:

> Por esso vos lo digo que byen lo entendades,
> mejor es dotrras tierras en la que vos morades,
> de todo bien conplida en la que vos estades;
> dezir vos he agora quantas a de bondades.
>
> Tyerra es muy tenprada syn grrandes calenturas,
> non faze en yvyerno destenprradas fryuras,
> non es tierra en mundo que aya tales pasturas,
> árboles pora fruta syquier de mil naturas . . .
>
> Com ella es mejor de las sus vezindades,
> assý sodes mejores quantos aquí morades,
> omnes sodes sesudos, mesura heredades,
> desto por tod el mundo muy grrand preçio ganades.
>
> Pero de toda Spanna Castyella es mejor
> por que fue de los otrros el comienço mayor,
> guardando e temiendo syenpre a su sennor,

quiso acreçentar la assý el Cryador.
Aun Castyella Vyeja, al mi entendimiento,
mejor es que lo hal por que fue el çimiento ...

(st. 144-5 and 155-7)

This theme is fairly frequent in medieval Spanish writing, both Latin and vernacular, and owes something to an acute awareness of the contrast between the (partly imaginary) glories of the Visigothic past and the harsh realities of present conflict between the Christian kingdoms and with the occupying Moors.[20]

The hero's relations with the monastery of San Pedro de Arlanza form an important part of the story. Fernán González loses his way when hunting (a frequent opening of an adventure in folklore). His quarry takes refuge in a hermitage, the hero is stricken with remorse for his unintentional violation of sanctuary, and promises to build an adequate monastery on the site. The monk Pelayo correctly prophesies a victory in the coming battle, and thereafter the destinies of Fernán González, Castile, and Arlanza are closely linked. The poem is designed to encourage others to emulate the Count's generosity, and to increase the monastery's attractiveness to pilgrims. The stimulation of pilgrims' interest by a collection of relics associated with a saint or a national hero, and best of all by his tomb, was a favourite tactic of medieval churches and monasteries. If a hero was commemorated by an epic poem, this was still more useful, and in some cases an epic was composed for this purpose. There is still vigorous disagreement among scholars on the relevance of tomb-cults to epics,[21] but it is clear that the *PFG* represents the use of epic material for ecclesiastical purposes. It is, however, not always realised that *PFG* is itself, despite its metre, an epic. The nature of its main narrative, the audience at which it appears to aim, the number of folk-motifs that it incorporates, and perhaps the irregularity of its metre (which seems to be much greater than that of other *cuaderna vía* poems)—all of these point to its being a heroic epic composed by a monk as propaganda.

The Arlanza poet based his work on an earlier epic, about which we know little, generally referred to as the *Cantar de Fernán González*. A version of this lost epic supplied to fourteenth-century chronicles and ballads material of clearly epic nature that they could not have obtained from *PFG*, so that we are able to deduce something of its content, independently of what is incorporated in *PFG*. The date and authorship of the *Cantar de FG* remain unknown. We can, however, be reasonably sure that the Arlanza poet added to it the episodes involving his monastery, and also the historical introduction; it is likely that he was responsible for a reorganisation of the epic's structure. In addition, he drew on a number of learned sources: the *Libro de Alexandre*, at least two of Berceo's poems, at least two Latin chronicles, and a vernacular chronicle, the *Liber regum*; several other sources have been suggested, but without sufficient proof. The economic interests of the monastery were the main but not the only motive of the *PFG* poet. His Castilian patriotism is strong, as we have seen, and he tends to identify Castile with the Reconquest and the best interests of Spain as a whole. This leads to some weakness in the poem's effect on its audience, since emotion tends to be divided between Castile and Fernán González, whereas in most epics it is concentrated on the hero as an embodiment of his country.

VI. 'SIETE INFANTES DE LARA'

One other epic dealing with the early years of autonomous Castile is known to us through Menéndez Pidal's reconstructions from the chronicles: the *Siete Infantes de Lara*.[22] The plot of this poem, set in the reign of Fernán González's successor, Garci Fernández, is almost wholly fictitious, though the political situation that is used as a background is authentic. The story is one of family feud, betrayal, and vengeance; it incorporates such familiar motifs as the letter of death (best known to English readers in *Hamlet*), the love of a girl for her brother's captive, and the hero of mysterious origins. In its outline and also—as far as can be judged from the reconstructed verse fragments— in its detail, it is a poem of great power. When the avenging hero, Mudarra, has killed the traitor Ruy Velázquez, he turns his attention to the woman who instigated the betrayal, Doña Lambra. She seeks protection:

> La mala de doña Lambra para el conde ha adelinado
> en sus vestidos grandes duelos, los rabos de las bestias tajados;
> llegado ha a Burgos, entrado ha en el palacio,
> echóse a los pies del conde e besóle las manos:
> '¡Merçed, conde señor, fija so de vuestra prima!
> Lo que don Rodrigo fizo yo culpa non avría,
> e non me desanparedes ca pocos serán los mis días.'
> El conde dixo: '¡Mentides, doña alevosa sabida!
> ca todas estas traiciones vos avedes bastecidas;
> vos de las mis fortaleças erades señora e reina.
> Non vos atreguo el cuerpo de oy en este día;
> mandaré a don Mudarra que vos faga quemar viva
> e que canes espedaçen esas carnes malditas,
> e, por lo que fezistes, el alma avredes perdida.'
> (538-51)

The story that the poem told was, although fictitious, one that carried conviction: the parish church at Salas de los Infantes displayed as relics seven skulls which were allegedly those of the betrayed brothers, while two monasteries claimed to possess the authentic seven tombs.[23]

It is easier to arrive at an approximate date of composition for the *Siete Infantes* than for the other lost epics. Although the main action of the poem is fiction, the political situation which provides the background is authentic: the poet's assumptions about relations between the Moors of Córdoba and the Christian kingdoms of the north reflect the situation of *c.* 990, and it would have been difficult for anyone to imagine such a state of affairs a generation later. The obvious objection is that the first surviving trace of the *Siete Infantes* is in *EE*, some three hundred years later, but it must be remembered that since the earlier chronicles concerned themselves only with royalty and the highest nobles, their silence cannot disprove an early date for the poem.[24] A learned poet could, of course, have been familiar with the political relationships of *c.* 990 long after ordinary people had forgotten them, but since they are not essential to the story, he would have had little reason to include them; a poem composed soon after the event might, however, continue to appeal long afterwards, if its plot and the vigour of its narration outweighed the unfamiliarity of its setting. Again, the use in the *Cantar de Mio Cid*, composed by a learned poet at the end of the twelfth century, of the remnants of oral-formulaic technique (see below, pp. 44-5, 49), points to a considerably earlier period when epics were orally composed. Thus an early date for the *Siete Infantes* is consistent with the general evidence of oral-formulaic technique. The simplest and most satisfactory conclusion is that an epic poem, resembling the *Siete Infantes* preserved by *EE*, was composed not much later than the year 1000.

We have now considered the date of the *Siete Infantes* at some length, and for good reason: the first decades of Castile's autonomous existence, filled with struggle and danger but also with a growing Castilian self-confidence, have the qualities needed for a heroic age. The *Siete Infantes* is a poem set in that period, and probably composed in it. The heroic ages of many cultures are a later nostalgic invention, but it is likely that Castile's heroic age — *c.* 1000 — was not merely a source of later poems but the period when the poems themselves originated.

VII. OTHER EPICS OF EARLY CASTILE

A number of other epics, now lost, are set in this period, although it is impossible to date them accurately. The most likely hypothesis is that several epics were orally composed at this time, and that they established a pattern not only for other poems about the early counts and their contemporaries, but also for poems about the Cid, and for epics inspired by the French Carolingian cycle.

One of the most interesting of the epics whose plots are roughly contemporary with that of the *Siete Infantes* is *La condesa traidora*, which deals with the private misfortunes of Count Garci Fernández. No text survives, but there is a brief summary in the Hispano-Latin *Crónica Najerense* (mid-twelfth century), a fuller one in Archbishop Rodrigo's *De rebus Hispaniae*, and a very full account in *EE*.[25] The poem tells of the adultery of the Count's first wife, his terrible revenge, the treachery of his second wife (French, like the first) which causes his death, her attempt to murder her son, and her own death from the poison she had prepared. This scandalous and sensationally-told tale makes it hard to believe in the accepted doctrine of the realistic sobriety of the Spanish epic; it may also come as something of a shock to realise that the poem has carefully-developed ecclesiastical connections. The story as told in *EE* begins with the foundation of a monastery by Garci Fernández, and with a miracle. It ends with the burial of Doña Sancha (the treacherous Countess) at the monastery of San Salvador de Oña, and with an explanation of the monastery's name. It is true that this is absent from the earliest chronicle summary of the poem, in the *Najerense*, but this ends with the burial of Garci Fernández at another monastery, San Pedro de Cardeña. As far back as we can trace the epic of *La condesa traidora*, its ending is of predominantly monastic interest. This does not necessarily mean that the poem had such an ending when first composed, but it may well have done so.

Two other epics of this group are the *Romanz del Infant García* and, more doubtfully, the *Abad don Juan de Montemayor*, both set in the early eleventh century. The former, which is mentioned by its title in *EE* (see above, p. 33), tells of the murder in León of the last count of Castile.[26] Like the *Siete Infantes* and *La condesa traidora*, the *Romanz* includes a highly-coloured version of the epic motif of vengeance: three of the murderers are burned alive, and García's fiancée is asked to decide the fate of the fourth:

> Estonces donna Sancha tomól et fizo justicia en él qual ella quiso, et fízola en esta guisa: tomó un cuchiello en su mano ella misma, et tajóle luego las manos con que él firiera all inffant et a ella misma, desí tajól los pies con que andidiera en aquel fecho, después sacóle la lengua con que fablara la traición; et desque esto ovo fecho, sacóle los ojos con que lo viera todo. Et desquel ovo parado tal, mandó adozir una azémila et ponerle en ella et levarle por quantas villas et mercados avie en Castiella et en tierra de León do él fiziera aquella traición... (*PCG* II, 472)

This epic also resembles the *Poema* (and the *Cantar*) *de Fernán González*, the *Siete Infantes*, and *La condesa traidora* in the important part played by a woman; and it further resembles them in its ecclesiastical connections. There were two competing tombs of García, in León and at San Salvador de Oña, with epitaphs giving different versions of the murder. The *Abad don Juan de Montemayor* is much less well documented: there is a reference in a Portuguese poem of the mid-fourteenth century, and a summary in a chronicle of the late fifteenth.[27]

VIII. THE CID

Two of the extant epics are concerned with the greatest of Spain's heroes, Rodrigo (or Ruy) Díaz, known as el Cid.[28] He was born at Vivar, near Burgos, c. 1043, and began his career as a knight towards the end of the reign of Fernando I, who had united Castile, León, and Galicia. When the kingdoms were divided at Fernando's death in 1065, Rodrigo rose to high office under Sancho, the king of Castile, whom he helped in the campaigns that gave him control of León and Galicia. When the king was murdered at the siege of Zamora in 1072, Rodrigo tried to avenge him. He inevitably found less favour under the new king, Alfonso VI, who had been in exile in Toledo since Sancho drove him from the throne of León. Nevertheless, Rodrigo was too powerful for Alfonso to make an enemy of him unnecessarily, and he seems already to have been regarded as to some extent a representative of a new and rising class, the lesser nobility of Castile. These nobles were for the most part energetic, talented, and ambitious, though few possessed these qualities to the same extent as Rodrigo; they had supported Sancho, and they were opposed not only to the Leonese nobility, but also to the well-established higher nobility of their own country, which they regarded as effete. These socio-political issues may be clearly seen in the *Cantar de Mio Cid*, where the hero's chief enemies are the Leonese Infantes de Carrión and the eminent Castilian noble García Ordóñez, all of whom are presented in an unattractive, and sometimes satirical, light.[29]

Alfonso VI attempted a reconciliation, arranging Rodrigo's marriage to Ximena Díaz, a Leonese noblewoman, in 1074, but tension continued, and Rodrigo was exiled from 1081 to 1087, and again from 1089. The Cid, as he was now known, took service with the Moorish king of Saragossa (a fact not reflected in the epic), and eventually conquered and ruled the Moorish city of Valencia, defending it against the Almoravids (puritanical and fanatical Moroccan warriors, who had rapidly overrun the highly cultured but politically and militarily decadent Hispano-Moorish kingdoms). He died in Valencia in 1099, and his body was later reburied at the monastery of San Pedro de Cardeña. Here a tomb-cult grew up, which involved the collection not only of relics but also of legends, probably known as the *Estoria del Cid*. These

stories seem to have acquired their definitive form about the middle
of the thirteenth century, but it is impossible to say when their collection
by the monks began. They consisted of the *Cantar de Mio Cid*,
historical material (including some from Arabic historians), and legends
of a type common in hagiography. This Cardeña *Estoria*, largely because
it was incorporated in *EE*, exercised a strong influence on many
generations' views of the Cid's career, displacing the much more
accurate account in the Latin *Historia Roderici*, which was composed
in the first half of the twelfth century.[30]

Although the *Historia Roderici* is unquestionably the most accurate
medieval work on the Cid, by far the best in literary quality is the
Cantar (or *Poema*) *de Mio Cid*. This poem survives in a single manuscript of disputed date, copied by one Per Abbat, and which now
contains some 3,700 lines; it has some gaps, and the beginning and
possibly the end are missing, but most has survived. In it, the Cid is
exiled and his property confiscated, so that he and his followers have
to live by raiding the Moors. They do this with increasing success, and,
with the capture of Valencia, attain far greater prosperity than before
the hero's exile:

> Los que foron de pie   cavalleros se fazen;
> el oro e la plata   ¿quién vos lo podrie contar?
> Todos eran ricos   quantos que allí ha.   (1213-15)

Despite his exile, the Cid has consistently maintained that he is a loyal
vassal of Alfonso, and has sent him gifts. Alfonso gradually relents,
allowing the hero's wife and daughters to join him in Valencia. There
had been an anguished leave-taking when the Cid left Castile:

> assís parten unos d'otros   commo la uña de la carne   (375),

but even at this stage his energy and optimism asserted itself:

> 'Aun todos estos duelos   en gozo se tornarán.'   (381)

Now the prophecy is fulfilled, as Ximena and her daughters are shown
the city that has been won for them. Alfonso pardons the Cid, and in
an attempt to compensate him, arranges the marriage of the hero's
daughters to two brothers, the Infantes de Carrión, members of the
Leonese nobility. The Cid is uneasy about the marriages, but accepts
them. The Infantes soon prove cowardly as well as vain and avaricious;
then, deciding that they have been slighted, they take their wives away
from Valencia, and in the depths of a forest:

> con las çinchas corredizas   májanlas tan sin sabor;
> con las espuelas agudas,   don ellas an mal sabor,
> ronpien las camisas e las carnes   a ellas amas a dos;
> linpia salie la sangre   sobre los çiclatones . . .

Canssados son de ferir   ellos amos a dos,
ensayandos amos   quál dará mejores colpes.
Ya non pueden fablar   don Elvira e doña Sol,
por muertas las dexaron   en el robredo de Corpes.   (2736-48)

The Cid demands justice, and the king convokes a court, at which the Infantes are outmanoeuvred and discredited. Their disgrace, and the vindication of the Cid and his daughters, are completed by their defeat in judicial duels, and by the remarriage of the daughters to the heirs to the thrones of Navarre and Aragon. Thus the Cid's honour will continue to grow, even after his death:

Oy los reyes d'España   sos parientes son,
a todos alcança ondra   por el que en buena naçió.   (3724-5)

The most noteworthy features of the *Cantar de Mio Cid* are not only its optimism, but also its realism and its moderation. Epics rarely concern themselves with the need to earn a living, but in *CMC* there is an acute awareness of these matters; when Moors try to recapture Valencia after the arrival of Ximena and the daughters, the Cid decides that they should watch the battle:

'mis fijas e mi mugier   veerme an lidiar;
en estas tierras agenas   verán las moradas cómmo se fazen,
afarto verán por los ojos   cómmo se gana el pan.'   (1641-3)

The same attitude is revealed in the frequency and precision with which the Cid's gains are mentioned, and in the accurate psychological depiction of the characters. It is also notably moderate: the great gains of the Cid and his followers remain within credible limits (though the virtual elimination of their casualties is less easy to believe in). We have already seen that vengeance in most Spanish epics is as bloody as in any other epic tradition, yet the Cid takes a legal revenge, which involves no deaths (the Infantes and their brother lose the duels, but survive to endure their ignominy). Such is the poet's skill that this moderation in vengeance not only avoids anti-climax, but provides an exciting and fitting end to the story.

The main theme of the poem is the Cid's honour, and the structure is based on its loss and restoration. His public, or political, honour is destroyed by the King's anger and the exile, and is restored by the conquest of Valencia and the King's pardon. The Cid is now at a higher point than before he was exiled, but this leads to the collapse of his private, family or sexual, honour in the outrage inflicted on his daughters. This, in turn, impels him to a vindication that leaves his honour at the highest point it has ever reached. Irony plays an essential part in this structure, since at the three turning-points of the action, intentions misfire and produce the opposite result to that intended: when Alfonso exiles the Cid, he unwittingly gives him the chance to become lord of Valencia; when he tries to make amends, he puts the Cid's honour in the hands of the Infantes de Carrión; and when the Infantes humiliate the Cid, they plant the seeds of his triumph and their own disgrace.

This contrast between intentions and their outcome is only one of the contrasts that make up the structure of the poem. Contrasts may be found at every level: within the individual line, between characters, and between early disaster and final triumph. These form an important means by which the poet expresses his judgments on the characters. The criterion for such judgments is clear: it depends on the attitude of the characters to the Cid. They are, however, seldom explicit (this is another way in which *CMC* departs from the normal characteristics of epic, and the artistic restraint required is another facet of the poem's moderation). The methods used to imply judgments include the use of symbols, parody, verbal oppositions and identifications, epic epithets with unusually strong connotations, and comparison and contrast of situations.[31] To take just one example from the last category, the Infantes are given hospitality by the Cid's Moorish friend Abengalbón. They plan to murder him for his money, but the plot is discovered, and Abengalbón spares their lives only because they are the sons-in-law of his ally. The Christian nobles are shown to fall far below the moral standard of the Moor; explicit comment by the poet is unnecessary.

Epic epithets are already an established device in Homer, and are still found in the oral epics of twentieth-century Yugoslavia. They usually take the form of noun-adjective combinations ('el burgalés leal') or of dependent clauses ('el que en buen ora çinxo espada'). Like other repeated phrases known as formulas if repeated exactly, or as formulaic phrases if repeated with variations, such epithets are essential to an oral poet. Studies of the Yugoslav epic singers by Milman Parry and his pupil Albert B. Lord have shown how they can improvise poems of great length, building up lines at high speed from their stock of formulas, and using their stock of motifs to construct whole poems.[32] Epic epithets, like other formulas, can be put to very sophisticated use, and those in *CMC* are used with particular skill as implied comments on the action and the theme.[33]

We must now consider the problems of *CMC*'s authorship. When Menéndez Pidal published his monumental edition of the poem, he argued that it was composed about 1140 by a Mozarabic *juglar* from what was then the Castilian frontier-town of Medinaceli. He rejected the possibility of ecclesiastical influence, and emphasised the poem's fidelity to the historical facts. Towards the end of his life, he revised his theories, maintaining that the poem had been composed *c.* 1110 by a native of San Esteban de Gormaz, and that the Medinaceli *juglar* of *c.* 1140 had reworked it, increasing the fictional element.[34] Recent research makes it clear that both the original and the revised versions of Menéndez Pidal's theories are, notwithstanding their virtually unanimous acceptance by historians of literature, mistaken. Taking in conjunction the evidence of style, versification, language, historical and geographical references, and the poem's treatment of legal and documentary matters, a very different picture emerges.[35] CMC was composed towards the end of the twelfth century, or perhaps at the beginning of the thirteenth, by a single author, a learned poet who may well have been a cleric and who had certainly had a legal and notarial training. He lived in the Burgos area, though he had not necessarily been born there, and he addressed his poem primarily to a Burgos audience; the degree to which he was influenced by the tomb-cult of the Cid at Cardeña, if there was any influence, remains uncertain. The poem was composed in writing, but was intended for oral diffusion by *juglares* to a popular audience. Its historical accuracy is considerably less than was once believed, and the whole story of the Infantes de Carrión and the Cid's daughters is fictitious.[36] It must in fairness be added that these conclusions remain controversial, despite the very strong evidence in their favour, and that Menéndez Pidal's views still enjoy distinguished support outside, as well as within, Spain.

CMC is not the only poem on the Cid. The first to be composed was almost certainly a literary epic in Latin, the *Carmen Campidoctoris*, which was probably written by one of his followers in 1093-94, and of which the first 129 lines survive.[37] Another Latin literary epic, the *Poema de Almería*, written between 1147 and 1157, refers to the Cid, and may possibly show knowledge of a vernacular poem about him.[38] No doubt some vernacular Cidian epics preceded CMC, and it may well be that the CMC poet used one or more as source material; this might explain his incorporation of local Medinaceli and San Esteban de Gormaz traditions. It must, however, be emphasised that we have no means of knowing what such poems were like. The untypical nature of CMC makes it improbable that any predecessors resembled it to a major extent, and there is no justification for the common assumption of a series of vernacular epics on the final stages of the Cid's career, each reworking its predecessor, until the extant text was composed.

We reach firmer ground with the *Cantar de Sancho II*, which deals with the murder of that monarch and Rodrigo's attempts to avenge him. The poem has been lost, but the main content and some lines of verse can be reconstructed from the chronicles, with help from ballads. Its date of composition is hard to establish: the epic is prosified in *EE*, and it may have been used in the *Crónica Najerense*, but it is equally possible that *Najerense* drew its material from, and perhaps prosified some lines of, a Latin literary epic, the *Carmen de morte Sanctii regis*, which was probably composed at the monastery of San Salvador de

Oña.[39] The *Cantar de Sancho II* may have ended with an episode in which Rodrigo compelled the new King Alfonso VI to swear three times that he was innocent of complicity in his brother's murder, but it is slightly more probable that this episode, the *Jura de Santa Gadea*, was composed later and separately, for the purpose of linking *Sancho II* and *CMC* into a cyclical poetic life of the Cid.[40]

Epic poets normally present their heroes at the height of their powers, and it is only at a fairly late stage in the development of an epic tradition that attention is focused on the hero's birth, childhood, and youth. The reason is simple: a hero's earliest years are generally unremarkable, and only an audience thoroughly familiar with his later career will demand stories of his youth. Poems about a hero's youth, in order to claim an audience's interest, tend to the fictitious and even the sensational. This is the case with the early part of the *Poema de Fernán González*, and even more with the *Mocedades de Rodrigo*.

The *Mocedades* tells of Rodrigo's ancestry, his killing of his father's enemy, and King Fernando's order that he should marry the dead man's daughter Ximena. The hero refuses to see Ximena again until he has won five battles; in these, he defeats the Moors (twice), an Aragonese champion, treacherous Castilian Counts, and usurpers who had deprived the Bishop of Palencia of his rights. At this point, the King of France, the Holy Roman Emperor, and the Pope demand a humiliating submission by Castile. Rodrigo encourages King Fernando to resist, and they lead a victorious army to the gates of Paris. In the middle of peace negotiations, the manuscript breaks off.

Chronicles of the first half of the fourteenth century prosify a lost predecessor of the *Mocedades*, and this lost epic was also the ultimate source of ballads on Rodrigo's youth.[41] Its content seems to have coincided fairly closely with the extant *Mocedades* in its outline of Rodrigo's career, but it probably differed substantially in two other respects. First, it was more moderate in tone: in the extant poem Rodrigo is presented as more emphatically a rebel vassal, and there is some exploitation of sexual scandal, in order to attract and retain the interest of an audience eager for novelty. Secondly, the extant *Mocedades* is much concerned with the history of the diocese of Palencia, which has nothing to do with the main subject, and does not appear in the lost poem.

The poet's evident interest in Palencia provides a clue to his background. Although the *Mocedades* is nearly always described as the work of a decadent *juglar*, it is in fact of learned authorship, and composed in the third quarter of the fourteenth century in order to support the claims of the diocese of Palencia at a critical moment in its history. It is not a good poem, though it is in some ways better than has been supposed.[42] Its main importance is not aesthetic but historical, since it is the earliest extant verse-text in the flourishing tradition of works on the Cid's youth (its lost predecessor gave rise to the ballads, the ballads to Guillén de Castro's play *Las mocedades del Cid*, and this play to Corneille's *Le Cid*); it is the latest extant epic of medieval Spain, and must have been one of the last ever to be composed; and it provides an unusually good opportunity for testing the theories of *neotradicionalismo*, the dominant Spanish school of thought on the epic.

IX. THE THEORY OF 'NEOTRADICIONALISMO'

The use of the epics by the chroniclers dies away in the fifteenth century; they repeat what their predecessors said, but very rarely add new material, and give no clear indication that they have made direct use of the poems. If any epics circulated at this time—which seems unlikely—it can only have been fitfully and in a stage of extreme decadence.[43] The *Mocedades de Rodrigo* already shows unmistakable signs of decadence in its technique and approach, and it confirms what students of the more abundant French epic tell us about the last stages of an epic tradition. Nevertheless, it is a genuine epic, and as we shall see, it was undoubtedly circulated by the *juglares*. Scholars have been almost unanimous in asserting that it is, in all respects except its decadence, typical of the Spanish epic, and that it can be fully explained by the doctrines of *neotradicionalismo*. This school of thought was foreshadowed in its essentials by the nineteenth-century scholar Manuel Milá y Fontanals, and was given definitive form by Menéndez Pidal.[44]

The main *neotradicionalista* theories about Spanish epic are that it has a continuous development from Visigothic times; that it is essentially, and not just accidentally, anonymous; that epics were composed at the time of the events described in them, and underwent a succession of reworkings (the epic 'vive en variantes y refundiciones'); that they were at the time of their composition faithful to the historical facts, though subsequent reworkings might introduce a good deal of fiction; and that they were composed by *juglares*, without any ecclesiastical influence—in other words, that they were entirely popular and lay in their authorship and inspiration. The third and fourth of these beliefs rely for their principal support on each other, rather than on any independent evidence: since we do not possess in its original form any Spanish epic that was composed at the time of the events, we can do no more than speculate about the historical accuracy of such a poem, and Menéndez Pidal's arguments on these points are circular. It may be significant that the one epic for whose early composition there is substantial evidence, the *Siete Infantes de Lara* (see above, p. 39), is accurate in its background but entirely fictitious in its main action; it is true that we know this poem only in a chronicle prosification some three centuries after the period in which the action is set, but it is also true that we do not have a shred of evidence to show that the original form of the *Siete Infantes* was faithful to history. The question of continuity from the Germanic epic of the Visigoths is one that we have already considered when discussing the supposed epic on the fall of Spain to the Moors. The *neotradicionalista* belief in the essential anonymity of epics is probably well founded: the manuscripts of *PFG*, *CMC*, and the *Mocedades* lack an author's name, though this is true of most Spanish poems before the fourteenth century. Finally, we come to the theory that Spanish epics were composed by lay *juglares*, who took no interest in ecclesiastical matters. The lost epics prosified in chronicles usually have connections with tomb-cults, though because of chronological difficulties we cannot be sure v hether the tomb-cult gave rise to the poem or vice versa. Evidence for the *Roncesvalles* fragment is lacking, but *PFG* is undoubtedly a work of ecclesiastical propaganda. *CMC*, too, is clearly the work of a learned poet, but it is harder to prove specifically ecclesiastical inspiration. The *Mocedades*, whose lay and popular nature has always been asserted as a matter of *neotradicionalista* principle rather than on the basis of the evidence, proves on examination to have a learned author whose aim was to serve the immediate interests of his diocese. A theory which leads to such errors needs some revision.

It should not be concluded that *neotradicionalismo* is necessarily wrong at every point; and we certainly cannot resolve all the problems of Spanish epic by the application of Bédier's theories of monastic origins. No single theory can explain the whole of epic poetry, or even the whole of Spanish epic. We must also remember that, when most clerics but few laymen could write, poems with ecclesiastical connections stood an above-average chance of preservation in writing; and we must bear in mind the far-reaching implications of the work of Parry and Lord (see above, p. 44).

X. ORAL-FORMULAIC STYLE

Parry began his studies of Homer in the late 1920s, and extended them to the epic singers of modern Yugoslavia a few years later; the work was continued and made better known by Lord. This major development in research was surprisingly slow to attract the attention of medievalists: a pioneer study discussed formulas in the Spanish ballads, but Anglo-Saxon specialists were the first to adopt the Parry-Lord approach very widely.[45] Not until the publication of Lord's book in 1960 were his ideas generally recognised by Hispanic medievalists, who then compensated for their delay by an over-eager acceptance. The difficulties of this approach have yet to be thoroughly explored.

It is necessary to distinguish two questions: first, do any Spanish epics show, by formulas and other features, that they were orally composed? Secondly, do any of the manuscripts derive from a text dictated by a *juglar* to a scribe? The second question is much easier to answer, since Lord reports that similar dictation in Yugoslavia will, if unskilfully done, produce metrical irregularity and passages of prose mixed with the verse, especially at the beginning. It is likely that the extant manuscript of the *Cantar de Mio Cid* descends from an ineptly dictated oral text, and it is virtually certain that this is true of the *Mocedades de Rodrigo* manuscript.[46] Some irregularity seems to have been a feature of a good deal of medieval Spanish verse, but extreme fluctuations in length of lines can be satisfactorily explained only by Lord's concept of the dictated oral text.

This, however, need not mean that the poem in question was orally composed. Even a written poem could be diffused by *juglares*, and then dictated by a *juglar* to a scribe; the effects of inept dictation would be the same as for an orally-composed poem. Irregularity may be, and extreme irregularity almost certainly is, evidence of oral diffusion followed by dictation, but it can tell us nothing about the method of composition. To decide whether a Spanish epic was orally composed, we must investigate its use of formulas, of motifs, and of enjambement, Lord's three essential tests of oral composition. Some scholars have concluded that by these tests *CMC* and *Roncesvalles* are orally-composed epics,[47] but other research suggests that the use of formulas in the extant Spanish epics is, though too frequent to be the product of mere chance, not frequent enough to indicate oral composition; the use of motifs in *CMC* supports this conclusion.[48] It is likely that a formulaic style was used at one period by Spanish epic poets as an aid to oral composition, but that the extant poems were composed in writing by poets who regarded formulas as a traditional and thus a necessary device, but who no longer depended on them. The role of the *juglares* was, at any rate for the poems we possess, not the composition of epics but their performance. In their performance the *juglares* seem to have relied much more on memory, and much less on improvisation, than the singers of modern Yugoslavia. They must have improvised to some extent, and dictation to scribes would also have caused changes, but the texts we possess today seem to be substantially what the poets composed, blending popular and learned elements, and making individual use—sometimes skilful, sometimes clumsy—of the formulaic tradition.

NOTES

1. C. M. Bowra, *Primitive Song*, Ch. 2, and 'The Meaning of a Heroic Age', *In General and Particular* (London, 1964), pp. 63-84. On origins, see also H. M. and N. K. Chadwick, *The Growth of Literature*, III (Cambridge, 1940), Part 4.

2. Bowra, *Heroic Poetry*, p. 5. This is the best treatment of the standard features of heroic epic.

3. Bowra, *From Virgil to Milton* (London, 1945), Ch. 1.

4. Bowra, 'Meaning of a Heroic Age'; Chadwick, *Growth of Literature*; H. M. Chadwick, *The Heroic Age* (Cambridge, 1912).

5. R. Menéndez Pidal, 'Los godos y el origen de la epopeya española', *Los godos y la epopeya española* (Madrid, 1956), pp. 9-57. The most recent version of this theory is Robert A. Hall's article, 'Old Spanish Stress-Timed Verse and Germanic Superstratum', *RPh*, XIX (1965-66), 227-34. This should not be confused with the much more likely theory that Germanic folk-tales and other traditions persisted among the Visigoths after their Latinisation; cf. Krappe and Entwistle (below, note 13).

6. Menéndez Pidal, *Reliquias*, pp. xvi-xx, and *En torno al Poema del Cid*, pp. 87-94; Martín de Riquer, 'Épopée jongleresque à écouter et épopée romanesque à lire', *La Technique littéraire des chansons de geste. Actes du Colloque de Liège (septembre 1957)* (BFPLUL, CL, Paris, 1959), 75-82.

7. Menéndez Pidal gives a full, though partisan, account of this matter in the Introduction to *Reliquias*.

8. *Primera crónica general*, II, 355. The reference here is to epics of French origin that exalt the deeds of Charlemagne. Another manuscript of the chronicle refers at this point to the part played by minstrels in the diffusion of the poems: 'maguer que los joglares cuentan en sus cantares de gesta que Carlos conquirió en España muchas çibdades . . .' Traditional theories of epic chronology and the relationship between chronicles and epics will be challenged in a forthcoming study by Keith Whinnom.

9. Henríquez Ureña, *Estudios de versificación*, p. 23n, gives an example of rhythmic and assonating prose in *EE* that came not from an epic but from a Latin prose-chronicle.

10. *La leyenda*; the reconstructed text is printed in *Reliquias*, pp. 199-239. Such reconstruction can be overdone: compare Julio Puyol y Alonso's reconstruction of the *Cantar de gesta de don Sancho II de Castilla* (Madrid, 1911) with the more cautious and sounder work of Carola Reig (1947). Most, though not all, of Menéndez Pidal's *Siete Infantes* reconstruction is reliable.

11. The *Romancero tradicional*, ed. Menéndez Pidal *et al.*, collects these texts with commentary.

12. Menéndez Pidal, '*Roncesvalles*. Un nuevo cantar'. Connections between ballads and the corresponding epics now seem less close than had been thought: see Paul Bénichou, *Creación poética en el romancero tradicional* (Madrid, BRH, 1968).

13. For the supposed epic, see Menéndez Pidal, *Floresta*; and *Reliquias*, Introduction and pp. 7-19. For analogous folklore, see A. H. Krappe, *The Legend of Rodrick, Last of the Visigoth Kings, and the Ermanarich Cycle* (Heidelberg, 1923); and cf. W. J. Entwistle, 'Remarks Concerning the Historical Account of Spanish Epic Origins', *RH*, LXXXI (1933), part 1, 352-77. The change of language among the Visigoths would, as previously noted, make their retention of Germanic epics very difficult, but Krappe rightly points out that folk-traditions were likely to be preserved. Arabic influence on the Spanish epic has also been suggested: Francisco Marcos-Marín, *Estudios épicos: los árabes y la poesía épica* (Montréal, 1970); Alvaro Galmés de Fuentes, 'Épica árabe y épica castellana (problema crítico de sus posibles relaciones),' *Atti dell' Accademia dei Lincei*, 139 (1970), 195-259. This question remains open.

14. See *Reliquias*, Introd. and pp. 22-6.

15. Jules Horrent, *La Chanson de Roland dans les littératures française et espagnole au Moyen Age* (BFPLUL, CXX, Paris, 1951).

16. Martín de Riquer, 'El fragmento de *Roncesvalles* y el planto de Gonzalo Gústioz', *Studi in onore di Angelo Monteverdi* (Modena, 1959), II, 623-8 (amplified version in *La leyenda del Graal y temas épicos medievales* (Madrid, 1968), pp. 205-20); Ruth H. Webber, 'The Diction of the *Roncesvalles* Fragment', *Homenaje a Rodríguez-Moñino* (Madrid, 1966), II, 311-21; Jacques Horrent, 'L'allusion à la chanson de Mainet contenue dans le *Roncesvalles*', *MRo*, XX (1970), 85-92.

17. Menéndez Pidal, *'Galiene la Belle* y los palacios de Galiana en Toledo', *Historia y epopeya*, pp. 263-84; reprinted in *Poesía árabe y poesía europea* (Madrid, Austral, 1941).

18. W. J. Entwistle, 'The *Cantar de gesta* of Bernardo del Carpio', *MLR*, XXIII (1928), 307-22 and 432-52; A. B. Franklin, 'A Study of the Origins of the Legend of B. del C.', *HR*, V (1937), 286-303.

19. A number of the folklore elements were pointed out by Entwistle, 'Historical Account', and by María Rosa Lida de Malkiel in a review of Zamora Vicente's edition, *NRFH*, III (1949), 182-5. On the questions of structure and of use of folklore, see J. P. Keller, 'Inversion of the Prison Episodes in the *PFG'*, *HR*, XXII (1954), 253-63; 'The Hunt and Prophecy Episode of the *PFG'*, *HR*, XXIII (1955), 251-8; 'El misterioso origen de Fernán González', *NRFH*, X (1956), 41-4; 'The Structure of the *PFG'*, *HR*, XXV (1957), 235-46. Although some of Keller's conclusions are of doubtful validity, these articles are essential reading for anyone interested in literary criticism of the poem. See also Lida de Malkiel, *La idea de la fama*, pp. 197-207; Joaquín Gimeno Casalduero, 'Sobre la composición del *PFG'*, *AEM*, V (1968), 181-206; and, for the treatment of history, Louis Chalon, 'L'histoire de la monarchie asturienne, de Pelayo à Alphonse II le Chaste, dans le *PFG'*, *MRo*, XX (1970), 61-7.

20. Gifford Davis, 'The Development of a National Theme in Medieval Castilian Literature', *HR*, III (1935), 149-61, and 'National Sentiment in the *PFG* and in the *Poema de Alfonso Onceno'*, *HR*, XVI (1948), 61-8; J. A. Maravall, *El concepto de España en la Edad Media* (2nd ed., Madrid, 1964); Stephen Reckert, *The Matter of Britain and the Praise of Spain* (Cardiff, 1967).

21. The opposing extremes are Joseph Bédier's theory that the French epics were born in the shrines along the pilgrim-routes, and Menéndez Pidal's denial of any ecclesiastical influence on epics. See Bédier, *Les Légendes épiques. Recherches sur la formation des chansons de geste* (4 vols, Paris, 1908-13); Menéndez Pidal, 'Problemas de la poesía épica', *Los godos*, pp. 59-87, and *La Chanson de Roland et la tradition épique des Francs* (2nd ed., Paris, 1960). For recent discussions of the problem, see Urban T. Holmes, 'The Post-Bédier Theories on the Origins of the *Chansons de Geste'*, *Sp*, XXX (1955), 72-81; Pierre Le Gentil, 'Le traditionalisme de D. Ramón Menéndez Pidal (d'après un ouvrage récent)', *BH*, LXI (1959), 183-214; D. M. Dougherty, 'The Present Status of Bédier's Theories', *S*, XIV (1960), 289-99; W. G. van Emden, ' "La bataille est aduree endementres": traditionalism and individualism in Chanson-de-geste studies', *NMS*, XIII (1969), 3-26; Italo Siciliano, *Les Chansons de geste et l'épopée—mythes-histoire-poèmes* (Torino, 1968).

22. *La leyenda*; *Reliquias*; see also his *'Los Infantes de Salas* y la epopeya francesa—influencias recíprocas dentro de la tradición épica románica', *Mélanges Lejeune*, I, 485-501.

23. P. E. Russell, 'San Pedro de Cardeña and the Heroic History of the Cid', *MAe*, XXVII (1958), 57-79, at pp. 57-8. This article gives details of the ecclesiastical connections of other epics. See also Deyermond, *Epic Poetry and the Clergy*, map I; and for an important discussion of the effect of tomb-cults on French epics, Stephen G. Nichols, 'The Interaction of Life and

Literature in the *Peregrinationes ad loca sancta* and the *Chansons de geste*', *Sp*, XLIV (1969), 51-77.
24. See Menéndez Pidal, *La leyenda*; W. J. Entwistle, 'Remarks Concerning the Order of the Spanish *Cantares de gesta*', *RPh*, I (1947-48), 113-23, at pp. 117-18; J. M. Ruiz Asencio, 'La rebelión de Sancho García heredero del Condado de Castilla', *Hispania Sacra*, XXII (1969), 31-67.
25. Chapters 729-32 and 763-4. See Menéndez Pidal, *Historia y epopeya*, pp. 1-27; Ruiz Asencio, 'La rebelión'. The best treatment is the unpublished dissertation of J. E. Plumpton, *An Historical Study of the Legend of Garcí Fernández* (University of St Andrews, 1962).
26. There is a reference to the poem in the *Najerense*, summaries by Lucas of Túy and Archbishop Rodrigo, and a much fuller summary in *EE*, chapters 787-9. See *Historia y epopeya*, pp. 29-98.
27. *Historia y epopeya*, pp. 99-233. It is possible that the chronicle incorporates not an epic but a prose romance.
28. Full details of the Cid's life are given in Menéndez Pidal's *La España del Cid*. Though this includes some fictitious elements derived from the epics, it also contains the original Latin and Arabic sources on which our knowledge of the hero largely depends.
29. Medieval Spanish society has not yet been adequately studied, but we cannot assume that conditions prevalent in the remainder of western Europe necessarily occurred in Spain; for example, Castile never had a full feudal system. For a courageous attempt to apply the techniques of social history to the *Cantar de Mio Cid*, see Nilda Guglielmi, 'Cambio y movilidad social en el *CMC*', *Anales de Historia Antigua y Medieval*, XII (1963-65), 43-65.
30. W. J. Entwistle, 'La Estoria del noble varón el Çid Ruy Díaz el Campeador, sennor que fue de Valencia', *HR*, XV (1947), 206-11; Russell, 'San Pedro de Cardeña'. The *Historia Roderici* is printed in *La España del Cid*.
31. *CMC* is one of the few medieval Spanish works to which a considerable amount of literary criticism has been devoted. See Menéndez Pidal's remarks in his CC ed.; Américo Castro, 'Poesía y realidad en el *Poema del Cid*', *Hacia Cervantes* (2nd ed., Madrid, 1960), pp. 37-51; Dámaso Alonso, 'Estilo y creación en el *Poema del Cid*', *Ensayos sobre poesía española* (Madrid, 1944), pp. 69-111; Pedro Salinas, 'El *CMC* (Poema de la honra)' and 'La vuelta al esposo', *Ensayos de literatura hispánica* (Madrid, 1958), pp. 27-56; Eleazar Huerta, *Poética del Mio Cid* (Santiago de Chile, 1948); M. Singleton, 'The Two Techniques of the *PMC*: an interpretative essay', *RPh*, V (1951-52), 222-7; T. R. Hart, 'The Infantes de Carrión', *BHS*, XXXIII (1956), 17-24, and 'Hierarchical Patterns in the *CMC*', *RR*, LIII (1962), 161-73; Ulrich Leo, 'La afrenta de Corpes, novela psicológica', *NRFH*, XIII (1959), 291-304; Louise H. Allen, 'A Structural Analysis of the Epic Style of the *Cid*', *Structural Studies on Spanish Themes*, ed. H. R. Kahane and A. Pietrangeli (Salamanca and Urbana, Illinois, 1959), pp. 341-414; Stephen Gilman, *Tiempo y formas temporales en el Poema del Cid* (Madrid, BRH, 1961); P. N. Dunn, 'Theme and Myth in the *PMC*', *R*, LXXXIII (1962), 348-69, and 'Levels of Meaning in the *PMC*', *MLN*, LXXXV (1970), 109-19; T. Montgomery, 'The Cid and the Count of Barcelona', *HR*, XXX (1962), 1-11; Paul R. Olson, 'Symbolic Hierarchy in the Lion Episode of the *CMC*', *MLN*, LXXVII (1962), 499-511; J. Horrent, 'La Prise de Castejón. Remarques littéraires sur un passage du *CMC*', *MA*, LXIX (1963), 289-97; A. N. Zahareas, 'The Cid's Legal Action at the Court of Toledo', *RR*, LV (1964), 161-72; E. Caldera, 'L'oratoria nel *PMC*', *Miscellanea di Studi Ispanici* (Pisa, 1965), pp. 5-29; J. Rodríguez Puértolas, 'Un aspecto olvidado en el realismo del *PMC*', *PMLA*, LXXXII (1967), 170-7; Edmund de

THE EPIC 53

Chasca, *El arte*; Cesáreo Bandera Gómez, *El PMC: poesía, historia, mito* (Madrid, BRH, 1969). These studies vary considerably in difficulty and reliability: Allen and Gilman are too technical for any but advanced students, while Bandera Gómez's is of doubtful validity. For a stylistic feature of the Spanish epic in general, see C. C. Smith and J. Morris, 'On "Physical" Phrases in Old Spanish Epic and Other Texts', *Proc. of Leeds Philos. and Lit. Soc., Lit. and Hist. Section*, XII (1967), 129-90.

32. Lord, *The Singer of Tales*; *The Making of Homeric Verse* [Parry's collected papers] (Oxford, 1971). Motifs are what Lord, rather confusingly, calls themes. See also Eugene Dorfman, *The Narreme in the Medieval Romance Epic. An introduction to narrative structures* (Toronto and Manchester, 1969).

33. Rita Hamilton, 'Epic Epithets in the *PMC*', *RLC*, XXXVI (1962), 161-78; de Chasca, *El arte*, Ch. 9. See also Ruth H. Webber, 'Un aspecto estilístico del *CMC*', *AEM*, II (1965), 485-96.

34. 'Dos poetas en el *CMC*', *R*, LXXXII (1961), 145-200; reprinted in *En torno*, pp. 109-62. A case for dual authorship had previously been argued by E. C. Hills, 'The Unity of the *Poem of the Cid*', *HBalt*, XII (1929), 113-18.

35. P. E. Russell, 'Some Problems of Diplomatic in the *CMC* and their Implications', *MLR*, XLVII (1952), 340-9, 'Where was Alcocer?', *Homenaje a J. A. van Praag* (Amsterdam, 1956), pp. 101-7, and 'San Pedro de Cardeña'; A. Ubieto Arteta, 'Observaciones al *CMC*', *Arbor*, XXXVII (1957), 145-70; D. G. Pattison, 'The Date of the *CMC*: a linguistic approach', *MLR*, LXII (1967), 443-50. Menéndez Pidal replies to some of these points in 'Sobre la fecha . . .', *En torno*, pp. 165-9; and 'Los cantores épicos yugoeslavos y los occidentales. El *Mio Cid* y dos refundidores primitivos', *BRABLB*, XXXI (1965-66), 195-225 (this article slightly modifies M.P.'s dual-authorship theory, suggesting that the San Esteban poet, now dated *c.* 1105, may himself have reworked a yet earlier poem). See also Jules Horrent, 'Tradition poétique du *CMC* au XIIe siècle', *CCMe*, VII (1964), 451-77, and 'Localisation du *CMC*', *Mélanges offerts à René Crozet* (Poitiers, 1966), I, 609-15.

36. Leo Spitzer, 'Sobre el carácter histórico del *CMC*', *NRFH*, II (1948), 105-17, reprinted in *Sobre antigua poesía española* (Buenos Aires, 1962), 7-25; R. Menéndez Pidal, 'Poesía e historia en el *Mio Cid*: el problema de la épica española', *NRFH*, III (1949), 113-29, reprinted in *De primitiva lírica esp. y antigua épica* (Buenos Aires, Austral, 1951); L. Chalon, 'A propos des filles du Cid', *MA*, LXXIII (1967), 217-37. See also M.P.'s articles on dual authorship.

37. Jules Horrent, 'Sur le *Carmen Campidoctoris*', *Studi Monteverdi*, I, 334-52. The text is printed in *La España del Cid*, II.

38. In *Chronica Adefonsi imperatoris*, ed. L. Sánchez Belda (Madrid, 1950). There is no adequate basis for the widely-held belief that the references in this poem prove that *CMC* was already in existence.

39. This Latin epic is now lost, except perhaps for the verse-epitaph on Sancho's tomb at Oña, which may derive from it. See W. J. Entwistle, 'On the *Carmen de morte Sanctii regis*', *BH*, XXX (1928), 204-19; Francisco Rico, 'Las letras latinas del siglo XII en Galicia, León y Castilla', *Abaco*, II (1969), 9-91, at pp. 83-5.

40. J. Horrent, 'La jura de Santa Gadea. Historia y poesía', *Studia Philologica. Homenaje ofrecido a Dámaso Alonso*, II (Madrid, 1961), 241-65.

41. S. G. Armistead's Princeton thesis (1955) is the standard work; a

revised version is to be published. See also Jole Scudieri Ruggieri, 'Qualche osservazione su *Las MR*', *CN*, XXIV (1964), 129-41.

42. S. G. Armistead, 'The Structure of the *Refundición de las Mocedades de Rodrigo*', *RPh*, XVII (1963-64), 338-45; Deyermond, *Epic Poetry and the Clergy*.

43. Menéndez Pidal, *Reliquias*, pp. lxxiii-lxxvi; and *Poesía juglaresca*, Ch. 12. For suggestions that the epic may have survived longer, see W. C. Atkinson, 'The Chronology of Spanish Ballad Origins', *MLR*, XXXII (1937), 44-61; and S. G. Armistead, *A Lost Version of the Cantar de gesta de las Mocedades de Rodrigo Reflected in the Second Redaction of Rodríguez de Almela's Compendio historial* (UCPMP, XXXVIII, no. 4, Berkeley and Los Angeles, 1963).

44. Typical statements of *neotradicionalista* theory may be found in Menéndez Pidal's 'Problemas de la poesía épica'; *Reliquias*, pp. vii-xiii; *Poesía juglaresca*, Ch. 13-14; and *La Chanson de Roland*, Ch. 11.

45. Ruth H. Webber, *Formulistic Diction in the Spanish Ballad* (UCPMP, XXXIV, no. 2, Berkeley and Los Angeles, 1951); F. P. Magoun, 'Oral-Formulaic Character of Anglo-Saxon Narrative Poetry', *Sp*, XXVIII (1953), 446-67.

46. L. P. Harvey, 'The Metrical Irregularity of the *Cantar de Mio Cid*', *BHS*, XL (1963), 137-43; Deyermond, 'The Singer of Tales and Mediaeval Spanish Epic', *BHS*, XLII (1965), 1-8, and *Epic Poetry and the Clergy*, pp. 55-8 and 200-2; R. A. Hall, 'Old Spanish Stress-Timed Verse'.

47. See de Chasca, *El arte juglaresco*; *Registro*; 'Composición escrita y oral en el *Poema del Cid*', *Fi*, XII (1966-67), 77-94; 'Toward a Redefinition of Epic Formula in the Light of the *CMC*', *HR*, XXXVIII (1970), 251-63. See also Ruth H. Webber, 'The Diction of *Roncesvalles*' and 'Un aspecto'; and J. M. Aguirre, 'Épica oral y épica castellana: tradición creadora y tradición repetitiva', *RF*, LXXX (1968), 13-43. Menéndez Pidal's views are given in 'Los cantores épicos yugoeslavos'. For the ballads, see Webber, *Formulistic Diction*; and Bruce A. Beatie, 'Oral-traditional Composition in the Spanish *Romancero* of the Sixteenth Century', *Journal of the Folklore Institute*, I (1964), 92-113.

48. I draw here on a forthcoming study by Margaret Chaplin.

Chapter 3

THE LITERATURE OF THE
THIRTEENTH-CENTURY EXPANSION: I

I. THE TWELFTH-CENTURY RENAISSANCE AND
SPAIN'S BELATEDNESS

THE CONCEPT OF THE MIDDLE AGES as a long and uniform period of intellectual stagnation, and of the Renaissance as a sudden awakening, has long since been abandoned. There was a revival of learning under Charlemagne, and an even greater revival in the twelfth-century renaissance. This century saw, in most of western Europe, not only a revival of learning whose most enduring achievement was the foundation of the universities, but also far-reaching changes in other aspects of life. The towns grew, and with them grew a money economy and an increasingly sophisticated nobility which seems closely linked with the spread of courtly love. New trade-routes were opened, pilgrimages flourished, and the Crusades (begun in 1096) were renewed throughout the century; early in the thirteenth century, European man's new mobility found further expression in the mendicant orders of travelling friars, the Franciscans and Dominicans. In Church and state, centralising tendencies made possible a greater stability which both fostered and benefited from the expansion of travel and the economy.

The cause of these developments and their relation to the intellectual revival are still disputed. The revival of learning took several forms. Translation of learned works into Latin, chiefly from Arabic but also from Hebrew and Greek, enriched the intellectual life of western Europe. This was one of the earliest aspects of the revival, and, paradoxically, it was undertaken first and most intensively in Italy and Spain, although in Italy the development of vernacular literature came late, and Spain was belated in almost all respects. Southern Italy, and above all Spain, were the only parts of Europe colonised by Arabic-speaking peoples, and the conditions were ideal for the transmission of Arabic culture; but the belatedness of Spain in other ways is less easily explicable.

Educational expansion was inevitably a major factor in the twelfth-century renaissance: the cathedral schools inherited from the earlier Middle Ages were enlarged and enriched, and the new institution of the *studium generale,* later known as the university, grew up in Italy, then in France, and later in England. Little is known of the Spanish cathedral schools, though it is likely that one flourished in Toledo; Spain may well have lacked universities until the early thirteenth century.[1] A prominent part was also played by lawyers (the blending of common law with an adapted Roman Law) and, of course, by philosophers: this was a period of wide-ranging and adventurous thought. Both lawyers and philosophers wrote in Latin, the language also of a flowering of sacred and secular lyric and narrative poetry, yet instead of stifling creative writing in the vernacular, the renaissance of Latin culture seems to have fostered it, at least north of the Alps and the Pyrenees. The first substantial body of cultured vernacular literature—the Provençal courtly poets, Chrétien de Troyes, and the first generations of German courtly lyric and narrative poets—dates from the twelfth century.[2]

Spain is an exception. Catalonia at this time was in most respects more French than Spanish, and the south was still Moorish, but the Christian kingdoms from Portugal to Aragon show a very different pattern from the remainder of western Europe. Except in the field of translation, the characteristic features of the twelfth-century French renaissance do not appear in Spain until the thirteenth. The first Spanish university was probably founded some time between 1208 and 1214, at Palencia. Cultured vernacular literature began at the end of the twelfth century in Portugal and Galicia (the Provençal-inspired lyric); in Castile—if we exclude epics which learned men composed in the traditional style, and one short play—it is not found until the early decades of the thirteenth century. The Gothic architecture which flourished in France from the 1140s onwards does not affect Spanish cathedrals until the 1220s. Our information about the social and economic conditions of twelfth-century Spain is still inadequate, but in this sphere also it seems probable that changes were slower in coming than they were north of the Alps.[3] Even in that other twelfth-century phenomenon, the Crusades, Spain was an exception to the European pattern: since the Muslims were an active danger within the Iberian Peninsula, there could be no question of the departure of many Spanish knights for the Holy Land, and even a lukewarm interest in the Crusades was not shown by Spanish monarchs until the thirteenth century was well advanced.[4] In Latin culture, the same situation occurs: twelfth-century Spain makes no great original contribution to the development of philosophy, and although the literary contribution is respectable, it is not outstanding; the Latin lyric is scarcely represented.[5] Even in small details, Spain's belatedness appears: for example, the poet of the thirteenth-century *Libro de Alexandre* states his literary aims in terms very similar to those used by Chrétien de Troyes in the previous century,[6] and there is an equal similarity and an equal time-lag between the literary programme of Gonzalo de Berceo and that of Wace and other Anglo-Norman poets.

This belatedness cannot be attributed to lack of foreign contacts: the eleventh century had been the high point of French penetration into Spain, with the thriving pilgrim-route to Santiago de Compostela, assistance against the Moors, the establishment of French commercial quarters in many Spanish towns, and the domination exercised over the Castilian Church by the reforming Cluniac monks. This domination led to the replacement of the native Spanish liturgy (the Mozarabic rite), and, less directly, of the native Spanish (Visigothic) script, by the standard western European forms.[7] Nor is the time-lag due to a very slow diffusion of literary works across the Pyrenees; when conditions were favourable, such influence could be quickly assimilated.

The cause of Spain's cultural belatedness is to be found in her twelfth-century history. The Cid's struggle to hold Valencia against the invading Almoravids has already been mentioned; his was an isolated example of successful resistance. When Alfonso VI took Toledo in 1085, the liberation of the entire Peninsula was in sight, but the intervention of the Almoravids undid the work of the Reconquest; when their power decayed, a fresh wave of fanatical Muslims, the Almohads, reached Spain. From the mid-1140s, the Spaniards were again on the defensive, and as late as 1195 they suffered a crushing defeat at the battle of Alarcos. Probably the most far-reaching effect of these invasions was that the mutual toleration which had long existed, despite warfare, between Christians, Muslims, and Jews was replaced by suspicion, intolerance, and persecution, though the towns kept the old attitude longer than the countryside. The prosperous and brilliant Jewish communities of Andalusia were driven to take refuge in the Christian north, whose economic and cultural life they enriched, but persecution spread to the Christian cities and Spain in the end deprived herself of the contributions that Moors and Jews had long made, and might have continued to make.

Not only the Almoravid and Almohad invasions darkened the twelfth century for Castile and León. In the first quarter, the reign of Queen Urraca was a period of discord and of Aragonese intervention; in the middle of the century, León and Castile again became separate kingdoms. Throughout this period, the nobles asserted themselves at the expense of the central authority, and the task of repopulating the previously deserted frontier areas so reduced the population of the north that it caused serious weakness. In these circumstances, the surprising thing is not the absence of a twelfth-century renaissance, but the ability of Castile and León to maintain a respectable level of Hispano-Latin literature and to develop a major centre of translating in Toledo. When circumstances changed, the literary and educational renewal came rapidly.

The decisive factor in the change was military. The defeat at Alarcos was avenged by the battle of Las Navas de Tolosa (1212), in which the united Castilian, Leonese, and Aragonese armies, with help from across the Pyrenees, broke the Almohad power. Five years later one of Castile's greatest kings, Fernando III (later to be canonised), came to the throne. In 1230 he reunited Castile and León, and soon afterwards the Reconquest was resumed on a scale unknown since the liberation of Toledo. Córdoba, which had been the centre of Moorish power, fell in 1236 (the Aragonese retook Valencia in the same year), Murcia in 1244, Seville in 1248, and Cadiz in 1250. Only the kingdom of Granada remained, and that might well have been reconquered had Fernando not died in 1252. Although Portugal and Aragon played a successful part, the main credit and the main benefits from the thirteenth-century Reconquest accrued to Castile. With the military expansion came economic recovery, abundant energy and self-confidence, and educational expansion. The University of Palencia was, as we have seen, founded about the time of Las Navas de Tolosa, and those of Salamanca and Valladolid followed within a few decades. Literary developments were equally impressive: by the middle of the century, Castile had a flourishing tradition of cultured narrative poetry, and the first substantial prose-works in the vernacular.

II. 'CUADERNA VÍA' VERSE

Some narrative poems of this period are in short and often irregular lines, but a different metre is used in an important and fairly homogeneous group of poems. This metre, *cuaderna vía*, has stanzas of four fourteen-syllable lines (alexandrines), each with a caesura in the middle, with full rhyme not assonance, and rhyming AAAA, BBBB, etc. There is in these poems far less metrical irregularity than in most Spanish verse of the period, and some poems come very near to total regularity; scholars still disagree, however, as to whether regularity can be assumed to be a standard feature of *cuaderna vía*. The term *mester de clerecía* is often used as a synonym for *cuaderna vía*, or to describe all poems in this metre, but this is misleading, especially if such use is coupled with references to *mester de juglaría* as the opposite of *clerecía*. Medieval Spanish narrative verse was not divided into two watertight compartments; neither did *juglares* compose all (or, indeed, many) of the non-*cuaderna vía* poems; nor can all *cuaderna vía* poems be grouped together.[8] It is, however, reasonable to apply the term *mester de clerecía* to the thirteenth-century *cuaderna vía* poems, since in addition to a common metre they have a common background, the monasteries of Old Castile (certain in the case of some poems, likely in others); a common period of origin (they were composed within a few decades of each other); and a mutual awareness (borrowings and reminiscences are frequent). The fourteenth-century *cuaderna vía* poems are very different.

III. GONZALO DE BERCEO

The chronology of this group of poems is still uncertain, but priority in the new metre belongs either to Berceo or to the *Libro de Alexandre*. The new form is undoubtedly an adaptation of a verse-form in another language; both French and Latin have their advocates.

Gonzalo de Berceo, unlike most of his contemporaries and immediate successors, tells us his name and other personal details; he is, indeed, the first Castilian poet whose name we know. He was born towards the end of the twelfth century, in the village of Berceo in La Rioja, and received at least part of his education in the nearby Benedictine monastery of San Millán de la Cogolla; it has been suggested that he studied at the University of Palencia. He served the monastery of San Millán not as a monk but as a secular priest. His service was primarily legal and administrative and involved a good deal of travelling; there is good reason to believe that he was notary to the abbot. Berceo was still alive in the early 1250s, but we do not know the date of his death.[9]

A few of Berceo's works may have been lost, but most of them survive. They fall into three groups: the hagiographic poems, three of them telling the lives of local saints and the fourth, which is incomplete, dealing with the martyrdom of St Lawrence; the poems devoted to the Blessed Virgin Mary—*Milagros de Nuestra Señora, Loores de Nuestra Señora*, and *Duelo que fizo la Virgen*; and two doctrinal works, *De los signos que aparescerán antes del Juicio* and *Sacrificio de la Misa*; in addition, three hymns are attributed to this poet.

The first of the hagiographic works to have been composed seems to be the *Vida de San Millán*. The patron saint of the monastery was a natural subject for Berceo's earliest poem, whose main source is the prose *Vita Beati Æmiliani* by Braulio, bishop of Saragossa. To this Berceo adds much material from the traditions of the monastery, and specifically from the Latin writings of his contemporary, the monk Fernandus (tentatively identified as Fernando Garcíez). The poem is divided into three sections: the outline of the saint's life, his miracles while alive, and the posthumous miracles (the *Vida de Santo Domingo* has the same division). The most important of the posthumous miracles is the appearance of San Millán and of Santiago (St James, the patron saint of Spain) in the skies during a crucial battle with the Moors; the terrified enemy flee, and the grateful Christian monarchs order the payment of perpetual tribute. The King of León decrees that his kingdom shall pay tribute to Santiago de Compostela, and Count Fernán

González orders that all Castile should make payment to San Millán de la Cogolla. It is very doubtful whether these decrees were ever made, but many Castilians were induced to pay the amounts due to the monastery, and the monks of San Millán possessed in the thirteenth century a Latin text of Fernán González's document, together with a Spanish translation. The document is a forgery, carried out by Fernandus when Berceo was closely associated with the monastery. Berceo (who, as a notary, would be an expert on such matters) must have known it was a forgery when he used it as the basis for the last part of his poem. Moreover, the poem is clearly designed to lead up to the story of the tribute:

> Qui la vida quisiere   de sant Millán saber
> e de la su istoria   bien certano seer,
> meta mientes en esto   que yo quiero leer:
> verá a do embían   los pueblos so aver.   (st. 1)

At the end, just before a few stanzas on some final miracles, Berceo points the moral for his audience:

> Si estos votos fuessen   lealment enviados,
> estos sanctos preciosos serien nuestros pagados,
> avriemos pan e vino,   temporales temprados,
> non seriemos com somos   de tristicia menguados.
>   Amigos e sennores,   entenderlo podedes
> qe a estos dos sanctos   en debda lis yazedes;
> d'esto seet seguros,   qe bien vos fallaredes
> si bien lis enviáredes   esto qe lis devedes.   (479-80)

The forgery of documents to replace ones that had been lost, or to support claims that were strongly and devoutly believed in, was an accepted part of ecclesiastical life in the Middle Ages, and there is no inconsistency between the composition of a devout hagiographic poem and the deliberate propagation of a forgery; indeed, Berceo would almost certainly have seen both actions as part of the same duty.

Berceo was not a simple and uncultivated country priest, as he claimed when he wrote that:

> Quiero fer una prosa[10] en román paladino,
> en qual suele el pueblo fablar con so vezino;
> ca non so tan letrado por fer otro latino:
> bien valdrá, como creo, un vaso de bon vino.
>   (*Santo Domingo*, 2)

and asserted his total dependence on his Latin source:

> Quando non lo leyesse, dezir non lo querría;
> ca en firmar la dubda grand peccado avría.
>   (*Santo Domingo*, 73)

Ca al non escrevimos sy non lo que leemos.

(*Santa Oria*, 89)

The claim that Berceo dared not add anything to his source is demonstrably untrue. He uses the favourite medieval device—often found in sermons—of citing the authority of *lo escripto*; this carried conviction to an illiterate public for whom the written word was almost magical. Protestation of ignorance is also traditional: the medieval manuals of rhetoric recommend the modesty-*topos* as one of the best ways of gaining the goodwill of an audience.

Berceo's self-deprecation is patently false. His career as an ecclesiastical administrator, his complicity in Fernandus's forgeries, his ability to transform a Latin prose-work aimed at the learned into a Spanish poem to which popular audiences would respond—all these testify to his sophistication and skill, and they are supported by a detailed analysis of his poems.[11] Two main traditions were available to him: the rhetorical-ecclesiastical and that of the minstrels.

Medieval rhetoric was extremely influential in literature. The *Artes poeticae*, or manuals of rhetoric (and sometimes of grammar), developed the techniques inherited from the Classical Latin writers (the *Rhetorica ad Herennium*, long attributed to Cicero, was an important stage in this transmission); the Latin writers had borrowed from the Greek rhetoricians. Rhetoric was one of the basic subjects of medieval education,[12] and no educated writer—which of course means no writer—could totally escape its influence. The *Artes poeticae* provided writers with a wide range of stylistic devices (e.g. several forms of repetition and of balanced construction, methods of amplification, and pleasing sound-patterns) and of commonplaces (e.g. the modesty-*topos*, assurances that the speaker will be brief, and appeals to authority).[13] They did not provide much help in questions of literary structure, but for this writers could turn to manuals of preaching (*Artes praedicandi*) and, in the late Middle Ages, to works on memory-training.[14]

Since so much of medieval literature was composed by the clergy, the influence of sermon-technique is almost as powerful as that of rhetoric.[15] Sermons were of two main types: the learned (*divisio intra*) sermon addressed to a clerical congregation and usually in Latin; and the popular (*divisio extra*), which was in the vernacular and addressed to a lay and largely illiterate congregation. Either of these would provide a structural model by which the medieval writer could arrange his material, but the popular sermon offered him in addition a rich store of illustrative material. The popular preacher had to make his message vivid if his audience was to grasp it; and having gained the attention of his congregation, he needed the skill to retain it. This need was made all the more urgent by the fact that from the thirteenth century onwards the parish priests were in competition with the travelling friars who preached in the market-place—and both had to compete with the minstrels. The sermon thus had to offer entertainment as well as edification, and relied heavily on *exempla* (illustrative stories drawn from the Bible, history, animal fables, and the preacher's real or imagined experience and observation); it also, especially towards the end of the Middle Ages, made use of satire and of the realistic presentation of popular speech.

A poet addressing a wide audience faced the same necessities as a popular preacher; often he would himself be a preacher, and there are medieval Spanish literary works which incorporate stories that the author had, in all probability, used in the pulpit and found that he enjoyed using. If a writer was to compete successfully with the *juglares*, he would have to adopt some of their techniques and even their subject-matter. Not all clerics took the same view of *juglares*: some are strongly hostile, while Berceo, whose use of minstrels' resources is particularly noteworthy, varies in his attitude, but refers to himself as a *juglar* four times in the *Vida de Santo Domingo*, as well as asking for a *juglar*'s reward, a 'vaso de bon vino'.

Berceo employs juglaresque devices in most of his poems, and makes some use throughout his poetic career of the formulaic style which narrative poets (and writers of prose narrative) inherited from a now vanished stage of orally-composed epic.[16] His use of epic subject-matter is on the other hand largely concentrated in the *Vida de San Millán*, the only one of Berceo's poems in which military action plays a decisive part, decisive in both the poem's structure (the battle is the last major incident, and the most notable of the saint's posthumous miracles) and its purpose (the battle is the occasion for Fernán González's decree that tribute should be paid to the monastery). Berceo, addressing a rural audience, frequently uses images of country life to refer to the saint; he also uses military images, and most of his reminiscences of epic fit into this pattern. The picture of the saint as knight balances that of the saint as peasant, and thus prevents any over-familiarity. Berceo incorporates this balance into the very structure of his poem. San Millán is a shepherd in his youth, and the beginning of his religious education is described in military imagery. Later in the poem, when he is a famous and influential priest, he is referred to figuratively as a shepherd, and at the end his most important posthumous miracle is the winning of a battle with the Moors. The rural and the military metaphors are of New Testament origin, and they correspond to two of the three Estates of medieval social theory.[17] Berceo shows us San Millán as a real shepherd and metaphorical knight who becomes a real knight and metaphorical shepherd; yet he is primarily, as the narrative never allows us to forget, a priest, so that the structural balance of two Estates is enclosed in a framework of the third.

The *Vida de Santo Domingo*, like the *Vida de San Millán*, is firmly rooted in medieval European hagiography, first a Latin and later a vernacular tradition. *Santo Domingo*, like most vernacular hagiography, has a Latin source; it is based on the *Vita Sancti Dominici* of Abbot Grimaldus, who had been the saint's pupil.[18] Perhaps the most remarkable feature for a modern reader is the help that Santo Domingo gives to a young girl who wishes to become a nun, and who is tormented by visions of the Devil in the form of a serpent (stanzas 315-33). The saint banishes the Devil, and the girl (perhaps the Oria whose *Vida* Berceo wrote later) can follow her vocation. This episode seems to incorporate an authentic record of a sexual dream—the description of the serpent is unmistakably phallic. This is typical of the matter-of-fact acceptance of human sexuality in much medieval religious writing. This poem again reveals Berceo's concern for his monastery. The resistance of Santo Domingo, Prior of San Millán de la Cogolla, to the King of Navarre's claim to the monastery's treasure (131-68) is described with a warmth that clearly indicates Berceo's emotional commitment. It is also relevant that the monastery of Santo Domingo de Silos, which the saint refounded, was allied to San Millán de la Cogolla. The direct and urgent economic motive which led to the writing of the *Vida de San Millán* is absent from Berceo's other poems, but loyalty to his monastery and awareness of its interest to pilgrims often remain; on several occasions, he writes of a feature that would be of special concern to pilgrims, as when he gives detailed directions for finding the tombs at the upper (older) monastery of San Millán (*Vida de Santa Oria*, 181-2).

Berceo wrote the *Vida de Santa Oria* at the end of his life: his own statement is supported by stylistic and historical evidence.[19] On this occasion, the Latin source (Berceo tells us that he bases his poem on the account written by Munio, the saint's confessor) is no longer extant, and the tripartite division of the material is concealed by the fact that Oria's visions, not her miracles, are the main subject. Yet the same basic arrangement exists, and the structure of the poem is at once tighter and more subtle than in the previous works. A series of misfortunes, of kinds common enough in medieval manuscripts, has blurred the structure in the extant text, but the correct order can be restored with reasonable certainty.[20] *Santa Oria* is more lyrical in tone than *San Millán* or *Santo Domingo*, largely because attention is concentrated not on good works in this world but on visions of Heaven (a reflection of Berceo's preoccupations as death approached). There is also a greater reliance on allegory than in his other lives of saints; again, the change in subject-matter is the reason. One final point: Berceo tells us directly that he is old and tired (st. 2), and also makes the point by a highly personal and moving use of a familiar metaphor:

Avemos en el prólogo mucho detardado;
siguamos la estoria, esto es aguisado.
Los días son non grandes, anochezrá privado,
escrivir en tiniebra es un mester pesado.   (10)

Although this metaphor is later used to indicate Oria's approaching
death ('a boca de noche era', 176), almost all critics have concluded
that Berceo was referring literally to the coming of night as a reason
for haste in completing his poem (which, of course, he had only just
begun).[21]

The position of the *Milagros de Nuestra Señora* within the chronological order of Berceo's works cannot be fixed with any certainty, but
since one of the stanzas refers to Fernando III as dead (he died in
1252), the final version must come late in Berceo's life, and may well
be just before *Santa Oria*. It too comes mainly from a Latin source, and
belongs to a widespread and flourishing tradition. Works devoted to
the Blessed Virgin Mary were as numerous and as widely diffused as
hagiographic works at this period. In the early centuries of the Church,
Mary received little or no special attention, and when popular devotion
to her began to grow, church Councils several times tried to discourage
it. Eventually the pressure of popular belief, the need to rely on a
maternal figure who could intercede on man's behalf, became too great,
and by the tenth century Marian devotion, which developed earlier in
eastern Europe, was firmly established in the West. Hymns were written
to the Virgin, feast-days and churches were dedicated to her, and she
began to take a prominent part in literature and the visual arts; this
began on a large scale in the eleventh century. There are three main
types of Marian literature: narrative (mainly miracle-stories), doctrinal,
and lyrical (often poems on the joys or the sorrows of Mary); the
lyrical works are closest in tone to the visual arts.

Collections of Marian miracle-stories began to be formed in Latin
in the eleventh century, and rapidly increased in bulk, in number, and
in circulation. The most intensive period for miracle-collections is the
twelfth to fourteenth centuries; they are diffused both orally (sermons,
recitation of poems) and in manuscript; they pass from Latin into
the vernacular, and spread throughout and beyond Europe (Berceo's
story of the *Ladrón devoto*, no. 6 in the *Milagros*, is found not only in
all the great Latin collections, in French, and in German, but also in
Arabic and Ethiopian). About one hundred stories occur with great
frequency, including some which have been adapted from a non-
Marian and even non-Christian tradition (for example, Berceo's no. 15,
La boda y la Virgen, which seems to have links with pre-Christian
folklore, and no. 20, *El monge embriagado*, whose ultimate origin is
probably a sermon-commentary on Psalm 22). There are three major
Hispanic collections of Marian miracles dating from the thirteenth

century, in three languages: besides Berceo's there are Alfonso X's *Cantigas de Santa Maria* in Galician-Portuguese, and Gil de Zamora's Latin prose-work, both of them more extensive than the *Milagros,* and each of them containing versions of most of the miracles that Berceo uses.

The Latin source for the *Milagros* is a prose collection of twenty-eight stories; a manuscript very similar to that used by Berceo survives.[22] The Spanish poet discards four of these miracles and adds an allegorical introduction and a local Spanish miracle not in the Latin source. The introduction describes a meadow which is in the medieval rhetorical tradition of the *locus amoenus,* a glade or garden which is often a setting for love; here the perfection of the meadow is explained as an allegory of the perfection of the Virgin Mary. There are occasional cross-references between this introduction and the miracles, which tighten the structure of the work, but in general the stories can be taken as independent poems without any appreciable loss. The purpose of the *Milagros* is less to give information about Mary than to inspire devotion to her, and stories in which her devotees are rewarded (although some display no other virtue) are much more numerous than those in which the wicked are punished; the severe teaching of the medieval Church on the difficulty of salvation is here replaced by a mother's care for her wayward children:

> El monge que por todo esto avía pasado,
> de la carga del vino non era bien folgado,
> que vino e que miedo avienlo tan sovado,
> que tornar non podió a su lecho usado.
>
> La Reina preciosa e de precioso fecho
> prísolo por la mano, levólo poral lecho,
> cubriólo con la manta e con el sobrelecho,
> púsol so la cabeza el cabezal derecho.
>
> Demás quando lo ovo en su lecho echado
> sanctiguól con su diestra e fo bien sanctiguado:
> 'Amigo,' díssol, 'fuelga, ca eres mui lazrado,
> con un poco que duermas luego serás folgado.'   (481-3)

But we should remember that the tone of the stories varies from tender and humorous to fierce, and that the doctrine varies from exaggeratedly Marian to Christ-centred. The structural skill varies also: the first and tenth miracles are weak in this respect, the second, ninth, and several others are particularly good.[23]

One other poem of Berceo's deserves special mention, since it includes a section not in *cuaderna vía.* This is the *Duelo de la Virgen,* which includes near the end a song of the Jewish guards set to watch over the Sepulchre. The extant text of this song, which has traces of parallelistic structure, does not easily make consecutive sense, and scholars have therefore tried to rearrange the stanzas so as to improve both the sense and the structure.[24] The present order can, however, be satisfactory if the stanzas are divided between two antiphonal groups. The song is probably inspired both by popular lyric and by the liturgy.[25]

IV. 'LIBRO DE ALEXANDRE'

The *Libro de Alexandre*—sometimes attributed to Berceo—is very different. Its subject is one that has fascinated men of every period, from Alexander the Great's own contemporaries to the twentieth century, but the spectacle of a brilliant and ambitious youth who overthrew the world's greatest empire yet failed to master his own nature, and who died, still young, at the hands of a traitor—this captured the medieval imagination more than that of any other period, and it was outdone in the Middle Ages only by the Christian story of man's fall and redemption.[26] The *Libro de Alexandre*, the earliest and the best of several Spanish treatments of the subject, is also one of the best in any language. It may be classified as either a literary epic or a romance; in medieval Spain, as in many other countries, romances (in prose or verse) were one of the most widespread and characteristic literary forms.[27]

Medieval works on Alexander descend from the romance known as Pseudo-Callisthenes and the largely historical tradition of which Quintus Curtius is the chief representative. (The accurate historical treatment of Alexander remained unknown in the Middle Ages.)[28] The main source of the *Libro de Alexandre* is the twelfth-century Latin *Alexandreis* of Gautier de Châtillon, which is in the Quintus Curtius tradition; this is supplemented by other sources, of which the two most important derive ultimately from Pseudo-Callisthenes: a French poem, the *Roman d'Alexandre*, and a Latin prose-work, the *Historia de preliis*.[29] These and other sources are blended with great care, and usually to excellent effect, into a complex structure. The many apparent digressions, especially the long narrative of the Trojan War which Alexander addresses to his army, have been thought irrelevant and structurally weak, but the *Alexandre* is unified in a way which is almost as frequent in medieval narrative as the simpler linear plot: it carefully interweaves themes and episodes.[30] Moreover, the apparent digressions contribute to the major themes: the overthrow of human greatness, the fatal flaw in the hero's character, and the workings of treachery. We are shown Alexander's increasing success, which can never satisfy him; his exploration of the skies and the depths of the sea, his growing pride and *cobdicia* (not avarice but a general lack of restraint, a desire for forbidden things); and the tragedy of his death:

Fue el rrey en todo esto la palabra perdiendo,
la nariz aguzando, la boz engordiendo.
Dixo a sus varones, 'Ya lo ydes veyendo;
arrenunçio el mundo, a Dios vos acomiendo.'
Acostó la cabeça sobre un fazeruelo,
non serie omne bivo que non oviese duelo.
Mandó que lo echasen del lecho en el suelo,
que avie ya travado del alma el anzuelo...
El gozo fue tornado en bozes e en planto.
'Señor,' dizían los unos, '¿quién vio atal quebranto?
A vos avíamos todos por saya e por manto;
señor, maldito sea quien nos guerreó tanto.'   (2645-8)

The poet's attitude to Alexander's salvation or damnation has been
much discussed.[31] We are certainly not told that the hero is saved, but
neither is it made clear that he is damned. The evidence in the poem
is conflicting, partly because the poet found it intellectually or emotionally difficult to resolve this point, partly because he wished to present
an exemplary case of fallen greatness, and the worldly fall was striking
enough for his purposes:

Alexandre, que era rrey de gran poder,
que mares nen tierra no lo podien caber,
en una fuessa ovo en cabo a caer,
que non podie de término doze pies tener.   (2672)

The themes of the poem are not at first presented by direct statement
but by a gradual building-up of episodes which prefigure, or fore-
shadow, Alexander's downfall and the reasons for it; this is the purpose
served by the apparent digressions, including the Troy narrative.[32]
Only towards the end of the *Alexandre* is this method reinforced by
explicit commentary from the poet.

The merits of the *Libro de Alexandre* are primarily structural and
thematic; they are to be seen in the poem as a whole, not in isolated
sections. Although there are passages attractive in themselves—the first
dawn that the Greek army sees on Asian soil, the May-song, the portents
in the skies before the hero's murder—they are still more impressive
when set in their context. The poet's medievalisation of classical antiquity must also be seen in the light of the work's themes. It is not naive
quaintness but deliberate policy, aimed at making the work meaningful to the poet's contemporaries; it is, moreover, carried out with
generally unobtrusive sophistication.[33]

Los votos del pavón, a Spanish version of another French Alexander
poem, *Les Voeux du paon*, is now lost. It was probably in *cuaderna
vía*, but we have no means of knowing how it treated its original.

V. 'LIBRO DE APOLONIO'

The *Libro de Alexandre* is probably one of the earlier *cuaderna vía* poems and may even have been composed at the very beginning of the thirteenth century.[34] A work which is almost certainly later is the *Libro de Apolonio*, whose plot and theme are stated at the outset by the poet:

> del buen rey Apolonio e de su cortesía.
> El rey Apolonio de Tiro natural,
> que por las aventuras visco grant tenporal,
> commo perdió la fija e la muger capdal,
> como las cobró amas, ca les fue muy leyal.   (1-2)

This work is in the tradition of the late classical Greek romance, the typical mechanism of whose plot is an arbitrary series of storms at sea and kidnappings by pirates; the families or lovers separated by these misfortunes are reunited in a recognition scene, and all ends happily. The source for the *Libro de Apolonio* is the *Historia Apollonii regis Tyri*, a Latin work of the late classical period written in the Greek tradition.[35] The *Historia* is weak in structure and inconsistent in motivation; this is partly due to the arbitrary nature of the typical Greek romance plot and the half-understood folk-traditions that persist in this story, but many of the faults are remedied by the Spanish poet.[36] *Libro de Apolonio*, whose plot and theme are stated at the outset by the in the famous description of the heroine as a *juglaresa*, st. 426-32), as is usual in medieval Spanish adaptations of a Latin work, and it is also superior in the intellectual qualities of consistency and organisation.[37]

The machinery of wanderings and separations is set in motion when Apolonio has to flee from the King of Antioch, whose incest he has revealed. The story is rich in folk-motifs, and traditions of incest and of succession to the throne through the female line seem to have played a major part in its origins.[38] A number of incidents which are difficult to account for in the present form of the story make immediate sense in the light of these underlying traditions, whose unconscious appeal must have been strong.

The *Apolonio* shows virtue rewarded. The happy ending for the hero and his family is a reward not for strength or intelligence but for unswerving virtue and trust in God. The arbitrary series of misadventures is brought to an arbitrary end, inevitably by a further storm which the poet clearly sees as God's work, so that in the final stanza he asks that

> El Sennyor que los vientos e la mar ha por mandar,
> él nos dé la ssu graçia e él nos denye guiar;
> él nos dexe tales cosas comedir e obrar
> que por la ssu merçed podamos escapar.   (656)

Conflict within the hero dominates the *Alexandre*, but in the *Apolonio* we have a straightforward contest between good and evil characters. Monotony is avoided by the poet's skill in narrative and characterisation, by the hidden tensions of the incest-motif, and by the striking contrast between the highly sophisticated hero and the primitive situations in which he is set.[39]

The other well-known *cuaderna vía* poem of the thirteenth century, the *Poema de Fernán González*, has already been dealt with (see above, pp. 36-8), but there is a lesser-known poem that deserves mention. The *Castigos y ejemplos de Catón* (written several decades later) has no narrative element, and in most ways resembles the prose-works of wisdom literature (see below, pp. 99-101), rather than the earlier *cuaderna vía* poems. It belongs to the flourishing medieval tradition of pseudo-Cato literature, purportedly the advice given by Cato to his son. By one of the quirks of literary fashion, it enjoyed a considerable circulation in sixteenth-century *pliegos sueltos* (chap-books) when much better *cuaderna vía* works were forgotten.[40]

VI. THE PROBLEM OF DIFFUSION

It is disputed whether these *cuaderna vía* poems were intended mainly for oral or for written diffusion. Phrases like 'I shall tell you', 'You will hear', seem to imply the presence of a listening audience; but similar phrases occur in prose-works that can hardly have been recited by *juglares*, and there are lines in *cuaderna vía* poems which refer to a written text. The debate continues.[41]

The problem also affects prose romances. Very often, such works might be read aloud to a small and homogeneous group, a situation which has much more in common with private reading than with recitation by a *juglar*: it allows for a sophisticated appeal and a high level of complexity.[42] This may well have been the way in which most thirteenth-century *cuaderna vía* poems were diffused. The *Poema de Fernán González* is, because of its epic nature, an exception: it was probably recited by *juglares* in much the same way as the *Cantar de Mio Cid* (though in both cases the manuscripts doubtless found private readers also). The *Libro de Alexandre*'s length, complexity, and intellectual sophistication make the private reader or the small educated group the natural public for the poem; the same may well be true, in a modified way, of the *Apolonio*. As we have already seen, some passages in Berceo's hagiographic poems seem designed for groups of pilgrims, whereas his emphasis on the tribute that is due to the monastery suggests that he aimed the *Vida de San Millán* at a wide and varied audience.

VII. 'VIDA DE SANTA MARÍA EGIPCIACA'

A hagiographic poem not in *cuaderna vía* but in rhymed couplets of short and sometimes irregular lines is the *Vida de Santa María Egipciaca*, an adaptation of the French *Vie de Sainte Marie l'Egyptienne*. This story, which occurs in the vernacular in several countries as well as in Greek and Latin, begins as a variant of that of Mary Magdalene. María, beautiful but self-centred and lustful, leaves home for Alexandria, where she disrupts society by her activities as a prostitute. When life there begins to pall, she goes to the Holy Land, paying with her body for her passage in a pilgrim ship. God begins to direct the course of her life: a storm springs up, and María thinks she will drown,

> Mas non le fizo nengún tuerto,
> que Dios la sacó a puerto. (399-400)

In Jerusalem, warrior-angels turn her away from the temple-door. She is filled with remorse, and goes into the wilderness to live a penitent life of solitude and hardship. Many years later, when she has become outwardly like a wild animal, she meets a monk to whom she tells her story, and he transmits it after her death.

This poem is built on a double contrast: María's outward youth and beauty is a mask for inner corruption, whereas later her aged, roughened, and hideous body houses the purified soul of a saint; appearance and reality change places. The literary resources of the time emphasise the poem's message and strengthen the structural contrast, and although most of these are present in the French *Vie*, some are added by the Spanish poet. For example, when María leaves home to go to Alexandria, she takes with her a songbird, a familiar feature of the Iberian lyric tradition; and the lyric note is reinforced when the description of her life of prostitution in Alexandria is prefaced and concluded by new lines in the parallelistic form of the *cantigas de amigo*:

> Solla ssalló como ladrón,
> que non demandó companyón:
> en ssu camino entró María,
> que non demandava companýa.
> Una aveziella tenie en mano,
> assí canta yvierno como verano;
> María la tenie a grant honor
> porque cada día canta d'amor. (139-46)

Although the surface attractions of María are emphasised by these devices, we are never allowed to lose sight for long of the inner squalor: the frequent association of sensuality with gold and silver, as when she says of her body

Fevos aquí mio tresoro,
mi argente e todo mi oro   (347-8),

reminds us that physical beauty and the passion it arouses are used
by her with calculated selfishness, and that lust is linked to other sins.[43]

VIII. 'TRES REYS D'ORIENT' AND '¡AY JHERUSALEM!'

A much shorter religious poem of the thirteenth century, the *Libre
dels tres reys d'Orient*, is preserved in the same manuscript as the *Vida
de Santa María Egipciaca*. There is no evidence for the frequent
assertion that this is a translation of a French or Provençal poem: it
seems, in fact, to be an original Spanish treatment of material from
the canonical, and still more from the apocryphal, Gospels. The familiar
story of the three Kings, Herod, the slaughter of the innocents, and the
flight into Egypt leads up to the Holy Family's encounter with two
robbers, one cruel and the other merciful. At the insistence of the good
robber, their lives are spared, and Mary bathes the leprous baby of their
benefactor in the water which has washed the infant Jesus. The leprosy
is miraculously cured, and the rest of the poem shows that this bathing
in sanctified water has had the effect of conferring grace by baptism:
the episode of the robbers and the Holy Family is immediately followed
by the Crucifixion, in which the robber who believes in Christ, dies
with Him, and is saved, turns out to be the one who was cured of
leprosy. The *Tres reys* is the only work in the tradition of the apocryphal Gospels which arranges the material in this way, and the only
one to make the theological point of the action of grace into the main
purpose of the narrative.[44] Theme and structure are interdependent.
The opening of the poem may seem only loosely attached to the rest,
but the difficulty vanishes when we recognise a pattern, running through
the three sections, which opposes belief and charity (the three Kings,
the good robber and his wife, their son Dimas) to rejection and cruelty
(Herod, the bad robber, and his son Gestas who is crucified with Christ
and refuses to believe). This opposition is traced both by structural
development and by verbal repetition, and is carefully linked to the
illustration of the workings of grace.[45]

These two poems were probably composed in or soon after the first
half of the century. More evidence of date is available in *¡Ay
Jherusalem!*[46] This is a rarity: a Spanish poem of the Crusades. The
fall of Jerusalem to the Saracens in 1244 shocked Europe, and Councils
of the Church were held at Lyons in 1245 and 1274 to organise the
city's recapture, but the attempts were unsuccessful. The poem was
inspired by one of these Councils, that of 1245 being more likely. The

poet made use of letters written from the Holy Land, describing the horrors of the city's capture and the desecration of the Holy Sepulchre; he blends narrative and lyrical traditions. The poem is indisputably a work of propaganda, aimed at recruiting Crusaders (and presumably Spanish Crusaders), and the sources and literary traditions used in it are directed principally to that end; but it is also a good poem in its own right. Its immediate purpose remained unfulfilled, since few Spaniards set out for the Holy Land and even fewer arrived, yet its lament for the lost city still has power to move us.[47]

IX. DEBATE-POEMS

One large and important group remains to be dealt with: the debate-poems. Some poems of this type are found in Arabic and Hebrew, and even further afield, but the main and most flourishing tradition is European, with its origins in Latin. Debate-poems are well established by the ninth century, and within a hundred years they are found in the Latin literature of Spain. They spread to the vernacular of almost every western European country, and seem to have been as successful with a popular audience as with their original learned public. A wide variety of topics is covered: theological (body and soul, Christianity and Judaism); social (knight's mistress and clerk's mistress, friar and layman, priests and peasants); erotic (love and an old man, heterosexual and homosexual love); philosophical (Fortune and the philosopher); economic (both theoretical, as in the debate between expansionist and restrictionist economics, and clashes of vested interests: wool and flax, wine and beer). In addition to the debates which relate directly to urgent issues of the day, there are others which are exercises on set topics: the three ages of man, summer and winter, the violet and the rose, Lazarus and Mary.[48]

These poems dramatise a clash between two (or occasionally more) points of view on a central issue. They reflect not only such literary sources as the Classical Latin eclogue, but also medieval social and educational conditions. The emphasis in warfare, and especially in epic and other narratives of battle, was on single combat, and a medieval tournament was a series of encounters between pairs of champions. In the legal custom of the judicial duel (which died out in medieval life but survived for much longer in literature), we find the same essential feature of a clash between the two protagonists, as we do when the law courts substitute words for blows. The tendency to think in terms of single combat was reinforced by the importance of logic, or dialectic, in the curriculum; it was believed that from the encounter of opposites, truth would emerge. Logic provided the structure, and rhetoric the technique, for the medieval scholastic disputation, a highly-skilled

contest between representatives of two opposing propositions which was
not only an educational instrument, but a means of debating important
real-life issues. There are, for instance, records of formal disputations
between Jewish and Christian champions, and between representatives
of the Eastern and Western Churches.[49]

All these factors, including the prevalence of formal disputations in
the universities and in the world outside, helped to form the medieval
debate-poems, and ensured their long-lived popularity. The style of
the poems was also affected by literary influences, in particular
the classical eclogues and, at a later stage, the dialogue-poems of
Provence. These, which sprang from the competitive atmosphere of a
small, self-consciously cultured society, are of two main types: the
partimen, concerned with theoretical questions, and the more personal
and satirical *tenso*. These had among their descendants the *preguntas*
and *respuestas* of fifteenth-century Castilian court poets (see below,
pp. 188-9) and had a relationship of mutual influence with the Latin
debate-poems. The *tenso* had little influence on subject-matter, but
a considerable influence on style, especially in the vernacular debates.
The scurrilous tone which is also found in other genres influenced by the
tenso, such as the Galician-Portuguese *cantigas d'escarnho e de
maldizer*, is unmistakable in such debates as *Elena y María* (see below,
pp. 74-5).

The earliest extant Spanish poem in this genre is the *Disputa del
alma y el cuerpo*, which survives in an incomplete form in a manuscript
of the very early thirteenth century; the poem may well have been
composed in the late twelfth century. The poet tells us of a vision in
which he sees a corpse and the soul, which has left it, in the form of a
naked child. The soul bitterly reproaches the body for damning them
both by its sins; the poem breaks off before the body's reply. This is an
adaptation of a French debate, and the Spanish poet makes intelligent
use of his source.[50] However, the *Disputa*, partly because it is so short
and fragmentary, does not have the literary merit or the interest of
later Spanish poems on the same subject. The body-soul debate appears
in verse and prose some two centuries later, and continues into the
sixteenth century. These later debates (see below, p. 189) derive not
from the first *Disputa* but from the general European tradition.

A few decades after the *Disputa* comes the best and most puzzling
of Spanish debate-poems, the *Razón de amor con los denuestos del
agua y el vino*; the first part of the title is taken from lines 3-4 of the
poem. The need for a twofold title arises from the apparent duality
of the poem. The first half is a love-narrative, lyrical in tone: in a
spring landscape which derives from the rhetorical *locus amoenus* (cf.
above, p. 65), the protagonist is visited by a maiden who sings of
the lover she has never met.[51] They recognise each other by the gifts
they had exchanged, and their love is consummated:

Yo connoçí luego las alfayas,
que yo gelas avía enbiadas;
ela connoçió una mi cinta man a mano,
qu'ela la fiziera con la su mano.
Toliós el manto de los onbros,
besóme la boca e por los ojos;
tan gran sabor de mi avía,
sól fablar non me podía.
'¡Dios senor, a ti loado,
quant conozco meu amado!
¡Agora e tod bien comigo
quant conozco meo amigo!'   (122-33)

The girl then goes away, leaving her lover despondent. A white dove bathes in a vessel of water which is hung in one of the trees, and spills the water into a vessel of wine. The debate between wine and water ensues, wine appropriately being more aggressive and water more rational, and its tone contrasts sharply with that of the poem's first half; even the rhythm is different. Such a strongly-marked difference is unprecedented among debate-poems, and it is natural that some critics should have concluded that a copyist combined two separate poems. This, however, will not do: there is no point at which a satisfactory division could be made, and all attempts to separate the supposed two poems have involved substantial changes in the order of lines. This is a single poem, but one which draws on two traditions. The Spanish poet, in adapting the Latin tradition of the wine-water debate (his model was probably the *Denudata veritate*), seems to have expanded the idealised landscape which is sometimes a setting for debates (as, for example, in a number of those between a knight's mistress and a clerk's mistress), making it into a love-narrative which drew heavily on the Galician-Portuguese lyric tradition.

If the *Razón* is, as argued above, a single poem, what is its theme? It has been held to be a Christian allegory, the girl representing the Virgin Mary; or a doctrinal expression of the persecuted Cathar heresy, with many of the key words having a double meaning. While the Cathar theory is not wholly satisfactory, it has weighty points in its favour; equally strong, however, is the theory that the poet shows the necessity of reconciling opposites, chaste and sensual love in the first half, water and wine in the second; the synthesis is worked out in action, and is then explored theoretically in the debate. Much work remains to be done on this enigmatic and brilliant poem; for instance, its resemblances to the ballad of *Fontefrida* have not yet been adequately explained.[52]

The other important debate-poem of thirteenth-century Spain, *Elena y María*, reflects one of the major social issues of medieval Europe.

Medieval society was, in theory, divided into three estates: clerks
(priests and other learned men), knights, and farmers or peasants. The
impulse to divide society into three is ancient and powerful, being
found as early as Plato and Aristotle, and as late as the post-revolution-
ary Russian classification of workers, peasants, and intellectuals. The
three estates of medieval theory were complementary, each carrying
out one of the vital functions of society; but in practice, there was
bound to be rivalry and dissension. Social changes made the classification less satisfactory. Educational expansion meant that an increasing
number of clerks were laymen, and the rise of the towns produced large
and powerful groups (in particular, merchants and an urban proletariat)
not easily assignable to any of the three estates.

The decreasing reality of the classification did not diminish the sense
of rivalry, especially between clerks and knights, which seems to have
become sharper and more personal, as we may see in the acrimonious
exchanges of *Elena y María*. As in most such debates, the protagonists
are not clerk and knight but their mistresses. The quarrel enables us to
see their lives from two points of view: Elena's optimistic picture of life
as a knight's mistress is followed by María's satirical account; similarly,
Elena is quick to deflate María's pretensions by giving her own version
of what it is like to be the mistress of a priest:

> 'Ca tú non comes con sazón
> esperando la oblación;
> lo que tú has a gastar
> ante la eglisa honrada lo ha a ganar;
> vevides como mesquinos,
> de alimosna de vuestros vecinos.
> Cuando el abad misa decía,
> a su mojer maldecía;
> en la primera oración
> luego le echa la maldeción.
> Si tú fueres misa escuchar,
> tras todos te has a estar . . .
> a mí levarán como condesa,
> a ti dirán como monaguesa.'   (203-20)

The girls agree to submit their argument to the court of King Oriol
for decision, but the manuscript of the poem breaks off before we can
learn what the decision was. In almost all Latin and French knight-
clerk debates, the clerk's mistress is the winner (the poems were written
by clerks), but the decision in the Spanish poem may have gone in
favour of Elena. A distinctively Spanish and popular tone has been
claimed for this debate, but this is doubtful in view of the uninhibited
satire to be found in many goliardic poems and in the Galician-
Portuguese *cantigas d'escarnho*, which inherit a Provençal tradition.[53]

Debate-poems continue in Spanish until long after the end of the Middle Ages, though until the fifteenth century each derives separately from Latin or French models, and there is no indigenous Spanish debate-tradition. The later poems are discussed in Chapter 7 below, but it may be worth noting now that debates are not confined to these poems. They are found in other forms of literature, being, for example, an important part of the *Libro de Buen Amor* in the fourteenth, and the *Corbacho* in the fifteenth, century.

NOTES

1. Hastings Rashdall, *The Universities of Europe in the Middle Ages*, new ed., ed. F. M. Powicke and A. B. Emden (Oxford, 1936). For Spanish universities, see C. M. Ajo G. y Sainz de Zúñiga, *Historia de las universidades hispánicas. Orígenes y desarrollo hasta nuestros días*, I (Madrid, 1957); and V. Beltrán de Heredia, *Los orígenes de la Universidad de Salamanca* (Salamanca, 1953). For a Toledo cathedral school, see P. E. Russell, *MLR*, XLII (1947), 394-5; he suggests that there may even have been a *studium generale*. On the belatedness of educational reforms, see Derek W. Lomax, 'The Lateran Reforms and Spanish Literature', *IR*, I (1969), 299-313. On the general issue of Spain's cultural belatedness, see E. R. Curtius, *European Literature and the Latin Middle Ages*, pp. 541-3.

2. There is no essential difference in type between the Latin and the vernacular poets; see, for example, Dronke's discussion in *Medieval Latin and the Rise of European Love-Lyric*.

3. When the towns of Old Castile, León, and Galicia asserted themselves in the twelfth century against their ecclesiastical overlords, the militant leadership was frequently made up of French settlers.

4. Steven Runciman, *A History of the Crusades* (3 vols., Cambridge, 1951-54); Eugenio Asensio, '*¡Ay Iherusalem!* Planto narrativo del siglo XIII', *NRFH*, XIV (1960), 251-70, reprinted in *Poética y realidad*, 2nd ed.; Runciman (I, 89-92) shows that foreign aid to the Spanish Christians against the Almoravids in the late eleventh century, which was blessed by the Pope as a holy task, may well have provided a model for the Crusades; Claude Cahen, 'An Introduction to the First Crusade', *Past and Present*, 6 (1954), 6-30. Spanish writers of the thirteenth and fourteenth centuries are more interested in the Crusades than are Spanish kings.

5. At least two Hispano-Latin literary epics date from this period, as do some important chronicles and an excellent parody of works on the discovery of saints' relics, by García, a canon of Toledo. See Francisco Rico, 'Las letras latinas del siglo XII en Galicia, León y Castilla', *Ábaco*, II (1969), 9-91, and Lida de Malkiel, 'La *Garcineida* de García de Toledo', *NRFH*, VII (1953), 246-58, reprinted in *Estudios de literatura española y comparada* (Buenos Aires, 1966), pp. 1-13. For the preceding period, see Manuel C. Díaz y Díaz, 'La circulation des manuscrits dans la Péninsule ibérique du VIIIe au XIe siècle', *CCMe*, XII (1969), 219-41 and 383-92.

6. Ian Michael, 'A Parallel between Chrétien's *Erec* and the *Libro de Alexandre*', *MLR*, LXII (1967), 620-8.

7. M. Defourneaux, *Les Français en Espagne au XIe et XIIe siècles* (Paris, 1949).

8. Many scholars have taken the opening stanzas of the *Libro de*

Alexandre, which use the terms *clerecía* and *joglaría*, as a literary manifesto accepted by all *cuaderna vía* poets; see A. D. Deyermond, 'Mester es sen peccado', *RF*, LXXVII (1965), 111-16, oversimplified in one respect, as J. C. Musgrave will show in a forthcoming article. See also Georges Cirot, 'Sur le *mester de clerecía*', *BH*, XLIV (1942), 5-16, and 'Inventaire estimatif du *m. de c*', *BH*, XLVIII (1946), 193-209; Julio Saavedra Molino, 'El verso de clerecía', *BFC*, VI (1950-51), 253-346.

9. Brian Dutton, 'The Profession of Gonzalo de Berceo and the Paris Manuscript of the *Libro de Alexandre*', *BHS*, XXXVII (1960), 137-45, and 'G. de B.: unos datos biográficos,' *Actas del Primer Congreso Internacional de Hispanistas* (Oxford, 1964), 249-54.

10. *Prosa* here means not 'prose' but 'poem'. Literary terminology of this period is extremely fluid; see Artiles, *Los recursos literarios*, pp. 13-18.

11. For general studies, see Georges Cirot, 'L'expression dans G. de B.', *RFE*, IX (1922), 154-70; C. Guerrieri Crocetti, 'La lingua di G. de B.', *SM*, n.s., XV (1942), 163-88; Bernard Gicovate, 'Notas sobre el estilo y la originalidad de G. de B.', *BH*, LXII (1960), 6-15; Jorge Guillén, *Language and Poetry* (Cambridge, Mass., 1961), Ch. 1; Frida Weber de Kurlat, 'Notas para la cronología y composición literaria de las vidas de santos de Berceo', *NRFH*, XV (1961), 113-30; Brian Dutton, *La vida de San Millán . . .*, and 'G. de B. and the *Cantares de gesta*', *BHS*, XXXVIII (1961), 197-205. See also Gormly, *Use of the Bible*, Ch. 1, and T. C. Goode, *G. de B.*, *El sacrificio de la Misa: a study of its symbolism and of its sources* (Washington, 1933).

12. The fundamental medieval curriculum was made up of the Seven Liberal Arts: the three word-based subjects of logic, grammar, and rhetoric (the *trivium*); and the four number-based subjects of arithmetic, geometry, astronomy, and music (the *quadrivium*). After this the student could proceed to one of the higher subjects (medicine, law, theology, philosophy).

13. For introductory treatment, see C. S. Baldwin, *Medieval Rhetoric and Poetic (to 1400) interpreted from representative works* (New York, 1928); and Curtius, *European Literature*. For more detail, see Edmond Faral, *Les Arts poétiques du XIIe et du XIIIe siècle. Recherches et documents sur la technique littéraire du Moyen Âge* (BÉHÉ, CCXXXVIII, Paris, 1924); Heinrich Lausberg, *Manual de retórica literaria. Fundamentos de una ciencia de la literatura* (3 vols., Madrid, BRH, 1966-68).

14. Frances Yates, *The Art of Memory* (London, 1966). Some stylistic features may also come from this source. For the structural guidance offered by rhetoric and grammar, see Douglas Kelly, 'The Scope of the Treatment of Composition in the Twelfth- and Thirteenth-Century Arts of Poetry', *Sp*, XLI (1966), 261-78.

15. Owst, *Literature and Pulpit*; T. M. Charland, *Artes praedicandi. Contribution à l'histoire de la rhétorique au Moyen Âge* (Paris and Ottawa, 1936). The diffusion of sermons and *artes praedicandi* in Spain is a neglected subject: see my review of Owst, *ELu*, VII (1963), 233-5; and Lomax, 'Lateran Reforms', 302-3.

16. The use of formulaic language in the thirteenth-century *clerecía* poems does not seem to be as great as in, for example, the *Cantar de Mio Cid*, perhaps for two reasons: the *clerecía* poets are one stage further removed from the oral epic than their fellow-clerks who composed epics in writing; and *cuaderna vía* lends itself to formulas less well than the epic line.

17. See below, p. 75; and Luciana de Stéfano, *La sociedad estamental de la baja Edad Media española a la luz de la literatura de la época* (Caracas, 1966).

4 *

18. A more famous St Dominic, the founder of the Dominican order of friars (who was also a Spaniard), may have been the subject of a verse life in the thirteenth century, and a prose *Vida de Santo Domingo*, which also depends on Latin sources, probably dates from the end of the century; see Warren F. Manning, 'An Old Spanish Life of St Dominic: sources and date', *Mediaeval Studies in honor of Jeremiah Denis Matthias Ford* (Cambridge, Mass., 1948), pp. 137-58. On hagiography, see Hippolyte Delehaye, *The Legends of the Saints* (London, 1962); Baudouin de Gaiffier d'Hestroy, 'L'hagiographe et son public au XIe siècle,' *Études critiques d'hagiographie et d'iconologie* (Bruxelles, 1967), pp. 475-507; S. C. Aston, 'The Saint in Medieval Literature,' *MLR*, LXV (1970), pp. xxv-xlii.

19. Weber de Kurlat, 'Notas para la cronología'; Dutton, *La vida de San Millán*.

20. Lida de Malkiel, 'Notas para el texto de la *Vida de Santa Oria*', *RPh*, X (1956-57), 19-33.

21. See Dámaso Alonso, 'B. y los *topoi*', *De los siglos oscuros al de oro* (*Notas y artículos a través de 700 años de letras españolas*) (Madrid, 1958), pp. 74-85. The correct interpretation is given by Perry, *Art and Meaning*, pp. 178-80.

22. Richard Becker, *G. de B.'s Milagros und ihre Grundlagen* (Strassburg, 1910); see Dutton, *Milagros*.

23. Agustín del Campo, 'La técnica alegórica en la introducción a los *Milagros de Nuestra Señora*', *RFE*, XXVIII (1944), 15-57; Thomas Montgomery, 'Fórmulas tradicionales y originalidad en los *Milagros de N.S.*', *NRFH*, XVI (1962), 424-30; Valeria Bertolucci, 'Contributo allo studio della letteratura miracolistica', *Miscellanea di Studi Ispanici* (Pisa, 1963), 5-72; Gariano, *Análisis;* Germán Orduna, 'La introducción a los *Milagros de N.S.* (El análisis estructural aplicado a la comprensión de la intencionalidad de un texto literario)', *Actas del Segundo Congreso Internacional de Hispanistas* (Nijmegen, 1967), pp. 447-56.

24. See Leo Spitzer, 'Sobre la cántica *Eya velar*', *NRFH*, IV (1950), 50-6, reprinted in *Antigua poesía*, pp. 29-38; and Wardropper, 'B.'s *Eya velar*', *RoN*, II (1960-61), 3-8.

25. Germán Orduna, 'La estructura del *Duelo de la Virgen* y la cántica *Eya velar*', *HumT*, 10 (1958), 75-104. For a different view, see Daniel Devoto, 'Sentido y forma de la cántica *Eya velar*', *BH*, LXV (1963), 206-37.

26. In western Europe, Arthurian romances were more popular, but stories of Alexander were serious rivals, and their appeal was not confined to the West. See George Cary, *The Medieval Alexander* (Cambridge, 1956); Lida de Malkiel, 'La leyenda de Alejandro en la literatura medieval', *RPh*, XV (1961-62), 311-18, and 'Datos para la leyenda de Alejandro en la Edad Media castellana', ibid., 412-23.

27. The importance of the romance in Spain has often been overlooked, and critics tend to describe romances as novels or epics, with unfortunate results; see my forthcoming 'The Lost Genre of Medieval Spanish Literature'. On romances in general, see Eugène Vinaver, 'From Epic to Romance', *BJR*, XLVI (1964), 476-503; Gillian Beer, *The Romance* (The Critical Idiom 10, London, 1970). For the literary epic, see above, pp. 31-2; borderline cases such as the *Alexandre* are rare.

28. D. J. A. Ross, *Alexander Historiatus: a guide to medieval illustrated Alexander literature* (Warburg Institute Surveys, I, London, 1963), and supplement in *JWCI*, XXX (1967), 383-8.

29. R. S. Willis, *Relationship*, and *Debt*. Alarcos, *Investigaciones*; latest information in Michael, *Treatment*, Ch. 2 and appendix.

30. Cf. Eugène Vinaver, *Form and Meaning in Medieval Romance* (Modern Humanities Research Association Presidential Address, 1966).

31. The controversy is summed up by Ian Michael, 'Estado actual de los estudios sobre el *Libro de Alexandre*', *AEM*, II (1965), 581-95, at pp. 591-2; see also *Treatment*; for a different conclusion, see Lida de Malkiel, *Idea de la fama*, pp. 167-97.

32. This method is a secularised use of typology, or *figura*, by which the Old Testament was believed to prefigure the life of Christ. See Deyermond, 'Exemplum, Allegoria, Figura', *IR* (in press).

33. See above, n. 29, and Willis, *'Mester de clerecía*. A Definition of the *Libro de Alexandre*', *RPh*, X (1956-57), 212-24. On other aspects, see A. G. Solalinde, 'El juicio de Paris en el *Alex*. y en la *General estoria*', *RFE*, XV (1928), 1-51; Georges Cirot, 'La Guerre de Troie dans le *L. de Alex*.', *BH*, XXXIX (1937), 328-38; Lida de Makiel, 'Alejandro en Jerusalén', *RPh*, X (1956-57), 185-96; Ian Michael, 'The Description of Hell in the Spanish *L. de Alex.*', *Medieval Miscellany presented to Eugène Vinaver* (Manchester, 1965), pp. 220-9; Dana A. Nelson, *'El L. de Alex.*: a reorientation', *SP*, LXV (1968), 723-52.

34. N. J. Ware, 'The Date of Composition of the *Libro de Alexandre*. A re-examination of stanza 1799', *BHS*, XLII (1965), 252-5.

35. See Ben E. Perry, *The Ancient Romances. A literary-historical account of their origins* (Sather Classical Lectures, XXXVII, Berkeley and Los Angeles, 1967), appendix II.

36. Deyermond, 'Motivos folklóricos y técnica estructural en el *Libro de Apolonio*', *Fi*, XIII (1968-69), 121-49.

37. On the literary quality of the *Apolonio*, see Manuel García Blanco, 'La originalidad del *Libro de Apolonio*', *Revista de Ideas Estéticas*, III (1945), 351-78; Lida de Malkiel, *La idea de la fama*, pp. 159-66.

38. Philip H. Goepp, 'The Narrative Material of *Apollonius of Tyre*', *ELH*, V (1938), 150-72; Margaret Schlauch, *Chaucer's Constance and Accused Queens* (New York, 1927); Deyermond, 'Motivos folklóricos'. There are also resemblances to a widely-diffused hagiographic tale: see A. H. Krappe, 'La leggenda di S. Eustachio', *Nuovi Studi Medievali*, III (1926-27), 223-58.

39. There are two other treatments of the story in Spanish: a fifteenth-century prose romance, the *Historia de Apolonio*, ed. Serís, *Nuevo ensayo*, I, 1, pp. 80-115; and the eleventh tale of Juan de Timoneda's *Patrañuelo* (1567).

40. Reprinted in facsimile by Antonio Rodríguez-Moñino, *Los pliegos poéticos de la colección del Marqués de Morbecq (siglo XVI)* (Madrid, 1962). For *pliegos sueltos*, see E. M. Wilson, *Some Aspects of Spanish Literary History* (Oxford, 1967); A. Rodríguez-Moñino, *Poesía y cancioneros (siglo XVI)* (Madrid, 1968), pp. 31-6; F. J. Norton and E. M. Wilson, *Two Spanish Verse Chap-Books* (Cambridge, 1969).

41. Menéndez Pidal, *Poesía juglaresca*, pp. 274-80; Ruth Crosby, 'Oral Delivery in the Middle Ages', *Sp*, XI (1936), 88-110; Chaytor, *From Script to Print*, Ch. 2 and 6; Gicovate, 'Notas sobre el estilo'; Ian Michael, 'A Comparison of the Use of Epic Epithets in the *Poema de Mio Cid* and the *Libro de Alexandre*', *BHS*, XXXVIII (1961), 32-41; G. B. Gybbon-Monypenny, 'The Spanish *Mester de clerecía* and its Intended Public: concerning the validity as evidence of passages of direct address to the audience', *Vinaver Miscellany*, pp. 230-44; Dutton, *La vida de San Millán*, p. 175n; Perry, *Art and Meaning*, p. 28n; Rodrigo A. Molina, 'Gonzalo de Berceo y el lenguaje oral', *QIA*, 37 (1969), 8-12; Michael, *Treatment*, p. 246n. We must remember that even the private reader was seldom silent, but rather read aloud to himself (Chaytor, pp. 14-19); and that medieval terminology in this matter, as in many

others, can be highly confusing (see Artiles, *Recursos*, part I), so that we do not really know what *leer*, for instance, meant on any particular occasion.

42. Roger M. Walker, 'Oral Delivery or Private Reading? A contribution to the debate on the dissemination of medieval literature', *FMLS*, VII (1971), 36-42.

43. See J. W. Rees, 'Notes on the Text of the *Vida de Santa María Egipciaca*', *Hispanic Studies in Honour of Ignacio González Llubera* (Oxford, 1959), pp. 259-68; M. Alvar, 'Fidelidad y discordancias en la adaptación española de la *VSME*', *GAKS*, XVI (1960), 153-65; Jerry R. Craddock, 'Apuntes para el estudio de la leyenda de SME en España', *Homenaje Moñino*, I, 99-110, which deals also with three prose versions: a Hispano-Latin text of the tenth century, its fourteenth-century Portuguese translation, and a fifteenth-century Spanish version of another Latin text.

44. Margaret Chaplin, 'The Episode of the Robbers in the *Libre dels tres reys d'Orient*', *BHS*, XLIV (1967), 88-95. The apocryphal Gospels were widely known in medieval Europe: see *The Apocryphal New Testament*, trans. M. R. James (Oxford, 1924).

45. I draw here on a forthcoming study by Vivienne Richardson.

46. Asensio, '*¡Ay Iherusalem!*'

47. Similar emotions could be evoked on the other side of the Muslim-Christian conflict: compare *¡Ay Jherusalem!* with a lament in an Arabic historian's account of the Cid's siege and capture of Valencia (*Primera crónica general*, Ch. 909-10).

48. See Le Gentil, *La Poésie lyrique*, I, 458-519, and Raby, *Secular Latin Poetry*, II, 282-308.

49. What purports to be the text of a Christian-Jew disputation, but is probably an imaginary reconstruction, survives in thirteenth-century Spanish prose: Américo Castro, 'Disputa entre un cristiano y un judío', *RFE*, I (1914), 173-80. It is of great historical interest but no literary merit.

50. A. G. Solalinde, 'La disputa del alma y el cuerpo. Comparación con su original francés', *HR*, I (1933), 196-207. The European tradition is studied by T. Batiouchkof, 'Le Débat de l'âme et du corps', *R*, XX (1891), 1-55 and 513-78, and Woolf, *English Religious Lyric*, pp. 89-102.

51. Falling in love by hearsay alone is an established, though not a frequent, feature of the European courtly tradition, e.g. the Provençal poet Jaufré Rudel and the Welsh *Mabinogion*). Life may have followed literature in this respect as in others.

52. Leo Spitzer, '*Razón de amor*', *R*, LXXI (1950), 145-65, reprinted in *Antigua poesía*, pp. 41-58; Alfred Jacob, 'The *Razón de amor* as Christian Symbolism', *HR*, XX (1952), 282-301; di Pinto, *Due contrasti*; Guillermo Díaz-Plaja, 'Poesía y diálogo: *Razón de amor*', *EstE*, 5 (1960), 7-43; Enrique de Rivas, 'La razón secreta de la *Razón de amor*', *Anuario de Filología*, VI-VII (1967-68), 109-27, reprinted in *Figuras y estrellas de las cosas* (Maracaibo, 1969), pp. 93-110. Two studies showing technical differences between parts of the poem are Giuseppe Tavani, 'Osservazioni sul ritmo della *Razón feyta d'amor*', *Studi di Letteratura Spagnola*, ed. C. Samonà (Roma, 1964), pp. 171-86; and Daniel N. Cárdenas, 'Nueva luz sobre *Razón de amor y denuestos del agua y del vino* (sugerida por un análisis fono-morfo-sintáctico)', *RHM*, XXXIV (1968), 227-41. For a general survey, see J. H. Hanford, 'The Mediaeval Debate between Wine and Water', *PMLA*, XXVIII (1913), 315-67.

53. Goliardic is a term used to describe Latin parodic or satirical verse of the twelfth and thirteenth centuries, or Latin drinking-, gambling-, and love-songs of the same period. The supposed Order of Golias is now known to have been a literary joke. See Raby, *Secular Latin Poetry*; Helen Waddell,

The Wandering Scholars (London, 1927), Ch. 6-9; J. H. Hanford, 'The Progenitors of Golias', *Sp*, I (1926), 38-58; O. Dobiache-Rojdesvensky, *Les Poésies des Goliardes* (Paris, 1931). For knight-clerk debates in general, see C. Oulmont, *Les Débats du clerc et du chevalier* (Paris, 1911); Tavani, 'Il dibattito sul chierico e il cavaliere nella tradizione mediolatina e volgare', *RJ*, XV (1964), 51-84. For criticism of *Elena y María*, see Menéndez Pidal's edition; di Pinto, *Due contrasti*; and G. Díaz-Plaja, 'Poesía y diálogo: *Elena y María*', *EstE* 6 (1960), 65-82.

Chapter 4

THE LITERATURE OF THE
THIRTEENTH-CENTURY EXPANSION: II

I. THE EARLIEST PROSE

POETRY DOMINATES THE VERNACULAR LITERATURE of the first half of the thirteenth century, as we have seen in the previous chapter. In the second half, the quantity and the quality of Spanish prose increase sharply, and there is a corresponding decline in poetic activity. It seems likely that these two changes are causally connected, and that talented and ambitious men, of the type who would in the previous generation have served the monastic orders and composed poems in *cuaderna vía*, were attracted to the Court of Alfonso X. It is dangerously easy to oversimplify this explanation, and there is no question of a deliberate redeployment of labour, but it would be very strange if Spaniards had not felt the pʳwerful attraction of financial reward, prestige, intellectual stimulus, and high cultural level which the Castilian Court exercised on scholars and poets from other European countries. When we take into account King Alfonso's preference for Castilian as the language of prose and Galician-Portuguese as the language of poetry, the changes become easy to understand.

It would, however, be wrong to conclude that Spanish prose began with Alfonso, and it would be an even greater mistake to neglect the tradition of medieval Hispano-Latin prose-writing. At every period of Latin literature there are prominent writers of Spanish origin: under the Roman occupation, Spain produced Seneca (and also such poets as Martial and Lucan); after the collapse of the Empire, St Isidore of Seville was one of the leading figures of Hispano-Visigothic culture; and in the sixteenth and seventeenth centuries, Spaniards—like other Europeans—frequently wrote in Latin. It was, however, in the period from the Moorish conquest to the end of the Middle Ages that Hispano-Latin literature flourished most strongly. Only sixty years after the fall of the Visigothic kingdom, the Spanish monk Beatus of Liébana wrote a commentary on the Apocalypse which became influential outside as well as within the Peninsula. There is a series of Latin chronicles from the end of the ninth century, beginning with the *Chronica Visegothorum* written in the kingdom of Asturias; at first, these are short and summary, but gradually they become more ambitious both in scope and in treatment.[1] By the twelfth century, writings in Latin are more diverse and more consciously literary, though they cannot compete with contemporary works north of the Pyrenees. There is, however, one sphere in which Spain excels: that of translation from Arabic and, to a lesser extent, from Hebrew.

The very high cultural and technological level attained by Moorish Spain, at a time when the Christian kingdoms of the Peninsula were backward and impoverished, provided a powerful incentive for the acquisition of knowledge by means of translation. This made available to Europe not only the original works of Arabic writers, but also Indian and Persian works that had previously been translated into Arabic, and a number of Greek works (including some of Aristotle's) that had been lost in the Western tradition but preserved, with the addition of commentaries, in Arabic versions.[2] Translations began as early as the tenth century in the Catalan monastery of Ripoll, which was one of the four major centres of monastic learning in the Peninsula (the others were San Millán, Silos, and Sahagún). At this stage there was no question of translation into the vernacular, and the use of Latin made the works accessible to scholars from beyond the Pyrenees, who consequently began to visit Ripoll in order to benefit from, and to share in, the work of translation.[3]

The reconquest in 1085 of Toledo, with its mixed population and its wealth of Arabic books, made possible the growth of translating activity in the centre of the Peninsula, and before long Toledo eclipsed Catalonia. The chief figure in this development is Raimundo, archbishop of Toledo from 1126 to 1152; he turned what had been a sporadic activity into an organised school of translators, which became one of the most important cultural centres of medieval Europe.[4] In the hundred years that separate Raimundo's death and Alfonso X's accession to the throne, there were built up in Toledo a tradition of translation, a team of scholars, translators, and scribes, and a major library of scientific and other works. Many Jews settled in the city as refugees from the Almohads (see above, p. 57), joining those whose families had been there for centuries. They played a vital part in the school of translators, not only for the obvious reason that they enriched it with the Hispano-Hebraic cultural tradition, but even more because they, unlike most Christian Spaniards of the north, were fluent in Arabic. The difficulty of direct translation from Arabic into Latin—few men would be proficient in both languages—may often have been overcome by a rough intermediate draft in Spanish: a Jew could produce a draft (perhaps not even in writing), which a Christian would then turn into Latin.[5] It may seem strange that, if this procedure was in fact followed, the Spanish version never went beyond a working draft discarded when it had served its purpose, but there was no demand for Spanish versions until literacy increased: those who were capable of reading a learned book would expect to read it in Latin. We must also bear in mind that the beginning of translation into Spanish did not mean the end of translation into Latin; on the contrary, Toledo remained until the fifteenth century one of the most important centres of activity, supplying Europe with Latin versions of Arabic and Hebrew works.

The belief that vernacular prose-works of any length began only in the thirteenth century is well founded, even though it has been strongly challenged by the discovery of an allegedly much earlier text. This is the *Fazienda de Ultra Mar*, a pilgrims' guide to the Holy Land, which combines geographical description with translations of extracts from the historical books of the Old Testament and the occasional insertion of material from classical antiquity; thus the pilgrim is given the historical background to the place he visits:

> Allí delante Monte Carmel, a parte de orient, es Sabast, e ovo nonbre Samaria; en ebreo ovo nonbre Somron, e era cabo del reysmo de Israel e de Samaria. Allí en Samaria era el rey de Israel. El rey de Syria avýa guerra con el rey de Samaria, e dixo a sos vasallos: 'En atal logar nos metremos en celada.' Todo esto sopo el rey de Israel, que lo dixo Helyseus el propheta, omne de Dios. Esto non fue una vez, mas muchas. Estonz el rey de Syria dixo a sos omnes: '¿Quál de vos me descubre de mi poridat al rey de Israel?' (125)

The text is preceded by two letters, one from 'Remont, por la gracia de Dios, arçobispo de Toledo, a don Almeric, arçidiano de Antiochia' asking him

> que tú me enbíes escripto en una carta la fazienda de Ultra Mar e los nombres de las cibdades e de las tierras como ovieron nonbre en latin e en ebraico, e quanto a de la una cibdat a la otra, e las mara-vyllas que Nuestro Sennor Dios fezo en Jherusalem e en toda la tierra de Ultra Mar (43);

and the other from Almeric, agreeing to produce the work. Such letters are a far from reliable form of authentication, and in some well-known cases are blatant forgeries. The belief that the text must have been composed during Raimundo's tenure of the see of Toledo is invalid on both linguistic and historical grounds. The *Fazienda* is syntactically far more complex than the first Castilian chronicles of the late twelfth and early thirteenth centuries; indeed, its syntax is closer to that of mid-thirteenth-century works. In other linguistic features, the *Fazienda* bears a considerable resemblance to the Aragonese chronicle *Liber regum* (see below, pp. 85-6). The historical objections are even stronger. Almeric was French, and seems never to have been in Spain. Raimundo was also French, and showed no interest in the production of vernacular

Spanish translations although, as we have seen, he organised a school of translators from Arabic into Latin. If Almeric and Raimundo corresponded, they might have used French, though Latin is a much more likely medium; a correspondence in Castilian would have been a near-impossibility. The extant text of the *Fazienda* is almost certainly of the thirteenth century, and cannot be the work of a French cleric in Antioch. If, however, we postulate a twelfth-century Latin compilation which was later translated into Spanish, the difficulties disappear. The *Fazienda* must, then, relinquish its claim to chronological priority, but this does not deprive it of interest. It remains a remarkably early vernacular rendering of the Bible, and there are good reasons for believing that it descends not from the Vulgate—the standard Latin Bible of the Middle Ages—but from a twelfth-century Latin translation of the Hebrew text.[6]

The earliest extant prose-work in Spanish is one of a group of very brief historical writings in Navarro-Aragonese which are found at the end of a manuscript legal code, the *Fuero general de Navarra*. One of these *Corónicas navarras* is dated by its editor at 1186, with amplification between 1196 and 1213. It is in the form not of a connected prose narrative but of annals, and cannot claim any literary merit. It does, however, possess considerable interest for the student of literature, since the first three entries are references to King Arthur (the first trace of Arthurian material in Spain), to Charlemagne, and to the epic hero García (see above, pp. 40-41):

Era D. LXXX. aynos fizo la bataylla al rey Artuyss con Modret Equibleno. Era DCCC. LXXX. VI. aynos morió Carle Magne. Era Mª. L. VIII. aynos mataron al yfant García en León. (40)

Another of these *Corónicas*, probably of the late twelfth century, is in narrative form, and seems to be a vernacular summary of the *Historia Roderici* (see above, p. 42). Very early in the thirteenth century come the *Anales toledanos primeros*, in Castilian, but neither in style nor in historical technique do these annals have much claim on our interest.

A slightly later work is of more interest: the Aragonese *Liber regum*, composed between 1194 and 1211, has a much fuller and sometimes more vivid narrative than its vernacular predecessors:

Est rei don Remiro fo muit bueno, & ovo muitas faziendas con moros e lidió muitas vezes con ellos e vencielos. Et a postremas vino sobr'éll el rei don Sancho de Castiella con grant poder de moros e con tod el poder de Çaragoza, qui era de moros. Vinieron ad él a Sobrarbe e gastoronle toda la tierra, et él vino ad ellos a batalla e lidió con ellos e matoron lo i en Grados. (37)

Even so, the intrinsic merit of this chronicle is limited, especially when it is compared with contemporary Latin or Arabic chronicles, and perhaps its main point of interest is its remarkably enduring influence. It was translated into Castilian *c.* 1220, and subsequently into Portuguese, and was still used as a literary source two centuries later.[7] The *Corónicas navarras, Anales toledanos*, and *Liber regum* are not representative of the Spanish historiography of the late twelfth century and the first half of the thirteenth, since the main stream is, until the reign of Alfonso X, made up of Latin chronicles. These chronicles were, until the mid-twelfth century, rooted in the north-west (first the kingdom of Asturias, then the successor kingdom of León) both by their authorship and by their concentration of interest on the history of that region. The first important chronicle to come from Castile was the *Crónica Najerense*, so called because it was composed at the Benedictine monastery (at that time a Cluniac centre) of Santa María de Nájera.[8] The *Najerense* set a pattern which was to be followed not only by subsequent Latin chronicles, but also by the Alfonsine historians: it drew fairly extensively on epic poems, and its range was progressively restricted: the history of the world in biblical and classical times, that of the Iberian Peninsula in the Visigothic period, and León and Castile thereafter. Other Latin histories in the twelfth century are notable innovations: the *Historia Roderici* deals with the career of a non-royal personage, the Cid (it remains, however, chronicle rather than biography, since it makes no attempt to assess its hero's character); and the *Historia Compostelana* presents the history of a diocese and of its archbishop, using extensive quotation of documents as well as narrative.[9]

Hispano-Latin historiography was, then, well established long before the thirteenth-century expansion, but that expansion nevertheless had its effect, since the second quarter of the century saw the composition of two lengthy, important, and influential chronicles. The *Chronicon mundi* of Lucas, bishop of Túy (el Tudense), completed in 1236, is the last significant work in the Leonese tradition, coinciding in method with the *Najerense*. Like most of his predecessors, Lucas is content to accept what his sources tell him without exercising independent historical judgement.[10] The other major chronicle is *De rebus Hispaniae*, of Rodrigo Ximénez de Rada, archbishop of Toledo (el Toledano); this was completed in 1243. Rodrigo's strenuous politicoecclesiastical career did not hinder his work as a historian: not only did he write a number of other chronicles, including a *Historia Arabum*, but he evolved a scholarly historical method, making skilful use of documents, drawing on Arabic sources (an especially valuable innovation, since at this time the Arabs alone understood the value of economic and social history), and applying an alert and critical mind to all his sources. Both el Tudense and el Toledano were soon translated into Spanish, and both were important sources for Alfonso X's vernacular *Estoria de España*. El Toledano continued to exercise a strong influence on Spanish historiography well into the fifteenth century.[11]

Geography played a much smaller part than history in Spanish writing of the thirteenth century, but there is one work of some importance: the *Semejança del mundo*, composed soon after 1222, in Castile. The principal direct sources are the *Etymologiae* of St Isidore, and the *Imago mundi* of Honorius (probably Honorius Inclusus, fl. 1100), itself indebted to the *Etymologiae*. The geographical picture inherited by the Middle Ages was the product of Greek science and exploration as interpreted by Latin writers (and, of course, distorted in the process), which was then adjusted to the biblical view of the world. This picture was accepted in the thirteenth century by the author of the *Semejança* and his contemporaries, inevitably colouring even first-hand observations.[12]

The *Semejança* gives not only the traditional description of the world, but also other material: a picture of Hell, the properties of precious stones, and accounts of animals, some of which are drawn from the bestiaries.[13] It reflects the medieval habit of dealing fully not only with the matter in hand but also with related matters, including the origins of names. The medieval world-picture was of elaborately organised hierarchies, harmonies, and correspondences, and it was thought unreasonable to treat one field of knowledge in isolation or to ignore its relation to the divine plan.

II. ALFONSO X

The Spanish prose-works surviving from the period before Alfonso X's accession to the throne are considerably fewer in number than the extant works composed during his reign and under his direction. Alfonso came to the throne of Castile and León in 1252, at the age of thirty. He was a mature man of great energy and talent, considerable military and diplomatic experience, and relentless ambition. His father, Fernando III, had been one of Castile's most successful monarchs, re-uniting the separated kingdoms, liberating much of Spain from the Moors, and securing an unprecedented increase in economic prosperity and cultural level. To succeed such a father could not have been easy for anyone, but for a man of Alfonso's temperament and ability it must have been intolerably difficult. The new king tried to assert his own and his country's supremacy in every possible way, and in most ways, almost inevitably, he failed.

At first, Alfonso showed prudence and restraint in his enterprises, but in two other major ventures he did not know when to stop, and the results wrecked his reign. In his prolonged attempts to become Holy Roman Emperor, he committed to the struggle far more of Castile's financial and military resources than the country could afford, and met with increasing opposition from the nobility and from his own family, until he was compelled to renounce his claim in 1275. The king's attempt to strengthen the royal authority at the expense of the great nobles was a far more justifiable policy, but proved equally disastrous. The principal cause of Alfonso's failure was a dispute over the succession to the throne; the king's vacillation provoked a rebellion led by his son, Sancho. The struggle was still going on when Alfonso died in 1284.[14]

It is impossible to separate Alfonso's political and literary careers, for the same motives inspire them, and they interact throughout his life. As we shall see, the formulation of an encyclopaedic legal code, the *Siete partidas*, was drastically affected by the struggles with the nobility. The use of the vernacular for scientific and historical works is paralleled by insistence on its use for official purposes. In the first case, the dominant factor is Alfonso's determination to assert himself and the royal authority; in the second, his equally intense Castilian patriotism. Until his accession to the throne, chancery documents had normally been in Latin, but he immediately changed this practice, using Spanish for all documents addressed to his subjects, and towards the end of his reign he even addressed documents to some foreign rulers in that language. This insistence on use of the vernacular sprang not, as has been suggested, from the influence of the king's Jewish collaborators in his scholarly work, but rather from his vigorous national consciousness and his wish to foster the only language common to the three races— Spaniards, Moors, and Jews—of his newly-expanded kingdom. Moreover, although use of the vernacular is more sudden and more thorough in Castile than elsewhere, there is a general tendency for educational expansion to be followed by a secularisation of learning, with wider use of the national language.[15]

Alfonso planned two major historical works, the *Estoria de España* and the *General estoria,* or history of the world. The latter remained unfinished, and the former, it now seems, was never completed in the form envisaged by Alfonso. Despite all the resources assembled by the king, the double task proved too large when the team of translators, scholars, and compilers was also engaged on extensive scientific and legal works. In his historical work, as in the attempt to become emperor, Alfonso seems to have overreached himself.

The dating of the *Estoria de España* and the numerous chronicles descended from it, and the relationships between them, are the subject of lively disagreement, owing to the number, length, and bewildering variety of manuscripts.[16] The apparent facts about the *Estoria de España* may be briefly stated, though new evidence may change the position. The work was begun fairly soon after Alfonso came to the throne, and was completed at least in a first draft before his death; Sancho IV was indifferent or even hostile to his father's scholarly enterprises, and seems to have drastically reduced, or even stopped, the payments to Alfonso's collaborators, so that there can be no question

of *EE*'s having been completed under Sancho. The first draft may
have been finished by the early 1270s. At least 400 chapters of *EE*
had been completed by the time Alfonso turned his attention to the
General estoria, and the work may have gone much further, but in
any case it is clear that the diversion of the energies of the king and
his team into the composition of a world history seriously hampered
the production of a final version of *EE*. The edition published by
Menéndez Pidal under the title of *Primera crónica general* faithfully
represents the earlier part of *EE*, but for the later part it relies on a late
and unsatisfactory manuscript, while the most authoritative manuscript
remains unpublished. It follows that the notorious self-contradictions of
the later chapters of the chronicle, seen at their most startling in the
treatment of the Cid's career, are not all the fault of Alfonso and his
compilers, whose organising skill probably deserves more credit than it
has so far received. It would be strange if the men who had earlier in
their work carefully blended such a wide variety of sources by a massive
intellectual effort of synthesis, had then grown utterly careless and
allowed their final version to contain blatant contradictions.

The *Estoria de España*, like the majority of full-scale medieval
Spanish chronicles, begins at the beginning, in this case with Moses,
continuing with pre-Roman Spain, and with Rome, whose history is
seen as an essential part of Spain's background. The bulk of *EE* is, of
course, devoted to the history of Spain, from the Germanic invasions to
the reign of Fernando III; the account breaks off during this reign.
The two major Hispano-Latin chronicles of the thirteenth century
provide a great deal of material, and el Toledano, because of his more
highly developed historical method, is a particularly important source.
Alfonso also uses other medieval Latin chronicles, the Bible, Classical
Latin historians and poets, ecclesiastical legends, vernacular epics, and
Arabic historians. There was ample precedent for the use of epic
sources, but none for the extent to which Alfonso used them: he summarises a few epics so fully that we can reconstruct the entire plot (*La
condesa traidora, Romanz del Infant García, Cantar de Sancho II*),
and prosifies others at length in a way that makes possible the recovery
of many lines of verse (*Siete Infantes de Lara, Cantar de Mio Cid*).[17]

The use of Arabic historians was valuable in three ways. It contributed vivid similes:

> et veno pora Xátiva assí como león fambriento va all enodio, et
> como la grand abenida del diluvio viene a dessora. (551)

It added historical perspective and balance, since the events were seen
by the Moors with a different bias. Finally, it brought into Alfonsine
historiography the Arabic concern for economic and social history (el
Toledano had already discovered the advantages of this). The effects
of the Cid's siege of Valencia are brought home to us by lists of food

prices, in which the prices rise and the quality of the food declines, and by the eventual abandonment of price-lists in favour of a narrative whose simple statement intensifies its horror:

> Et aquellos a que fincava algún poco de pan, soterrávanlo et non lo osavan mostrar por esto que les fazie. Et non fallavan poco nin mucho a conprar caro nin refez. Et los que algo avien tornávanse a comer las yervas, et las raýzes, et cueros, et nervios, et los lectuarios de los especieros, et esto todo muy caro. Et los pobres comien la carne de los omnes. (583)[18]

The *General estoria* was planned as a full-scale history of the world, but was never completed, breaking off when it reaches the parents of the Virgin Mary. Even so, it is of enormous length, and its publication has not yet been completed. Indeed, since the *General estoria* does not seem to have been begun until 1272, it may well be that the king's declining hopes of success in the long struggle to secure recognition as emperor led him to undertake this extraordinarily ambitious history as compensation: if he could not impose his authority outside Spain as a political leader, then he would do so as a historian.

The sources of *GE* are even more numerous and diverse than those of the *Estoria de España*, and are on the whole well combined, with the Old Testament as the chief source, into which the other material is woven. The structural models are the *Jewish Antiquities* of Josephus (in a Latin translation), whose novelistic presentation of biblical episodes and interest in the characters' motivation clearly attracted Alfonso, and the twelfth-century *Historia scholastica* of Peter Comestor, which set an influential precedent for the combination of biblical narrative with historical and pseudo-historical material from other sources. Although Alfonso wished to present the history of the world as a moral mirror for Christians, his interest in secular history is notably greater than Peter Comestor's, and this interest is consistent with other features of *GE*: the literal interpretation of Scripture is preferred to the three hidden levels of meaning which it was at that time common practice to seek with the help of the patristic techniques of exegesis; the extensive treatment of classical mythology (over which *GE* expresses some uneasiness); and the more secular tone given to the Creation story.

The work contains a number of sections which are in effect full Spanish versions of classical stories such as the siege of Troy, the life of Alexander, and the tragic family feud of Thebes; in the last case, Alfonso and his collaborators seem to have translated into Spanish a French prose version of the *Roman de Thèbes*. Indeed, much of *GE* resembles a library of translations, whose compilers worked hard and, on the whole, successfully to integrate their diverse sources into a coherent narrative.[19]

The legal works produced under Alfonso's direction show the same massive effort at synthesis, and the same insistence on the vernacular (there was a precedent here, since the old Visigothic legal code, the *Forum judicum*, had been translated earlier in the century under the title of *Fuero juzgo*).[20] These works may also, like the two histories and Alfonso's political enterprises, show a deep-rooted inability to match ambitious plans with the capacity to carry them through to a successful conclusion. Of the four legal works compiled in his reign, only an early one, the *Fuero real*, was promulgated as a legal code in his lifetime.

When Alfonso came to the throne, there was no unified code of laws for the kingdom as a whole. Many towns had their individual *fueros* (charters), León preserved the Visigothic code, and Castile—more radical than León in its legal institutions, just as it was in linguistic features—had abandoned this code in favour of common law. Alfonso wished first of all to provide for the entire kingdom a code which would supplement existing *fueros*, and thus establish some degree of uniformity; with the *Fuero real*, he achieved this objective, even though the code was not immediately applied to all towns. The other early legal work of the reign is the *Setenario*, whose compilers tell us that it was begun by Alfonso at Fernando III's request, and completed after his accession. It is concerned almost exclusively with ecclesiastical matters, and its compilers have been careful to base its organisation on the magic number seven (hence the title). It gives an encyclopaedic treatment of the sacraments, and a considerable part of the book is devoted to an explanation of various types of pagan nature-worship. It is, then, a combination of legal code, encyclopaedia, and manual for priests.[21]

By far the most important of the Alfonsine legal works is the long *Siete partidas*, which legislates for all aspects of national life—ecclesiastical and secular, civil and criminal law—and explains the subjects with which it deals. Although the *Siete partidas* was not promulgated in Alfonso's reign, it had a wider and more lasting influence than the great majority of his works (its only rivals in this respect being the *Estoria de España* and the *Tablas alfonsies*), for it was promulgated in 1348 by Alfonso XI, its validity was accepted for centuries, and its influence is still discernible today.

The *Siete partidas* draws on a wide range of sources, among the most important being previous Spanish law (*Fuero juzgo*, *Fuero real*, and, for the first *partida*, the *Setenario*, which may well have been a first draft of this section); Roman Law (especially Justinian, with the glosses of later Italian jurists); church law (especially the *Decretum* of Gratian and the collections of canon law known as Decretals); the Bible; and literary sources (both *exempla* from the *Disciplina clericalis*, and *sententiae* from wisdom literature such as the *Bocados de oro*—

see below, pp. 97, 99-100). The distinction between legal codes and literature would not have been a meaningful one to most medieval writers, and legal education seems to have contributed both to the formation of a genre (the debate-poems—see above, pp. 72-3), and to individual works (e.g. *La Celestina*—see below, p. 177, n.53).[22]

There are two versions of the first *partida*, one considerably shorter than the other. The shorter version probably represents the views of Alfonso and of his closest advisers, while the version which eventually gained general acceptance is much closer to the views of Sancho and the nobles who supported him. What is involved here is a clash between two theories of royal power. The *Siete partidas* was composed between 1256 and 1265, but the date of the longer version of the first *partida* is uncertain. It may have been composed late in Alfonso's reign, under pressure from Sancho's party, but it may date from Sancho's own reign (1284-95) or that of his successor, Fernando IV (1295-1312).

The fourth legal work to be considered is of much less importance: the *Espéculo*. It was never promulgated; its date of composition and its relation to the *Siete partidas* are obscure, but it is probably late, and may well have been composed under Sancho IV or Fernando IV.[23]

The numerous scientific works produced under Alfonso's direction are mostly treatises on astronomy or astrology. They are translated from Arabic and in some cases the ultimate source is Greek. The most important of the works for scientific history, though not as literature, is the *Tablas alfonsíes*, tables of the movements of the planets; the original was compiled by an eleventh-century Arabic astronomer from Córdoba, al-Zarkali, and the revision based on observations carried out in Toledo between 1262 and 1272 by Alfonso's scientists. In this form they became known in France, and in an early fourteenth-century French astronomer's revision they were diffused throughout Europe, and were used well into the Renaissance.

Among the scientific productions of Alfonso's reign are a collection of astronomical treatises (the *Libros del saber de astronomía*), and two astrological works, the *Libro de las cruzes* and the *Libro conplido en los judizios de las estrellas*. What seems to have been a major collection of treatises, the *Libro de las formas*, has been lost except for the table of contents, from which it can be seen that it consisted (or was intended to consist) of eleven lapidaries. A group of four such works on the properties of stones has survived, three of them extremely short. The extant manuscript of the *Lapidario* (as this group is generally known) is, like many manuscripts emanating from the royal scriptorium, rich in illustrations: there are nearly fifty drawings of the animals and other symbolic figures for divisions of the zodiac.[24] Another feature of the scientific works is that a number of the prefaces give valuable information about the methods of Alfonso and his collaborators.[25]

Of the extant Alfonsine works, one minor and one major category remain to be considered: the recreational and the religious works (for *exemplum* and wisdom literature of this reign, see below, pp. 97-100). In the first category, a work on chess and other games was translated from the Arabic, amended, and profusely illustrated: the *Libro de axedrez, dados e tablas*.[26]

The religious works are unique among the serious Alfonsine production in that they are not in Castilian. Bernardo de Brihuega, canon of Seville, compiled a Latin volume of saints' lives, probably at Alfonso's request, though not under his immediate direction.[27] The *Cantigas de Santa Maria* are probably much less a collective enterprise than the historical, legal, or scientific works, and very many of them may be individual compositions by the king. A personal tone is especially noticeable in songs of praise to the Virgin and in stories where Alfonso or his relatives are central figures.

The 427 poems are in Galician-Portuguese, and in a great variety of verse-forms, though all are refrain-based (see above, pp. 23-4). Alfonso's reasons for choosing Galician-Portuguese are disputed, but he may have wished to experiment with versification, and found a greater choice offered by the Galician-Portuguese tradition. This would help to explain why he chose to cast his miracle stories in metres not really suitable for continuous narrative.

Of the *Cantigas*, every tenth poem is a *cantiga de loor*. These songs of praise were, like many of the other poems, set to music, and may be regarded as vernacular hymns, a category which developed in the thirteenth century alongside the writing and use of hymns in Latin. Most of the final *Cantigas* may be seen in this light, since from number 400 onwards very few are miracle stories; instead, we have a poem on the Sorrows of Mary, a series for Marian festivals in the Church's calendar, and so on.[28]

Berceo's *Milagros de Nuestra Señora* was almost entirely derived from a single source (see above, p. 65), but the origins of Alfonso's much longer collection are more varied: a number of Latin miracle-collections, and probably one or two vernacular ones, Spanish and German folklore (Alfonso's mother was German), and the king's own experiences. The inclusion of the author or organiser of the collection as a character in some of the stories is a novelty in this particular context. There is, however, a precedent to be found elsewhere: in popular sermons, preachers often used allegedly autobiographical *exempla* to add vividness.

There are four manuscripts of the *Cantigas*, and at least some of these are products of the royal scriptorium. Carefully and lavishly produced, they have preserved not merely the texts of the poems, but their music and a large number of exquisite miniatures which illustrate the action of the stories. One of the manuscripts contains a further element of great interest: summaries in Castilian of the first 25 *Cantigas*.[29]

There are other Galician-Portuguese poems which are almost certainly Alfonso's individual work, whatever doubts remain as to the extent of his authorship of the Marian poems. These are, with few exceptions, *cantigas d'escarnho e de maldizer* (see above, pp. 14-15), and are addressed to nobles, ecclesiastics, and poets. Some, for example, are directed at Pero da Ponte, one of the leading poets of Fernando III's Court, and it is possible to trace a quarrel that may well have begun before Alfonso ascended the throne. These poems show great ingenuity and an apparently inexhaustible enjoyment of scurrilous abuse of those who have irritated the king.

Some Alfonsine works have been lost, including two of the most interesting, but we are able to form some impression of them from extant translations. One of these works is *Picatrix*, translated in 1256 under Alfonso's direction from what has been described as the outstanding medieval work on astrological magic, the Arabic *Goal of the Sage*, which was composed in Spain in the eleventh century. This was influenced by Hermetism, the secret religion that arose in Hellenistic Egypt in the second and third centuries A.D. The Arabic original survives, and so does a Latin version based on the Spanish.[30]

Another lost work is an account, translated from Arabic, of Mohammed's vision of Heaven and Hell. The book was translated into medieval French under the title of *Livre de leschiele Mahomet*, and if the prologue of the French text is to be believed, this also was prepared under Alfonso's direction, from the Spanish, in 1264.[31] The Arabic narrative of Mohammed's vision enjoyed considerable currency in thirteenth-century Spain: a shorter text was translated into Latin by Rodrigo of Toledo in his *Historia Arabum*, from which a Castilian version was made for the *Estoria de España* (chapters 488-9); and at the end of the century St Pedro Pascual, bishop of Jaén, included Mohammed's vision in an anti-Muslim polemical work. In addition, a Christian narrative of an other-world journey, the *Purgatory of St Patrick*, was translated from Latin into Castilian, perhaps by Alfonso's team.[32]

Alfonso was not only a patron,[33] but also an active editor. It is clear that he chose the subjects of works to be compiled or translated, that he guided his collaborators, and that he inspected the results closely. How far he took an actual part in the labour of translation and of preparing prose drafts cannot be known, but there is no doubt as to the intensity of his involvement in all aspects of editorial work. Also beyond doubt is his concern for language. This was not restricted to a patriotic determination that Castilian should be used for prose-works, but extended to a detailed care for the development of an adequate linguistic standard in the vernacular. Both of these points are attested by the prologue to the *Libro de la ochava esfera* in a well-known passage:

tolló las razones que entendió eran sobejas et dobladas et que no eran en castellano drecho, et puso las otras que entendió que complían; et cuanto en el lenguage, endreçólo él por síse.

The main linguistic problems confronting Alfonso were of syntax and vocabulary. Without a more flexible and varied syntax than had previously been used in Spanish prose, even a moderately sophisticated treatment of ideas would have been impossible. We must not exaggerate the change brought about in Alfonso's reign: even in the later works, the syntax can be rudimentary, and even at its best, it cannot compete with the resources of Latin. Nevertheless, the development is unmistakable and substantial; some of the features both of Latin and of Arabic syntax are used to enrich Spanish. In the field of vocabulary, it was necessary to introduce words for things and concepts not previously dealt with in the vernacular. The problem was usually resolved by borrowing a Latin word (sometimes one from another language), and making the minimum changes necessary to adapt it to the Castilian habits of pronunciation. Such a word was defined the first time it was used in any work, but thereafter readers were assumed to be familiar with its meaning. A number of sound-changes also seem to date from Alfonso's reign, but these, although important for the history of the language, are much less significant culturally than the expansion of vocabulary or the sophistication of syntax. The main picture is, then, one of regularisation and of an increase in the resources of the language. A final point to be noticed is that the linguistic norm now took account of New Castile: the centre of gravity of Castilian shifted from Burgos towards Toledo. Stress has been laid in this chapter on Alfonso's repeated failure, both in political life and in literary undertakings, to match ambition with completed performance, and it is therefore only right to emphasise now that in linguistic development and in the organisation and direction of a team of scholars, translators, scribes, artists, and musicians, he not only achieved his objectives, but did so in a way that conferred lasting cultural benefits on his country. Fernando III had incorporated Andalusia, with its large Moorish population, into Castile. The need to unify this expanded, diverse kingdom helps to explain Alfonso's wish to provide a legal, cultural, and linguistic standard.

The picture of Alfonso given here must also be modified in another way. National pride and personal ambition were powerful motives in his intellectual life, just as they were in his political activities. They were, almost certainly, the dominant motives throughout his reign, but they did not have exclusive power over him. He was inspired also by his religious faith and hence by his concern with morality and personal behaviour, as is revealed by his choice of subjects for his works: religion, law, history (which offered examples to follow and to avoid), astronomy and astrology (which determined the limits within which man's moral choice could be exercised).[34]

III. BIBLE TRANSLATIONS

The thirteenth century also saw the growth of Bible translations, collections of *exempla*, and wisdom literature, all of them parts of a general movement to bring Christian instruction to the people in their own language (even though much of the original material is of non-Christian origin). The Bible translations brought the word of God directly to those who were literate in the vernacular, and to small groups who heard the Scriptures read aloud; *exemplum*-collections and wisdom literature were probably designed for the use of preachers, who fortified and enlivened their popular sermons with illustrative stories and pithy sayings, but these collections must also have had their private readers.

The Catholic Church in the Middle Ages was suspicious of vernacular Bibles, partly for fear that error in translation might convey false doctrine, and partly because direct access to biblical texts by the people might undermine the Church's authority. The Protestant reformers were active in the work of translation, and at an earlier period the Greek Orthodox Church and the Cathars saw this as one of their main religious tasks. Catholics were notably more attached to vernacular Bibles in Spain than in other western European countries, but this does not seem to have been due to Jewish influence. At a later stage, there were Judeo-Spanish versions of the Old Testament, for the use of Jewish communities expelled from the Peninsula (Judeo-Spanish remains the official language of Sephardic synagogues in several countries even today); but this scriptural tradition is quite separate from that of the Spanish Christian translations which began in the early thirteenth century. These translations were not confined to the Bible: the *Setenario*, for instance, contains a vernacular version of most of the Canon of the Mass, together with a number of other prayers.

The tradition of Spanish vernacular Bibles is both rich and persistent, and substantial translations of the Old Testament are combined with other material in the *Fazienda de Ultra Mar* and the *General estoria*. Official rulings were the same as in other Catholic countries—the Council of Tarragona prohibited vernacular scriptures in 1233—but they were more often disregarded in Spain than elsewhere, and disregarded at a higher social level: some kings and masters of military orders read the Bible in Spanish. Perhaps the circumstances of the Reconquest led to the tacit condoning of this practice, just as they caused explicit relaxation of other rules.[35]

IV. 'EXEMPLUM'-COLLECTIONS

The importance of *exempla* in the *divisio extra*, or popular, sermon has already been mentioned (see above, p. 62); this use of illustrative stories derives from the parables of the New Testament and the exemplary figures of classical rhetoric. *Sententiae*, or sayings of famous men which conveyed wisdom in concentrated form, were also frequently used in sermons, and they too have both a rhetorical and an early Christian ancestry; the later medieval and Renaissance use of proverbs is a development of this tradition. With these two techniques at his disposal, the popular preacher could entertain his audience while edifying them, and he could shield himself from criticism by the invocation of the authority of the past. The collection of *exempla* and *sententiae* began in the Classical Latin period (the *Factorum et dictorum memorabilium libri ix* of Valerius Maximus), and the practice was greatly increased in the Middle Ages. Almost anything could be used as an *exemplum*: Aesopic fables, historical and biblical events and persons, classical mythology (this was less frequent in sermons than in formal literature), and events which the preacher had, or claimed to have, witnessed or experienced.[36]

No priest or friar could be expected to gather an adequate stock of *exempla* from his own reading and observation, and *exemplum*-collections proliferated, at first in Latin, and then in the vernacular. By far the earliest collection to be compiled in Spain is the *Disciplina clericalis* of Pedro Alfonso (born *c.* 1062), a Jew who was converted to Christianity in 1106, spent some time in England, and became a physician to Henry I. He also wrote a polemical treatise in Latin against Judaism, and astronomical works whose original language is unknown. The language in which the *Disciplina* itself was first composed is uncertain, since the prologue says 'Deus . . . me librum hunc componere et in latinum transferre compulit.' Perhaps the first version was in Hebrew, but it may equally well be that, since most of the thirty-four *exempla* are of oriental origin, Pedro Alfonso was referring to the task of assembling the material from different sources and then writing the book as a whole in Latin. The precise sources of the book remain to be established, but the stories belong to the common stock of international popular tales, and embody a great many folk-motifs; this is, indeed, true of all *exemplum*-collections. Groups of *sententiae* (often derived from wisdom literature) are interposed between some of the stories; and the *Disciplina* is constructed on a thin narrative framework in which a father instructs his son by means of *exempla*.[37] There is a fairly widespread belief that this book was translated into medieval Spanish, but though it is an important source for three fifteenth-century Spanish *exemplum*-collections, there is no reason to suppose that they used a vernacular text. Although the *Disciplina* had considerable influence in Spain (it was also used as a source of the *Siete partidas* and other works), its vogue seems to have been much greater in the rest of Europe.

A fairly wide range of morals could be drawn from any of the stories in the *exemplum*-collections, which meant that preachers were encouraged to produce their own variations on the stories; this led eventually to a highly individual literary use of *exempla*, as we shall see in dealing with the *Libro de Buen Amor*. Another result of the adaptability of *exempla* was that stories of non-Christian origin presented no difficulty to the preacher. The first vernacular collections in Spain, the *Libro de los engaños e los asayamientos de las mugeres* and *Calila e Digna*, have much in common. Both were translated into Spanish from an Arabic intermediary, the original collection having come from further east, India in the case of *Calila*, India or Persia in the case of the *Libro de los engaños*. Both are supposed to have been translated in the mid-thirteenth century, *Calila* under the auspices of Alfonso before he came to the throne, *Engaños* at the instigation of his brother Prince Fadrique. Both set the *exempla* within a narrative framework. Both stress worldly wisdom rather than a Christian moral. The chief structural and didactic features of these two collections are characteristic of Eastern collections of tales. Their purpose is to teach men to live virtuously, but above all prudently, in the world as they find it. As to the structure, there are three main types of frame-story which serve as pretexts for the tales included in them. The telling of tales to postpone an execution (*The Thousand and One Nights* is the most familiar example) and the use of tales by a master to answer his pupil's questions, or in an argument, are oriental frame-stories, while the third type, the telling of tales to while away a journey or a tedious period of waiting, is late and Western (*The Canterbury Tales* and the *Decameron* exemplify this type).

Calila e Digna descends, through Persian and Arabic translations, from an Indian collection made perhaps two centuries before Christ, the *Panchatantra*. Some of the *Panchatantra* is omitted from *Calila*, and some new material introduced. The protagonists in the frame-story are animals who exchange tales and advice, but for part of the book these give way to a philosopher who answers a king's questions; in the *Libro de los engaños* (a version of the *Book of Sindibad*, or *Sendebar*), the frame-story concerns a prince who rebuffs the advances of his father's concubine and is accused by her of attempted rape. (This blends the folk-motif of the wicked stepmother and the story familiar in biblical tradition as that of Potiphar's wife.) He is sentenced to death, and since a mysterious fate compels him to remain silent, wise men of the Court tell stories to gain time until he can defend himself. Inevitably, the stories have an anti-feminist tinge, and the concentration on women's sexual guile means that this book is the first substantial collection of *fabliaux* in Spanish: [38]

> Señor, oý dezir que un omne que era, çeloso de su muger; e conpró un papagayo e metiólo en una jaula e púsolo en su casa, e mandóle que le dixiese todo quanto viese fazer a su muger, e que non le en-

cubriese ende nada; e después fue su vía a rrecabdar su mandado; e entró su amigo della en su casa do estava. El papagayo vio quanto ellos fizieron, e quando el omne bueno vino de su mandado, asentóse en su casa en guisa que non lo viese la muger; e mandó traer el papagayo, e preguntóle todo lo que viera . . .   (p. 15)

The origins of the *Book of Sindibad*, and the channel by which it reached Europe, are disputed. There are numerous European versions of the work, including two later Spanish ones, the *Scala celi* of Diego de Cañizares, and the *Siete sabios de Roma*. The stories in these versions, and the details of the frame, differ, but they are unmistakably members of the same family.[39]

Later in the century comes the *Castigos e documentos para bien vivir ordenados por el rey don Sancho IV* (Sancho's responsibility for the work is disputed). This is less clear-cut than *Calila e Digna* or *Libro de los engaños*, since the frame is more tenuous (it consists of Sancho's advice to his son, and has no narrative interest), the *exempla* of oriental origin are mixed with borrowings from the patristic and medieval European tradition, and the book has some of the features of wisdom literature. It also resembles the European genre of the *speculum principis*, the book of advice to a king on how to rule, though the resemblance probably arises from a common purpose rather than from any conscious debt.[40]

A work that has affinities with the *exemplum*-collections of oriental origin is the *Libro de la vida de Barlaam y del rey Josapha de India*, a Christianised version of the legend of Buddha, which came via Greek and Latin; this Spanish text (there are also later medieval Spanish versions of the legend) was composed in either the thirteenth or the fourteenth century. In it, a young prince is shielded from the knowledge of death until he encounters successively an aged man, a corpse, and an ascetic hermit; he learns wisdom and virtue, and sees this world in its true light. In this main story are set a number of *exempla*.[41]

V. WISDOM LITERATURE

The *exemplum*-collections inevitably include a number of *sententiae*. Similarly, the wisdom literature so prevalent in thirteenth-century Spain incorporates some brief exemplary tales. Nevertheless, the distinction between the two groups of texts is clear and important. Most of the wisdom literature is derived directly or indirectly from Arabic, and most of the Spanish texts are related to one another, either by descent from common sources or by direct influence. For example, the *Flores de filosofía* is an abridgement of the *Libro de los cien capítulos*, and the third book of the *Libro del cavallero Zifar* (see below, pp. 157-8) is an amplified rearrangement of the *Flores de filosofía*. Similar works are the

Libro de los buenos proverbios, the *Libro de los doce sabios,* the *Bonium* or *Bocados de oro,* and the *Libro del consejo e de los consejeros* attributed to Maestre Pedro, whose identity is obscure. The titles do not always give an accurate impression of the works: for instance, the *Libro de los cien capítulos* in fact contains fifty chapters, and though the table of contents lists a further fifty, the book's modern editor concludes that they were never written. In most of these works, the *sententiae*—which either originate in the Arabic tradition or have been filtered through it—are not attributed to particular wise men by name. The *Libro del consejo* (probably early fourteenth century) is an exception, since names are frequently given, and they are generally names from classical antiquity or from the Bible. The chief source for this book is not Arabic, but the *Liber consolationis et consilii* (1246), of Albertano of Brescia. Even in this case, however, there is a considerable amount of overlap with the *Flores de filosofía* and *Bocados de oro.* The *Bocados* presents something of a paradox, since it is firmly within the Arabic tradition, yet attributes its *sententiae* to Greek philosophers. The description of the *sabio* at the beginning of each chapter is the most lively part; the form of the *sententiae* tends to be rigidly repetitive. The *Poridat de las poridades* purports to be the advice given by Aristotle to his pupil Alexander the Great (it coincides to some extent with Aristotle's advice in the *Libro de Alexandre*). Many Aristotelian works were translated into Arabic, and, as we have already seen, a number of these reached the Latin West only through their Arabic versions; thus there was no reason for medieval readers to query the Aristotelian credentials of this spurious work. The *Poridat* is a translation direct from the Arabic, whereas most European vernacular versions derive from the Latin *Secretum secretorum.* Even in Spain, the Latin text seems to have been more influential than the *Poridat.*[42]

Very few of the *sententiae* contained in thirteenth-century wisdom literature are biblical, although many of them could be turned to an edifying purpose in sermons. Early in the fourteenth century, Pedro López de Baeza, an officer of the Order of Santiago, adapted the *Flores de filosofía* so as to give explicitly Christian advice, under the title of *Dichos de santos padres.*[43]

Two works lie on the fringes of *exemplum* and wisdom literature: the *Historia de la donzella Teodor* and the *Lucidario.* The first of these derives (either directly or via Latin) from a story of *The Thousand and One Nights.* Teodor, a slave-girl, saves herself from dishonour and her kind master from bankruptcy by answering all the riddles and factual questions that the wisest men of the kingdom can put to her. In different versions (the *Historia* remained popular in Spain for centuries) the content of the questions changes. The process of imparting information by question and answer was, of course, familiar to medieval Christians from the catechism (normally Latin, but occasionally vernacular), but the process was also used for scientific education, so that Teodor's adventure represents the popular end of a chain which leads to highly sophisticated medical and scientific questions.[44] The *Lucidario* is also based on question and answer; in this case, a pupil asks about theological matters and natural phenomena, and receives detailed replies from his master. The general tone is consciously rational and matter-of-fact. The chief source is the *Elucidarium* of Honorius of Autun (*c.* 1095), very considerably adapted.[45] The *Lucidario* was probably composed in the reign of Sancho IV, and serves to remind us that Alfonso's opponent and successor was not irrevocably hostile to literary and scientific culture. Nevertheless, the level of literary production does seem to have fallen sharply, and one cannot easily see Sancho's reign as part of the thirteenth-century cultural expansion. It is likely, however, that education continued to expand, and the level of literacy to rise, with all the consequences that those developments imply for the future of literature.

NOTES

1. See Menéndez Pidal's introduction to *Reliquias de la poesía épica*. These chronicles are being published in the collection of Textos Medievales, directed by A. Ubieto Arteta (Valencia, 1961-).
2. J. M. Millás Vallicrosa, 'La corriente de las traducciones científicas de origen oriental hasta fines del siglo XIII', *CHM*, II (1954-55), 395-428; Millás Vallicrosa, *Traducciones, Estudios*, and *Nuevos estudios*; Thorndike, *History of Magic*, II, 66-93; R. Menéndez Pidal, 'España y la introducción de la ciencia árabe en Occidente', *España, eslabón entre la Cristiandad y el Islam* (Madrid, Austral, 1956), pp. 33-60; D. M. Dunlop, *Arabic Science in the West* (Karachi, n.d.).
3. J. M. Millás Vallicrosa, *Assaig d'història de les idees físiques i matemàtiques a la Catalunya medieval* (Barcelona, 1931).
4. A. González Palencia, *El arzobispo don Raimundo de Toledo* (Barcelona, 1942).
5. On linguistic knowledge, see Bernhard Bischoff, 'The Study of Foreign Languages in the Middle Ages', *Sp*, XXXVI (1961), 209-24.
6. Cf. the reviews of Lazar's edition by F. Lecoy, *R*, XC (1969), 574-6; and Alberto Vàrvaro, *RPh*, XXIII (1969-70), 239-44.
7. L. F. Lindley Cintra, 'O *Liber regum*, fonte comum do *Poema de Fernão Gonçalves* e do *Laberinto* de Juan de Mena', *BF*, XIII (1952), 289-315.
8. ed. A. Ubieto Arteta (Textos Medievales 15, Valencia, 1966). See R. Menéndez Pidal, 'Relatos poéticos en las crónicas medievales', *RFE*, X (1923), 329-72, and *Reliquias*, pp. xxxviii-xliii; Rico, 'Las letras latinas', 81-5.
9. *Historia Roderici*, ed. Menéndez Pidal, *La España del Cid*, II; A. Ubieto Arteta, 'La *HR* y su fecha de redacción', *Saitabi* (Valencia), XI (1961), 241-6. *Historia Compostelana*, in *España sagrada*, XX, and in J. P. Migne, *Patrologia latina*, CLXX; Anselm G. Biggs, *Diego Gelmírez. First Archbishop of Compostela* (Catholic University of America Studies in Mediaeval History, n.s., XII, Washington, 1949); Bernard F. Reilly, 'The *HC*: the genesis and composition of a twelfth-century Spanish *gesta*', *Sp*, XLIV (1969), 78-85; Rico, 'Las letras latinas', 51-8.

10. ed. Andreas Schott, *Hispaniae illustratae*, IV (Francofurti, 1608); Paul Högberg, 'La Chronique de Lucas de Tuy', *RH*, LXXXI, 1 (1933), 404-20.

11. ed. Schott, *Hisp. illus.*, II (1603); ed. M. D. Cabanes Pecourt (Textos Med. 22, Valencia, 1968); Javier Gorosterratzu, *Don Rodrigo Jiménez de Rada, gran estadista, escritor y prelado* (Pamplona, 1925); Diego Catalán and María S.A. Castellanos de Pliego, 'El *Toledano romanzado* y las *Estorias del fecho de los Godos* del s.XV', *Estudios dedicados a James Homer Herriott* (Universidad de Wisconsin, 1966), pp. 9-102.

12. John K. Wright, *The Geographical Lore of the Time of the Crusades. A study in the history of medieval science and tradition in Western Europe* (2nd ed., New York, 1965).

13. Bestiaries are largely fanciful, though occasionally accurate, descriptions of animals, in which authority weighs more heavily than direct observation (they include legendary animals also); the descriptions are then interpreted in Christian terms. Numerous works of literature and art show the influence of the bestiaries, in Spain as elsewhere, though there is no evidence that a Spanish bestiary ever existed. See A. D. Deyermond, *Traces of the Bestiary in Medieval Spanish Literature* (London, 1971).

14. Robert A. MacDonald, 'Alfonso the Learned and Succession: a father's dilemma', *Sp*, XL (1965), 647-53. See also a letter and two wills by Alfonso (*Antología*, pp. 218-42).

15. On the growth of literacy, see below, pp. 136-7.

16. See Menéndez Pidal's introduction to his ed. of *Primera crónica general* (i.e. *Estoria de España*); Sánchez Alonso, *Historia de la historiografía*, I; Theodore Babbitt, 'Observations on the *Crónica de once reyes*', *HR*, II (1934), 202-16, and *La crónica de veinte reyes. A comparison with the text of the Primera crónica general, and a study of the principal Latin sources* (YRS, XIII, New Haven, 1936); L. F. Lindley Cintra's introd. to his ed. of *Crónica geral de Espanha de 1344*, I (Lisboa, 1951); Diego Catalán, *De Alfonso X*, 'El *Toledano romanzado*', and articles in *R*, LXXXIV (1963), and *HR*, XXXI (1963); J. Gómez Pérez's articles in *RABM*, LXVII (1959), *Sc*, XVII (1963), and *His*, XXV (1965); Samuel G. Armistead, 'New Perspectives in Alfonsine Historiography', *RPh*, XX (1966-67), 204-17.

17. See, however, above, p. 50, note 9.

18. On *EE*, in addition to the studies already cited, see A. G. Solalinde, 'Una fuente de la *Primera crónica general*: Lucano', *HR*, IX (1941), 235-42; Dorothy Donald, 'Suetonius in the *PCG* through the *Speculum historiale*', *HR*, XI (1943), 95-115; J. R. Ashton, 'Putative *Heroides* Codex AX as a Source of Alfonsine Literature', *RPh*, III (1949-50), 275-89; C. E. Dubler, 'Fuentes árabes y bizantinas en la *PCG*', *VR*, XII (1951-52), 120-80; Antoinette Letsch-Lavanchy, 'Éléments didactiques dans la *CG*', *VR*, XV (1956), 2, 231-40; A. M. Badía Margarit, 'La frase de la *PCG* en relación con sus fuentes latinas. Avance de un trabajo de conjunto', *RFE*, XLII (1958-59), 179-210, and 'Los *Monumenta Germaniae historica* y la *PCG* de A. el sabio', *Strenae. Estudios Manuel García Blanco* (Salamanca, 1962), pp. 69-75.

19. A. G. Solalinde, 'El juicio de Paris en el *Alexandre* y en la *General estoria*', *RFE*, XV (1928), 1-51, 'El *Physiologus* en la *GE* de Alfonso X', *Mélanges d'histoire littéraire générale et comparée offerts à Fernand Baldensperger*, II (Paris, 1930), 251-4, and 'Fuentes de la *GE* de A. el Sabio', *RFE*, XXI (1934), 1-28 and XXIII (1936), 113-42; L. B. Kiddle, 'A Source of the *GE*: the French prose redaction of the *Roman de Thèbes*', *HR*, IV (1936),

264-71, and 'The Prose *Thèbes* and the *GE*: an illustration of the Alphonsine method of using source material', *HR*, VI (1938), 120-32; J. Engels, *Études sur l'Ovide moralisé* (Groningen, 1943); G. H. London and R. J. Leslie, 'A Thirteenth-Century Spanish Version of Ovid's *Pyramus and Thisbe*', *MLR*, L (1955), 147-55; Lida de Malkiel, 'La *GE*: notas literarias y filológicas', *RPh*, XII (1958-59), 111-42, and XIII (1959-60), 1-30, and 'Josefo en la *GE*', *Hispanic Studies in Honour of I. González Llubera*, pp. 163-81; Gormly, *Use of the Bible*, Ch. 2; Margherita Morreale, 'La fraseología bíblica en la *GE*. Observaciones para su estudio', *Literary and Linguistic Studies in Honor of Helmut A. Hatzfeld* (Washington, 1964), pp. 269-78; M. M. Lasley, 'Secularization of the Creation Story in the *GE*', *RHM*, XXXIV (1968), 330-37.

20. *Fuero juzgo en latín y castellano* (Madrid, Real Academia Española, 1815); V. Fernández Llera, *Gramática y vocabulario del FJ* (Madrid, 1929).

21. Such manuals were normally in Latin, but some vernacular ones are extant, including a short thirteenth-century Castilian manual on confession. This work, *De los diez mandamientos*, is published by Alfred Morel-Fatio, *R*, XVI (1887), 379-82; it is of interest for its references to popular song, and for comparison with *leyes* 98-103 of the *Setenario*.

22. See also Lomax, 'The Lateran Reforms', 310.

23. *Setenario*, ed. Kenneth H. Vanderford (Buenos Aires, 1945); *Siete partidas* (3 vols., Madrid, RAE, 1807); *Fuero Real* and *Espéculo* in *Opúsculos legales* (2 vols., Madrid, Real Academia de la Historia, 1836). Samuel P. Scott, introd. to transl. of *Siete partidas* (Chicago, 1931); Ángel Ferrari Núñez, 'La secularización de la teoría del Estado en las *Partidas*', *AHDE*, XI (1934), 449-56; J. Homer Herriott, 'A Thirteenth-Century Manuscript of the *Primera partida*', *Sp*, XIII (1938), 278-94, and 'The Validity of the Printed Editions of the *PP*', *RPh*, V (1951-52), 165-74; María del Carmen Carle, 'La servidumbre en las *P*', *CHE*, XX (1949), 105-19; Alfonso García Gallo, 'El *Libro de las leyes* de A. el sabio. Del *Espéculo* a las *P*', *AHDE*, XXI-XXII (1951-52), 345-528; José Jiménez, 'El *Decreto* y las *Decretales*, fuentes de la primera *P* de A. el sabio', *Anthologica Annua*, II (1954), 239-48; José M. Gárate Córdoba, *Espíritu y milicia en la España medieval* (Madrid, 1967), 263-330.

24. *Lapidario* (facsimile of MS., Madrid, 1881); ed. María Brey Mariño (Madrid, Odres Nuevos, 1968). See J. H. Nunemaker's articles in *PQ*, VIII (1929), 248-54; *RFE*, XVI (1929), 161-8, and XVIII (1931), 261-2; *PMLA*, XLV (1930), 444-53; *MP*, XXIX (1931-32), 101-4; *Sp*, VII (1932), 556-64, and XIV (1939), 483-9; *HR*, II (1934), 242-6; cf. Joan Evans, *Magical Jewels of the Middle Ages and the Renaissance, particularly in England* (Oxford, 1922).

25. *Libros del saber de astronomía*, ed. Manuel Rico y Sinobas (5 vols., Madrid, 1863-67); *Tratado del cuadrante*, ed. J. M. Millás Vallicrosa, 'Una nueva obra astronómica alfonsí: el *Tratado del cuadrante "sennero"* ', *Al-An*, XXI (1956), 59-92 (repr. in *Nuevos estudios*, Ch. 13); Aly Aben Ragel, *El libro conplido en los iudizios de las estrellas*, ed. Gerold Hilty (Madrid, 1954); *Libro de las cruzes*, ed. Lloyd A. Kasten and Lawrence B. Kiddle (Madrid and Madison, 1961). In addition to the studies cited above in notes 2 and 24, see J. L. E. Dreyer, 'On the Original Form of the *Alfonsine Tables*', *Monthly Notices of the Royal Astronomical Society*, LXXX (1920), 243-62; Evelyn S. Procter, 'The Scientific Works of the Court of A.X of Castile: the King and his collaborators', *MLR*, XL (1945), 12-29; A. R. Nykl, 'Libro conplido en los juizios de las estrellas', *Sp*, XXIX (1954), 85-99; Gerold Hilty, 'El libro conplido . . .', *Al-An*, XX (1955), 1-74.

26. ed. A. Steiger (R Hel 10, Zurich, 1941); J. B. Trend, 'A. el Sabio and the Game of Chess', *RH*, LXXXI, 1 (1933), 393-403. There are other works not attributed in the MSS. to Alfonso, though they are probably of his reign and may well have been composed under his direction, e.g. the *Libro de los caballos*, a translation of a thirteenth-century Latin treatise (ed. Georg Sachs, *RFE* anejo XXIII, Madrid, 1936).

27. R. Beer, 'Los cinco libros que compiló B. de B.', *BRAH*, XI (1887), 363-9; M. C. Díaz y Díaz, 'La obra de B. de B., colaborador de A.X', *Strenae*, 145-61; Mário Martins, 'B. de B., compilador do *Livro e legenda que fala de todolos feitos e paixões dos santos mártires*', *Brot*, LXXVI (1963), 411-23, and 'B. de B., compilador dos *Autos dos apóstolos*', *BF*, XXI (1962-63), 69-85. Others connected with Alfonso wrote in Latin, e.g. Gil de Zamora, author of historical works and miracles of the Virgin Mary, but there is less reason to connect the works themselves with the king than in Brihuega's case.

28. Poems on the Joys and on the Sorrows of Mary were frequent in the Middle Ages: see Le Gentil, *La Poésie lyrique*, I, and Woolf, *English Religious Lyric*.

29. Higinio Anglés, *La música de las Cantigas de Santa María del rey A. el sabio* (Barcelona, 1943); José Guerrero Lovillo, *Las Cantigas. Estudio arqueológico de sus miniaturas* (Madrid, 1949); Dorothy C. Clarke, 'Versification in A. el Sabio's *C*', *HR*, XXIII (1955), 83-98; John E. Keller, 'Folklore in the *C* of A. el Sabio', *Southern Folklore Quarterly*, XXIII (1959), 175-83; Keller and Robert W. Linker, 'Some Spanish Summaries of the *CSM*', *RoN*, II (1960-61), 63-7; Emilio Carilla, 'El rey de las *C*', *Estudios de literatura española* (Rosario, 1958), pp. 7-23; Bertolucci, 'Contributo'; Francisco Márquez Villanueva, 'La poesía de las *Cantigas*', *RO*, n.s. XXV (1969), 71-93; Sara Sturm, 'The Presentation of the Virgin in the *CSM*', *PQ*, XLIX (1970), 1-7; John G. Cummins, 'The Practical Implications of Alfonso el Sabio's Peculiar Use of the *Zéjel*', *BHS*, XLVII (1970), 1-9.

30. Henry and Renée Kahane and Angelina Pietrangeli, 'Hermetism in the Alfonsine Tradition', *Mélanges Lejeune*, I, 443-57, and 'Picatrix and the Talismans', *RPh*, XIX (1965-66), 574-93; Thorndike, *History of Magic*, II, 813-24 (and, for medieval hermetic books, II, 214-28).

31. ed. Peter Wunderli (R Hel 77, Bern, 1968); Wunderli, *Études sur le Livre de l'eschiele Mahomet* (Winterthur, 1965). W. believes that the French translation was probably made from the Latin. Miguel Asín Palacios, *La escatología musulmana en la Divina Comedia* (2nd ed., Madrid, 1943), argues that Dante owed much to Muslim traditions of the other world, and that this text was the means by which he knew them. The question remains undecided.

32. A. G. Solalinde, 'La primera versión española de *El purgatorio de San Patricio* y la difusión de esta leyenda en España', *Homenaje a Menéndez Pidal* (Madrid, 1925), II, 219-57. See Patch, *The Other World*.

33. His patronage was not confined to Spaniards: Geoffrey the Englishman dedicated his *Ars epistolaris ornatus* to Alfonso, and intended it to be used at Salamanca University; see Valeria Bertolucci Pizzorusso, 'Un trattato di *Ars dictandi* dedicato ad A.X', *SMV*, XV-XVI (1968), 9-88.

34. On Alfonso's functions as patron and editor, and the linguistic aspects of his work, see A. G. Solalinde, 'Intervención de A.X en la redacción de sus obras', *RFE*, II (1915), 283-8; J. M. Millás Vallicrosa, 'El literalismo de los traductores de la corte de A. el sabio', *Al-An*, I (1933), 155-8 (repr. in *Estudios*, Ch. 12); Américo Castro, *España en su historia*, pp. 478-87, and 'Acerca del castellano escrito en torno a A. el sabio', *FiR*, I, 4 (1954), 1-11; Gonzalo Menéndez Pidal, 'Cómo trabajaron las escuelas alfonsíes', *NRFH*, V (1951),

363-80; Badía Margarit, 'La frase'; Rafael Lapesa, *Historia de la lengua española* (5th ed., Madrid, 1962), Ch. 9; Diego Catalán, 'El taller histórico alfonsí. Métodos y problemas en el trabajo compilatorio', *R*, LXXXIV (1963), 354-75. On other aspects of Alfonso, see Frank Callcott, *The Supernatural in Early Spanish Literature*, studied in the works of the court of A. el Sabio (New York, 1923); John E. Keller, *A.X, el Sabio* (New York, 1967).

35. *Biblia medieval romanceada, según los manuscritos escurialenses I-j-3, I-j-8 y I-j-6: Pentateuco*, ed. Américo Castro, Agustín Millares Carlo, and Angel J. Battistessa (Buenos Aires, 1927); *El evangelio de San Mateo según el manuscrito escurialense I.I.6*, ed. Thomas Montgomery (*BRAE* anejo VII, Madrid, 1962); *Biblia medieval romanceada judía-cristiana. Versión del Antiguo Testamento en el siglo XIV*, ed José Llamas (2 vols., Madrid, 1950-55); *Escorial Bible I.j.4*. I, *The Pentateuch*, ed. O. H. Hauptmann (Philadelphia, 1953). Samuel Berger, 'Les Bibles castillanes', *R*, XXVIII (1889), 360-408 and 508-42; Jesús Enciso, 'Prohibiciones españolas de las versiones bíblicas en romance antes del tridentino', *Estudios Bíblicos*, III (1944), 523-54; George E. Sachs, 'Fragmento de un estudio sobre la Biblia medieval romanceada', *RPh*, II (1948-49), 217-28; Margherita Morreale, 'Apuntes bibliográficos para la iniciación al estudio de las traducciones bíblicas medievales en castellano', *Sef*, XX (1960), 66-109, 'Libros de oración y traducciones bíblicas de los judíos españoles', *BRABLB*, XXIX (1961-62), 239-50, 'El canon de la Misa en lengua vernácula y la Biblia romanceada del siglo XIII', *Hispania Sacra*, XV (1962), 203-19, 'Aspectos no filológicos de las versiones bíblicas medievales en castellano', *ACLLS*, V (1962), 161-87, 'Las antiguas Biblias hebreo-españolas comparadas en el pasaje del cántico de Moisés', *Sef*, XXIII (1963), 3-21, and *The Cambridge History of the Bible*. II, *The West from the Fathers to the Reformation*, ed. G. W. H. Lampe (Cambridge, 1969), pp. 465-91; Spurgeon W. Baldwin, 'Two Old Spanish Versions of the Epistle to the Romans', *Mediaeval Studies in Honor of Urban Tigner Holmes, Jr.* (UNCSRLL 56, Chapel Hill, 1965), 29-42; H. Vidal Sephiha, 'Bibles Judéo-espagnoles: littéralisme et commentateurs', *IR*, II (1970), 56-90. Cf. Gormly, *Use of the Bible;* Diego Catalán, 'La Biblia en la literatura medieval española', *HR*, XXXIII (1965), 310-18; Beryl Smalley, *The Study of the Bible in the Middle Ages* (2nd ed., Oxford, 1952). Later in the Middle Ages, some MSS. of Latin Bibles contained both verbal and pictorial amplifications of the text.

36. J. T. Welter, *L'Exemplum dans la littérature religieuse et didactique du Moyen Âge* (Paris, 1927); Owst, *Literature and Pulpit*, Ch. 4; Curtius, *European Literature*, pp. 57-61; Salvatore Battaglia, 'L'esempio medievale', *FiR*, VI (1959), 45-82, and 'Dall'esempio alla novella', *FiR*, VII (1960), 21-84.

37. Haim Schwarzbaum, 'International Folklore Motifs in Petrus Alfonsi's *Disciplina clericalos*', *Sef*, XXI (1961), 267-99, XXII (1962), 17-59 and 321-44, and XXIII (1963), 54-73; Thorndike, *History of Magic*, II, 68-73.

38. Joseph Bédier, *Les Fabliaux. Études de littérature populaire et d'histoire littéraire du Moyen Âge* (Paris, 1893); Per Nykrog, *Les Fabliaux: étude d'histoire littéraire et de stylistique médievale* (Copenhague, 1957); Jean Rychner, *Contributions à l'étude des fabliaux: variantes, remaniements, dégradations* (Neuchâtel and Genève, 1960).

39. Domenico Comparetti, *Researches respecting the Book of Sindibad* (Publications of the Folklore Society 9, London, 1882); George T. Artola, '*Sindbad* in Medieval Spanish: a review article', *MLN*, LXXI (1956), 37-42; B. E. Perry, 'The Origin of the *Book of Sindbad*', *Fabula*, III

(1959-60), 1-94; *Tales of Sendebar. An edition and translation of the Hebrew version of the Seven Sages*, ed. Morris Epstein (Philadelphia, 1967); Enrique de Rivas, 'Huellas del simbolismo esotérico medieval en el *Libro de los engaños* y en el enxemplo once del *Conde Lucanor'*, *Figuras y estrellas*, pp. 73-89. For later versions, see *Versiones castellanas del Sendebar*, ed A. González Palencia (Madrid and Granada, 1946); Killis Campbell, introd. to *The Seven Sages of Rome* (Boston, 1907); A. H. Krappe, 'Studies on the Seven Sages of Rome', *Archivum Romanicum*, VIII (1924), 386-407, IX (1925), 345-65, XI (1927), 163-76, XVI (1932), 271-82, and XIX (1935), 213-26.

40. Gormly, *Use of the Bible*, Ch. 3.

41. ed. F. Lauchert, *RF*, VII (1893), 331-402.

42. *Flores de filosofía*, ed. H. Knust, *Dos obras didácticas y dos leyendas* (SBE, XVII, Madrid, 1878); *El Libro de los cien capítulos*, ed. Agapito Rey (IUHS 44, Bloomington, 1960); *Libro de los buenos proverbios*, ed. Hermann Knust, 'Mittheilungen aus dem Eskurial', *Bibliothek des Litterarischen Vereins in Stuttgart*, CXLI (1879), 1-65; *Bocados de oro*, ed. Knust, 'Mittheilungen', 66-394; *Libro del consejo*, ed. Agapito Rey (Biblioteca del Hispanista 5, Zaragoza, 1962); *Poridat de las poridades*, ed. Lloyd A. Kasten (Madrid, 1957). See Thorndike, *History of Magic*, II, 246-78; M. Zapata y Torres, 'Breves notas sobre el *Libro de los cien capítulos* como base de las *Flores de filosofía*', *Smith College Studies in Modern Languages*, X, 2 (1929), 41-54, and 'Algo sobre el *Libro del consejo e consejeros* y sus fuentes', ibid., XXI (1940), 258-69; Kahane and Pietrangeli, 'Hermetism'; cf. A. H. Gilbert, 'Notes on the Influence of the *Secretum secretorum'*, *Sp*, III (1928), 84-98. For other links between the Alexander tradition and wisdom literature, see Ross, *Alexander Historiatus*, pp. 7-9.

43. ed. Derek W. Lomax, *Miscelánea de Fuentes Medievales*, I (in press).

44. Marcelino Menéndez y Pelayo, 'La doncella Teodor (Un cuento de *Las mil y una noches*, un libro de cordel y una comedia de Lope de Vega)', *Homenaje a D. Francisco Codera* (Zaragoza, 1904), pp. 483-511. For vernacular catechisms, see Lomax, 'Lateran Reforms', 304-5. Cf. Brian Lawn, *The Salernitan Questions: an introduction to the history of medieval and Renaissance problem literature* (Oxford, 1963).

45. The information changes as time passes, though the framework is preserved. The *Elucidarium* was on the whole confined to theological matters, but the *Lucidario* introduces a great deal of natural philosophy. J. Nachbin, 'Noticias sobre el *Luc.* español y problemas relacionados con su estudio', *RFE*, XXII (1935), 225-73, XXIII (1936), 1-44 and 143-82.

Chapter 5

DECAY AND INNOVATION IN FOURTEENTH-CENTURY POETRY

I. THE DECAY OF 'CUADERNA VÍA'

THE DOMINANT CASTILIAN LITERARY FORM of the first half of the thirteenth century, *cuaderna vía* verse, was neglected by the writers of the second half of the century (see above, p. 82), although the earlier poems do not appear to have fallen from public favour. There is no way of knowing how often, if at all, they were recited, but we do have valuable evidence in the copying of manuscripts. Only Berceo's *Vida de Santo Domingo* survives in a thirteenth-century copy, but no fewer than seven extant manuscripts of Berceo, the *Alexandre*, the *Apolonio*, and the *Fernán González* date from the fourteenth century, from which fact two conclusions may safely be drawn: the total number copied must have been much greater, and there must have been a persistent and substantial demand for these poems from the public, even if we assume that some manuscripts were required by the monasteries of San Millán de la Cogolla and San Pedro de Arlanza for their own purposes.

It was not, then, a change in public taste, but a competing development that brought about the collapse of the *cuaderna vía* school of poetry. The intellectual resources of thirteenth-century Castile could not sustain two major vernacular literary movements at the same time.

In the late thirteenth century and the first half of the fourteenth, there were two conflicting tendencies in the external circumstances that affected literature. The great efforts of the earlier expansion brought about a reaction in which depopulation and a stagnant economy were the chief features; the industrial and commercial development of Catalonia at this time had no counterpart in Castile. To these difficulties must be added the civil strife of the closing years of Alfonso's reign, and the political troubles brought about by the accession of two child-kings, Fernando IV in 1295 and Alfonso XI in 1312. Against all this must, however, be set the increasing pace of intellectual development: the founding of new universities and schools, and the expanded activities of the Church. When we add the technological advances (see below, pp. 136-7), the political, social, and economic troubles of Castile are on the whole outweighed, and the general situation is one in which literature has a chance to grow. That growth included the composition of new poems in *cuaderna vía*, but there was no restoration of the monastic school of *clerecía* poets; the Alfonsine competition had been decisive. The clerical monopoly of the form was broken, and among the fourteenth-century poets are to be found a rabbi and a lay politician. The poems that attempt to deal with religious and moral themes in the old way are at best uninspired and at worst painfully weak. Real merit is confined to the poets who, in subject-matter or versification or both, break away from the previous conventions of the genre: Juan Ruiz, Santob, and, less certainly, Pero López de Ayala.

The *Vida de San Ildefonso* is by a 'beneficiado de Úbeda' of whom nothing else is known. In the form in which it has come down to us, it consists of over a thousand lines. The text is clearly very corrupt: many of the stanzas are incomplete, and the rhymes are often seriously defective. To the extent that we can judge the literary quality when the text is, presumably, so far from what the author wrote, the poem is pedestrian in tone and unremarkable in structure. The subject is a favourite one for Spanish hagiography: apart from Latin works, St Ildefonso (archbishop of Toledo) is portrayed in the first of Berceo's *Milagros*, and in a prose Life by the Archpriest of Talavera. The priest of Úbeda's poem contains a number of favourable references to Toledo, but there is no reason to suspect an economic motive as in Berceo's *Vida de San Millán*; nor does the poem fit into the new category of hagiography springing from the mendicant orders.[1]

Morality fared no better than hagiography. The *Libro de miseria de omne* is an adaptation of Pope Innocent III's *De contemptu mundi*, and like its source it warns in the gloomiest tones against the miseries of mortal life, the sins of the individual, and the evils of the world. Innocent III drew on a wide range of religious and secular works, and the Spanish poet does not attempt to widen this choice, though he amplifies the Latin prose of his model (a standard feature of medieval vernacular adaptations of Latin). On a few occasions, the poet's own emotions take control, and the writing acquires new force, as in the comparison of the lives of the rich and the poor (stanzas 114-21).[2] The versification has one unusual feature: instead of the fourteen-syllable line normal in *cuaderna vía*, the poet consistently uses lines of sixteen, divided into two hemistichs. This may well show the influence of the ballad line (see below, p. 126), which consists of eight-syllable hemistichs; but if so, the poem must have been composed towards the end of the century.

A less consistently gloomy outlook is found in the *Proverbios de Salamón*, in very irregular *cuaderna vía*. The poem presents the doctrine of the Book of Ecclesiastes, whose aphoristic style and attribution to Solomon account for the Spanish title. It summarises the source, sometimes quotes directly, and draws on other books of the Bible. Here also, emphasis is placed on the relations between rich and poor, and although this theme is biblical, the additional importance attached to it by fourteenth-century poets (including Juan Ruiz and Rodrigo Yáñez, author of the *Poema de Alfonso XI*) may reflect the troubled state of Castile for most of the century and the consequent sufferings of the common people. The didactic aim is conveyed by aphorisms and by a simple and clear structure, though the fragmented style is a hindrance.

The *Doctrina de la discriçión* (or *Tractado de la doctrina*) of Pedro de Veragüe is a similar work of basic religious instruction, but differs in two ways from the *Proverbios de Salamón*. It is not in *cuaderna vía* but in monorhymed octosyllabic tercets, with an unrhymed half-line to end each tercet; and its first part falls into a standard form of medieval religious writing, the catechism, which aims to provide instruction for the laity (compare the vernacular prose-catechism of Gutierre de Toledo, bishop of Oviedo 1377-89). Veragüe then turns to general moral advice, of which worldly prudence is the keynote. Here, and in the aphoristic nature of much of the advice, the *Doctrina* resembles the prose-works of wisdom literature (see above, pp. 99-100) and parts of the *Proverbios de Salamón*, though it has little of the popular phrasing which distinguishes the latter poem.[3]

II. 'LIBRO DE BUEN AMOR'

A far longer and more complex work owes a great deal to the traditions of religious writing discussed so far. The *Libro de Buen Amor* is strongly influenced by the techniques of both the learned and the popular sermons, *exemplum*-collections, the catechism, treatises on confession, and the religious lyric. It also owes much to Ovid, the *fabliaux*, courtly love, medieval Latin secular drama, Goliardic poetry, and the popular lyric. The *Libro de Buen Amor*'s most striking features are its diversity, its exuberance, the difficulty of placing it firmly within a single tradition or of assigning to it a single meaning, and, the most obvious of all, its autobiographical form.

In most works composed before the fifteenth century, the author gives neither his name nor a title for the book, so that we have to turn for information to often unreliable copyists. In this work, however, the author tells us his name, Juan Ruiz, his position, Archpriest of Hita, and the title he chose for the work: 'Buen Amor dixe al libro' (stanza 933). It might be assumed that a poet who was so careful to provide information about himself and his work would be anxious to make things clear to his readers in other ways, but this is far from being the case. *LBA* has only the outward appearance of autobiography, and not a single one of the incidents narrated or referred to can be accepted as factually correct. There are frequent exhortations to understand the book rightly, but such an understanding is constantly impeded by the poet's irony and ambiguity. Certainly this is a book about good love, but *buen amor* at some points in the work means the love of God, and at others, skilled sexual love. It is hardly surprising that in the face of these deliberately contrived obstacles, two scholars conclude that not even the poet's name can be accepted as genuine.[4]

LBA begins with a *cuaderna vía* invocation to God and the Virgin Mary, asking for help in the author's troubles. This is followed by a prose prologue to the book, which takes the form of a learned sermon, of the type addressed to clerics and therefore devoid of *exempla* and the other aids to an uneducated public that characterise the popular sermon. The learned, or *divisio intra*, sermon was nearly always in Latin, but one vernacular sermon of this type survives from the end of the fourteenth century, and there must have been others. At the end the Archpriest tells us that, although he wishes to warn people against 'el amor loco del pecado del mundo', nevertheless,

> por que es umanal cosa el pecar, si algunos, lo que non los conssejo, quisieren usar del loco amor, aquí fallarán algunas maneras para ello.

It is very hard to take this seriously. Medieval preachers undoubtedly used bad examples to show their congregations what to avoid, but when we consider the Archpriest's choice of words, together with the content of much of the book (for example, the advice by Don Amor on how to effect a seduction), it seems clear that this is a parody of the *divisio intra* sermon, and an attempt at the outset to confuse readers or audiences about the basic intention behind *LBA*. It is possible that this is a defence against criticism, but more likely that it is the result of the Archpriest's mischievous sense of humour and his dislike of being irrevocably committed to a single point of view.[5]

The remainder of *LBA* is in verse: *cuaderna vía*, of considerable irregularity, is interspersed with lyrics in various metres. The Archpriest says in his sermon-prologue that one of his aims is to

> dar algunos leçión e muestra de metrificar e rrimar e de trobar; ca trobas e notas e rrimas e ditados e versos, que fiz conplidamente, segund que esta çiençia rrequiere.

There is no hint of humour here; the Archpriest always takes himself very seriously as an artist. The metrical virtuosity that is claimed in the prologue is fully achieved in the main body of the *LBA*, both in the use of different kinds of metre and in a far greater adventurousness in the use of rhyme than is found in any other *cuaderna vía* poet.[6]

The first narrative element is a comic tale, one of many which the book contains. This is the story of the dispute in sign-language between the Greeks and the Romans. The Archpriest tells us that we are to learn from this story not to misunderstand his work, yet the message of the story seems to be that the wise and the foolish are equally wrong, or equally right, in their interpretations. Placed as it is at the beginning of the narrative, this has been regarded by commentators as crucially important to our view of *LBA*, yet it leaves a feeling of uncertainty, and this feeling will persist to the end. The story of the Greeks and the Romans also takes up, in a much more open way, the technique of parody first seen in the prose sermon: four simultaneous parodies are built into the story.[7]

The first narrative is followed by the first autobiographical episode. The protagonist falls in love, and sends a female go-between to his lady, who twice refuses to listen, supporting each refusal by an animal-story. This is, on a small scale, a technique which the Archpriest is to develop fully at a later stage of the book: *exempla* set within a frame-story and used as part of a debate, so that two major medieval genres are blended. The popular tales used as *exempla* by the Archpriest come from a variety of sources, and they are almost all of the type that were frequently used in sermons. However, the connection between the tale as told in *LBA* and the point that it is supposed to illustrate may be rather tenuous, and it seems likely that here (as, in a different way, with Juan Manuel's *Conde Lucanor*—see below, pp. 138-9) we have the final development of the sermon *exemplum*, which was eventually elaborated for its own sake rather than for the sake of the didactic message. It is highly probable that the Archpriest had already used many of these tales in his own sermons, found that he enjoyed telling them, and embroidered them to the point at which we find them in *LBA*. Much the largest category of tales that he used is the Aesopic animal-fable, and in this respect he conformed to Spanish and indeed European taste.[8]

The protagonist's second love is the humiliating but hilarious story of the man who sees his go-between (a youth named Ferrand García) win the girl, a baker's wife, for himself. The girl's name is Cruz, and this and her husband's occupation lead to a series of sacrilegious and obscene double meanings, making the six lyric stanzas, and the *cuaderna vía* narrative in which they are set, into a concentrated display of verbal ingenuity:

> Cruz cruzada panadera
> tomé por entendedera,
> tomé senda por carrera
> commo andaluz.

> Coydando que la avría,
> dixielo a Fferrand Garçía
> que troxiese la pletesía
> e fuese pleytés e duz.

> Dixo me quel' plazía de grado
> e fizo se de la cruz privado;
> a mí dio rrumiar salvado,
> el comió el pan más duz ...   (116-18)[9]

The Archpriest describes this as a *troba cazurra*; *cazurros* were the lowest type of *juglar*, and since he tells us elsewhere that he wrote songs for them, for students, for blind beggars, and for other *juglares*, we see the range covered by the man who parodied a learned sermon in a way that only clerics could appreciate. Virtually the whole of fourteenth-century Castilian society was the audience, as well as the subject-matter, for his art.

A third failure in love precedes a vision, in which the protagonist denounces a personified Love for letting him down; this is half personal grumble and half a popular sermon against sensual love, which is accused of responsibility for all the deadly sins.[10] Don Amor's reply takes the form not of self-justification but of advice on how to succeed in love-affairs; thus the moral element in the denunciation is ignored, and this is tacitly accepted by the protagonist. The advice derives from Ovid's *Ars amatoria*, well known throughout the Middle Ages, but here it is modified in a few respects by awareness of courtly love. This reply includes a satire, adapted from a Latin model, on the power of money. Such satires seem to have been a conservative reaction to the new financial policies of the Papacy, which were part of the general expansion of activity of the Church after the Fourth Lateran Council.[11]

Acting on Don Amor's advice, the protagonist consults Venus, who offers substantially the same guidance. The Archpriest here begins his long adaptation of *Pamphilus*, a twelfth-century Latin elegiac comedy (so called because of the metre in which these comedies were written). *Pamphilus* summarises Ovidian doctrine (hence Venus' repetition of Don Amor's advice) and then shows it being put into practice. The protagonist, now named not Juan Ruiz but Don Melón de la Huerta, although there has been no break in the first-person narrative (another example of the Archpriest's delight in mystification), is at last successful, with the help of the go-between Trotaconventos. This old woman persuades the young widow Endrina, after an argument in which *exempla* are exchanged, to visit her house, and there the seduction takes place. The lovers marry, but the Archpriest intervenes to warn ladies against the wiles of men.[12]

The scene now shifts to the Guadarrama mountains, between Hita and Segovia, where the protagonist (now the Archpriest again) encounters four *serranas*, mountain women, three of whom are strong and terrifying. In these misadventures he is knocked down, carried off to a *serrana*'s hut, and raped. This is a parody of the pastourelle (see above, p. 19) which reverses every feature of its model, and which draws on the wild-woman folklore of the Middle Ages. Here the use of both *cuaderna vía* and lyric stanzas for each episode makes it possible to see the encounters in double focus, and the perspective thus gained is especially ironic in the case of the fourth *serrana*, where the courtly tones of the lyric are rendered absurd by the grotesque vision presented in *cuaderna vía*.[13]

After a group of religious lyrics (discussed below), we have a mock epic, a battle between Carnival and Lent, in which the soldiers are joints of meat and fish. The Archpriest is here drawing on a flourishing European tradition of Carnival and Lent poems, and clearly enjoys the opportunity for humorous development that it offers.[14] Don Carnal's army is defeated and he is captured; while he is in prison (i.e. during the season of Lent), he feigns repentance and his confession is heard. This section has been regarded as humorous by some critics, but the Archpriest is giving his considered views on one of the major controversies of the fourteenth-century Church, that on methods of confession and rights of jurisdiction.[15] He was, it seems, less likely to take a humorous view when his own duties and prerogatives were involved. In due course, Don Carnal escapes and, when Doña Cuaresma has fled, rides in triumph through the town with Don Amor; the welcome given to the conquerors by various branches of the clergy is one of the goliardic anti-clerical satires that are a feature of *LBA* and of the writing of a good many priests in medieval Europe.

The narrator of this supposed autobiography plays only a minor part in the reception of Amor and Carnal, but in the next episode he returns to the centre of the story. Trotaconventos persuades him that it is best to love a nun, and on his behalf she approaches Doña Garoza. The nun and the go-between argue at length, their argument being the frame for a good many *exempla* and also for a description of the protagonist which early critics regarded as authentic, but which is now seen as carefully constructed to create an impression of the inner and not the outer man.[16]

The outcome of the courtship of the nun is uncertain: some critics believe that the Archpriest intended to show us a man who hoped for sexual love but received the love of God; others, that it is a love-affair, though unconsummated; others, that Garoza is seduced. Whatever the truth of this, the nun dies, and so, soon after, does Trotaconventos, for whom the Archpriest composes a lament. The denunciation of death is entirely serious, and may well have been composed as a separate poem in the first instance.[17] It is followed by a treatise on the Arms of the Christian, the deadly sins, the sacraments, the virtues, the gifts of the Holy Ghost, and the works of charity. This is, in its origins, a catechism (see above, p. 109), but it has been made much more complex by an attempt to establish correspondences between all of these sevenfold categories. The attempt fails, however, partly because Don Amor had been accused of responsibility not for seven but for eight deadly sins.

This is the end of the main narrative, but it is not the end of *LBA* as we have it. There are religious and secular lyrics still to come, together with a satire on clerical concubinage (compare some sections of *Elena y María*—above, p. 75) and a final, but still highly ambiguous, statement on the nature and purpose of the book. The lyrics deserve further attention, for three reasons. First of all, if taken with those occurring elsewhere in *LBA*, they represent a wide variety of metrical forms and of lyric genres, and this becomes much wider when we add to it the genres which, though not directly represented in the book, are parodied: dawn-song, spring-song, and pastourelle. Even if we disregard the occasions when the Archpriest tells us that a lyric is to follow though, in the extant manuscripts, it does not (critics cannot agree on whether these poems were ever included), the wealth and the range of his lyric poetry is astonishing at a time when cultured lyric was seldom composed in Castilian, and popular Castilian songs were not yet recorded in writing. Secondly, the songs for students and blind beggars again stress the wretched situation of the poor in fourteenth-century Castile, and whether deliberately or not, contrast it with the life of the rich. The Archpriest shared the concern expressed by other poets of this century (see above, pp. 108-9), and gave it both theoretical formulation and a vivid imaginative reconstruction. Thirdly, there are the religious lyrics (or hymns).

LBA includes two poems on the Crucifixion, but the great majority of its religious lyrics are dedicated to the Virgin Mary. Although most of these lyrics occur at the end of the work, and may never have been intended to form an integral part of it, some are inserted between episodes (for example, one Marian poem and the two on the Crucifixion divide the *serrana* section from the battle between Doña Cuaresma and Don Carnal). A favourite theme is the Joys of the Virgin, lyric meditations on the most significant events of Mary's life (Annunciation, Nativity, and so on, up to the Bodily Assumption):

Madre de Dios gloriosa,	Fue tu alegría quarta
Virgen Santa Marýa,	quando ovyste mandado
fija e leal esposa	del hermano de Marta,
del tu fijo Mexía,	que era rresuçitado
tú, Señora,	tu fijo duz,
da me agora	del mundo luz,
la tu graçia toda ora,	que viste morir en cruz,
que te sirva toda vía. . . .	que era levantado. (1635-9)

The oldest tradition is of five Joys, but the Franciscans expanded the list to seven, and this is the model followed by the Archpriest in his *gozos*. Further expansion of the list to twelve or fifteen Joys is to be found in some poets; for instance, an anonymous fourteenth-century *Gozos de la Virgen* (preserved in the same manuscript as the *Libro de miseria de omne*) contains twelve. The structure of the anonymous *Gozos* is simple and coherent, but the work does not attain the same level as the Archpriest's four poems on this subject.[18] The contrast in verse-form is of great importance: the anonymous *Gozos*, like Berceo's hymns in the previous century, uses *cuaderna vía*, whereas the Archpriest uses metres comparable to those chosen by Alfonso X for his Marian lyrics. There are no other surviving examples of the refrain-based lyric forms (see above, pp. 23-5) in Castilian religious poetry before the fifteenth century, and it is entirely possible that no others were written. Just as the Archpriest may have been an innovator in composing sophisticated versions of beggars' songs which had previously circulated orally, so he may have been the first to compose in Castilian poems of a type which had previously been confined to Galician-Portuguese. It is even possible that his stated programme of 'dar algunos leçión e muestra de metrificar e rrimar e de trobar' refers to such an innovation.

LBA must have been widely read in the first hundred years of its existence. Three manuscripts survive, none complete, but each with a very large proportion of the text; these are the manuscripts known as *S*[alamanca], *G*[ayoso], and *T*[oledo]. In addition, fragments are included in a miscellany scribbled at the end of a chronicle manuscript (usually, but not altogether convincingly, described as the repertoire of a *juglar cazurro*); fragments survive of a fourteenth-century Portuguese translation; it is possible that Chaucer knew *LBA* and was influenced by it; it is quoted in the mid-fifteenth century by the Archpriest of Talavera, and referred to by the marqués de Santillana; and some lines are quoted in a sixteenth-century commonplace-book.[19] It is highly probable that parts of the Archpriest's work were circulated orally, but it is hard to imagine any occasion on which the whole book could have been presented in this way. As a unified work, it must have been intended for the private reader, or for reading aloud to small groups.

LBA was not always a unified work, however: many sections were composed independently, and probably over a considerable period, although some must have been written at the time when the Archpriest decided to bring his work together into a single book. In particular, the main autobiographical framework is likely to belong to this late stage, even though some apparently autobiographical episodes are probably much earlier. There is little chance of dating most of the individual sections, but we have information about the date of the completed work: manuscript *G* tells us that *LBA* was finished in 1330, and manuscript *S* says 1343. Since *S* contains material that seems never to have been included in the manuscript family represented by *G* and *T*, it would appear that the Archpriest prepared an amplified version thirteen years after he had first assembled his poems into a unified *LBA*.[20]

The Archpriest was profoundly affected by his ecclesiastical background (see above, pp. 108-10) and by his earlier studies of rhetoric. His sources also include much secular literature in Latin and Castilian, and probably in French, Provençal, and Galician-Portuguese. All the sources are European; even though some of the material has its origins in the East (some *exempla*, the *Secretum secretorum*, the Bible), it reaches the Archpriest through a Latin and Christian culture.[21]

It would be surprising if a work built on European sources owed its structure and main inspiration to Arabic or Hebrew traditions, yet this view has been argued in some detail, and *LBA* presented as a supreme example of *mudéjar* art (coming, that is, from a peculiarly Spanish fusion of Eastern and Western cultures). Américo Castro maintains that *LBA* owes to Hispano-Arabic literature its complex and fluid structure, its bewildering transitions between fiction and reality, its erotic autobiography, its exuberance, its metrical variety; and he sees a special debt to *The Dove's Neck-Ring* of Ibn Ḥazm (994-1064). Yet *The Dove's Neck-Ring* is far from typical of Hispano-Arabic literature; there is no firm evidence that the Archpriest either knew this work or could read Classical Arabic (though he shows some familiarity with the Vulgar Arabic of singers); and all the features that Castro declares to be Arabic may be found within the medieval European traditions on which the Archpriest can be shown to have drawn.

María Rosa Lida de Malkiel points to a Hispano-Hebraic genre, the *maqāmat*, and in particular to the *Book of Delights* by Yosef ben Meir ibn Sabarra (born *c.* 1140); but a first impression of strong resemblance between this work and *LBA* is not confirmed by closer inspection, most of the difficulties in the way of accepting Castro's theory apply in this case also, and there is the additional point that the Archpriest seems less likely to have known Hebrew than Arabic.

Attempts to find European models are more fruitful. There is a group of works which identify the protagonist with the author by name, present him in a sympathetic light as the courtly lover, and insert into the narrative lyrics which are linked with the love-affair. The theory that *LBA* parodies such works is an attractive one, and is consistent with the discovery that the elegiac comedy *De vetula* coincides with *LBA* in erotic autobiography (the protagonist in *De vetula* is supposedly Ovid), in doctrinal digressions, in the use of a prose prologue, and in a large number of minor features. *De vetula* was very widely known in medieval Europe, and the Archpriest's familiarity with another elegiac comedy, *Pamphilus*, is undisputed. There is, in short, an overwhelming case for seeing the structure of *LBA*, as well as its individual episodes, within the European tradition.[22]

Mystification can hardly have been the only reason that made the Archpriest write a pseudo-autobiography. Medieval preachers often chose a first-person narrative to add vividness to their didactic message, and it is reasonable to assume that the Archpriest adopted this technique in his own sermons. If he wanted to convey a message in *LBA*—and, despite the ambiguities and ironies, he probably did—then his identification of himself with the protagonist of the story was a shrewd move.[23] The Archpriest's precise purpose is hard to define. It can scarcely be the simple and wholehearted denunciation of sexual sin: the ambiguities, the subversion of a moral position by parody, the delight in expanding an *exemplum* even at the expense of its message, all rule out a simplistic moral explanation of the book. It is equally hard to maintain that Juan Ruiz was a loose-living sceptic, determined to ridicule the Church and exalt the joys of the flesh: the evidence is in his insistence on the ludicrous aspects of sexual love, his patently sincere religious lyrics, what we now know to be his entirely serious treatment of the problem of confession, and in many other parts of the book. It seems certain that he felt the attractions of the world—of love, poetry, and humour. It seems certain also that he felt the love of God, that he disapproved of unworthy priests, and that he feared for his own soul.

Different emotions must have been dominant in Juan Ruiz at different times, as they are in all men, and since much of *LBA* was originally composed as separate poems, we receive one main impression from one part of the book, and a quite contrary impression from another. The Archpriest cannot have failed to be aware of this, and it does not seem that the discrepancy worried him very much. Indeed, he seems to have been reluctant to abandon either attitude irrevocably, just as he was reluctant to discard poems he had written or *exempla* he had elaborated. He incorporated poems and *exempla* into a single yet diverse book which he bound together by apparently autobiographical narrative, and to which the prevalence of parodic technique and ironic tone gave further coherence. Parody was for the Archpriest not merely a convenient device but a way of looking at the world; there were few things he could contemplate without seeing at the same time their parodic possibilities. This made it possible for him to come very close to reconciling the irreconcilable: the two sides of his own nature, the impulses of priest and of poet, the reality of fourteenth-century Castile and the doctrines of the Church. These conflicts could be made bearable only by laughter —and even that solution was soon to become impossible.

In the 1330 version of *LBA*, the dominant notes are irony, ambiguity, and parody. Nevertheless, the sexual adventures which characterise the first half of the book (with progress from early failures to success with Doña Endrina) are replaced at the end by emphasis on death. The Archpriest may not have composed his poems in the order in which they occur in the book, but he chose to arrange them in an order which gives an impression—even though a far from consistent one—of progress towards old age and death. The artistic pattern of *LBA*, then, is broadly that of any human life, including its author's. Most of the changes made in the 1343 version may well have been designed to strengthen the didactic message, and the references to *presión* added in 1343 probably reflect the sufferings of old age, which would have concentrated the poet's mind on thoughts of the next world. Even so, parody is never far away: the prose sermon is among the extra material of 1343. The Archpriest's contradictions, and their near-resolution in laughter, persist to the end.[24]

III. THE MID-CENTURY CRISIS

The *Libro de Buen Amor* was composed in the reign of Alfonso XI (1312-50). Alfonso was only one year old when he inherited the throne, and his minority was marked by the struggles of the great nobles of the kingdom, who wanted to seize the real power for themselves, and by the depredations of the lesser nobility, who in their turn sought wealth and advancement through violence. When Alfonso came of age, he reasserted the central authority in a way that was equally welcome to the Church and to the ordinary people of Castile (in 1348 he promulgated the *Siete partidas*—see above, pp. 91-2), and he resumed the work of the Reconquest. Morocco had taken advantage of the weakened state of Castile to invade Andalusia, but at the battle of the Salado (1340), Alfonso gained a decisive victory with the help of Aragon and Portugal (a Portuguese narrative poem by Afonso Giraldes commemorates the event). Invasion from across the Straits of Gibraltar was never again a threat, and this victory was followed by the liberation of part of the remaining Moorish-held territory. While besieging Gibraltar in 1350, Alfonso died of the plague; had he lived longer, he might well have completed the Reconquest.

Alfonso XI was succeeded by his legitimate son, Pedro I, who tried to continue his father's work of stabilising the kingdom by strengthening the power of the Crown at the expense of the nobles. Under his rule, Castile began an economic recovery which was cut short by the ravages of the Black Death and of civil war. The Black Death (pneumonic and bubonic plague) first struck Spain in 1348, with further epidemics in 1362 and the 1370s. This by itself would have had disastrous economic and demographic results, but matters were made far worse by a savage and prolonged war between Pedro and his illegitimate half-brother Enrique de Trastámara. Foreign powers intervened on both sides, and even after Pedro's murder in 1369, the fighting continued. By the mid-1370s, therefore, the vigour and confidence of the early 1340s was replaced by apathy, fear, and almost universal misery. These events are decisive for the poetry of Castile and León from the *Libro de Buen Amor* until the end of the century.

IV. 'POEMA DE ALFONSO XI'

In 1348, Rodrigo Yáñez wrote, probably in Leonese, the *Poema de
Alfonso XI*. This poem narrates the life of the king from his accession
to the capture of Algeciras from the Moors in 1344, at which point the
manuscript breaks off. It consists, in its extant form, of nearly ten
thousand octosyllabic lines, rhyming ABAB. As well as a narrative of the
political and military events of the reign, there are passages of praise to
Alfonso and to his mistress Leonor de Guzmán. (Yáñez shows some
signs of embarrassment here, but it would have been tactless to omit any
reference to Leonor, and she could hardly be criticised.) There are
spirited accounts of battles, which draw on some of the resources of the
epic, and on several occasions the sufferings of the people at the hands
of the nobles are described with obvious strength of feeling:

> En este tienpo los señores
> corrían a Castilla,
> los mezquines labradores
> pasavan grant manziella:
> los algos les tomavan
> por mal o por codiçia,
> las tierras se hermavan
> por mengua de justiçia. (72-3)

One of the deeds for which Alfonso is praised is his firm action to deal
with this menace:

> Mató luego los mayores
> que ssolían andar robando
> e fuéronse los menores
> por aquesto castigando. (268)

The main source of the *Poema de Alfonso XI* has not yet been
established, but it is clear that the poem is, in some way still to be
determined, related to the chronicle tradition of this reign. Yáñez drew
on vernacular poetic tradition as well, using epic epithets with some
skill, together with other devices of the traditional epic style. He borrowed from the *Libro de Alexandre* and the *Poema de Fernán González*. In addition, there are important similarities between the *Poema
de Alfonso XI* and Afonso Giraldes's Portuguese poem, but since Giraldes's work has survived only in fragments, it is impossible to decide
whether he borrowed from Yáñez or vice versa.[25]

The *Poema* is generally successful as narrative. There are tedious
passages, but these are more than compensated for by the vigour of the
battle descriptions and social commentary already referred to, by the
clear narrative structure, and by a number of stylistic successes (for
example, the use of hunting imagery to describe the struggles with the

Moors). Another effective feature is the use of prophecy as a structural device: the European vogue of the Arthurian romances meant that Merlin's fame as a magician, and hence as one able to foretell the future, could be adapted to local circumstances, and Yáñez makes Merlin prophesy, in order that we may see the prophecies come true later in the poem.[26]

V. SANTOB DE CARRIÓN

The tone of Yáñez's work is optimistic: his belief in the continued progress of social stability and of the Reconquest is not merely a panegyric convention, but arises out of the state of the country in the closing years of Alfonso's reign. The *Proverbios morales* of the Rabbi Šem Ṭob ibn Ardutiel ben Isaac, known as Santob de Carrión, provides a strongly-marked contrast. A new king, Pedro I, is on the throne, and his kingdom is beset by troubles. Santob's outlook on the world is one of caution tinged with melancholy, and sometimes approaches a resigned pessimism.

Santob was one of the leading Hebrew writers of fourteenth-century Spain, and although the *Proverbios morales* seems to be his only work in Spanish, his extant production in Hebrew includes liturgical prose and poetry, a debate in rhymed prose between Pen and Scissors, and a cabbalistic treatise; phrases apparently taken from two of these works appear in the *Proverbios*. There is, however, no suggestion that this is a Spanish translation of a work originally written in Hebrew. It is, rather, an expression of Jewish thought in Spanish poetic form. Nevertheless, the poem cannot be fully understood without a knowledge of its Hebrew cultural background: contemporary Hebrew poems have the same concision and dignity, the same inclination towards experimental syntax, the same close connection with the tradition of wisdom literature; and some of the thought expressed in the *Proverbios* derives from doctrinal controversies between Conservatives and Rationalists in the Castilian synagogues of Santob's day.

However, the poem is addressed to a Christian king: there is an explicit appeal for help at the beginning and end, and an implicit appeal in the praises of royal qualities scattered throughout the work. This is a poem that belongs to both Jewish and Christian cultures: its sources are chiefly biblical, Talmudic, and Arabic, but they also include Latin and vernacular Spanish works. The acceptability of the *Proverbios* to both communities is illustrated by the fact that of the three extant manuscripts, one is written in Hebrew characters, and the other two in Roman script.

It may be that some of the *Proverbios* was composed in the reign of Alfonso XI, but in any case it is clear that the work as a whole was directed to Pedro I. Although Spanish Jews were not systematically persecuted until the end of the fourteenth century, there were already grounds for disquiet in Alfonso XI's reign, and perhaps the *Proverbios* was partly intended to secure the king's goodwill for the Jewish community as well as for Santob personally. There is certainly more than a hint of anxiety in the poem's most famous lines:

Por nasçer en el espino,	non val la rrosa çierto
menos, nin el buen vyno	por salyr del sarmiento.
Non val el açor menos	por nasçer de mal nido,
nin los enxenplos buenos	por los dezyr judío. (st. 63-4)

The poem is attractive in its commonsense, the agreeable personality that it reveals (the personal note is much stronger than is usual in wisdom literature), its technical skill, its intellectual force (Santob's enthusiasm for books and learning is explicit), and its lyricism.

The nature of the *Proverbios*' verse-form is disputed. It can be seen either as pairs of rhyming alexandrines, with full internal rhyme, or as quatrains of seven-syllabled lines rhyming ABAB. On balance, it is probably better to take the former view, and to see this poem as a development of *cuaderna vía*. There is, however, some inconsistency in doing so unless we also accept the verse-form of the *Poema de Alfonso XI* as couplets with internal rhyme (in which case, the octosyllabic basis of the *Alfonso XI* would correspond to the type of *cuaderna vía* found in the *Libro de miseria de omne*—see above, p. 108—in the same way as the heptasyllables of the *Proverbios morales* correspond to the more orthodox type of *cuaderna vía*).[27]

VI. OTHER LATE 'CUADERNA VÍA' POEMS

A very different work from the same background is the *Coplas de Yoçef*, of which fifty stanzas survive; this section begins with God's command to Jacob that he should join Joseph in Egypt and ends with Joseph's last illness. This text also is in Hebrew characters, and its purpose may have been to provide a vernacular poem (perhaps for the celebration of the Purim festival) to be read to Jews who could not understand Hebrew. The Bible narrative is supplemented by borrowings from Josephus, the *Sefer hayašar* (a collection of medieval Jewish legends), and perhaps vernacular Spanish Bibles. There are similarities with the Morisco *Poema de Yúçuf*, which are to be explained by common sources. The probable date of the *Coplas* is the first half of the fourteenth century. The verse-form may reflect an earlier stage in the break-up of the *cuaderna vía* than we find in the *Proverbios morales*: the strengthened caesura has led to the introduction of internal rhyme; most hemistichs are of six syllables. These features correspond on the whole to those of some verse in the *Historia troyana polimétrica* and the

Conde Lucanor (see below, pp. 138 and 160). The historical interest of the *Coplas de Yoçef* is much greater than its literary value: the style is dull and the structure lacks coherence.[28]

The *Poema de Yúçuf* also tells the story of Joseph. The background from which the poem sprang is not, however, that of the Jewish communities of Castile, but the Moors of Aragon. The main source is the Koran's account of Joseph's life, but this is copiously supplemented from medieval traditions, especially the *Sefer hayašar*. The story begins with the jealousy which Joseph excites in his brothers, and breaks off when the brothers return from their mission to Joseph in Egypt. The versification is a degenerate form of *cuaderna vía*, though without internal rhyme. In style and structure, the *Poema* is not much better than the *Coplas de Yoçef*, and its lack of literary distinction is typical of *aljamiado* literature (works in Spanish, written in Arabic script, by Muslims or the superficially Christian Moriscos). It is generally thought that this is a fourteenth-century work, but recent research suggests that it may be much later.[29]

VII. PERO LÓPEZ DE AYALA

For the last significant work of *cuaderna vía*, we return to a Christian background, and to the poems deeply affected by contemporary history. Pero López de Ayala (1332-1407), chancellor of Castile, was the author of several chronicles (see below, p. 150), and translated a number of Latin works into Spanish. His poetry is contained in a heterogeneous work known as the *Rimado de palaçio*, though only part of it is about court life. Like the *Libro de Buen Amor*, the *Rimado* is made up of poems composed over a number of years, and has only a retrospective unity. There is, however, an important difference: whereas the Archpriest of Hita gave his work a narrative structural unity by devising an autobiographical frame, Ayala was content to group his poems together according to general subject, without attempting a structural link between the three main sections.

The first section of the *Rimado*, occupying just under half of the work, is composed of religious, moral, and didactic *cuaderna vía*. After the customary invocation, there begins a confession whose structure is based on that of the confessors' manuals inspired by the decisions of the Fourth Lateran Council. (It is very similar to that of contemporary catechisms.) Ayala lists his sins under the commandments, the seven deadly sins, the seven corporal works of mercy, and the five senses, but it is very doubtful whether this was a deeply-felt personal confession. He seems to be following the conventional procedure largely because it was conventional; certainly the similarities between his verse confession and a vernacular prose example of the genre (the late fourteenth-century *Libro de la justiçia de la vida espiritual*) are very marked. Once Ayala had shown the way, others followed, and the verse confessions of Fernán Pérez de Guzmán and Ruy Páez de Ribera in the fifteenth century may well depend on his precedent.

Before the end of the usual confession sequence, Ayala turns to social criticism, which begins under the heading of the seven spiritual works of mercy and continues during observations on the government of the state. Even in the confession section, he had shown himself to be increasingly interested in making general points rather than a personal statement, and this generalising tendency is now given full scope. He shows considerable gusto in his denunciation, and enlivens it with *exempla*. Ayala's view of society is a gloomy one; this is partly justified by the state to which the Black Death and a savage civil war had reduced Castile, but he seems to paint an even blacker picture than the reality justifies. The last part of this section is still more generalised, since it consists mainly of reflections on the art of government and fit conduct for a king; here Ayala relies partly on Egidius Romanus's treatise *De regimine principum* (which was available to him not only in the original but also in Juan de Castrojeriz's mid-fourteenth-century Spanish translation and commentary).[30] He also relies, naturally enough, on his observations and experience in his own political and administrative career.

The first section is followed by a much shorter group of Marian lyrics, prayers, and reflections on the Great Schism which had divided the Catholic Church since 1378. It is only in the lyrics that Ayala seems concerned with style, and it is only in this middle section that he experiments with versification: apart from the lyric verse-forms, with their shorter lines and more intricate rhyme-schemes, he here introduces the *arte mayor*, which was to become for the fifteenth century what *cuaderna vía* had been for the thirteenth, a substantial form able to carry the weight of a long narrative or didactic poem. It normally consists of twelve-syllable lines, but the essential feature is not syllabic regularity but the presence in each line of four strongly-marked beats; the stanzas have eight lines. This form, whose origin is still in dispute, began to appear in Castilian towards the end of the fourteenth century; there is no possibility of Ayala's being the innovator.[31]

In the very long third section, Ayala returns to *cuaderna vía*, and to moral issues. The issues are now scarcely related either to the poet's own life or to contemporary Castile, for this section is an adaptation of Gregory the Great's *Moralia* on the Book of Job. Ayala felt a stronger affinity with Job than with any other book of the Bible: he translated it into Spanish prose, produced a Spanish prose version of the *Moralia*, and was probably responsible also for the *Flores de los Morales de Job*, a selection from Gregory's commentary. The reason for this affinity is obvious enough. The dominant tone of the *Rimado* is melancholy, that of a man who felt himself isolated and who took a pessimistic view of human nature and especially of human society. Ayala's lifetime was a depressing period for a devout Christian who loved his country: the Great Schism, the Trastámaran civil war and its aftermath, the economic and demographic weakness of Castile, provided ample reason for gloom. To this must be added Ayala's personal circumstances. He was captured at the battle of Aljubarrota, and spent a year in a Portuguese prison. Some of the *Rimado*, including the lyrics, seems likely to have been composed then. Much more important, however, is the fact that Ayala's political advancement was obtained by treachery: he deserted Pedro I for the winning Trastámaran side, and if he was not to express guilt in his poetry he had to fix the blame on external things, the evil times, the society in which he was compelled to live. This would explain not only the emotional but also the stylistic contrast between the *Rimado* and the *Libro de Buen Amor*, the absence from Ayala's poetry of the exuberant inventiveness that is so marked a feature of Juan Ruiz.[32]

VIII. RISE OF THE BALLAD

The breaking-down of *cuaderna vía*—the writing of dull works within the established conventions, and of major poetry that breaks out of those conventions—dominates the history of Castilian fourteenth-century poetry. There are two other changes, neither of which is reflected in a series of important poems within the century, but which taken together involve a drastic remodelling of the poetic landscape. In 1300, cultured Castilians wrote their lyrics in Galician-Portuguese, and popular audiences listened to epics. In 1400, Galician-Portuguese was largely neglected, and cultured poets were writing in Castilian, while the ballad had generally replaced the epic in popular esteem.

The second half of the fourteenth century was a period of extreme decadence in the Spanish epic (see above, pp. 46-7). This decadence may have been hastened by the Trastámaran war. A major function of heroic epic is to unify a society, but in the third quarter of the fourteenth century few Castilians were concerned with unity, and self-interest reigned supreme. In this atmosphere, epic would have no place, but political poetry, inciting hatred and contempt for the other side, could flourish, and did (see below, pp. 125-6). Although the evidence is not totally conclusive, and although there are signs that epics circulated to some extent in the fifteenth century, it seems fairly clear that from the end of the fourteenth century their popularity had declined almost to vanishing point, that new epics were no longer being composed, and that the process of reworking old epics had virtually ceased.

Scholars' opinions on the relations between epics and ballads have changed greatly in the past hundred years. It used to be widely believed that ballads came first, and that out of these short narrative poems, longer ones were built up, until in the course of time epics arose on the same subjects. This theory was shown by Manuel Milá y Fontanals to be untenable. Epics precede ballads in Spain (and in most other countries that have both genres), and whenever a relationship between them can be demonstrated, it is the epic that gives rise to the ballad.[33] This lesson has, if anything, been too well learned, and it is often assumed that Spanish ballads as a whole derive from epics. The most that can reasonably be said is that epics provide the verse-form for the ballads in general, the subject for a considerable number, and the detailed content for a few; and some scholars would dispute even this limited assertion, and would argue that the two verse-forms are distinct and independent.

We are immediately confronted with problems of chronology. There are no extant medieval manuscripts of individual ballads, and the earliest datable printed editions come in the 1530s. This is, of course, implausibly late, and it can be shown without difficulty that ballads circulated throughout the fifteenth century. The earliest clear record is a text which Jaume de Olesa, a law-student from Majorca, wrote down in his notebook in 1421; this is a freak survival, and it seems certain that many other ballads circulating at that time must have gone unrecorded.[34] Towards the end of the century, other texts occasionally appear in *cancioneros*; and increasingly frequent references to ballads are made by fifteenth-century writers. Such references are unfavourable or at best ambiguous in the first half of the century (we are faced by the familiar difficulty of medieval critical terminology), but in the second half ballads began to find favour at Court, and this was especially the case under the Catholic Monarchs, Fernando and Isabel.

Is it possible to trace the history of ballads before the fifteenth century? If we consider the subject-matter, this can be done. Some ballads seem to arise directly out of a historical event, particularly if the event roused political passions. It is said that the existence of a ballad on the death of Fernando IV in 1312 proves that it was composed at the time of the event, but this is not so, since a king's death in dramatic circumstances would long be remembered, and a ballad could be composed on the subject at any time. The earliest datable ballad is that on the defiance of the king by the prior of San Juan, which refers to, and arises directly out of, an event of 1328.[35]

The first substantial group of early ballads that can be dated with any accuracy arises out of the Trastámaran civil war. They were composed to vilify Pedro; and though they were answered by counter-accusations in other ballads, most of these have not survived, since the

Trastámarans won the war, and it would have been dangerous to continue to circulate pro-Pedro ballads. It is most improbable that poems of this sort, whose aim is to influence public opinion, would have been composed much after the event, and we may safely conclude that from the 1320s at the latest there were ballads in Castile, and that not later than the 1360s they were very well established. These dates may be too cautious an estimate.[36]

Ballads on epic subjects cannot be dated in the same way as those arising directly from a historical event, and we cannot tell which group arose earlier. Most of the subjects of Spanish epics, both extant and lost, have their cycles of ballads: the Cid, Fernán González, Bernardo del Carpio, the Siete Infantes de Lara, Roncesvalles, and others. It is sometimes possible, by comparison of texts, to decide that a section of an epic was detached and developed as a separate poem, but in most cases the ballad is a new poem inspired by the subject of the epic.

It is impossible to decide whether the ballads deriving from the text of an epic really are the earliest (in which case they simply continued the verse-form of the parent epic), or whether they are modelled on pre-existing historical ballads. Even in the latter case, however, there are very strong arguments for believing that the epic verse-form was the model adopted. Epic lines in medieval Spain were, to varying degrees, irregular (see above, p. 49), but it is possible to establish an average for the number of syllables that they contain. The early epics have an approximate norm of fourteen syllables to the line, whereas in the fourteenth century the average is sixteen: all Spanish epic lines are grouped in series of widely differing length but each with a single assonance. Ballads have a single assonance, their length differs greatly, and their lines have sixteen syllables, though there may have been more variety in the fifteenth century. The similarity is certainly very striking, and whereas the comparative regularity of the ballad-line is not easy to reconcile with the irregularity of epic verse, it still seems right to conclude that ballad versification has an epic origin.

Spanish ballads are usually divided by scholars into *romances viejos* (of which *romances noticieros* are a subdivision), *juglarescos,* and *artificiosos,* but the classification used by W. J. Entwistle is more helpful. He divides ballads into historical, literary (including epic), and adventure ballads. The historical category, as is implied above, consists of ballads which arise directly from the historical event; if a ballad about a real event is derived from a chronicle or an epic, then it is not historical but literary. The earliest known historical ballads are followed by *romances fronterizos*, poems about the frontier wars with the Moors. When Granada fell in 1492, the Moors were no longer seen as a threat; they had always been treated with some sympathy by the ballad-poets, as in this poem on the siege of Baza (1489):

Sobre Baza estaba el rey,   lunes, después de yantar;
miraba las ricas tiendas   que estaban en su real;
miraba las huertas grandes   y miraba el arrabal,
miraba el adarve fuerte   que tenía la ciudad,
miraba las torres espesas   que no las puede contar.
Un moro tras una almena   comenzóle de fablar:
'Vete, el rey don Fernando,   no querrás aquí invernar,
que los fríos desta tierra   no los podrás comportar;
pan tenemos por diez años,   mil vacas para salar;
veinte mil moros hay dentro,   todos de armas tomar,
ochocientos de caballo   para el escaramuzar;
siete caudillos tenemos   tan buenos como Roldán,
y juramento tienen hecho   antes morir que se dar.'

Now they are regarded indulgently in the *romances moriscos*, where the typical Moor is seen as a noble but rejected lover.[37]

The most important class of literary ballads in Spanish is based on epics, both indigenous and from the Roland tradition. Some of these share the characteristic tone of the Spanish epic (to which the *Cantar de Mio Cid* constitutes a notable exception, as we saw above, on p. 43), but others are more elaborate and sophisticated. Also among the literary ballads are those deriving from chronicles, and in this group the ballads on the fall of Spain to the Moors are of particular interest, not only because of the event with which they deal, but also because they have so often been taken as evidence of an early epic which, as far as one can judge, never existed (see above, pp. 34-5).

The third category is that of adventure ballads or, as Spanish critics call them, *romances novelescos*. This is a miscellaneous grouping of ballads tied directly neither to a historical event nor to a literary text: ballads of love, revenge, mystery, or, literally, adventure. Because they normally lack local detail, they travel easily, and because of the perennial human interest of their themes they are well received in any country. For this reason, many of the Spanish adventure ballads belong to an international stock comparable to that of the folktale or the Marian miracle. Ballads in this category may have poignant lyricism:

Que por mayo era, por mayo,   cuando hace la calor,
cuando los trigos encañan   y están los campos en flor,
cuando canta la calandria   y responde el ruiseñor,
cuando los enamorados   van a servir al amor;
sino yo, triste, cuitado,   que vivo en esta prisión,
que ni sé cuándo es de día   ni cuándo las noches son,
sino por una avecilla   que me cantaba al albor.
Matómela un ballestero,   ¡ déle Dios mal galardón!

The language of Spanish ballads is generally archaic, and includes a number of phrases inherited from the epic tradition. There is, in addition, considerable use of formulaic language, which raises questions of oral composition in at least some cases (cf. above, on pp. 48-9). There is characteristically, though not invariably, a sobriety and impersonality of tone, manifested in, for example, a very sparing use of adjectives. Most ballads begin in the middle of the action, without explaining the background, and many of them end before the story has been fully worked out. This is, of course, a weakness in the hands of a mediocre poet, but a poet of genius can convert it into a strength. In particular, the enigmatically sudden ending, which Menéndez Pidal felicitously called *saber callar a tiempo*, produces some of the most moving and most characteristic of Spanish ballad achievements (by contrast, the unexplained ballad-opening is a European rather than a specifically Spanish feature). Perhaps the best example of *saber callar a tiempo* is *Conde Arnaldos*:

¡ Quién hubiese tal ventura   sobre las aguas del mar
como hubo el conde Arnaldos   la mañana de San Juan!
Con un halcón en la mano   la caza iba a cazar,
vio venir una galera   que a tierra quiere llegar.
Las velas traía de seda,   la ejercia de un cendal;
marinero que la manda   diciendo viene un cantar
que la mar hacía en calma,   los vientos hace amainar
los peces que andan al hondo   arriba los hace andar,
las aves que andan volando   en el mástil las hace posar.
Allí habló el conde Arnaldos,   bien oiréis lo que dirá:
'Por Dios te ruego, marinero,   dígasme ora ese cantar.'
Respondióle el marinero,   tal respuesta le fue a dar:
'Yo no digo esta canción   sino a quien conmigo va.'

A longer version was discovered in the present century; in this version, Arnaldos is kidnapped by the sailors but then proves to be their long-lost prince. It is a fine poem, which may have great depth of meaning, but the shorter version is finer.[38]

The creation of a different and better poem by the omission of the ending raises questions both of authorship and of transmission. Each ballad must originally have been composed by a single poet, who is none the less individual for being unknown to us, but he cannot be considered the sole author of the ballad as we have it today. Each of these poems may have been revised in the course of transmission, and in this sense it is reasonable to talk of collaborative authorship. Undoubtedly the poems were at first sung or recited by *juglares*; in the reign of the Catholic Monarchs they were sung at Court, to tunes composed by court musicians; from the early sixteenth century they circulated very widely in chap-books. A *juglar* who recited a ballad from memory might easily introduce small changes, and these could be incorporated into the traditional form of the poem; an especially talented *juglar* might deliberately make alterations which improved the ballad. One point on which we can be fairly certain is that there was little improvisation in the Yugoslav manner (see above, p. 44): the extraordinary stability of Spanish ballad-texts over the centuries cannot be reconciled with the techniques observed by Parry and Lord. Changes were often made by court poets and musicians, and it may be to them that we owe the shortening of a number of ballads; in particular, when musical styles became more elaborate, the texts of ballads were bound to be affected. The printing of ballads in *pliegos sueltos* is also an important textual influence, and an underestimated one: printers of these cheap popular editions would often need to shorten texts in order to fit them into the available space, and oral performances of ballads frequently originated not from memory but from chap-book texts.[39]

The sixteenth century is, to judge from printed evidence (chap-books and the great collections known as *romanceros*), the chief period of popularity of the Spanish ballad, but we have seen that the tradition of these poems goes back much further—to the early fourteenth century in the case of historical ballads. And it comes forward to our own times: in the nineteenth century ballads began to be collected by scholars from the oral tradition of Portugal, Galicia, Andalusia, and Catalonia, though they seemed to have been long extinct in Castile. In May 1900, Menéndez Pidal heard a fifteenth-century ballad being sung in the town of Osma, and the search began. Thousands of texts and variants have been collected, and although under the advance of literacy the tradition is running thin, more remain to be collected. Ballads were carried overseas, and many of them—often of great antiquity—have been recovered from the oral traditions of Spanish America and of the Spanish-speaking Jews of Mediterranean countries whose ancestors fled or were expelled from Spain (it was in Morocco that the long version of *Conde Arnaldos* was found).[40]

IX. THE CULTURED LYRIC: FROM GALICIAN-PORTUGUESE TO CASTILIAN

Galician-Portuguese was accepted as the appropriate language for cultured lyric not only in the areas where it was normally spoken, but far outside them, and this fact was recorded in the fifteenth century by the marqués de Santillana (see above, p. 20). The use of Galician-Portuguese by Castilian poets depended, however, on the continued existence of a flourishing lyric tradition within Portugal, and from the mid-fourteenth century this was no longer present. King

Dinis (1261-1325) was perhaps the greatest of the Galician-Portuguese poets, and certainly (as befitted a grandson of Alfonso X) their greatest patron. A near-contemporary said of him that when he died, poets never wrote in Portugal again; though this is an exaggeration, it is clear that the removal of Dinis's patronage virtually destroyed the Court at Lisbon as a poetic centre. The last poet to be included in the *cancioneiros* is Dinis's son Pedro, count of Barcelos, who died in 1354. Thereafter, the few poems written in Galician-Portuguese are to be found in Castilian *cancioneros* of the following century.

The ending of royal patronage seems to have been the decisive factor, though it was no doubt reinforced by the increasingly commercial outlook of the Portuguese ruling classes, the decline of the archiepiscopal Court at Santiago de Compostela (which meant that Galicia was unlikely to replace Portugal as the centre of this poetry), and perhaps the warfare between Portugal and Castile, culminating in the battle of Aljubarrota in 1385, which severely limited the cultural links between the two countries and thus broke the previous unity (if we exclude Catalan) of the Hispanic court lyric. All this is more than enough to account for the decadence of the Galician-Portuguese tradition. It was the Portuguese decline that gave Castilian lyric poetry a clear field in which to develop, and not the Castilian development which helped to undermine the Portuguese tradition. There are analogous changes elsewhere: Italian and Catalan poets originally wrote in Provençal, but the collapse of Provençal culture after the Albigensian Crusade in the early thirteenth century helped to stimulate the composition of lyrics in the national language.[41]

In the period from, approximately, 1350 to 1450 traces of the Galician-Portuguese tradition are still found: poems in that language by Castilians, linguistically mixed poems, and works in Castilian by Galician poets who continue to show awareness of the old traditions. In this transitional period, poets gradually became accustomed to writing cultured lyrics in Castilian.

The transition may be seen in the first of the Castilian anthologies of the fifteenth century, the *Cancionero de Baena*, whose compilation was begun in or just before 1445, and to which poems were added until 1454. This *cancionero* covers the poetry of the previous seventy or eighty years; the earlier poems are in Galician-Portuguese, the later ones almost invariably in Castilian. The career of one poet gives the best indication of the change: Alfonso Álvarez de Villasandino began writing c. 1370, and continued until his death, c. 1424. He was a fluent and adaptable poet whose livelihood depended on his verse. He, far more than the majority of writers, had to sense the coming of new tendencies and conform to them. Consequently, Villasandino wrote in the old lyric language at the beginning of his career, but by about 1400 he was consistently using Castilian.[42]

This change coincided roughly with the beginnings of Italian poetic influence in Castile, where French had previously been the most influential of the vernaculars. Other changes followed from it, most notably the appearance in writing of the popular *villancicos* (see above, pp. 21, 26), and the appearance of a flourishing and brilliant circle of court poets in Castile. Within a hundred years, more than a few Portuguese poets found it natural to write their lyrics in Castilian.

NOTES

1. Ángel Custodio Vega, 'De patrologia española. San Ildefonso de Toledo . . .', *BRAH*, CXLV (1969), 35-107, at pp. 97-106. For mendicant hagiography, see Giuliano Gasca Queirazza, 'Una *Vita* di San Fransesco d'Assisi in antico castigliano', *Studi di Lingua e Letteratura Spagnola*, ed. G. M. Bertini (Torino, 1965), pp. 219-44; Lomax, 'Lateran Reforms', 307-8; and above, p. 78, n. 18.

2. Dámaso Alonso, 'Pobres y ricos en los libros de *Buen Amor* y de *Miseria de omne*', *De los siglos oscuros*, pp. 105-13.

3. Raúl A. del Piero, 'Explicación literal de la *Doctrina de la discriçión*', *PMLA*, LXXXIII (1968), 1334-46. On Gutierre de Toledo, see Antonio C. Floriano, 'Un catecismo castellano del siglo XIV', *Revista Española de Pedagogía*, III (1945), 87-99. For an early and fragmentary verse catechism, see *NRFH*, XIV (1960), 246-7.

4. L. G. Moffatt, 'The Evidence of Early Mentions of the Archpriest of Hita or of his Work', *MLN*, LXXV (1960), 33-44; anon., 'The Archpriest's Jokes', *TLS*, 13 October 1966, 941. On the title, see Menéndez Pidal, 'Notas al libro del Arcipreste de Hita', *Poesía árabe y poesía europea* (Madrid, Austral, 1941), pp. 137-57. On the meaning of *buen amor*: G. B. Gybbon-Monypenny, 'Lo que b.a. dize con rrazon te lo prueuo', *BHS*, XXXVIII (1961), 13-24; Gonzalo Sobejano, 'Escolios a la b.a. de Juan Ruiz', *Homenaje Alonso*, III (1963), 431-58; F. Márquez Villanueva, 'El b.a.', *RO*, n.s., III (1965), 269-91; Brian Dutton, 'B.a.: its meaning and uses in some medieval texts', *LBA Studies*, pp. 95-121. References in the first few stanzas to *presión* have led many to believe that the Archpriest prepared the expanded version of *LBA* while in prison, but this is an error. There is no evidence for imprisonment, and *presión* here probably means not prison but anguish: see L. G. Moffatt, 'The Imprisonment of the AP', *HBalt*, XXXIII (1950), 321-7, and Lida de Malkiel, 'Nuevas notas para la interpretación del *LBA*', *NRFH*, XIII (1959), 17-82 (repr. in *Estudios*, pp. 14-91).

5. Pierre L. Ullman, 'J.R.'s Prologue', *MLN*, LXXXII (1967), 149-70; Janet A. Chapman, 'J.R.'s "Learned Sermon" ', *LBA Studies*, pp. 29-51; Deyermond, 'Some Aspects of Parody in the *LBA*', ibid., pp. 53-78, at pp. 56-7; Richard P. Kinkade, 'Intellectum tibi dabo . . . The function of free will in the *LBA*', *BHS*, XLVII (1970), 296-315. *LBA* quotations in this chapter are taken from the Salamanca manuscript. For the vernacular learned sermon by Pedro de Luna, see *BH*, XLIX (1947), 38-46, and L (1948), 129-46. Cf. Diego de San Pedro's *Sermón* (below, p. 164).

6. Kenneth W. J. Adams, 'J.R.'s Manipulation of Rhyme: some linguistic and stylistic consequences', *LBA Studies*, pp. 1-28. See also Oreste Macrí's highly technical *Ensayo de métrica sintagmática (Ejemplos del LBA y del*

Laberinto de Juan de Mena) (Madrid, BRH, 1969); Adams, 'Rhythmic Flexibility in the *LBA*', *N*, LIV (1970), 369-80.

7. Discussions of this episode are summed up by Sara Sturm, 'The Greeks and the Romans: the AP's warning to his reader', *RoN*, X (1968-69), 404-12.

8. George C. Keidel, 'Notes on Aesopic Fable Literature in Spain and Portugal during the Middle Ages', *ZRP*, XXV (1901), 721-30; Ian Michael, 'The Function of the Popular Tale in the *LBA*', *LBA Studies*, pp. 177-218.

9. André S. Michalski, 'J.R.'s *troba cazurra*: "Cruz cruzada panadera" ', *RoN*, XI (1969-70), 434-8.

10. Morton W. Bloomfield, *The Seven Deadly Sins: an introduction to the history of a religious concept, with special reference to medieval English literature* (Michigan, 1952); Robert Ricard, 'Les péchés capitaux dans le *LBA*', *LR*, XX (1966), 5-37.

11. J. A. Yunck, *The Lineage of Lady Meed: the development of mediaeval venality satire* (University of Notre Dame Publications in Mediaeval Studies 17, Notre Dame, 1963).

12. Jorge Guzmán, *Una constante didáctico-moral del LBA* (University of Iowa Studies in Spanish Language and Literature 14, México, 1963); Gybbon-Monypenny, ' "Dixe la por te dar ensienpro": J.R.'s adaptation of the *Pamphilus*', *LBA Studies*, pp. 123-47.

13. Thomas R. Hart, *La alegoría en el LBA* (Madrid, 1959), Ch. 4; Le Gentil, *La Poésie lyrique*, I, and 'A propos des *Cánticas de serrana* de l'AP de H., *Wort und Text: Festschrift für Fritz Schalk* (Frankfurt, 1963), pp. 133-41; R. B. Tate, 'Adventures in the *Sierra*', *LBA Studies*, pp. 219-29.

14. Kemlin M. Laurence, 'The Battle between Don Carnal and Doña Cuaresma in the Light of Medieval Tradition', *LBA Studies*, pp. 159-76.

15. Rita Hamilton, 'The Digression on Confession in the *LBA*', *LBA Studies*, pp. 149-57.

16. Elisha K. Kane, 'The Personal Appearance of J.R.', *MLN*, XLV (1930), 103-9; Peter N. Dunn, 'De las figuras del arçipreste', *LBA Studies*, pp. 79-93. Kane sees the description as symbolic of sexual potency, while Dunn finds evidence of a sanguine temperament hampered by the influence of Saturn.

17. Rafael Lapesa, 'El tema de la muerte en el *LBA*', *De la Edad Media*, pp. 53-75; cf. Peter Dronke, *Poetic Individuality in the Middle Ages: new departures in poetry 1000-1150* (Oxford, 1970), Ch. 4.

18. M. Artigas, 'Unos *Gozos de la Virgen*, del siglo XIV', *Homenaje a Menéndez Pidal*, I, 371-5. Le Gentil, 'L'*Ave Maria* de l'AP de H.', *Fin du Moyen Âge et Renaissance. Mélanges de philologie française offerts à Robert Guiette* (Anvers, 1961), pp. 283-95; Raymond S. Willis, '*LBA*: the fourth Joy of the Virgin Mary', *RPh*, XXII (1968-69), 510-14. Le Gentil, *La Poésie lyrique*, I; Woolf, *English Religious Lyric*.

19. All MSS and fragments are printed by Criado de Val and Naylor. See Menéndez Pidal, *Poesía juglaresca*, pp. 233-9 and 388-92; L. G. Moffatt, 'An Evaluation of the Portuguese Fragments of the *LBA*', *S*, X (1956), 107-11, and 'Álvar Gómez de Castro's Verses from the *LBA*', *HR*, XXV (1957), 247-51; T. J. Garbáty, 'The *Pamphilus* Tradition in Ruiz and Chaucer', *PQ*, XLVI (1967), 457-70.

20. Menéndez Pidal, 'Notas al libro del AP de H.'; Gybbon-Monypenny, 'The Two Versions of the *LBA*: the extent and nature of the author's revision', *BHS*, XXXIX (1962), 205-21; Chiarini, pp. xvi-xxx; Rigo Mignani, 'Le due redazioni del *LBA*', *QIA*, 37 (1969), 1-7; Alberto Vàrvaro, 'Lo stato originale del ms. *G* del *LBA* di J.R.', *RPh*, XXIII (1969-70), 549-56. On textual problems raised by recent editions, see Giuliano Macchi, 'La tradi-

zione manoscritta del *LBA* (a proposito di recenti edizioni ruiziane)', *CN*, XXVIII (1968), 264-98; Vàrvaro, 'Nuovi studi sul *LBA*, I: problemi testuali', *RPh*, XXII (1968-69), 135-57; Gybbon-Monypenny, 'The Text of the *LBA*: recent editions and their critics', *BHS* (in press). 1330 and 1343 are dates of composition; the extant manuscripts are some decades later.

21. Lecoy is the main authority for *LBA*'s sources. See also H. J. Chaytor, 'The Influence of Provençal Literature upon the *LBA* of J.R.', *MHRA*, 18 (1939), 10-17; María Rosa Lida, 'Notas para la interpretación, influencia, fuentes y texto del *LBA*', *RFH*, II (1940), 105-50; Le Gentil, *La Poésie lyrique*, I; A. H. Schutz, 'La tradición cortesana en dos coplas de J.R.', *NRFH*, VIII (1954), 63-71; Irma Césped, 'Los *Fabliaux* y dos cuentos de J.R.', *BFC*, IX (1956-57), 35-65; Zahareas, *Art*; Deyermond and Roger M. Walker, 'A Further Vernacular Source for the *LBA*', *BHS*, XLVI (1969), 193-200; Walker, 'J.R.'s Defence of Love', *MLN*, LXXXIV (1969), 292-7; Dunn, 'De las figuras'.

22. Castro, *España en su historia*, Ch. 12; Claudio Sánchez-Albornoz, *España, un enigma histórico*, Ch. 8, and 'Originalidad creadora del AP frente a la última teoría sobre el *BA*', *CHE*, XXXI-XXXII (1960), 275-89; Emilio García Gómez, introd. to *El collar de la paloma* (Madrid, 1952); Lida de Malkiel, 'Nuevas notas' and *Masterpieces*. There are English translations of *The Dove's Neck-Ring* (A. R. Nykl, 1931) and the *Book of Delights* (M. Hadas, 1932). Gybbon-Monypenny, 'Autobiography in the *LBA* in the Light of some Literary Comparisons', *BHS*, XXXIV (1957), 63-78; Francisco Rico, 'Sobre el origen de la autobiografía en el *LBA*', *AEM*, IV (1967), 301-25.

23. Cf. Paul Lehmann, 'Autobiographies of the Middle Ages', *Transactions of the Royal Historical Society*, 5th ser., III (1953), 41-52; Leo Spitzer, 'Note on the Poetic and the Empirical "I" in Medieval Authors', *Romanische Literaturstudien 1936-1956* (Tübingen, 1959), pp. 100-12; George Kane, *The Autobiographical Fallacy in Chaucer and Langland Studies* (London, 1965).

24. Roger M. Walker, 'Towards an Interpretation of the *LBA*', *BHS*, XLIII (1966), 1-10, and ' "Con miedo de la muerte la miel non es sabrosa": love, sin and death in the *LBA*', *LBA Studies*, pp. 231-52. On humour, in addition to works already cited, see Otis H. Green, 'On J.R.'s Parody of the Canonical Hours', *HR*, XXVI (1958), 12-34, and *Spain and the Western Tradition*, I, Ch. 2. On language, see J. M. Aguado, *Glosario sobre J.R., poeta castellano del siglo XIV* (Madrid, 1929); H. B. Richardson, *An Etymological Vocabulary to the LBA* (New Haven, 1930); Corominas's notes; and Margherita Morreale's series of articles, reviews, and privately-issued commentaries. On other aspects, add to Bibliography and previous notes: Stephen Gilman, 'The Juvenile Intuition of J.R.', *S*, IV (1950), 290-303; L. G. Moffatt, 'Pitas Payas', *South Atlantic Studies for Sturgis E. Leavitt* (Washington, 1953), pp. 29-38; J. A. Chapman, 'A Suggested Interpretation of Stanzas 528 to 549a of the *LBA*', *RF*, LXXIII (1961), 29-39; Leo Spitzer, 'En torno al arte del AP de H.', *Lingüística*, Ch. 3; R. S. Willis, 'Two Trotaconventos', *RPh*, XVII (1963-64), 353-62; Roger M. Walker, 'A Note on the Female Portraits in the *LBA*', *RF*, LXXVII (1965), 117-20; Robert Ricard, 'Sur l'invocation initiale du *LBA*', *BH*, LXXI (1969), 463-75. Gybbon-Monypenny, 'Estado actual de los estudios sobre el *LBA*', *AEM*, III (1966), 575-609.

25. Diego Catalán, 'La historiografía en verso y en prosa de Alfonso XI a la luz de nuevos textos', *BRAH*, CLIV (1964), 79-126, *BRAH*, CLVI (1965), 55-87, and *AEM*, II (1965), 257-99. For Giraldes's poem, see João Gaspar Simões, *História da poesia portuguesa das origens aos nossos dias*, I (Lisboa,

1955), 81-5. Gifford Davis, 'The Debt of the *Poema de Alfonso Onceno* to the *Libro de Alexandre*', *HR*, XV (1947), 436-52, and 'National Sentiment in the *Poema de Fernán Gonçález* and in the *PA*', *HR*, XVI (1948), 61-8.

26. Lida de Malkiel, *La idea de la fama*, pp. 220-29, and (with Yakov Malkiel) review of Catalán, *RPh*, VIII (1954-55), 303-11; Diego Catalán, 'Hacia una edición crítica del *PA* (El cerco de Algeciras)', *Llubera Studies*, pp. 105-18, and 'Las estrofas mutiladas en el MS. *E* del *PA*', *NRFH*, XIII (1959), 325-34; Emilio González López, 'El *PA* y el Condado de Trastamara', *Miscelânea de Estudos a Joaquim de Carvalho*, 9 (1963), 963-83; Dorothy C. Clarke, *Morphology of Fifteenth Century Castilian Verse* (Pittsburgh and Louvain, 1964), pp. 30-32.

27. P. Mazzei, 'Valore biografico e poetico delle *Trobas* del Rabí don Santo', *Archivum Romanicum*, IX (1925), 177-89; Castro, *España en su historia*, Ch. 14; I. González Llubera, 'A Transcription of MS. *C* of Santob de Carrión's *Proverbios morales*', *RPh*, IV (1950-51), 217-56; E. Alarcos Llorach, 'La lengua de los *PM* de don Sem Tob', *RFE*, XXXV (1951), 249-309; Sánchez-Albornoz, *España, un enigma*, Ch. 9; Régine Gartenlaub's unpublished thesis, summarised *BH*, LIX (1957), 82-3; Joel H. Klausner, 'Reflections on S. de C.', *HBalt*, XLVI (1963), 304-6, and 'The Historic and Social Milieu of S.'s *PM*', *HBalt*, XLVIII (1965), 783-9.

28. For another poem of roughly the same period which is probably of Jewish origin, see Kenneth R. Scholberg, 'Nota sobre "El Dio alto que los çielos sostiene..." ', *RoN*, X (1968-69), 400-3.

29. J. Saroihandy, 'Remarques sur le *Poème de Yúçuf*', *BH*, VI (1904), 182-94. A. R. Nykl, 'A Compendium of *Aljamiado* Literature', *RH*, LXXVII (1929), 409-611. For dating, I draw on an unpublished paper by L. P. Harvey.

30. Helen L. Sears, 'The *Rimado de palaçio* and the *De regimine principum* Tradition of the Middle Ages', *HR*, XX (1952), 1-27; K. E. Shaw, 'Provincial and Pundit: Juan de Castrojeriz's version of *De regimine principum*', *BHS*, XXXVIII (1961), 55-63.

31. Julio Saavedra Molina, *El verso de arte mayor* (Santiago, 1946); Clarke, *Morphology of Fifteenth Century Castilian Verse*, pp. 51-61; Giuseppe Tavani, 'Considerazioni sulle origini dell'*arte mayor*', *CN*, XXV (1965), 15-33; Barclay Tittman, 'Further Remarks on the Origins of *Arte mayor*', *CN*, XXIX (1969), 274-82.

32. Selections from *Rimado*, ed. Kenneth W. J. Adams (Salamanca, Biblioteca Anaya, in press). *El libro de Job*, ed. Francesco Branciforti (Messina and Firenze, 1962); *Flores de los morales de Job*, ed. Branciforti (Messina and Firenze, 1963). Franco Meregalli, *La vida política del Canciller Ayala* (Milano, 1955); Luis Suárez Fernández, *El Canciller P.L. de A. y su tiempo (1332-1407)* (Vitoria, 1962). Branciforti, 'Regesto delle opere di P.L. de A.', *Saggi e ricerche in memoria di Ettore li Gotti*, I (Palermo, 1962), 289-317. Fernando Rossello, 'Nota sul moralismo di P.L. de A.', *SMV*, VIII (1960), 211-34; Germán Orduna, 'El fragmento *P* del *RP* y un continuador anónimo del Canciller A.', *Fi*, VII (1961), 107-19; Joaquín Gimeno Casalduero, 'P.L. de A. y el cambio poético de Castilla a comienzos del siglo XV', *HR*, XXXIII (1965), 1-14; Clarke, *Morphology*, Ch. 9; E. B. Strong, 'The *RP*: L. de A.'s proposals for ending the Great Schism', *BHS*, XXXVIII (1961), 64-77, and 'The *RP*: L. de A.'s rimed confession', *HR*, XXXVII (1969), 439-51. For the *Libro de justiçia*, see Amador de los Ríos, *Historia crítica de la lit. esp.*, V (Madrid, 1864), 223-33.

33. Milá, *De la poesía heroico-popular castellana* (Barcelona, 1959; first

published 1874); John G. Cummins, 'The Creative Process in the Ballad "Pártese el moro Alicante" ', *FMLS*, VI (1970), 368-81.

34. Ezio Levi, 'El romance florentino de Jaume de Olesa', *RFE*, XIV (1927), 134-60.

35. Diego Catalán Menéndez Pidal, 'Un romance histórico de Alfonso XI', *EMP*, VI (Madrid, 1956), 259-85 (revised in *Siete siglos*, Ch. 1); N. E. Gardiner, 'The Ballads of the Prior de San Juan', *MLR*, XXXIV (1939), 550-56.

36. W. J. Entwistle, 'The *Romancero del rey don Pedro* in Ayala and the *Cuarta crónica general*', *MLR*, XXV (1930), 306-26; Catalán, ' "Nunca viera jaboneros tan bien vender su jabón". Romance histórico del rey don Pedro, del año 1357', *BRAE*, XXXII (1952), 233-45 (revised in *Siete siglos*, Ch. 2); *Romancero del rey don Pedro (1368-1800)*, ed. Antonio Pérez Gómez (Valencia, 1954). Cf. Juan B. Avalle-Arce, 'Bernal Francés y su romance', *AEM*, III (1966), 327-91.

37. H. A. Deferrari, *The Sentimental Moor in Spanish Literature before 1600* (Philadelphia, 1927).

38. Leo Spitzer, 'The Folkloristic Pre-Stage of the Spanish *romance Conde Arnaldos*', *HR*, XXIII (1955), 173-87, and XXIV (1956), 64-6 (repr. in *Antigua poesía*, pp. 87-103); Thomas R. Hart, '*El CA* and the Medieval Scriptural Tradition', *MLN*, LXXII (1957), 281-5; A. Hauf and J. M. Aguirre, 'El simbolismo mágico-erótico de *El infante Arnaldos*', *RF*, LXXXI (1969), 89-118. For literary analysis of other ballads, see Leo Spitzer, 'El romance de *Abenámar*', *Antigua poesía*, pp. 61-84; Eugenio Asensio, '*Fonte frida*, o encuentro del romance con la canción de mayo', *NRFH*, VIII (1954), 365-88 (revised in *Poética y realidad*, pp. 241-77); Edmund de Chasca, *Estructura y forma en el Poema de Mio Cid*, pp. 147-54; Wilson, *Tragic Themes*; Bénichou, *Creación poética*.

39. Norton and Wilson, *Two Spanish Verse Chap-Books*; J. M. Aguirre, 'Épica oral y épica castellana: tradición creadora y tradición repetitiva', *RF*, LXXX (1968), 13-43; Diego Catalán Menéndez-Pidal, 'Memoria e invención en el Romancero de tradición oral', *RPh*, XXIV (1970-71), 1-25 and 441-63.

40. Samuel G. Armistead and Joseph H. Silverman, *Diez romances hispánicos en un manuscrito sefardí de la Isla de Rodas* (Pisa, 1962), and numerous articles on Judeo-Spanish ballads; *La flor de la Marañuela: romancero general de las Islas Canarias*, ed. Diego Catalán (2 vols., Madrid, 1969). In addition to studies already cited, see Ruth H. Webber, *Formulistic Diction in the Spanish Ballad;* Bruce A. Beatie, 'Oral-traditional Composition in the Spanish *Romancero* of the Sixteenth Century', *Journal of the Folklore Institute*, I (1964), 92-113; Joseph Szertics, *Tiempo y verbo en el romancero viejo* (Madrid, BRH, 1967); Daniel Devoto, 'Un no aprehendido canto. Sobre el estudio del romancero tradicional y el llamado "método geográfico" ', *Ábaco*, I (1969), 11-44; Jules Horrent, 'Traits distinctifs du romancero espagnol', *MRo*, XX (1970), 29-38.

41. M. Rodrigues Lapa, *Lições de literatura portuguesa. Época medieval*, Ch. 8.

42. The poetry of these transitional decades is discussed more fully below on pp. 179-80.

Chapter 6

LEARNED PROSE AND THE
RISE OF FICTION, 1300-1500

I. THE GROWTH OF LITERACY

SPANISH PROSE TEXTS from the fourteenth and fifteenth centuries, and poems from the fifteenth, survive in far greater quantity than the works that we have so far considered. Movements and general characteristics now become clearly visible, even though the best works obstinately refuse to conform entirely to the main tendencies. The increased number of texts is not caused to any great extent by the fact that the fifteenth century is closer to us than the thirteenth, and that accidental losses have had less time in which to occur. The main reason is that more works were in fact produced, and produced because there was a demand for them. Moreover, prose and the more sophisticated poems must have been directed primarily at the literate. Their public would in practice have been confined to those who could read fairly easily and to those who, while not possessing this skill, had nevertheless reached a moderate level of culture and were in regular contact with those who could read. The private reader and the small cultured group to whom books were read aloud were essential to the expansion of literary production (cf. above, p. 69). A combination of educational and technological factors seems to have brought about this change. The educational reforms decreed by the Fourth Lateran Council were slow in affecting Spain, but by the end of the thirteenth century they had begun to take effect; the Church's growing insistence on education was partly a deeply-felt spiritual obligation, and partly a recognition of the needs of an increasingly complex urban society. It was assisted by two technological developments: the widespread use of paper, and the manufacture of spectacles.

Paper, first used in China, reached Europe by the mid-twelfth century, and was being widely used by the end of the thirteenth. All manuscripts had previously been of parchment or of the still scarcer and more expensive vellum, whereas paper was plentiful and cheap once the technique of manufacture had been mastered. The need to copy out manuscripts by hand was still a limiting factor, which would persist until the introduction of printing with moveable type, but the use of paper brought books within the reach of a much wider public. Spectacles prolonged the reading life of the old: convex lenses to aid failing sight appeared in the late thirteenth century, and were in common use by the middle of the fourteenth (concave lenses to correct short sight were a much later development).[1]

These educational and technological factors combined with the results of Alfonso X's enthusiasm for the vernacular, since the availability of serious vernacular works encouraged the habit of reading. Not only were more copies of a book produced, but more works were composed: the circumstances that produced more readers also produced more men capable of literary and scientific work. Style, structure, and genre were affected: sophistication of style and complexity of structure were acceptable to private readers and small groups where they would have baffled and repelled a *juglar's* audience in the marketplace; and the growth of a reading public led to the composition of consciously literary works where previously there had been a strongly utilitarian purpose. It can hardly be an accident that in the first decades of the fourteenth century, Juan Manuel converted the *exemplum*-collection from a preaching aid into a highly-polished work, the *Conde Lucanor*, in which he took a craftsman's pride, and that at the same time the prose romance, which had previously been confined to a historical function (for example, the *Estoria de Tebas* in the *General estoria*—see above, p. 90), now appeared as an independent work, both in translation from French and as an original reworking and combination of diverse materials. The combination of religious or historical objectives with a firm artistic consciousness produces a new kind of work; some features of the *Libro de Buen Amor* (see above, p. 111) are due to a similar evolution. The great increase in vernacular prose-writing did not mean the end of Hispano-Latin literature, which continued steadily throughout the fourteenth century and increased in the fifteenth.

II. DIDACTIC LITERATURE

The prose literature of these two hundred years falls for the most part into the three main categories of didactic writing, chronicles, and fiction. These overlap to some extent, and there are important subsidiary groups such as biographies, travel-books, and political tracts, but it will be convenient to follow these main lines.

An early and interesting didactic writer in both Latin and Castilian is St Pedro Pascual, who was born *c.* 1227, became bishop of Jaén in 1296, was captured by the Moors, and was martyred in 1300. Much of his work was written in captivity, perhaps including the *Impunación de la seta de Mahomah* (see above, p. 94).[2]

Juan Manuel (1282-1348), the nephew of Alfonso X, is of much greater stature. The two most noteworthy features of his life are strongly reflected in his books: his devotion to the Dominican order (for whom he founded the monastery of Peñafiel), and his obsessively self-conscious ambition; the wish to reconcile these conflicting impulses may well have been his dominant literary motive. His association with the Dominicans influenced the thought of several works and the choice of *exempla* for the *Conde Lucanor*. His ambition, concern for reputation, and suspicion of others are often noticeable, and are openly stated in the general prologue to his works:

> Así commo ha muy grant plazer el que faze alguna buena obra, sennaladamente si toma grant trabajo e la faz quando sabe que aquella su obra es muy loada et se pagan della mucho las gentes, bien así ha muy grant pesar et grant enojo quando alguno a sabiendas o aun por yerro faze o dize alguna cosa por que aquella obra non sea tan preciada o alabada commo devía ser ... Et recelando yo, don Johan, que por razón que non se podrá escusar, que los libros que yo he fechos non se ayan de trasladar muchas vezes, et por que yo he visto que en el transladar acaeçe muchas vezes, lo uno por desentendimiento del scrivano, o por que las letras semejan unas a otras, et que en transladando el libro porná una razón por otra, en guisa que muda toda la entençión et toda la suma, et será traýdo el que la fizo non aviendo y culpa; et por guardar esto quanto yo pudiere, fizi fazer este volumen en que están scriptos todos los libros que yo fasta aquí he fechos ... Et ruego a todos los que leyeren qualquier de los libros que yo fiz, que, si fallaren alguna razón mal dicha, que non pongan a mí la culpa fasta que bean este volumen que yo mesmo concerté ...

Six of Juan Manuel's works have been lost. The *Libro de la cavalleria* was, to judge from the excerpts included in the *Libro de los estados,* a didactic work for knights, and the nature of the *Libro de las cantigas* (or *de los cantares*) is obvious. Probably a more serious loss is the *Reglas de trovar*, which would, assuming it was in Castilian, have provided us with the earliest treatise on poetry in that language. The other lost works are the *Crónica conplida*, the *Libro de los sabios,* and the *Libro de los egennos.*

The *Conde Lucanor*, or *Libro de Patronio* (completed 1335), is the most famous of Juan Manuel's works, and rightly so. The main part of the book consists of fifty-one *exempla*, set in the familiar framework of master instructing pupil (see above, p. 98). Lucanor asks his tutor Patronio for advice on a problem, Patronio tells a story and derives the solution from it, and Juan Manuel then sums up the moral in two lines of bad verse. Two features, apart from the couplets, are unusual among *exemplum*-collections: a generalising tendency is built into the frame-story, and is then reinforced by Juan Manuel's comment; secondly, the author does not merely sum up each moral, but appears as a character, referred to in the third person: 'Et quando don Johan falló este exiemplo, tóvolo por bueno . . .' This appearance within his own work is not confined to the *Conde Lucanor*, and the impression that it gives of self-centredness corresponds to his concern for his literary reputation, and to his frequent reference to, and even quotation from, his own writings.

The *exempla* of the *Conde Lucanor* come from a variety of sources. Many are of oriental origin; others are taken from Spanish historical traditions, both Moorish and Christian; from the Crusades (Richard the Lionheart is the hero of the third *exemplum*); from Aesop; and from the Church. The Dominicans made especially frequent use of *exempla* in their sermons, and were responsible for important *exemplum*-collections, which probably gave Juan Manuel many of his stories.

Whereas the Archpriest of Hita develops the humorous possibilities of his stories, often attaching them fairly loosely to the moral which he draws, Juan Manuel's treatment is serious, and is subjected to much tighter intellectual control. The *Conde Lucanor* ends with four short sections, most of which are in the tradition of wisdom literature, using *sententiae* to express the same kind of moral (worldly prudence rather than ascetic renunciation) as is embodied in the *exempla*. Nearly all of the *sententiae* are of learned origin, and the proverbs which play a part elsewhere in Juan Manuel's works are here neglected.[3]

The *Libro del cavallero et del escudero* (1326) uses the method of question and answer to convey a great deal of information, rather as the *Lucidario* (see above, p. 101) uses a different question-and-answer situation. A squire, who subsequently goes to Court and is knighted, spends some time with an aged knight who has retired from the world, and who instructs him not only in chivalry but also in religious matters and in natural philosophy. The *Llibre del orde de la cavayleria* of Ramón Llull is an important source of part of this work, together with the *Lucidario*, the works of Alfonso X, and Latin encyclopaedic sources. The *Libro infinido* is also didactic, but in a much more personal way: it is addressed to the author's son Fernando, and contains spiritual, and a great deal of worldly, advice. The major source here seems to be Juan Manuel's own *Libro de los estados*, which he composed in the early 1330s.

The *Libro de los estados* is an adaptation of the story of Barlaam and Josaphat (above, p. 99), with two major changes: the three encounters are reduced to a single meeting with a corpse; and its message is not the asceticism of the original, but the one familiar in Juan Manuel's other works: how man can live a good and prudent life in this world.

Of the other works, the *Crónica abreviada* (early 1320s) summarises the Alfonsine *Estoria de España*; the *Libro de la caza* deals (like most medieval Spanish books on hunting) with falconry, a favourite pastime of the author's; the *Tratado de la Asunción* represents a much more intellectual approach to Marian devotion than do the lyrics of the *Libro de Buen Amor*; and finally, the *Libro de las armas* gives us valuable biographical information, being devoted to the author's claims to status and power. Juan Manuel cannot have been a likeable man, but he was a considerable literary artist, and his life and personality are revealed in his works in a way that makes them a fascinating study.[4]

He was important as a writer but not as a patron or organiser. More important in these respects was Juan Fernández de Heredia (*c.* 1310-1396), an Aragonese noble who belonged to the Knights Hospitallers and became Grand Master of Rhodes. He was responsible for Aragonese versions of two widely-diffused works of wisdom literature, under the titles of *Secreto secretorum* and *Libro de actoridades*, and also for the *Rams de flores*, a selection from the *Summa collationum* of the thirteenth-century Franciscan John of Wales.[5]

Other didactic works of the fourteenth century are in the tradition of prose hagiography, and still others derive from the sacraments, and in particular from that of confession: the *Libro de la justiçia de la vida espiritual* (see above, pp. 122-3), and the manual for confessors by Martín Pérez. The latter work, now lost, was composed in the vernacular (aiming both at priests with an insecure command of Latin and at an educated laity); in 1399 it was translated into Portuguese, and thus its content has been preserved.[6] The *Vergel de consolaçión*, now known to be a translation of a work by an Italian friar, Jacopo da Benevento, is based on the catechism, and gives an amplified treatment of the vices and virtues, with some use of *exempla* from biblical and patristic sources.[7] In another, roughly contemporary, work, the aim really is to console. This is the *Libro de las consolaciones de la vida humana* by Pedro de Luna, who from 1394 to 1423 was the antipope Benedict XIII; the consolations of Christianity are systematically set against the miseries and dangers of life in this world.[8]

Pedro de Luna was, as we have already seen (above, p. 131, n.5), the author of a learned sermon in the vernacular, which was a rarity. Popular sermons were, of course, always in the vernacular, but at this time the few written records of them are mostly summaries in Latin. An extant vernacular homily is *Qué sinifica el hábito de los frailes de Santiago*, by Pedro López de Baeza, who early in the century held high office in the Order of Santiago; it is not certain, however, that this homily was intended for oral delivery.[9] Written vernacular texts of sermons are more frequent from the end of the fourteenth century. The most famous preacher of this period, St Vincent Ferrer, belongs not to Castilian but to Catalan literature, but he provides important evidence of sermon influence on literary technique (see below, p. 143), and his sermons against the Jews are closely connected with a major change in Spanish society.

Until the Almoravid invasions, Christians, Moors, and Jews had co-existed in an atmosphere of comparative religious tolerance, even when Moorish and Christian states were at war (the absence from Spanish epic of the crusading mentality found in the *Chanson de Roland* is well known). Even at a later stage, the Jewish communities in Christian Spain were largely immune from religious attacks, although there was social and economic discrimination, and although converts to Christianity wrote books designed to persuade other Jews to follow them; Alfonso de Valladolid (1270-1349), author of *Monstrador de justiçia* and *Libro de las tres graçias*, is a prominent example. In Spain, as throughout Europe, Jews were often blamed for the Black Death, but massacres were still avoided. The precarious balance of toleration survived until 1391, when popular despair, caused by the economic collapse which swept Europe in the last two decades of the century, was fanned by popular preachers into a hatred of the Jews, and then into massacres. The prosperous and culturally brilliant Jewish communities of Spain never really recovered from this blow, and many Jews sought safety in a usually reluctant and often superficial conversion to Christianity. Some *conversos* (the term includes the converts' descendants) continued the secret practice of Judaism, and many more were suspected, and the successful careers of many *conversos* in Church and state were bitterly resented by the *cristianos viejos*. There persisted throughout the fifteenth and sixteenth centuries a sense of the *conversos* as a separate and suspect group, who owed their success to sharp practice and conspiracy, and a natural consequence was a feeling of solidarity and of resentment among this group.

The effects of all this on late medieval Spanish life were far-reaching: certainly the establishment of the Inquisition, probably the prevailing anti-intellectualism of the nobility, and possibly a deeper pessimism among some *converso* writers than among their *cristiano viejo* contemporaries.

Some works in the fifteenth century were written in the general form of a sermon, but designed for private reading, as with the *Vençimiento del mundo*, which Alonso Núñez de Toledo sent at the end of 1481 to Leonor de Ayala for her edification. This work warns against the temptations of the world, and counsels asceticism, using the familiar pulpit devices. The whole of history is seen as an illustration of the truths that the author wishes to convey, so that Adam's downfall is followed immediately by a moral comment on the battle of Aljubarrota.[10]

A book of much greater literary merit than the *Vençimiento*, and which has travelled further from its sermon origins, is variously known as the *Corbacho* (because it was mistakenly thought to derive from

6 * *

Boccaccio's misogynistic *Corbaccio*), *Reprobaçión del amor mundano*, and *Arçipreste de Talavera*. This last title is the one given in the manuscript, but is confusing, since the author, Alfonso Martínez de Toledo, was Archpriest of Talavera. Martínez completed the *Corbacho* in 1438, when he was in his fortieth year and had already achieved great success in the Church (treasurer of Toledo Cathedral, chaplain to King Juan II). He wrote other works in the next few years, both historical (*Atalaya de las corónicas*, 1443) and hagiographic (*Vida de San Isidoro* and *Vida de San Ildefonso*, 1444—the latter supplemented by a translation of Ildefonso's work on the perpetual virginity of Mary). The date of his death is unknown, but he was still alive in 1482.

The *Corbacho* is a treatise against the sin of lust, and to an even greater extent than the *Vençimiento del mundo* it uses the techniques of the popular sermon in order to make its point. It gives the impression of a number of sermons fused into a single work; Martínez himself calls it 'un conpendio breve'. It is divided into four parts, which deal with the disastrous effects of lust on body and soul (the catechism is an important structural source for this section), the vices of women, the four humours in relation to lust, and miscellaneous topics which include astrology. It is frequently asserted that Martínez's chief aim in this book was to attack women, and that he belongs to a late medieval tradition of anti-feminist satire, but though lustful women are denounced, the attack on lustful men is equally severe. Martínez drew also on the opposing tradition of idealistic love-literature, in order to compare the pretensions of courtly lovers with the discreditable reality.

The range of sources and techniques used in the *Corbacho* is wide. Martínez relies to a great extent on Book III of Andreas Capellanus's *De amore*, which denounces the courtly love that Andreas had, at least on the surface, been exalting; and the allegorical dispute between Fortune and Poverty derives from Boccaccio. Other sources provide him with *exempla* and *sententiae*: St Augustine, the Archpriest of Hita, pseudo-Cato, pseudo-Aristotle, the Catalan Francesch Eiximenis, all of whom he seems to know directly, and many others whom he probably read only in extracts in one or more of the *florilegia* which were so important to the medieval writer and preacher. The *sententiae* include proverbs; these summings-up of popular philosophy had appeared spasmodically in prose-works and poems from the thirteenth century, but a substantial interest in them does not appear until the fifteenth, when a few collections were made, including one by the marqués de Santillana.[11]

Martínez's *exempla*, like those of any good preacher of *divisio extra* sermons, are extremely varied, both in source and in content. Some are very brief, but others are given a fuller treatment, and occasionally a story acquires a firm structure and great dramatic power, as in the *exemplum* of a dissolute hermit (pp. 188-92). Even more noteworthy is a device common enough in actual sermons, both in Spain and in other countries (it may be seen in the extant sermons of St Vincent Ferrer): the realistic presentation of popular speech. This is not merely a question of trying to reproduce some of the sounds of popular speech, as in the stylised language of peasants in the early drama (*sayagués*), but is an attempt to convey the impression that we are listening to real speech. This was, of course, an invaluable way of catching an audience's interest for a sermon, and Martínez must, like other priests, have used it often. In the *Corbacho* he transfers the technique, with triumphant success, to formal literature:

¡Yuy! ¡Dexadme! ¡Non quiero! ¡Yuy! ¡Qué porfiado! ¡En buena fe yo me vaya! ¡Por Dios, pues, yo dé bozes! ¡Estad en ora buena! ¡Dexadme agora estar! ¡Estad un poco quedo! ¡Ya, por Dios, non seades enojo! ¡Ay, paso, señor, que sodes descortés! ¡Aved ora vergüenza! ¿Estáys en vuestro seso? ¡Avad ora; que vos miran! ¿Non vedes que vos veen? ¡Y estad, para synsabor! ¡En buena fee que me ensañe! ¡Pues, en verdad, non me río yo! ¡Estad en ora mala! Pues, ¿querés que vos lo diga? ¡En buena fe yo vos muerda las manos! ... (130)

It is this technique which was inherited from the *Corbacho* by *La Celestina*. Just as impressive as Martínez's renderings of popular speech are his full-scale satirical descriptions: the lover swaggering through the town, the woman in borrowed finery, and several others. In both of these developments, we are given not a mere transcript of what the author has seen and heard, but an artistic re-creation, in which selection and emphasis produce the maximum effect. Martínez's grasp of overall structure is, however, less impressive.

It is noteworthy that he seldom shows bitterness to those whom he attacks; only the go-between and the homosexual are portrayed with real hatred, and in other cases humour accompanies the denunciation.[12]

The misogynistic bitterness that is lacking in the *Corbacho* is abundantly present in Luis de Lucena's *Repetición de amores* (*c.* 1497). The most famous poetic attack on women is by Pere Torrellas, who for this reason appears as a character in Juan de Flores's sentimental romance *Grisel y Mirabella* (see below, p. 165). The case for the defence is found at the end of Diego de San Pedro's romance *La cárcel de Amor* (see below, pp. 164-5), in the *Defensa de virtuosas mugeres* of Diego de Valera (1412-88?), and in the *Libro de las virtuosas e claras mugeres* (1446), by Álvaro de Luna, constable of Castile (1390?-1453). Both sides in the argument about women belong to a European tradition, and both sides spread from treatises into other genres.[13]

One other work of great interest is harder to classify within this debate: the *Tractado cómo al ome es nescesario amar*, by Alfonso de

Madrigal, known as el Tostado (1400?-55). El Tostado, who became bishop of Ávila, was an exceptionally prolific Latin writer, and also produced a substantial body of work in Spanish: a *Confesional*, a *Tratado sobre la Misa*, commentaries on religious texts, and the philosophical *Catorce questiones*. The *Tractado cómo al ome* deals first with the inevitability of sexual love, and then with its effects: mental disturbance, illness, and even death (cf. above, p. 28, n.21). There is plentiful reference to authority, and use of *exempla* from the Bible and from classical mythology. The effects of love are better suited to illustration by *exempla* than is its inevitability, and perhaps for this reason there is a marked ambiguity of tone. Most of the *exempla* and a number of *sententiae* are biased against love, or even against women, yet el Tostado says that he does not regret falling in love, even though it turned out badly for him; this conflict remains unresolved.[14]

A type of didactic work that flourished in the thirteenth century but then seems to have lapsed (except for Juan Manuel's consciously literary development of it—see above, pp. 138-9) is the *exemplum*-collection. This reappears in the fifteenth century, but within a different tradition. The earlier collections (see above, pp. 96-9) were either translations of oriental works, or drew very heavily on oriental material, whereas at least two of the fifteenth-century books of *exempla* have Latin sources (though, of course, a number of *exempla* are still oriental in origin). In these works, the device of the frame-story has virtually been abandoned.

The oddly-named *Libro de los gatos* contains animal *exempla* of different origins (Aesop, the beast-epic of Reynard the Fox, bestiaries, and oriental tales). It is a version of the *Fabulae*, or *Narrationes*, of the thirteenth-century Anglo-Latin writer Odo of Cheriton; most of the morals seem to have been supplied by the Spanish author. There is a strong note of social satire, directed against the rich and powerful in Church and state, and the style is clear and direct. The *gatos* of the title may be liars and hypocrites, and the word of Arabic origin; they cannot be literally cats, and an attempt to read the title as *Libro de los cuentos* has been discredited.[15]

Another Latin work from thirteenth-century England, the Franciscan *Speculum laicorum*, was translated as *Espéculo de los legos*, and here the title reflects the main purpose of such collections, the instruction of the laity. This is a much longer work, and contains a fair amount of encyclopaedic information, as well as a large number of *exempla*.[16]

The *Libro de los exenplos por A.B.C.*, by Clemente Sánchez de Vercial, uses a structure almost as popular in the Middle Ages as the frame-story: the alphabetical arrangement. This is often used for lists of *sententiae*, and a collection of *exempla* arranged under the key-words of their morals was of particular value to a hard-pressed preacher. Several works of this sort exist in Latin—for instance, the

Alphabetum narrationum of the fourteenth-century Dominican Arnold de Liège—and there are vernacular versions as well. Sánchez de Vercial (died 1434?) was a canon of León Cathedral, and wrote a devotional work, the *Sacramental*, which was widely read down to the mid-sixteenth century. The *Exenplos* is by far the largest *exemplum*-collection in Spanish, with nearly 550 stories (there is sometimes more than one story to a single heading).[17]

Other Spanish *exemplum*-collections of the fifteenth century are of types familiar to us from previous chapters: the two *Book of Sindibad* versions (see above, p. 99), and the *Ysopete ystoriado*, one of the many Aesop versions which circulated in the Middle Ages (see above, p. 111). This *Ysopete*, however, includes a good deal of other material from the *Disciplina clericalis*, the Latin tales of Poggio Bracciolini, and other sources.[18]

Many other didactic works survive from the fifteenth century, both in Latin and the vernacular. Some offer spiritual guidance, others advise on how to live prudently in this world, while a few combine the two types. Characteristic works are the *Doctrinal de caballeros*, the *Glosa a San Juan Crisóstomo*, the *Memorial de virtudes*, and the *Defensorium unitatis christianae* of Alfonso de Cartagena (1384-1456), the *converso* bishop of Burgos; the *Carro de dos vidas* of García Gómez, which compares the active and contemplative lives; the *Breve e muy provechosa doctrina de lo que debe saber todo christiano* and *Glosa sobre el Ave Maria* of Fray Hernando de Talavera (1428-1507), the first archbishop of reconquered Granada; the *Breviloquio de virtudes, Espejo de verdadera nobleza*, and *Tratado de providencia contra fortuna* of Diego de Valera (cf. above, p. 143); the works of two Augustinian friars of the first half of the century, Juan de Alarcón (*Libro del regimiento de los señores*) and Lope Fernández de Minaya (*Espejo del alma, Libro de las tribulaciones*); and the *Compendio de la fortuna* and *Jardin de nobles doncellas* (not a courtly work, but a treatise on how a Christian woman should behave) of their fellow-Augustinian Martín Alfonso de Córdoba (end of fourteenth century-1476?).[19] An Islamic equivalent of such treatises is the *aljamiado* (see above, p. 122) *Kitab segobiano* (1462), by Ice de Gebir. Three other works need fuller comment.

In the late 1430s, Alfonso de la Torre wrote the *Visión deleitable*, a compendium of medieval knowledge within the allegorical framework. The *Visión* deals with the seven liberal arts, and then with the higher studies of natural philosophy, ethics, and theology. It draws on Isidore of Seville for encyclopaedic content, on Martianus Capella (fourth century) and Alain de Lille (twelfth century) for allegory, and also on Arabic scientists and Maimonides's *Guide for the Perplexed* (see above, p. 2). No source is later than the twelfth century, and Alfonso de la Torre applied his wide reading, great intellectual energy, and considerable powers as a stylist to producing an encyclopaedia of knowledge as it had been some two and a half centuries previously; moreover, the *Visión* was copied out, printed, and translated well into the Golden Age. Not merely is it a supreme example of Spain's cultural belatedness (see above, pp. 55-7), but it shows that such belatedness was entirely acceptable to Renaissance Italy.[20]

A shorter work with a marked ecclesiastical bias, but again with encyclopaedic aims, is the *Invencionario* of Alfonso de Toledo. The first version of this book, which is often mistakenly attributed to the author of the *Corbacho*, was written *c.* 1460, and the final version was completed in 1474. The chief sources are the Bible, the Decretals, and Peter Comestor, and the author's interest is chiefly concentrated on the origins of the institutions with which he deals: in order to illustrate these origins, he draws on some remarkable anecdotal material.[21]

Thirdly, the *Libro de vita beata* of Juan de Lucena is an imaginary dialogue between Alfonso de Cartagena, Juan de Mena, and the marqués de Santillana, on how to attain true happiness; Lucena, character as well as author, joins in the conversation at the end; an ironic and satirical review of society includes a defence of the *conversos*. The identity of Lucena has been a matter of some doubt, but it seems highly probable that he was a *converso*, a scholar who served in Italy as a diplomat and became a printer on his return to Spain, and that he fled to Rome *c.* 1481 to escape the Inquisition. The author also of an *Epístola exhortatoria a las letras* (in praise of Isabel the Catholic) and the *Tractado de los gualardones* (on knighthood and heraldry), he is one of the most interesting intellectual figures of late medieval Spain.[22]

On the fringes of didactic literature are treatises on hunting, and especially on falconry. A *Libro de la montería* is sometimes attributed to Alfonso X, but is more likely to date from the reign of Alfonso XI. Its sources include the *Tratado de las enfermedades de las aves de caza* (probably thirteenth-century) which—like so much of medieval falconry-lore—has an Arabic basis, and also Spanish versions (which also may well date from the thirteenth century) of the treatises known as *Dancus rex* and *Guillelmus falconarius*. Juan Manuel wrote on falconry (see above, pp. 139-40), and so did Pero López de Ayala. Ayala's *Libro de la caza de las aves* was probably written while he was in a Portuguese prison (see above, p. 124), and incorporates a translation of Pero Menino's *Livro de falcoaria*, but half of the work is Ayala's own contribution. His book is, in its turn, incorporated into a compendium by Juan de Sahagún, falconer to King Juan II.[23]

In the fifteenth century, the most interesting group of miscellaneous prose-works is undoubtedly that concerned with language. What begins as a commentary on Dante's *Divina Commedia* turns into a surprisingly sophisticated handling of linguistic concepts,[24] and in the closing decade of the century two reference works of fundamental importance were published: Alfonso de Palencia's *Universal vocabulario en latín y romance* was printed in 1490, and Antonio de Nebrija's *Gramática de la lengua castellana* in 1492.

The introduction of paper had solved only half of the problem of producing cheap books (see above, p. 136); the other half was solved when, between 1440 and 1450, Johann Gutenberg invented moveable type (so that the type could be used again and again for different books) and a suitable ink and printing-press. Men were slow to realise the full implications of Gutenberg's work, but the commercial possibilities were too great to be overlooked, and printing spread rapidly throughout Europe; by the early 1470s it was established in Spain. The early printers (among whom Germans were, in Spain as elsewhere, dominant for some decades) were also publishers, booksellers, and very often editors; their cultural influence was thus substantial. At first, the books printed were those which had proved popular in manuscript, but before long, some books were written for immediate printing.[25]

The Italian humanistic influence is dominant in Nebrija, who was not as isolated a figure as he liked to believe. By this time, Italian humanists were very active in Spain. In the middle of the century, the Neapolitan Court of Alfonso V, the Magnanimous, of Aragon attracted the leading humanistic writers of Italy, but their influence hardly penetrated to Castile.[26] There, Juan II was a patron of scholars, but his example seems to have carried little weight, and when his long reign ended in 1454, twenty years of strife, corruption, and frivolity under the well-meaning but ineffectual Enrique IV made the intellectual outlook even bleaker. Under the Catholic Monarchs, however, a tradition of Italian influence and educational expansion to some extent compensated for the intellectual impoverishment that Spain inflicted on herself with the expulsion of the Jews and the persecution of the *conversos*.

In the closing decades of the fifteenth century, then, there was powerful support for humanistic culture, even though most men seem still to have viewed it with grave suspicion. In the remainder of the century, however, suspicion of any learning other than theology was almost universal. It was widely believed that a love of books might indicate a dabbling in magic, was incompatible with nobility and military prowess, and was characteristic of *conversos*. It may well be that the self-conscious erudition and complexity which we find in Mena's *Laberinto de Fortuna* (below, pp. 186-8) and in some of Villena's work is a defensive reaction from an isolated minority.[27]

Perhaps the most interesting case of a man who defied the anti-intellectual pressures of his time is Enrique de Villena (1384-1434).

A descendant of the royal houses of both Castile and Aragon, Villena was intensely ambitious (he appears, in the hope of advancement, to have connived at his wife's liaison with Enrique III), but his life ended in political failure. His ambitions were also intellectual: he prided himself on his linguistic attainments and the range of his interests. His contacts with Catalan culture were strong, and one of his earliest works, the *Doze trabajos de Hércules*, was written in Catalan and then translated into Castilian by Villena himself. He had Jewish and Moorish friends, and cites many Arabic and Hebrew authors in his works. His citations of authorities are lavish even for a period when this was the accepted practice, and it is highly probable that many of the works referred to were known to him only through extracts in *compendia* or at second hand. His style is in general heavily Latinised, both in syntax and vocabulary.

The *Doze trabajos de Hércules* (before 1417) follows a complex and ambitious plan, an adaptation of the fourfold exegesis used for biblical texts. Villena narrates the story of each labour, and follows it with an allegorical interpretation, the historically correct explanation of the story, and its application to one of twelve subdivided groups, thus providing an effective synopsis of early fifteenth-century Spanish society. The structure of the work is firm and clear, without any sign of the abridgement which the author claims. The opening of the first narrative gives a fair picture of Villena's style:

> Afírmase que fue un gigante a quien llaman Uxio el qual se enamoró de Juno deesa del aire, fija de Saturno e madrastra de Hércules. Aqueste gigante aviendo logar e vagar quiso con la dicha Juno carnalmente juntarse, mas non consintió ella nin por voluntad se inclinó al loco deseo de Uxio. Non enbargante que se viese en poder de tal gigante en logar apartado guardó con todo eso su onestad, defendiéndose non por fuerça corporal mas por engenio e presto consejo de muger entendida, formando en el aire imajen fantástica de muger en la niebla espesa que era entre Uxio e ella a figura de sí muy aína e casi sin tiempo por arte divinal.

Another early work is the *Arte de trovar*, which has survived only in fragmentary form. It is dedicated to Santillana, and combines observations on poetry with a good deal of linguistic material. The section on poetry has a strongly Provençal and Catalan bias.

Other works of Villena's are the *Tratado de la lepra* (*c.* 1417), *Tratado de la consolación* (1423), the *Arte cisoria* (1423), and a commentary on a verse of Psalm 8 (1424). The *Tratado del aojamiento* was mostly written in 1422, and completed two or three years later. This, the only extant work in which Villena's interest in magic is given free rein, deals with the nature of the evil eye and the different types of remedy for it. The *Libro de astrología* may have suffered at the hands of its copyist, and it is therefore not easy to judge its worth. Two other works, with two translations, complete the range of Villena's interests as far as it is known to us: the *Libro de la guerra* and *Epístola a Suero de Quiñones*, and the Spanish prose versions of the *Aeneid* and the *Divina Commedia*; the translations are probably among his last works (1427-28).

Villena's interest in magic made him an object of serious suspicion in his lifetime, and when he died Bishop Lope de Barrientos burned some fifty of the books from his library, supposedly on the orders of Juan II. His reputation as a magician persisted, and traditional tales about sorcerers became attached to his name.[28]

III. TRANSLATIONS

A growing number of translations became available to Spaniards of the fourteenth and fifteenth centuries. This is, admittedly, an artificial distinction in a medieval context, since many books are summaries, amplifications, or adaptations of foreign works, or incorporate partial translations within their own structure. Medieval writers regarded other books (in their own or some other language) as raw material in the same way as their own lives or the world around them, and a list of the works which contain some element of translation would include most of the masterpieces not only of medieval Spanish literature but of any other vernacular literature of this period. Nevertheless, some works are presented as translations, and attempt to give an accurate rendering of the original (the degree of success in this aim varies widely): the products of the Toledo school, the Alfonsine translations, and the vernacular Bibles. Translations from the Arabic continue, but to these are now added works from Classical Latin (Virgil, Livy, Cicero, Seneca, Ovid, Sallust), from Greek (Plato and Plutarch via Latin, Thucydides perhaps direct), from French (Brunetto Latini), from the Latin and vernacular writings of Dante, Petrarch, and Boccaccio, and (via a Portuguese intermediary) from English—Gower's *Confessio amantis*. Among those involved in the work of translation were Villena, Diego de Valera, López de Ayala, Alfonso de Cartagena, Pero Díaz de Toledo, Fernán Pérez de Guzmán, and Alfonso de Palencia; Santillana and Juan Fernández de Heredia were leading patrons of this work.

IV. CHRONICLES

We have seen in the *Visión deleitable* (above, pp. 145-6), the extraordinary conservatism of some Spanish didactic writing, and its ready acceptance in Renaissance Europe. When we turn to the chronicles of the fourteenth and fifteenth centuries, we find a similar conservatism. The Alfonsine *Estoria de España* was copied, abridged, and blended with a translation of el Toledano (see above, p. 86) in numerous chronicles down to the late fifteenth century. When, in the middle of the sixteenth century, there was a public demand for a comprehensive historical work, Florián de Ocampo met it with his 1541 edition of what is generally known as the *Tercera crónica general*, a text which may—extreme caution is necessary here—already have been 150 years old, and which derived in its essentials from the thirteenth century. What is more, Ocampo's edition was reprinted as late as 1604. It would, however, be pointless to attempt to trace the development of neo-Alfonsine historiography in the fourteenth and fifteenth centuries, for the reasons already explained (above, p. 88).

In the fourteenth century a series of chronicles of individual reigns began where the *Estoria de España* broke off. This treatment of a short and clearly defined segment of history made it easier to draw conclusions and to point a moral, thus opening the way for the fifteenth-century moralising *semblanza* (see below, pp. 153-4), and also for Pero López de Ayala's disguised Trastámaran propaganda in his *Crónica del rey D. Pedro*. This is the first example in Spanish of political history rewritten by a defector who wanted to justify himself to his contemporaries, to future generations, and, most difficult, to himself. For factual accuracy on the civil war, combined with open support for one side, we have to turn to a brief Latin work by Fernán Álvarez de Albornoz, archbishop of Seville.[29]

There are also in the fourteenth century more general histories that owe something to the Alfonsine tradition without being its direct descendants: for example, the writings of Fray García Eugui, bishop of Bayonne, and the *Crónica de San Juan de la Peña* (in Latin and Aragonese texts) are chiefly concerned with the eastern kingdoms of the Peninsula.

Juan Fernández de Heredia's *Grant crónica de Espanya* makes substantial use of the *General estoria*; his other historical works reflect directly or indirectly the Catalan venture in Greece. The *Crónica del moro Rasis*, which seems to derive from Arabic via Portuguese, incorporates a good deal of fictional material; and the lost *Estoria de los reyes del Señorío de África* was probably legendary monastic history (cf. the Cardeña *Estoria del Cid*, above, pp. 41-2).[30] On the other hand, a Latin chronicle by Gonzalo de Hinojosa, bishop of Burgos (died 1327), owes little or nothing to fiction or to the Alfonsine tradition.

In the fifteenth century, both the extant chronicles and the types represented are more numerous than in the fourteenth. There is usually a choice of chronicles for any reign, and in one case, the *Crónica de Juan II*, different chronicles are combined into a single work. This, like much of the historical writing of the fifteenth century, is more

detailed and livelier than works in the Alfonsine tradition. Though
the change began in the fourteenth-century chronicles of Sancho IV
and Alfonso XI, the decisive factor seems to have been the use by
historians of the techniques of vivid presentation which had been
evolved in fiction and in such sermon-based works as the *Corbacho*.
There is even a case—the *Crónica sarracina* (c. 1430), by Pedro del
Corral—which is a pseudo-historical romance set within a chronicle.
Corral's work has an account of the Visigothic kings of Spain (based
on el Toledano), and a summary of Spanish history down to Enrique
III, but its principal aim is to tell the story of the fall of Spain to the
Moors, and for this Corral draws on the *Crónica del moro Rasis* while
increasing still further the fictional element in the account.

The historiography of Juan II's reign is dominated by the personality of Álvaro de Luna (see above, p. 143) who, as chief adviser to
the king, virtually ruled the country for some years. Luna's aims were
to break the power of the nobility (the old struggle which had begun in
the reign of Alfonso X was still unresolved), and to use a strengthened
central administration in order to restore prosperity and complete the
Reconquest. His enemies proved in the end too powerful, and in 1453
he was dismissed and quickly executed. The official chroniclers of the
period are hostile to Luna, but the views of his supporters continued
to find expression, even after the *coup d'état* which destroyed him, in
the *Crónica de don Álvaro de Luna*. The probable author is Gonzalo
Chacón (died 1517), who had been one of Luna's servants, and who
appears in the narrative, as at the moment when the Constable knows
he is doomed:

> Díxole pues estonçe el Gonçalo Chacón:
> 'Señor, ¿para qué nos dais este aver? Pensáis nos fazer en ello
> merçed, e fazéysnos daño.'
> El Maestre le respondió:
> 'Dóvosle porque más no vos puedo dar, para que lo podáys con
> vosotros llevar, e para que si vos guardaren los seguros que el
> Rey mi señor vos ha dado, recojáis todos esos criados míos que a
> vosotros acudieren, e les fagáis buen acogimiento e buena conpañía,
> fasta que lleguéis a la condesa mi muger, e al conde mi fijo, si Dios
> allá vos llebare' . . .
> E después que aquella provisión fue fecha, el Maestre demandó
> sus sellos, e un martillo, e él mismo por sus manos los desfizo, e los
> despedaçó, a fin que con ellos ninguna maldad le pudiese ser fecha.
> (pp. 398-9)[31]

For the reign of Enrique IV, and still more for that of the Catholic
Monarchs, we have a wealth of chronicles, all of which have stylistic
polish and historical skill, though it remains true that the greatest
Peninsular historian of the fifteenth century is not a Spaniard but a

Portuguese, Fernão Lopes, who is outstanding both in historical method and in narrative technique.

Besides the chronicles of single reigns, other types of historical work flourish in the fifteenth century: Latin general histories of great sophistication (Alfonso de Cartagena, Rodrigo Sánchez de Arévalo); vernacular general histories of different kinds; excerpts from the Alfonsine tradition which deal in a popular manner with Castilian heroes of the distant past (*Crónica de Fernán González, Crónica particular del Cid, Crónica popular del Cid*); and such curiosities as Lope García de Salazar's *Libro de las bienandanzas e fortunas*, a vast miscellany of traditions and local history.[32]

The *Crónica sarracina* is a romance with the trappings of history. One strictly historical work reads like a romance: Pero Rodríguez de Lena's *Libro del passo honroso*. In 1434, a young knight named Suero de Quiñones obtained the permission of Juan II to hold a bridge in León against all comers in tribute to the lady he loved, and with nine friends he held it for a month, fighting sixty-eight Spanish and foreign knights, of whom one was killed; many were wounded on both sides. Rodríguez de Lena, a notary, was present as a witness, and the *Libro* is his account of the adventure. What is extraordinary is not that Suero de Quiñones undertook this feat and persuaded friends to join him, but that society as a whole accepted such conduct as normal in this and other cases.[33]

Some of the chronicles discussed above come close to being biographies or political tracts, and a number of other fifteenth-century works fall more or less clearly into these two categories. Of the clearly political works, the best known is the Latin speech made by Alfonso de Cartagena at the Council of Basle in 1434, asserting Castile's precedence over England and using the historical arguments embodied in his Latin chronicle. Cartagena's follower Rodrigo Sánchez de Arévalo wrote two works of political theory: *Suma de la política* and *Vergel de príncipes* (a *speculum principis*, concerned with pastimes and with martial qualities, whose title brings us back again to the familiar allegorical garden of medieval literature); some of the works already mentioned under the heading of didactic literature could easily be added to this group. Two other books have a more immediate concern with fifteenth-century Castile, and both have been overlooked until recently. One is the *Libro de la consolación de España*, and the other is Fernán Díaz de Toledo's *Instrucción del Relator*. Both are by *conversos*; the former is a pessimistic meditation on the condition of Spain, and the latter (possibly intended for oral delivery) was composed in late October 1449 as a political document against the rebels who had seized Toledo and were persecuting the *conversos*. Alfonso de Cartagena's *Defensorium unitatis christianae* (see above, p. 145) is a reaction to the same event, but takes up a general philosophical attitude, in contrast to Fernán Díaz's more polemical approach.[34] The Toledo revolt was the most serious of many outbreaks against the *conversos*, and this growing popular prejudice led the Catholic Monarchs to establish the Spanish Inquisition (totally distinct from the Papal Inquisition) in 1481.

V. BIOGRAPHY

There are three principal types of biographical writing in the period with which we are concerned: the biography of a single person (which, of course, overlaps with the chronicles of individual reigns), the collection of sketches known as *semblanzas*, and the much rarer autobiographical memoir.

A very early example of the single-subject biography is the *Historia Roderici* (above, p. 42); later comes the short Latin work on King Afonso III of Portugal composed by Juan Gil de Zamora towards the end of the thirteenth century. In the fifteenth century, very full biographies were written, and two of the most interesting vernacular works are lives not of kings but of nobles. Gutierre Díez de Games (1378?-after 1448) wrote most of the *Victorial*, or *Crónica de don Pero Niño*, by 1435, and completed it in 1448. Pero Niño, conde de Buelna, was the author's patron, but although the tone of the biography is firmly favourable, it avoids flattery. The assumptions that govern the work are chivalresque; not merely are there ample descriptions of tournaments and similar activities, but the characters are judged by the standard of chivalry.[35]

The anonymous *Relación de los hechos del condestable Miguel Lucas de Iranzo* covers events in the constable's life between 1458 and 1471. Its particular interest is that its descriptions of festivities provide evidence for semi-dramatic forms in the fifteenth century.[36] At the end of the century, a very different kind of biography was written by Gonzalo García de Santa María (1447-1521): the *Serenissimi principis Joannis secundi Aragonum regis vita*. This work, whose model is Sallust, has been described as the first humanistic biography written in Spain.

Outstanding among collections of biographical sketches is the *Generaciones y semblanzas* of Fernán Pérez de Guzmán (c. 1378-1460?). Most of this collection was written c. 1450, but some sketches are later. The prologue is a most interesting theoretical discussion of history and the responsibilities of the historian; Fernán Pérez here does for history what Santillana had done for poetry a year or so before (see below, p. 186). He stresses responsibility to the men he is writing about, and the effectiveness of fame as a moral force; and these aims are, on the whole, fulfilled in the body of the work.

Fernán Pérez writes of his contemporaries but, in an effort to attain an objective view, he writes only after their death. He rejects the practice, common at the time, of presenting a historical character as an *exemplum* of a particular vice or virtue, and shows that most of his subjects are mixtures of good and bad. He had been an opponent of Álvaro de Luna, but he cannot pretend that the great nobles with whom he sided were disinterested patriots:

No callaré aquí nin pasaré so silençio esta razón, que quanto quier que la prinçipal e la original cabsa de los daños de España fuese la remisa e nigligente condiçión del rey e la cobdiçia e ambiçión exçesiva del condestable, pero en este casso non es de perdonar la cobdiçia de los grandes cavalleros que por creçer e avançar sus estados e rentas, prosponiendo la conçiençia e el amor de la patria por ganar, ellos dieron lugar a ello. E non dubdo que les plazía tener tal rey, por que en el tienpo turbado e desordenado, en el río buelto fuesen ellos ricos pescadores. (p. 47)

Nevertheless, full objectivity is unattainable, and the author's opinions govern much of his selection and presentation.

Fernán Pérez owes to rhetoric both some stylistic devices and the structure of his portraits, which follow a standard pattern while allowing for amplifications and brief digressions. The style is restrained and effective both in description and in formulation of judgments. These judgments are based on a Christian concept of a noble's duty to his country, and differ from the values of the chivalresque romances which inspire the *Victorial*. Fernán Pérez's descriptive and evaluative techniques in the *Generaciones y semblanzas* make an interesting comparison with his portraits of men of the distant past in the *Mar de historias* (a translation of the fourteenth-century *Mare historiarum* of Giovanni della Colonna), and with the *Claros varones de Castilla* of Hernando del Pulgar (*c.* 1425-after 1490). Pulgar, who was also a chronicler and author of letters, some of which become independent essays, consciously takes Fernán Pérez's work as a model for the *Claros varones*; he differs from his model, however, in a more ambitiously literary style, and in a tendency to subordinate candour to diplomacy, although his psychological penetration and use of irony overcome these obstacles.

Autobiography is represented by the *Memorias* of Leonor López de Córdoba (1363-1412), which seems to have been composed towards the end of her life. The style is simple and sometimes awkward—this is not the simplicity born of literary skill and long practice, as with Pérez de Guzmán—and perhaps for this reason it conveys effectively the events of Doña Leonor's life and the emotions they aroused in her. Her family and her husband's were on the losing side in the Trastámaran war, and one of the most moving passages describes their imprisonment:

Y estuvimos los demás que quedamos presos nueve años, hasta que el Sr. Rey D. Enrique fallesció; y nuestros maridos tenían sesenta libras de hierro cada uno en los pies, y mi hermano D. Lope López tenía una cadena encima de los hierros en que había setenta eslabones; él era niño de trece años, la más hermosa criatura que había en el mundo. E a mi marido en especial poníanlo en el algibe de la hambre, e teníanlo seis o siete días que nunca comía ni bebía, porque era primo de las Señoras Infantas, hijas del Rey D. Pedro.

The authentic personal note, the depiction of someone who was, although well connected, relatively obscure, and the authorship by a woman, all combine to make this one of the most remarkable works of its time.[37]

VI. TRAVEL

There is one other group of works written in the first person, and usually from personal experience: travel-books. The earliest book of travel in Spanish, if we exclude pilgrims' guides such as the *Fazienda de Ultra Mar* (see above, pp. 84-5), is the *Libro del conoscimiento de todos los reinos e tierras e señoríos que son por el mundo*. The author, a Spanish Franciscan friar, tells us that he was born in 1305, and the work seems to have been composed in 1350-60. There is serious doubt as to whether the author really did travel as he claimed; his descriptions of journeys in Europe and part of West Africa are accurate enough, but lack any element of personal observation. When he moves further afield, he no longer carries any conviction, and much of what he says about Asia seems to derive from the Alexander romances. The literary merit of the book is small, and most of it is mere catalogue.

The *Embajada a Tamorlán*, by Ruy González de Clavijo, is a very different kind of book. In 1403, Enrique III decided to send an embassy to the Mongol emperor, Tamburlaine the Great (Europe was threatened by the Turks, and the embassy was a result of the recurrent European dream of making an alliance that would surround the Eastern enemy—the quest for Prester John was an unusually long-lived variant). This embassy was led by Clavijo, and in three years it travelled to Samarkand and back. In the six years that elapsed between his return and his death in 1412, Clavijo wrote a full account of the journey (possibly with the help of his travelling-companion, the Dominican Alfonso Páez de Santamaría). He is scrupulous in his regard for factual accuracy, and there are so many descriptions of Eastern scenes and of local customs, strung on the strictly chronological thread of the journey, that the whole book is extremely vivid. The style moves more easily in the later parts. The structure is good, and Clavijo makes use of inserted passages of direct speech, and of address to the reader, in order to strengthen it.

Some thirty years after Clavijo's journey, Pero Tafur travelled extensively in Europe and the Mediterranean (1436-39), not as an ambassador, nor to preach the Christian faith, but for his own interest and enjoyment. The pleasure he took in strange sights and legends is vividly communicated by part of his *Andanças e viajes*, and he makes no attempt to match Clavijo's objectivity. He wrote long after his journey, and his imagination supplemented his observation at some points. Like Clavijo, he incorporates local legends, but usually with fewer safeguards. The *Victorial* (above, p. 153) devotes much space to Pero Niño's travels, and it too incorporates legends.

There can be no doubt of the attraction which such narratives had for Spaniards. The two most famous travel-books of medieval Europe were translated: an Aragonese version of Marco Polo's narrative of his journey to China was made for Juan Fernández de Heredia in the fourteenth century, and both Marco Polo and the curious and fanciful book attributed to Sir John Mandeville were translated into Castilian in the fifteenth. The impulse behind such works, and the demand for them from readers, continue into the period of the discovery and conquest of America.[38]

VII. ROMANCES

The Arthurian romances were read or listened to throughout western Europe in the closing centuries of the Middle Ages. They were translated, amplified, abridged, combined; they were given new emphasis, and they acquired characters and motifs that originally had nothing to do with the story of Arthur and his knights. The earliest Arthurian reference in Spanish comes at the end of the twelfth century, and by the fourteenth century poets are assuming their audiences' familiarity with the romances. The Iberian Peninsula was not one of the centres of innovation in the Arthurian romances, except for the creation of an artistically successful and widely influential neo-Arthurian work, *Amadis de Gaula* (see below, p. 159); as far as the Arthurian cycle itself was concerned, Iberian writers and audiences were content to accept the French romances with comparatively little change. The form in which the romances reached Spain was not the cycle known as the Vulgate, but a Post-Vulgate cycle (1230-40) at one time attributed to Robert de Boron, and now called the *Roman du Graal*.

The Post-Vulgate *Roman du Graal* follows the Vulgate closely in some parts, but changes it drastically in others. When the French original is lost, it is hard to know whether the differences between the Vulgate and the Hispanic texts were already present in the Post-

Vulgate cycle, or whether they represent Hispanic innovations, but it is clear that the Post-Vulgate cycle (and hence the Hispanic texts) drops the *Lancelot* branch of the Vulgate, thus removing the love of Lancelot and Guinevere from the centre of the action, and attributing the downfall of the Kingdom of Logres to mischance, which is associated with Arthur's unwitting sin of incest.

The original Hispanic version of the Post-Vulgate cycle (attributed in the manuscripts to Brother Juan Vivas) is lost, and its language is in dispute (Castilian, Portuguese, and Leonese all have their supporters). It gave rise to the extant texts and fragments in Castilian and Portuguese (the Catalan texts are, on the whole, independent), and was in three branches, dealing with the early history of the Grail (Spanish *Libro de Josep Abarimatía* and a Portuguese equivalent), Merlin (Spanish *Estoria de Merlín*; the *Baladro del sabio Merlín* printed at the end of the fifteenth century represents this branch with the addition of other material), and the Quest of the Grail and the death of Arthur (*La demanda del Sancto Grial*, printed at the beginning of the sixteenth century, which also has a Portuguese counterpart). A much earlier Spanish fragment of the *Demanda* is called *Lançarote* by the copyist, but does not derive from the French *Lancelot*, which is represented by a fragmentary *Lançarote de Lago*. Finally, there are two fourteenth-century *Tristán* fragments (one Castilian, the other Galician-Portuguese), and the *Tristán de Leonis* first printed in 1501, which represent one translation of the story of Tristram and Iseult, and an Aragonese *Cuento de Tristán de Leonis*, which represents another translation. Both branches seem to come from the same source, which may have been not a French but an Italian text. The 1501 edition is to some extent affected by the sentimental romance then in vogue (see below, pp. 162-6)—the concentration of the Tristram story on love made it especially susceptible to such influence—but the main features remain unaffected.

Manuscripts of the Spanish Tristram and Lancelot romances survive from the mid-fourteenth century, but are probably not the originals, and the romances may well date from the beginning of the century. The same is true of Juan Vivas's translation of the Post-Vulgate cycle: we know that a Portuguese manuscript (now lost) was copied in 1313. Thus the Hispanic Arthurian romances seem to belong to the very early fourteenth century, and may even be a little earlier.[39]

At the same time as the translation of the Arthurian romances, the first indigenous Spanish romance was composed. This is the *Libro del cavallero Zifar* (*c.* 1300), probably the work of Ferrán Martínez, a Toledo priest. The author tells us that he has translated the story from Chaldean (i.e. Arabic), and although the *Zifar* does not seem to be a translation of any Arabic work, it owes stylistic features and the names of many characters and places to Arabic, and the main plot resembles a story which may have been included in *The Thousand and One Nights*. The origin of the story concerned is far from clear, both because of the very confused textual tradition of *The Thousand and One Nights*, and because of the story's resemblance to the legend of Placidas, who became St Eustace, and to the late classical Greek romance (cf. the *Libro de Apolonio*—see above, pp. 68-9).

Zifar has to leave his native country through undeserved misfortune, and travel with his wife and sons. Further misfortunes separate the family, but in the end a combination of virtue, piety, and good sense brings them together again in great prosperity (Zifar becomes King of Mentón). Zifar addresses to his sons lengthy advice (*Castigos del rey de Mentón*) which is a reworking of the *Flores de filosofía* (see above, p. 99), and the younger son, Roboán, then sets out on adventures of his own, becoming an emperor in his turn. The *Libro del cavallero Zifar* includes diverse elements such as *exempla* and supernatural episodes but it possesses a tight and complex structural unity of the interwoven type (see above, p. 66). The *Castigos* sums up the lessons to be derived from Zifar's rise from poverty to wealth and power, and these lessons are then applied in the last book by Roboán. The entertainment function of the romance and the didactic function of wisdom and *exemplum* literatures are thus satisfyingly blended.

The stylistic debt of the *Zifar* to Arabic has already been mentioned, but it also owes much to the epic tradition. There are strong traces of formulaic language and of the physical phrases which abound in the epic; the author, in the absence of an established vernacular style for extended prose fiction, evidently turned to the narrative style of the epic for a model. It has long been known that the medieval prose romances derived much of their content from the epic, and the *Zifar* now presents clear evidence of a stylistic debt in addition.[40]

The *Gran conquista de Ultramar* was probably composed only a few years after the *Zifar*. It is a chronicle of the Crusades, but fictionalised: its main sources are not only a history (a French translation of William of Tyre), but also poems, such as the *Chanson d'Antioche* and the *Conquête de Jérusalem*. A dominant motive is the wish to associate the crusading hero Godfrey of Bouillon with his legendary ancestor, the Swan Knight, and to show the working-out of God's favour through several generations. The romance of the *Caballero del Cisne* is incorporated into the historical narrative, and links are established between the romance characters and their descendant Godfrey, who is presented as the central figure of the crusading enterprise.

The story of the Swan Knight (this also has a French source) is one of a number of widely-diffused tales of humans turned into animals, and also belongs in part to the group of stories about unjustly-accused queens and the rearing of their children in humble circumstances. Its folkloric implications are far-reaching, and it seems to have had a powerful appeal, since eminent families were anxious to establish their descent from the Swan Knight, and swans became an important heraldic device; hence, in the *Gran conquista*, the thematic association of virtue, God's favour, and success in battle with descent from the Swan Knight. However, the *Gran conquista* is not in the same category as the *Zifar*: its Spanish author has not imposed a thematically-relevant structural unity on diverse materials; the crusading cycle of French poems had already exploited the structural and thematic possibilities of Godfrey, his supposed ancestry, and his part in the Crusades, and the *Gran conquista* takes this over without adding significantly to the achievements of its source.[41]

The most famous of Spanish romances of chivalry, *Amadís de Gaula*, was printed in 1508, in a version reworked *c.* 1492 by Garci Rodríguez de Montalvo, but references to *Amadís* are found from the mid-fourteenth century onwards. A French original has been suggested, implausibly, and there have been claims for a first version in Portuguese, but this is an indigenous Spanish romance.

Amadís is the son of a secret marriage between a princess and a neighbouring king: his birth is concealed, since by the *ley de Escocia* sexual relations outside the bounds of canonical marriage were punishable by death. He is brought up in a strange land, wins fame as a knight, and also wins the love of the princess Oriana, who is the inspiration for his chivalresque deeds. Love is, here as elsewhere, the motivating force of the chivalresque romance.

The discovery of a manuscript fragment of *Amadís de Gaula*, copied about 1420 and containing the character of Esplandián, son of Amadís and Oriana, shows that Montalvo did not, as had been thought, expand the original, but compressed it in order to make room for his own Book IV. This discovery also tends to confirm María Rosa Lida de Malkiel's theory that the original version ended tragically, Esplandián killing his father whom he had failed to recognise, and Oriana committing suicide.

Amadís is in its essentials the Arthurian story transposed into a new setting: many of the names, the motifs, and the sequence of the episodes are so strongly reminiscent of the Arthurian romances that the whole *Amadís* story must be regarded as neo-Arthurian, though the Troy romances were also influential. It is by far the most original contribution that Spain made to the literature of Arthur, and its influence was correspondingly great.[42]

The siege and destruction of Troy was another of the stories that captured the imagination of medieval Europe, matching two of the deepest preoccupations of the age: courtly love, and the downfall of greatness. The love of Paris and Helen set the whole tragic train of events in motion, and another love-story, that of Troilus and Cressida, grew from an insignificant place in the original story to a dominant position in some medieval treatments of it.

Homer's version of the story was available to the Middle Ages in a poor Latin text, the *Ilias latina*, but this had little influence, and then only among the learned (it is used by the poet of the *Libro de Alexandre* and by Juan de Mena). More influential was the *Excidium Troiae*, and more influential still were two supposed eyewitness accounts which, although spurious, were widely accepted. These are the *Ephemerides belli Troiani*, allegedly the work of Dictys of Crete, a soldier in the Greek army, and *De excidio Troiae historia*, attributed to Dares the Phrygian, who was believed to have fought on the Trojan side. From Dares, with some elements taken from Dictys, comes the fundamental Troy-book of medieval Europe, the *Roman de Troie* of Benoît de Sainte-Maure (mid-twelfth century), and Benoît is the source of the *Historia destructionis Troiae* of Guido delle Colonne (thirteenth century). The account in Alfonso X's *General estoria* is a combination of Dares, Dictys, and Benoît, but the next two Spanish works derive from Benoît alone. These are a prose translation of the *Roman de Troie*, commissioned by Alfonso XI and done in 1350 (this was translated into Galician-Portuguese before 1373), and a prose version with inserted poems, now known as the *Historia troyana polimétrica*.

The *Historia troyana polimétrica* (possibly *c.* 1270, but perhaps as late as the fourteenth century) translates Benoît fairly closely in the prose passages, but the poems are so much amplified that they must be regarded as original compositions inspired by the most emotionally intense parts of the *Roman de Troie*. The prose sections are a workmanlike translation of Benoît, but the real literary merit of this book is in the poems, some of which are of outstanding quality in their ability to convey the emotions of the characters, and in their construction. Three features of the poems are of special interest: their metrical variety, their presentation of the fighting and of Trojan society in medieval terms (as with the *Libro de Alexandre*, this is a deliberate policy), and, as a part of medievalisation, the courtly love emphasis that is given to the relationship of Troilo and Breseyda.

This is far from exhausting the list of medieval Spanish Troy romances. In the fourteenth century, the influential *Sumas de historia troyana*, by Leomarte (we know nothing else about him), derives from Guido delle Colonne, the *General estoria*, and other sources, and there are versions of Guido in Castilian (the incomplete *Corónica troyana*), Aragonese, and Catalan; a complete Castilian version dates from the mid-fifteenth century. Late in the fifteenth century, there came not a romance but a translation of the *Iliad*, made by Pedro González de Mendoza from Pier Candido Decembrio's Latin.[43]

We have considered many romances in this chapter, and to these must be added the thirteenth-century *Alexandre*, *Apolonio*, and *Estoria de Tebas.* There are many more, and most of them have been largely neglected by scholars (cf. above, p. 78, n.27), even though they are the dominant fictional genre of the fourteenth and fifteenth centuries in Spain. All that space allows here is a brief mention of some of the works concerned, and some attempt to classify them.

Some of the romances are descended from French epic (the transformation of epic into romance is a familiar occurrence in French and English, but is less common in Spanish): the *Cuento del emperador Carlos Maynes* concentrates attention on an accused queen, the *Historia de Enrique fi de Oliva* may also have a French epic origin, and the *Cuento del enperador Otas* is based on a French epic which in turn is related to an oriental legend. A story similar to that of *Otas* was given a hagiographic emphasis by Gautier de Coincy but eventually became a Spanish romance, the *Fermoso cuento de una saneta enperatriz.* Another hagiographic legend, that of St Eustace, or Placidas, is particularly well represented among Spanish romances: not only is there *De un cavallero Plácidas,* but the French poem *Guillaume d'Angleterre* (sometimes attributed to Chrétien de Troyes, but probably not by him), is based on the St Eustace legend and gives rise to two Spanish texts, the *Chrónica del rey don Guillermo de Ynglaterra* and the *Estoria del rey Guillelme.*

The *Ystoria del noble Vespesiano enperador de Roma* has, as the title suggests, a basis in classical antiquity, and so, in another way, does the prose *Historia de Apolonio,* which, like the thirteenth-century verse romance, derives from the late classical romance in the Greek style; the *Historia,* however, does not come directly from *Historia Apollonii regis Tyri,* but is a translation of the version in an *exemplum*-collection, the *Gesta Romanorum.*

Flores y Blancaflor, París y Viana (of which there is a Morisco version), the *Libro del esforçado cavallero Partinuplés,* and the *Historia del muy valiente Clamades y de la linda Clarmonda* are stories of lovers, usually separated by fate and the malice of others but reunited (as in the Apollonius story). The folkloric content in these is strong, and there is usually an oriental element; these two features are also found in the *Crónica sarracina* (see above, p. 151).

Finally, the *Historia de la linda Melusina* is the story of a woman who, as a punishment, is turned into a serpent from the waist down once a week (in some versions, she becomes a mermaid). Nevertheless, she marries and for a long time succeeds in concealing her weekly transformation from her husband, but the story, as all such stories, ends unhappily because of the husband's discovery of the secret. There are two separate Spanish translations of this French romance, both of which were printed. Most of the romances mentioned above have a French origin, and they use their sources with varying degrees of independence. A number of others were printed early in the sixteenth century, and may well have been composed in the fifteenth, but enough has been said to indicate the extent of the available material.[44]

Sixteenth-century readers are known to have taken the chivalresque romances very seriously, but the romances of the fourteenth, and especially of the fifteenth, centuries seem to have exercised just as powerful an influence. The *Libro del passo honroso* is doubtless the most extreme case (see above, p. 152), but the knights-errant of the chivalresque romances had many other imitators in real life. Moreover, the vogue of the romances had important historical consequences. The Spanish and Portuguese explorers and conquerors were often inspired by, and formed their expectations on, the model of what they read in the romances, while the chroniclers of discovery and conquest wrote in similar terms. The emotional life of late medieval Spaniards was also profoundly affected. Chivalresque romances were, as we have just seen, not the only type, and a wide range of emotional experiences was available as models to those who read the works or heard them read aloud: love as the mainspring of vigorous external action, as in the Arthurian cycle and *Amadis*; lovers persecuted by fate but happily united, as in *Flores y Blancaflor* or, in the case of husband and wife, the different versions of the Apollonius and William of England stories; and a tragic love where fate or society is too strong for the lovers, as in *Melusina*, the episode of Troilus and Cressida in the Troy romances, or the story of Tristram. In the last group, exploration of the emotions very often takes precedence over the external action, and this process is carried further in the sentimental romances of the second half of the fifteenth century. These, more than any other, provided the standard by which upper-class Spaniards measured their emotional lives, and while we must not fall into the error of assuming that this literature reflected the reality of the times, there is no doubt that life to some extent copied literature, as it always does.

The sentimental romances are much shorter than the chivalresque works; they devote little space to external action but instead concentrate on emotional analysis; like other romances, they abstract their characters from the real world, and, even when real geographical names are used, they are merely conventional; the prevailing atmosphere is one of refined courtliness; and the ending is unhappy, being either a despairing frustration or consummation followed by disaster. The methods used for emotional analysis include the debate (*Grisel y Mirabella, Cárcel de Amor*), allegory (*Siervo libre de amor, Cárcel de Amor, Sátira de la felice e infelice vida*), and the exchange of letters (*Siervo libre de amor, Arnalte e Lucenda, Cárcel de Amor, Grimalte y Gradissa*).

The literary ancestry of the sentimental romances is complex. One important element is the chivalresque romance (there are obvious Arthurian elements in the external action of most of these works), but this is blended with the Italian tradition of sentimental fiction (especially the *Historia de duobus amantibus* of Aeneas Sylvius, and Boccaccio's *Fiammetta*—both of these were translated into Spanish in the late fifteenth century, and *Grimalte y Gradissa* is presented as a sequel to *Fiammetta*). Verse is almost as important as prose in the ancestry of the sentimental romances: the allegorical love-poems of France and Italy have a strong influence on the poets of fifteenth-century Spain, and the use of allegory in these romances is largely due to that influence; and the shorter love-poems of the fifteenth-century *cancioneros* are influential both in their mixture of religious and sexual emotion and in their melancholy tone. The earlier sentimental romances tend to have a high proportion of verse (*Triste deleytación, Arnalte e Lucenda*); in the later works, the poetic influences have been more thoroughly assimilated. These are the main influences, though there are others, including folklore: the concentration of strong sexual emotion within the extremely stylised and sophisticated conventions of late medieval courtly love was bound to produce conflict and tension, and for this reason, in a number of sentimental romances, the incongruous folkloric figures of the wild man and wild woman, embodiments of anti-social and violent self-assertion, become a central part of courtly love.[45]

The prototype of the sentimental romance is to be found in the *Siervo libre de amor* of Juan Rodríguez del Padrón (or de la Cámara), a minor Galician noble of the first half of the fifteenth century, who was a priest and ended his life as a Franciscan friar. His works, in both verse and prose, are concerned with love and nobility. He defended women against their detractors in the *Triunfo de las donas* (cf. above, pp. 142-3), wrote a treatise on nobility, the *Cadira de honor*, and translated Ovid's *Heroides* (whose subject is women in love) under the title *Bursario*. The *Siervo libre* is largely autobiographical (the accuracy of its references to events is confirmed by external evidence), and tells of the author's unhappy love-affair. In this work is set a short sentimental romance, the *Estoria de dos amadores*, in which the love of Ardanlier and Liessa ends in violent death (this is based on the story of Inês de Castro, who was mistress of a Portuguese prince and was murdered at the king's orders). Ardanlier and Liessa find happiness, even though it is finally destroyed, but their fulfilled love is contrasted with the unrequited love of Princess Yrena for Ardanlier; the countryside becomes an image for reciprocated, and the Court for unreciprocated, love. The external action occupies a very small proportion of the romance, the bulk of which is taken up with discussion and analysis of the emotions. The basic inspiration in the *Siervo libre de amor* comes from the chivalresque romances and *cancionero* verse; the influence of Italian fiction is not felt until the last quarter of the century. The same inspiration is found in the *Triste deleytaçión*, written in Castilian by a Catalan known only by his initials.[46]

The work of Dom Pedro (1429-66), constable of Portugal and for a short time king of Aragon, is difficult to classify, but one of his books comes close to being a sentimental romance. This is the *Sátira de la felice e infelice vida*, written, like virtually all of his work, in Castilian. It most closely resembles the *Siervo libre de amor*, being an allegorical treatment of Pedro's unhappy love-affair. The *Sátira* (medieval terminology may mislead—there is nothing satirical in the work) is dedicated to Pedro's sister, Queen Isabel of Portugal, and her death in 1455 was the occasion for another work, the *Tragedia de la insigne reina doña Isabel* which, like one of its sources, the *De consolatione philosophiae* of Boethius, alternates verse and prose.[47]

The two most important authors of sentimental romances are Diego de San Pedro and Juan de Flores, of whose lives very little is known. San Pedro wrote two sentimental romances, a parodic sermon on the rules of love, two important long poems and a number of short ones. One of the long poems, the *Desprecio de la Fortuna* (for the other, see below, pp. 196-7), is an apparently sincere palinode in which he rejects his own erotic writings (such a palinode is fairly frequent among medieval writers: for instance, Chaucer, Chrétien de Troyes, Andreas Capellanus, and Boccaccio). However, it seems that San Pedro was also sincere when he praised courtly love in his two sentimental romances (his attitude in the *Sermón* is markedly ambiguous).

The earlier of the romances is the *Tractado de amores de Arnalte e Lucenda*, in which San Pedro tells us he met Arnalte living in a wilderness (symbolic of frustration), and heard the unhappy lover's story. Arnalte's friend Elierso, who had been acting as go-between, had married the girl Arnalte loved; Arnalte killed him in a duel, and Lucenda retired to a convent. Arnalte's love for her is a willingly-accepted suffering, an attitude full of the conventions of courtly love at its most frustrated; he never has any real hope of possessing Lucenda.

In the *Cárcel de Amor*, both the structure and the situation are different. El Autor is a character in the romance, not merely the man to whom the story is told. He meets Leriano on his way to the allegorical prison of the title, which represents unresolved tension between hope and despair. El Autor, who soon becomes emotionally committed to the success of his mission, brings Leriano and the princess Laureola together. A jealous rival falsely accuses the lovers of unchastity, and the King condemns his daughter to death (*ley de Escocia*), despite Leriano's vindication of her in a judicial duel. Leriano, in a scene borrowed from the Lancelot and Guinevere section of the Arthurian cycle, rescues her, but triumph turns to disaster, for Laureola can never marry Leriano, lest she give substance to the accusation. The rejected lover commits suicide in a scene with overtones of the death of Christ:

El lloro que hazía su madre de Leriano crecía la pena a todos los que en ella participavan; y como él sienpre se acordase de Laureola, de lo que allí pasava tenía poca memoria. Y viendo que le quedava poco espacio para gozar de ver las dos cartas que della tenía, ... hizo traer una copa de agua, y hechas las cartas pedaços echólas en ella; y acabado esto, mandó que le sentasen en la cama, y sentado, bevióselas en el agua y assí quedó contenta su voluntad. Y llegada ya la ora de su fin, puestos en mí los ojos, dixo: 'Acabados son mis males', y assí quedó su muerte en testimonio de su fe. (p. 211)

El Autor is left desolate in a tragedy of which he has been a partial and unwitting cause; his emotional involvement is made explicit in a sequel by Nicolás Núñez, where he is visited by Leriano's ghost.

In the *Cárcel*, San Pedro integrates the narrator with the action, and sharpens the tragedy by making Laureola reciprocate Leriano's love, and by making honour conflict with love. He integrates allegory (of which elaborate colour-symbolism forms a part) with chivalresque action, and eliminates the verse sections which were a virtual irrelevance in *Arnalte e Lucenda*. The general outline of the two works is similar, but the *Cárcel* shows greater structural mastery and a concentration on essentials. *Arnalte* is a first attempt which was superseded, not only in merit but in public esteem. There is also a marked stylistic change: the prose of *Arnalte* is elaborately Latinate, making conspicuous use of stylistic adornment. In the *Cárcel*, the promises of brevity reflect a real determination to simplify and compress the style, as the result of new literary ideals upheld by the humanists.

Arnalte was first printed in 1491, and the *Cárcel* in the following year, but the structural and stylistic differences imply a gap longer than a year. It is likely that *Arnalte* was composed early (perhaps about 1480), circulated in manuscript, met with some success, and was printed, whereupon San Pedro was encouraged to write another romance, which was printed almost immediately and enjoyed a great vogue both in Spain and abroad.[48]

Juan de Flores also composed two romances, *Grisel y Mirabella* and *Grimalte y Gradissa*. Both were printed c. 1495, but the date of their composition remains unknown; we cannot therefore reach a conclusion on influences between Flores and San Pedro. *Grisel* is the story of a pair of lovers caught *in flagrante delicto*. In order to discover which lover is more guilty, the King, Mirabella's father, arranges a debate between Braçayda (i.e. Cressida of the Troy romances) and Torrellas, the poet who had written anti-feminist *Coplas*. Torrellas wins unfairly, thus bringing about the deaths of both lovers, but revenge is taken by the Queen and the ladies of the Court, who torture Torrellas to death in a scene of ritual murder which combines the elements of the Last Supper and of primitive cults:

Desnudo fue a un pilar bien atado, y allí cada una trahía nueva invención para le dar tormentos, y tales hovo que con tenazas ardiendo, y otras con unyas y dientes raviosamente le despedeçaron . . . y depués que fueron ansí cansadas de tormentarle, de grande reposo la Reyna y sus damas a çenar se fueron allí çerca dell porque las viesse . . . y después que fueron alçadas todas las mesas fueron juntas a dar amarga cena a Torrellas . . . y esto duró hasta quel día esclareció, y después que no dexaron ninguna carne en los huessos, fueron quemados, y de su seniza guardando cada qual una buxeta por reliquias de su enemigo, y algunas hovo que por cultre en el cuello la trahían . . . (pp. 369-70)

Flores pronounces firmly in favour of the ladies, and his condemnation of Torrellas's cynicism is clear. There is no doubt that he is interested in the debate, and in the discussion of human behaviour that the debate implies, but his commitment to the values of courtly love remains unaffected.

In *Grimalte y Gradissa* the influence of Italian fiction is greatly strengthened. *Grimalte* is a deliberate experiment with Italian fictional material: the main characters of Boccaccio's *Fiammetta* reappear here as Fiometa and Pánfilo, in a new situation brought about by Gradissa's determination to give the old story a happy ending. She gives her suitor Grimalte the task of reconciling the estranged couple, but (as with El Autor in the *Cárcel*) he achieves temporary success at the price of final disaster, since Fiometa, abandoned again, commits suicide.

Flores differs from San Pedro in that he assumes the naturalness of a consummated love, but the outcome is, as with San Pedro's unconsummated affairs, shown to be tragic. He differs also in that he regards it as natural for women to fall in love and to say so openly, but again he keeps within the courtly conventions, since women too could write courtly love-poetry, and their poems sometimes imply physical satisfaction. Anyone who fundamentally challenges the courtly ideal is discredited and condemned (Torrellas), or repents at the end (Pánfilo). If the endings of Flores's two romances had been lost, it would have been easy to see him as wishing to subvert the courtly ideal by humour and realistic cynicism, but the endings make his intention clear: he wants to test the courtly ideal in new situations, and to vindicate it by these tests.[49]

VIII. 'LA CELESTINA'

The term 'romances' has been consistently used in the foregoing discussion, because the works concerned are, although fiction in prose, not novels, and if we think of them as novels we shall judge them by irrelevant criteria. There is, however, one novel at the end of the Spanish Middle Ages: *La Celestina*.

La Celestina is a story of passionate love that ends in disaster. Calisto falls in love with Melibea, is rebuffed, and, on the advice of his corrupt servant Sempronio, enlists the help of Celestina, an aged go-between and witch. Her plans are strenuously opposed by the honest servant Pármeno, but Calisto will not listen to him. Celestina gains access to Melibea by witchcraft; and by her psychological skill (possibly by witchcraft also) she wins the girl over; soon Melibea will confess her love for Calisto. Meanwhile, Celestina breaks Pármeno's resistance: Calisto's ingratitude has weakened his resolve, and his subversion is completed by Celestina's skill and his own desire for her protégée, the whore Areusa. Calisto meets Melibea secretly, and almost immediately his servants quarrel with Celestina over the lavish reward that he has given her; they murder the old woman, are gravely injured in an attempt to escape, and are summarily executed. The next night, Calisto enters Melibea's garden (a *locus amoenus* which has become a setting for realistic action) and seduces her. In the original version of *La Celestina*, Calisto falls to his death on leaving the garden, Melibea is unable to live without him, confesses to her father, Pleberio, and commits suicide. The book ends with Pleberio's lament for the desolation that he must now face alone (he places no reliance on his wife Alisa):

Del mundo me quejo, porque en sí me crió, porque no me dando vida, no engendrara en él a Melibea; no nacida, no amara; no amando, cesara mi quejosa y desconsolada postrimería. ¡O mi compañera buena, y mi hija despedazada! ¿Por qué no quisiste que estorbase tu muerte? ¿Por qué no hobiste lástima de tu querida y amada madre? ¿Por qué te mostraste tan cruel con tu viejo padre? ¿Por qué me dejaste, cuando yo te había de dejar? ¿Por qué me dejaste penado? ¿Por qué me dejaste triste y solo in hac lachrymarum valle? (XXI, p. 236)

In the expanded version, Calisto returns home safely after the seduction, and the lovers' meetings continue for a month, but Areusa and Elicia (Sempronio's mistress and another of Celestina's protégées) plan revenge on the lovers, and as the result of a chain of events set in motion by their plan, Calisto falls to his death when trying to defend two more of his servants from a non-existent danger. Thereafter, the plot continues as before, with Melibea's suicide and Pleberio's lament.

The first extant edition (Burgos, 1499) is divided into sixteen acts, and is entitled *Comedia de Calisto y Melibea*. Not later than 1502 (no editions survive from this year), five new acts (the *Tratado de Centurio*) were added, with interpolations in most of the other acts; the title of the work was changed from *Comedia* to *Tragicomedia*. In the first edition there is no hint of the author's identity. In subsequent editions he is revealed, by various devices such as acrostics (a poem in which the initial letters of the lines spell out name and description), as Fernando de Rojas, a law student from Puebla de Montalbán, who says that the first act and the beginning of the second were the work of another author; that he found it, admired it, and decided to continue the story. Evidence of sources and language shows that Rojas certainly did not write Act I at the same time as the rest of the work, and probably did not write it at all; he did, on the other hand, write the five new acts and the other interpolations. The authorship of Act I and the beginning of Act II remains a mystery: Rojas's introductory matter suggests the fifteenth-century poets Juan de Mena and Rodrigo Cota. Of these two, Cota is the more likely, but a stronger possibility is that this was the unfinished work of a previous student at Rojas's university of Salamanca.[50]

Fernando de Rojas was a *converso*. He suffered some discrimination, and relatives were brought before the Inquisition, but Rojas built up a successful legal career and held office in his town of Talavera, dying in 1541 and being buried as a lay member of a religious order.[51]

The change of title from *Tragicomedia de Calisto y Melibea* to *La Celestina* was the decision not of Rojas but of the printers, whose chief concern was to increase sales. The change testifies to the hold that Celestina established on the imagination of readers. Her vitality, her vividness of speech, and her psychological power make her memorable, and the effect is increased by the tragedy that she brings on herself by turning Pármeno from a virtuous servant into a corrupt but resentful accomplice, and then (her usual perception dimmed by avarice) by making too obvious a display of her hold over others.

Celestina is the most vivid character, but nearly all are presented in depth and with great realism. This is not merely a surface realism, with colourful pictures of low life, but extends to psychological realism (the conversation between Celestina and Melibea in Act IV is the supreme example) and to realism of speech. This takes two forms: the presentation of popular speech in a way that carries conviction (cf. above, p. 143); and a remarkable innovation of Rojas's own, the changing of speech-levels according to the person being addressed. In previous works, however skilful, the characters had their appropriate levels of speech (plebeian, aristocratic, and so on), and they kept to them whatever the circumstances. Rojas shows us plebeian characters who take on protective coloration when they talk to their social superiors, and who therefore, for the first time in Spanish literature, talk in the flexible way that is found in real life:

¡En hora mala acá vine, si me falta mi conjuro! ¡Ea pues! Bien sé a quién digo. ¡Ce, hermano, que se va todo a perder! . . . Tu

temor, señora, tiene ocupada mi desculpa. Mi inocencia me da osadía,
tu presencia me turba en verla airada, y lo que más siento y me pena
es recibir enojo sin razón ninguna.   (IV, pp. 95-6)

La Celestina is a novel in dialogue. Any information that we are to
receive about the characters must therefore come through their own
words. This is a limitation, but the author of Act I overcomes it, and
Rojas turns it into a strength. We learn about the characters as we learn
about the people that we meet, by building up a picture from their
words, their memories of their past lives, other people's descriptions of
them, and their descriptions of others. In the provision of a solid
background for the characters and the action, the use of memory
plays a crucial part, and it can also be used to express the characters'
individuality.[52]

As with most medieval works, La Celestina draws on a variety of
sources, especially for the sententiae which occur so plentifully. Many
of these sources would have been known not at first hand but through
compendia, but some were certainly known directly to Rojas or his
predecessor: for instance, Aristotle, Boethius, and el Tostado in Act I,
and Petrarch, Mena, and San Pedro elsewhere. Rojas's legal training
seems also to have provided material. By far the most important source
for Rojas is the Latin works of Petrarch: not only does he obtain
numerous exempla and sententiae from these works, but his outlook is
profoundly influenced by Petrarch's in his demonstration of the im-
permanence of earthly happiness and of the destructive effects of the
passions. Rojas's pessimism, however, goes deeper than Petrarch's,
and in Pleberio's final speech the consolations of Petrarchan Stoicism
are rejected, while those of Christianity are not even considered.

The main structural source of La Celestina is the humanistic comedy,
which arose in Italy in the fourteenth century, and reached its peak
in the fifteenth. It is an imitation (in Latin) of the Classical Latin
comedy; its plots treat of low life, or a seduction, or both. La Celestina
is an attempt to write a humanistic comedy in Spanish, but it grew in
the writing to a point where its length and its complexity ruled out
any possibility of a stage performance. (It has been staged in recent
years but in an adapted form, like any other novel that is presented on
the stage.) In the poem at the end, where Alonso de Proaza (who saw
one edition through the press) gives advice, he clearly envisages the
reading of the text aloud to a group. We can be sure that neither Rojas
nor his predecessor thought of the book as a novel; the term had not
been introduced. This, however, does not matter. Medieval literary
terminology is imprecise and inconsistent, and we must take our own
decisions on the categories to which medieval works belong. La Celestina
has the qualities that we look for in a modern novel: complexity, the

solidity of an imagined but real world, psychological penetration, a convincing interaction between plot, theme, and characters.

The humanistic comedy provided the starting-point for *La Celestina*, but humanistic comedies do not have tragic endings. They end either cheerfully, or, if the girl is abandoned by her lover, cynically. The tragic ending of *La Celestina*, the disaster which follows consummation, are characteristics of the sentimental romance, which was at the height of its popularity when Rojas was writing. The dominant influences are, then, in different ways, Petrarch, the humanistic comedy, and the sentimental romance.[53]

The purpose of *La Celestina* has been much disputed. It is not, as has been claimed, a protest against the treatment of the *conversos*, nor a warning to young nobles to choose their servants more carefully. It is not, on the other hand, an exaltation of romantic love. We cannot know what the first author's intentions were, but it seems clear that Rojas wished to show the destructive effects of the passions (love of power, avarice, and a desire for security, as well as the obvious sexual passion). It is likely that he wished to discredit courtly love, since his parody of the courtly lover in Calisto is by no means entirely sympathetic. To sum up, Rojas was a pessimistic moralist, who saw results following inexorably from their causes in human nature (the strict causality of the plot is often underestimated).[54]

The realism of *La Celestina*, its humour (present despite the pessimism), its vitality, and its style—and also, perhaps, its uncompromising view of life—made it an immediate success. Spanish editions multiplied, translations appeared, sequels were written, and the book's influence was prolonged and powerful. That is part of the story of Golden Age literature; what is relevant to the literary history of medieval Spain is that, although the romances were in full vigour and would long continue, Spanish fiction here evolved its first novel.[55]

NOTES

1. V. H. Galbraith, 'The Literacy of the Medieval English Kings', *PBA*, XXI (1935), 201-38; J. W. Thompson, *The Literacy of the Laity in the Middle Ages* (Berkeley, 1939); Carlo M. Cipolla, *Literacy and Development in the West* (Harmondsworth, Penguin, 1969), pp. 42-6; Charles Singer *et al.*, *A History of Technology*, II (Oxford, 1956), 187-90 and 771; Charles Singer and E. Ashworth Underwood, *A Short History of Medicine* (2nd ed., Oxford, 1962), p. 641.

2. *Obras de San Pedro Pascual*, ed Pedro Armengol Valenzuela (4 vols., Roma, 1905-08). R. Menéndez Pidal, 'Sobre la bibliografía de San P.P.', *BH*, IV (1902), 297-304.

3. A. H. Krappe, 'Le Faucon de l'Infant dans *El Conde Lucanor*', *BH*, XXXV (1933), 294-7; Menéndez Pidal, 'Nota sobre una fábula de don Juan Manuel y de Juan Ruiz', *Poesía árabe*, pp. 150-57; Lida de Malkiel, 'Tres

THE RISE OF FICTION, 1300-1500 171

notas sobre don J.M.', *RPh*, IV (1950-51), 155-94 (repr. in *Estudios*, pp. 92-133), and *La idea de la fama*, pp. 207-20; M. Ruffini, 'Les sources de don J.M.', *LR*, VII (1953), 27-49; Ernesto Lunardi, *El CL di don J.M.* (Lugano, 1955); Diego Marín, 'El elemento oriental en don J.M.: síntesis y revaluación', *CL*, VII (1955), 1-14; Fernando de la Granja, 'Origen árabe de un famoso cuento español', *Al-An*, XXIV (1959), 319-32; Kenneth R. Scholberg, 'A Half-Friend and a Friend and a Half', *BHS*, XXXV (1958), 187-98, and 'Sobre el estilo del *CL*', *KFLQ*, X (1963), 198-203; Alberto Vàrvaro, 'La cornice del *CL*', *Studi di Letteratura Spagnola*, ed. Carmelo Samonà (Roma, 1964), pp. 187-95; Enrique de Rivas, 'Huellas del simbolismo', *Figuras y estrellas*, pp. 73-89; Harlan Sturm, 'The *CL*: the first *ejemplo*', *MLN*, LXXXIV (1969), 286-92; Ian Macpherson, ' "Dios y el mundo"—the didacticism of *El CL*', *RPh*, XXIV (1970-71), 26-38.
4. For editions, see Bibliography; see also *Crónica abreviada*, ed. R. L. and M. B. Grismer (Minneapolis, 1958); *Libro de la caza*, ed. J. M. Castro y Calvo (Barcelona, 1945). J. M. Castro y Calvo, *El arte de gobernar en las obras de don J.M.* (Barcelona, 1945); Félix Huerta Tejadas, 'Vocabulario de las obras de don J.M.', 1282-1348', *BRAE*, XXXIV (1954)-XXXVI (1956); Delia L. Ísola, 'Las instituciones en la obra de don J.M.', *CHE*, XXI-XXII (1954), 70-145; Scholberg, 'Modestia y orgullo: una nota sobre don J.M.', *HBalt*, XLII (1959), 24-31, and 'J.M., personaje y autocrítico', *HBalt*, XLIV (1961), 457-60; Luciana de Stefano, 'La sociedad estamental en las obras de don J.M.', *NRFH*, XVI (1962), 329-54; Daniel Devoto, 'Cuatro notas sobre la materia tradicional en don J.M.', *BH*, LXVIII (1966), 187-215; J. A. Maravall, 'La sociedad estamental castellana y la obra de don J.M.', *Estudios de historia del pensamiento* (Madrid, 1967), pp. 451-72; Ramón Esquer Torres, 'Dos rasgos estilísticos en don J.M.', *RFE*, XLVII (1964), 429-35; Giuseppe di Stefano, 'Don J.M. nel suo *Libro de la caza*', *Studi di Lingua e Letteratura Spagnola*, ed. G. M. Bertini (Torino, 1965), pp. 379-90. Ian Macpherson, '*Amor* and Don J.M.', *HR* (in press).
5. M. Serrano y Sanz, *Vida y escritos de D. Juan Fernández de Heredia, Gran Maestre de la Orden de San Juan de Jerusalén* (Zaragoza, 1913); José Vives, 'J.F. de H., gran maestre de Rodas. Vida, obras, formas dialectales', *Analecta Sacra Tarraconensia*, III (1927), 121-92.
6. Mário Martins, *Estudos de literatura medieval* (Braga, 1956), pp. 81-92.
7. Amador de los Ríos, *Historia*, IV (1863), 331-9; Martins, *Estudos*, pp. 60-73.
8. The text is in BAE, LI.
9. ed. Derek W. Lomax, *Miscelánea de fuentes medievales*, I (in press).
10. Raúl A. del Piero and Philip O. Gericke, 'El *Vençimjento del mundo*, tratado ascético del siglo XV: edición', *HispI*, 21 (1964), 1-29; del Piero, 'El *VM*. Autor, fecha, estructura', *NRFH*, XV (1961), 377-92.
11. Eleanor S. O'Kane, *Refranes y frases proverbiales españolas de la Edad Media* (BRAE anejo II, Madrid, 1959).
12. Arnald Steiger, 'Contribución al estudio del vocabulario del *Corbacho*', *BRAE*, IX-X (1922-23); A. F. G. Bell, 'The Archpriest of Talavera', *BSS*, V (1928), 60-7; Anna Krause, 'Further Remarks on the *AP* of *T*', *BSS*, VI (1929), 57-60; D. P. Rotunda, 'The *Corvacho* Version of the Husband-locked-out Story', *RR*, XXVI (1935), 121-7; R. A. del Piero, 'El *Arcipreste de Talavera* y Juan de Ausim', *BH*, LXII (1960), 125-35; Erich von Richthofen, 'El *Corbacho*: las interpolaciones y la deuda de la *Celestina*', *Homenaje Moñino*, II, 115-20. On Martínez's other works, see José Madoz, *San Ildefonso de Toledo a través de la pluma del Arcipreste de T*. (Biblioteca de Antiguos Autores Cristianos Españoles II, Madrid, 1943), and *Vidas de San*

Ildefonso y San Isidoro, ed. Madoz (Madrid, CC, 1952); R. A. del Piero, 'La *Corónica de Muhamad* del AP de T.', *NRFH*, XIV (1960), 21-50, and 'La tradición textual de la *Atalaya de las corónicas* del AP de T.', *PMLA*, LXXXI (1966), 12-22; Madeleine Pardo, 'Remarques sur l'*Atalaya*, de l'archiprêtre de T.', *R*, LXXXVIII (1967), 350-98.

13. Jacob Ornstein, 'La misoginia y el profeminismo en la literatura castellana', *RFH*, III (1941), 219-32; Whitbourn, *The Arcipreste de Talavera*, Ch. 1. *Repetición de amores*, ed. Jacob Ornstein (UNCSRLL 23, Chapel Hill, 1954); Barbara Matulka, 'An Anti-Feminist Treatise of Fifteenth-Century Spain: Lucena's *Repetición de amores*', *RR*, XXII (1931), 99-116; Margherita Morreale, 'La *RA* di L. de L.: alcuni aspetti della prosa spagnola del Quattrocento', *QIA*, III (1956), 177-81. For Torrellas, see Matulka, *The Novels of Juan de Flores. Defensa de las virtuosas mugeres* is in BAE, CXVI; César Real de la Riva, 'Un mentor del siglo XV; Diego de Valera y sus epístolas', *RLit*, XX (1961), 271-305; Luna's treatise is ed. Marcelino Menéndez y Pelayo (SBE, XXVIII, Madrid, 1891); César Silió, *Don Álvaro de Luna* (Madrid, Austral, 1940). Teresa de Cartagena, a *conversa* nun, asserts in *Admiraçión operum Dey* that women are entitled to write about religion (*Arboleda de los enfermos. Admiraçión...*, ed. J. L. Hutton, *BRAE* anejo XVI, Madrid, 1967).

14. El Tostado's *Catorce questiones* is in BAE, LXV.

15. James F. Burke, 'More on the Title *El libro de los gatos*', *RoN*, IX (1967-68), 148-51, sums up the controversy.

16. *El espéculo de los legos*, ed. J. M. Mohedano Hernández (Madrid, 1951); see, however, the review by P. E. Russell, *MLR*, XLIX (1954), 94.

17. A. H. Krappe, 'Les sources du *Libro de exemplos*', *BH*, XXXIX (1937), 5-54, and 'Shepherd and King in *LE*', *HR*, XIV (1946), 59-64. See also H. G. Pfander, 'The Mediaeval Friars and some Alphabetical Reference-Books for Sermons', *MAe*, III (1934), 19-29.

18. *Fabulas de Esopo* (facsimile), ed. E. Cotarelo y Mori (Madrid, 1929); John E. Keller and J. H. Johnson, 'Motif-Index Classification of Fables and Tales of *Ysopete ystoriado*', *Southern Folklore Quarterly*, XVIII (1954), 85-117; Spurgeon W. Baldwin, 'The Role of the Moral in *La vida del Ysopet con sus fabulas historiadas*', *HBalt*, XLVII (1964), 762-5.

19. Most of these works are included in BAE, CXVI and CLXXI.

20. J. P. Wickersham Crawford, 'The Seven Liberal Arts in the *Visión delectable* of Alfonso de la Torre', *RR*, IV (1913), 58-75, and 'The *VD* of A. de la T. and Maimonides's *Guide of the Perplexed*', *PMLA*, XXVIII (1913), 188-212; Curtius, *European Literature*, pp. 542-3.

21. Raúl A. del Piero, 'Sobre el autor y fecha del *Invencionario*', *HR*, XXX (1962), 12-20.

22. Margherita Morreale, 'El tratado de Juan de Lucena sobre la felicidad', *NRFH*, IX (1955), 1-21; Rafael Lapesa, 'Sobre J. de L.: escritos suyos mal conocidos o inéditos', *De la Edad Media*, pp. 123-44; Ángel Alcalá, 'J. de L. y el pre-erasmismo español', *RHM*, XXXIV (1968), 108-31. The mordant satire of the *Libro de vita beata* links it to the satirical *Coplas* of the period, but it lacks their frequent scurrility (cf. below, p. 195).

23. James E. Harting, *Bibliotheca Accipitraria. A catalogue of books ancient and modern relating to falconry* (London, 1891), pp. 111-35; Marcelle Thiébaux, 'The Mediaeval Chase', *Sp*, XLII (1967), 260-74; Duque de Almazán, *Historia de la montería en España* (Madrid, 1934). *Libro de la montería*, ed. J. Gutiérrez de la Vega (2 vols., Madrid, 1877); Hakan Tjerneld, 'Una fuente desconocida del *LM* del Rey Alfonso el sabio', *SN*, XXII (1949-50), 171-93. *Tratado de las enfermedades de las aves de caza*, ed. Bertil Maler

(Stockholm, 1957). *Traducción española de Dancus Rex y Guillelmus Falconarius*, ed. Gunnar Tilander (Cynegetica XIV, Karlshamm, 1966). Ayala, *Libro de la caza de las aves*, ed. J. Gutiérrez de la Vega, in *Libros de cetrería de el Príncipe y el Canciller* (Madrid, 1879); ed. José Fradejas Lebrero (Valencia, Odres Nuevos, 1959); Giuseppe di Stefano, 'Il *Libro de la caza* di Pero López de Ayala e il *Livro de falcoaria* di Pero Menino', *Miscellanea di Studi Ispanici* (Pisa, 1962), 7-32, and 'Una nota su moralismo e didattica nel *LC* di P. L. de A.', *AION, Sez. Rom.*, VII (1965), 229-35.

24. Edwin J. Webber, 'A Spanish Linguistic Treatise of the Fifteenth Century', *RPh*, XVI (1962-63), 32-40. On science and medicine in this period, see Guy Beaujouan, *La Science en Espagne au XIVe et XVe siècles* (Paris, 1967); J. D. Latham, 'Isaac Israeli's *Kitāb al-ḥummayāt* and the Latin and Castilian Texts', *JSS*, XIV (1969), 80-95 (this work, translated as *Tratado de las fiebres*, shows that translation from Arabic continued during the fifteenth century).

25. E. P. Goldschmidt, *Medieval Texts and their First Appearance in Print* (London and Oxford, 1943); F. J. Norton, *Printing in Spain 1501-1520* (Cambridge, 1966).

26. Andrés Soria, *Los humanistas de la corte de Alfonso el Magnánimo* (Granada, 1956).

27. Nicholas G. Round, 'Renaissance Culture and its Opponents in Fifteenth-Century Castile', *MLR*, LVII (1962), 204-15, and 'Five Magicians, or the Uses of Literacy', *MLR*, LXIV (1969), 793-805; P. E. Russell, 'Arms versus Letters: towards a definition of Spanish fifteenth-century humanism', *Aspects of the Renaissance: a symposium*, ed. A. R. Lewis (Austin and London, 1967), pp. 47-58. For a different view of the cultural situation, see Lida de Malkiel, *Juan de Mena, poeta del prerrenacimiento español* (México, 1950), pp. 9-11, and *La idea de la fama*, pp. 231-2.

28. *Arte de trovar*, ed. F. J. Sánchez Cantón (Madrid, 1923); *Lepra, Consolación*, and *Aojamiento*, ed. J. Soler [R. Foulché-Delbosc], 'Tres tratados', *RH*, XLI (1917), 110-214; *Arte cisoria*, ed. Federico Sainz de Robles (Madrid, 1967); *Guerra*, ed. Lucas de Torre, *RH*, XXXVIII (1916), 497-531; *Astrología*, ed. Francisco Vera, *Erudición Ibero Ultramarina*, I (1930), 18-67. Emilio Cotarelo y Mori, 'Una obra desconocida de don Enrique de Villena', *RH*, II (1895), 97-101; Mario Schiff, 'La première traduction espagnole de la *Divine Comédie,' Homenaje a Menéndez y Pelayo* (Madrid, 1899), I, 269-307; J. M. Millás Vallicrosa, 'El *Libro de astrología*, de don E. de V.', *RFE*, XXVII (1943), 1-29; Doris K. Arjona, 'E. de V. and the *Arte cisoria*', *HBalt*, XLIII (1960), 209-13; Leonie F. Sachs, 'E. de V.: portrait of the magician as outsider', *SP*, LXIV (1967), 109-31.

29. W. J. Entwistle, 'The *Romancero del rey don Pedro* in Ayala and the *Cuarta crónica general*', *MLR*, XXV (1930), 306-26; Claudio Sánchez-Albornoz, 'El canciller Ayala, historiador', *HumT*, 2 (1953), 13-46; R. B. Tate, 'L. de A., Humanist Historian?', *HR*, XXV (1957), 157-74 (repr. in *Ensayos*, pp. 33-54); P. E. Russell, *The English Intervention in Spain and Portugal in the Time of Edward III and Richard II* (Oxford, 1955), pp. 18-19, and 'The *Memorias* of Fernán Álvarez de Albornoz, Archbishop of Seville, 1371-80', *Llubera Studies*, pp. 319-30.

30. Diego Catalán, 'La *Estoria de los reyes del señorío de África* del maestro Gilberto o Sujulberto. Una obra del siglo XIII perdida', *RPh*, XVII (1963-64), 346-53.

31. Lida de Malkiel, *La idea de la fama*, pp. 240-51; Henry N. Bershas, 'The Composition of the *Crónica de don Álvaro de Luna*', *Papers of the Michigan Academy of Science, Art and Letters*, XXXVIII (1953), 445-50;

7 * *

174 THE MIDDLE AGES

Giuseppina Ledda, 'L'ideale cavalleresco nella *Crónica de don Álvaro*', *Studi Ispanici*, I (1962), 93-8.
32. *Las bienandanzas e fortunas*, ed. Ángel Rodríguez Herrero (4 vols. Bilbao, 1967).
33. Ed. Martín de Riquer (Madrid, 1970); facsimile, ed. F. Arroyo Ilera (Textos Med. 38, Valencia, 1970). P. G. Evans, 'A Spanish Knight in Flesh and Blood. A study of the chivalric spirit of Suero de Quiñones', *HBalt*, XV (1932), 141-52; Riquer, *Caballeros andantes*, pp. 52-99.
34. Works by Cartagena and Sánchez de Arévalo are included in BAE, CXVI. *Libro de la consolación de España*, ed. Julio Rodríguez-Puértolas, *Misc. de fuentes medievales*, I (in press). Nicholas G. Round, 'Politics, Style and Group Attitudes in the *Instrucción del Relator*', *BHS*, XLVI (1969), 289-319.
35. Derek W. Lomax, 'A mais antiga biografia de El-Rei D. Afonso III de Portugal', *Ocid*, LXXI (1966), 71-5. Madeleine Pardo, 'Un épisode du *Victorial*: biographie et élaboration romanesque', *R*, LXXXV (1964), 259-92; Lida de Malkiel, *Idea de la fama*, pp. 232-40; Marichal, *Voluntad de estilo*, pp. 53-76; Maria T. Ferrer i Mallol, 'Els corsaris castellans i la campanya de Pero Niño al Mediterrani (1404). Documents sobre *El Victorial*', *AEM*, V (1968), 265-99.
36. ed. Juan de Mata Carriazo (Colección de Crónicas Españolas 3, Madrid, 1940). Charles V. Aubrun, 'La *Chronique de M. L. de I.*', *BH*, XLIV (1942), 81-95; Lida de Malkiel, *Idea de la fama*, pp. 253-7; Inoria Pepe, 'Sulla datazione e la paternità degli *Hechos del Condestable D. M. L. de I.*', *Miscellanea di Studi Ispanici* (Pisa, 1962), 195-215.
37. J. L. Romero, 'Fernán Pérez de Guzmán y su actitud histórica', *CHE*, III (1945), 117-51; Francisco López Estrada, 'La retórica en las *Generaciones y semblanzas* de F. P. de G.', *RFE*, XXX (1946), 310-52; Carlos Clavería, 'Notas sobre la caracterización de la personalidad en las *GS*', *Anales de la Universidad de Murcia*, X (1951-52), 481-526; Lida de Malkiel, *Idea de la fama*, pp. 269-76. Pulgar's *Letras*, ed. J. Domínguez Bordona (Madrid, CC, 1929). For fifteenth-century biographical techniques, see J. L. Romero, 'Sobre la biografía española del s. XV y los ideales de la vida', *CHE*, I-II (1944), 115-38. For Leonor López de Córdoba, see Russell, *Intervention*, pp. 163-4, 550.
38. *Libro del conosçimiento*, ed. Marcos Jiménez de la Espada (Madrid, 1877). Francisco López Estrada, 'Sobre el manuscrito de la *Embajada a Tamorlán* del British Museum', *AFA*, VIII-IX (1956-57), 121-6; J. García Lora, 'Dos enfoques sobre el gran Tamorlán de Persia: Marlowe y Clavijo', *PSA*, XII (1959), 52-72. R. Ramírez de Arellano, 'Estudios biográficos: Pero Tafur', *BRAH*, XLI (1902), 273-93; A. Vasiliev, 'P.T., a Spanish Traveler of the XVth Century and his Visit to Constantinople, Trebizond, and Italy', *Byzantion*, VII (1932), 75-122, and 'A Note on P.T.', ibid., X (1935), 65-6; José Vives, '*Andanças e viajes* de un hidalgo español, 1436-1439, con una descripción de Roma', *GAKS*, VII (1938), 127-206. Tafur's book was either written or retouched after 1453; the *Libro del Infante don Pedro de Portugal*, which purports to be an account of a voyage in the 1420s, seems to be a sixteenth-century work. *El libro de Marco Polo* [Aragonese], ed H. Knust and R. Stuebe (Leipzig, 1902); *Libro de las cosas maravillosas de Marco Polo* [Castilian], ed. Rafael Benítez Claros (SBE, n. s., XX, Madrid, 1947). W. J. Entwistle, 'The Spanish Mandevilles', *MLR*, XVII (1922), 251-7. See also Wright, *The Geographical Lore*; *Travel and Travellers of the Middle Ages*, ed. Arthur P. Newton (London and New York, 1926); John Hale, 'A World Elsewhere: geographical horizons and mental horizons', *The Age of the Renaissance*, Ch. 11.

39. Roger S. Loomis, *The Development of Arthurian Romance* (London, 1963); Lida de Malkiel, 'Arthurian Literature in Spain and Portugal', *Arthurian Literature in the Middle Ages: a collaborative history*, ed. Roger S. Loomis (Oxford, 1959), Ch. 31; Fanni Bogdanow, *The Romance of the Grail* (Manchester and New York, 1966); M. Rodrigues Lapa, *Lições*, Ch. 6. *Baladro* and *Demanda*, ed. Bonilla, *Libros de caballerías*, I; fragments ed. Bonilla, *Anales de la literatura española* (Madrid, 1904), pp. 25-8, and *Las leyendas de Wagner en la lit. esp.* (Madrid, 1913), pp. 73-107. P. Bohigas Balaguer, 'El *Lanzarote* español del manuscrito 9611 de la Biblioteca Nacional', *RFE*, XI (1924), 282-97, and 'Más sobre el *Lanzarote* español', *RFE*, XII (1925), 60-2; Pamela Waley, 'Juan de Flores y *Tristán de Leonís*', *HispI*, 12 (1961), 1-14; Daymond Turner, 'Tristan the Hungry', *RoN*, VIII (1966-67), 128-32.

40. Charles P. Wagner, 'The Sources of *El caballero Cifar*', *RH*, X (1903), 5-104; and 'The *Caballero Zifar* and the *Moralium dogma philosophorum*', *RPh*, VI (1952-53), 309-12; A. H. Krappe, 'La leggenda di S. Eustachio', *Nuovi Studi Medievali*, III (1926-27), 223-58, 'Le mirage celtique et les sources du *CC*', *BH*, XXXIII (1931), 97-103, and 'Le lac enchanté dans le *CC*', *BH*, XXXV (1933), 107-25; Jules Piccus, 'Consejos y consejeros en el *Libro del CZ*', *NRFH*, XVI (1962), 16-30, and 'Refranes y frases proverbiales en el *LCZ*', *NRFH*, XVIII (1965-66), 1-24; Roger M. Walker, 'The Unity of *El LCZ*', *BHS*, XLII (1965), 149-59, and 'The Genesis of *El LCZ*', *MLR*, LXII (1967), 61-9; Kenneth R. Scholberg, 'La comicidad del *CC*', *Homenaje Moñino*, II, 157-63; James F. Burke, 'Names and the Significance of Etymology in the *LCC*', *RR*, LIX (1968), 161-73, 'Symbolic Allegory in the Portus Salutaris Episode in the *LCC*', *KRQ*, XV (1968), 69-84, and 'The Meaning of the Islas Dotadas Episode in the *LCC*', *HR*, XXXVIII (1970), 56-68. I draw also on Walker's forthcoming book.

41. Gaston Paris, *R*, XVII (1888), 513-41, XIX (1890), 314-40 and 562-91, XXII (1893), 345-63; George T. Northup, '*La gran conquista de Ultramar* and its Problems', *HR*, II (1934), 287-302; Agapito Rey, 'Las leyendas del ciclo carolingio en la *GCU*', *RPh*, III (1949-50), 172-81; Suzanne Duparc-Quioc, *Le Cycle de la Croisade* (Paris, 1955), Ch. 6; J. Gómez Pérez, 'Las leyendas del ciclo carolingio en España', *RLit*, XXVIII (1965), 5-18. Cf. Margaret Schlauch, *Chaucer's Constance and Accused Queens*; John Cherry, 'The Dunstable Swan-Jewel', *Journal of the Archaeological Association*, 3rd ser., XXXII (1969), 38-53; Jeanne Lods, 'Encore la légende des enfants-cygnes', *Mélanges Lejeune*, II, 1227-44; Runciman, *Hist. of Crusades*, I. I draw also on an unpublished study by Janet Bickle.

42. G. S. Williams, 'The *Amadis* Question', *RH*, XXI (1909), 1-167; Lida de Malkiel, 'El desenlace del *A* primitivo', *RPh*, VI (1952-53), 283-9 (repr. in *Estudios*, pp. 149-56); Antonio Rodríguez-Moñino, *et al.*, 'El primer manuscrito del *A. de G.*', *BRAE*, XXXVI (1956), 199-225.

43. A. G. Solalinde, 'Las versiones españolas del *Roman de Troie*', *RFE*, III (1916), 121-65; Leomarte, *Sumas de historia troyana*, ed. Agapito Rey (*RFE* anejo XV, Madrid, 1932); *La coronica troyana*, ed. Frank P. Norris (UNCSRLL 90, Chapel Hill, 1970). See also Margaret R. Scherer, *The Legends of Troy in Art and Literature* (New York and London, 1963).

44. Pedro Bohigas Balaguer, 'Orígenes de los libros de caballería', *Historia general de las literaturas hispánicas*, ed. G. Díaz-Plaja, I (Barcelona, 1949), 521-41; and 'La novela caballeresca, sentimental y de aventuras', *ibid.*, II (1951), 189-212. *Otas*, ed. Amador de los Ríos, *Hist. crít. de la lit. esp.*, V (Madrid, 1864), 391-468; *Enrique*, ed. Pascual de Gayangos (SBE 8, Madrid, 1871); *Plácidas*, *Chrónica del rey don Guillermo*, and *Estoria del rey Guillelme*, ed. Hermann Knust, *Dos obras didácticas y dos leyendas* (SBE 17, Madrid,

176 THE MIDDLE AGES

1878); *Vespesiano*, ed. R. Foulché-Delbosc, *RH*, XXI (1909), 567-634; *Historia de Apolonio*, ed. Serís, *Nuevo ensayo*, I, 1, 80-115; *Flores y Blanca-flor*, ed. Adolfo Bonilla y San Martín (Madrid, 1916); *París y Viana* (Morisco), ed Âlvaro Galmés de Fuentes (Madrid, 1970); *Carlos Maynes*, *Partinuplés* and *Clamades*, ed. Bonilla, *Libros de caballerías*. See Helaine Newstead, 'The Traditional Background of *Partonopeus de Blois*', *PMLA*, LXI (1946), 916-46; Howard S. Robertson, 'Four Romance Versions of the William of England Legend', *RoN*, III (1961-62), 2, 75-80; Diego Catalán, *Por campos del romancero* (Madrid, 1970), pp. 77-117; Krappe, 'S. Eustachio'; and Schlauch, *Chaucer's Constance*.

45. Carmelo Samonà, *Studi sul romanzo sentimentale e cortese nella letteratura spagnola del Quattrocento*, I (Roma, 1960); J. L. Varela, 'Revisión de la novela sentimental', *RFE*, XLVIII (1965), 351-82; H. T. Oostendorp, *El conflicto entre el honor y el amor en la literatura española hasta el siglo XVII* (Publicaciones del Instituto de Estudios Hispánicos... de Utrecht 4, La Haya, 1962), Ch. 3; Pamela Waley, 'Love and Honour in the *Novelas sentimentales* of Diego de San Pedro and Juan de Flores', *BHS*, XLIII (1966), 253-75; Charles E. Kany, *The Beginnings of the Epistolary Novel in France, Italy and Spain* (UCPMP, XXI, 1, Berkeley, 1937); Deyermond, 'El hombre salvaje en la novela sentimental', *Fi*, X (1964), 97-111; Richard Bernheimer, *Wild Men in the Middle Ages: a study in art, sentiment and demonology* (Cambridge, Mass., 1952).

46. Carlos Martínez-Barbeito, *Macías el enamorado y Juan Rodríguez del Padrón. Estudio y antología* (Santiago de Compostela, 1951); Lida de Malkiel, 'JRP: vida y obras', *NRFH*, VI (1952), 313-51, 'JRP: influencia', *NRFH*, VIII (1954), 1-38, and 'JRP: adiciones', *NRFH*, XIV (1960), 318-21; Edward Dudley, 'Court and Country: the fusion of two images of love in JR's *El siervo libre de amor*', *PMLA*, LXXXII (1967), 117-20; M. Nozick, 'The Inez de Castro Theme in European Literature', *CL*, III (1951), 330-41. Riquer, '*Triste deleytación*, novela castellana del siglo XV', *RFE*, XL (1956), 33-65.

47. *Sátira*, ed. A. Paz y Melia, *Opúsculos literarios de los siglos XIV a XVI* (SBE 29, Madrid, 1892); *Tragedia*, ed. Carolina Michaëlis de Vasconcellos (2nd ed., Coimbra, 1922). Andrés Balaguer y Merino, *Don Pedro, el condestable de Portugal, considerado como escritor, erudito y anticuario. Estudio histórico-bibliográfico* (Gerona, 1881); J. E. Martínez Ferrando, *Tragedia del insigne Condestable don Pedro de Portugal* (Madrid, 1942).

48. Anna Krause, 'El "tractado" novelístico de Diego de San Pedro', *BH*, LIV (1952), 245-75; Bruce W. Wardropper, 'Allegory and the Role of El Autor in the *Cárcel de Amor*', *PQ*, XXXI (1952), 39-44, and 'El mundo sentimental de la *CA*', *RFE*, XXXVII (1953), 168-93; Keith Whinnom, 'D. de S.P.'s Stylistic Reform', *BHS*, XXXVII (1960), 1-15, and 'Two San Pedros', *BHS*, XLII (1965), 255-8; Francisco Márquez Villanueva, '*CA*, novela política', *RO*, n.s., XIV (1966), 185-200; Haydée Bermejo Hurtado and Dinko Cvitanovic, 'El sentido de la aventura espiritual en la *CA*', *RFE*, XLIX (1966), 289-300. Núñez's sequel is ed. by M. Menéndez y Pelayo, *Orígenes de la novela*, II (NBAE, VII). Márquez Villanueva suggests that a change in San Pedro's political views is reflected in the *Cárcel*, and he revives the theory of *converso* origin, discredited by Whinnom, *BHS*, XXXIV 1957), 187-200.

49. Pamela Waley, 'Juan de Flores y *Tristán de Leonís*' and 'Fiammetta and Panfilo Continued', *ISt*, XXIV (1969), 15-31.

50. R. Foulché-Delbosc, 'Observations sur la *Célestine*', *RH*, VII (1900), 28-80 and 510, IX (1902), 171-99, and LXXVIII, 1 (1930), 544-99; Ruth Davis, *New Data on the Authorship of Act I of the Comedia de Calisto y Melibea* (Univ. of Iowa Studies in Sp. Lang. and Lit. 3, Iowa City, 1928);

Anna Krause, 'Deciphering the Epistle-Preface to the *C. de C. y M.*', *RR*, LXIV (1953), 89-101; Giulia Adinolfi, 'La *C* e la sua unità di composizione', *FiR*, I, 3 (1954), 12-60; D. W. McPheeters, *El humanista español Alonso de Proaza* (Valencia, 1961); Manuel Criado de Val, *Índice verbal de la C* (*RFE* anejo LXIV, Madrid, 1955); Martín de Riquer, 'F. de R. y el primer acto de la *C*', *RFE*, XLI (1957), 373-95; Fernando González Ollé, 'El problema de la autoría de la *C*. Nuevos datos y revisión del mismo', *RFE*, XLIII (1960), 439-45; J. Homer Herriott, 'The Authorship of Act I of *La C*', *HR*, XXXI (1963), 153-9, *Towards a Critical Edition of the C: a filiation of early editions* (Madison and Milwaukee, 1964), and 'Notes on Selectivity of Language in the *C*', *HR*, XXXVII (1969), 77-101; Norton, *Printing in Spain*, pp. 141-56; Keith Whinnom, 'The Relationship of the Early Editions of the *C*', *ZRP*, LXXXII (1966), 22-40.

51. M. Serrano y Sanz, 'Noticias biográficas de F. de R . . .', *RABM*, VI (1902), 245-60; Fernando del Valle Lersundi, 'Documentos referentes a F. de R.', *RFE*, XII (1925), 385-96, and 'Testamento de F. de R. . . . ', *RFE*, XVI (1929), 366-88; Otis H. Green, 'F. de R., *converso* and *hidalgo*', *HR*, XV (1947), 384-7; Stephen Gilman, 'The Case of Álvaro de Montalbán', *MLN*, LXXVIII (1963), 113-25, 'F. de R. as Author', *RF*, LXXVI (1964), 255-90, and (with Ramón Gonzálvez), 'The Family of F. de R.', *RF*, LXXVIII (1966), 1-26.

52. Samonà, *Aspetti;* Gilman, *Art;* P. E. Russell, 'The Art of F. de R.', *BHS*, XXXIV (1957), 160-7; Lida de Malkiel, *Masterpieces, Originalidad*, and 'El ambiente concreto en la *C*', *Estudios Herriott*, pp. 145-65; Jane Hawking, 'Madre Celestina', *AION*, Sez. Rom., IX (1967), 177-90; Severin, *Memory*.

53. Castro Guisasola, *Fuentes;* J. de Vallata, *Poliodorus: Comedia humanística desconocida*, ed. J. M. Casas Homs (Madrid, 1953), pt. 2, Ch. 14; Deyermond, *Petrarchan Sources*, and 'The Text-Book Mishandled'. The importance of legal sources has been discovered by P. E. Russell, and will be documented in a forthcoming study.

54. Garrido Pallardó, *Problemas;* Bataillon, *Célestine;* Aguirre, *Amantes;* Russell, 'Ambiguity in *La C*', *BHS*, XL (1963), 35-40; Castro, *Contienda*.

55. On other aspects, and for general studies, see Menéndez y Pelayo, *Orígenes;* Ramiro de Maeztu, *Don Quijote, don Juan y la C. Ensayos de simpatía* (Madrid, 1926); Rachel Frank, 'Four Paradoxes in the *C*', *RR*, XXXVIII (1947), 53-68; Inez Macdonald, 'Some Observations on the *C*', *HR*, XXII (1954), 264-81; D. W. McPheeters, 'The Element of Fatality in the *Tragicomedia de C. y M.*', *S*, VIII (1954), 331-5, and 'The Present Status of *C* Studies', *S*, XII (1958), 196-205; Clara L. Penney, *The Book called C. in the Library of the Hispanic Society of America* (New York, 1954); Stephen Gilman, 'The *Argumentos* to *La C*', *RPh*, VIII (1954-55), 71-8; Pedro Bohigas, 'De la Com. a la Tragicom. de *C. y M.*', *EMP*, VII, 1 (1957), 153-75; P. E. Russell, 'La magia como tema integral de la *Tr. de C. y M.*', *Homenaje Alonso*, III, 337-54, and 'Literary Tradition and Social Reality in *La C*', *BHS*, XLI (1964), 230-7; Oostendorp, *El conflicto entre el honor y el amor*, Ch. 4; Berndt, *Amor;* Maravall, *Mundo;* Bruce W. Wardropper, 'Pleberio's Lament for Melibea and the Medieval Elegiac Tradition', *MLN*, LXXIX (1964), 140-52; Cándido Ayllón, *La visión pesimista de la C* (México, 1965); Charles F. Fraker, 'The Importance of Pleberio's Soliloquy', *RF*, LXXVIII (1966), 515-29; Jacqueline Gerday, 'Le remaniement formel des actes primitifs dans *La C de 1502*', *AION*, Sez. Rom., X (1968), 175-82; Dorothy C. Clarke, *Allegory, Decalogue and Deadly Sins in La C* (UCPMP 91, Berkeley and Los Angeles, 1968); Martin, *Love's Fools;* J. Homer Herriott, 'Estado actual de los estudios sobre *La C*', *AEM* (in press).

Chapter 7

COURT AND CHURCH POETS OF THE FIFTEENTH CENTURY

I. THE 'CANCIONEROS'—TYPES OF VERSE

THE CASTILIAN POETS OF THE FIFTEENTH CENTURY are known to us chiefly through a series of anthologies; manuscripts of a single poet's work are rare. The Castilian *cancioneros* survive in bewildering number and variety, and their complex interrelationship is still to be clarified. Some have come down to us in the form in which the compiler left them (though that is, unhappily, no guarantee that he included the correct texts of the poems), and some later *cancioneros*, including one of the most important, were immediately printed.[1]

The *cancioneros* contain two main types of poem: the lyric *canción* (short, originally intended to be sung, and usually a love-poem, though religious and panegyric *canciones* also occur), and the doctrinal, panegyric, narrative or satirical *decir* (considerably longer, intended to be read or recited). The *canción* uses lines of eight syllables (in some poems these are interspersed at regular intervals with half-lines; this device is known as *pie quebrado*). The lines have regular and fully consonantal rhymes and show great flexibility in their stress-pattern. Regularity in the number of syllables is late in being established, and at the end of the fifteenth century Juan del Encina has to protest against poets whose verse is irregular. The octosyllable has a long history in other languages —Latin, Provençal, and Galician-Portuguese; once established in Castilian, it flourished, and is still widely used today. Whereas the *canción* is virtually confined to a single metre, the *decir* uses either the octosyllable or *arte mayor*, a twelve-syllable line with a strongly-marked caesura and two strong beats in each hemistich. *Arte mayor* was once thought to derive from a Galician-Portuguese form, but this now seems doubtful (see above, p. 123). The number of syllables can fluctuate, since the distinctive feature of this verse-form is its pattern of fixed beats, which may be seen in the opening lines of the greatest of *arte mayor* poems, Juan de Mena's *Laberinto de Fortuna*:

> Al múy prepoténte / don Juán el segúndo,
> aquél con quien Júpiter / tóvo tal zélo . . .

178

Even in the pattern of beats, total regularity is not always obtained, and in the 1420s there were two opposing tendencies, one favouring freedom (found in the work of Pablo de Santa María and Mahomat el Xartosse), and the other a restricted form (Villasandino, Baena). The restricted form, with modifications, triumphed, and the danger of formal incoherence was averted. Eventually excessive rigidity set in, and *arte mayor*, unlike the octosyllable, was exhausted by the end of the fifteenth century and could not compete with the new Italian metres when these were successfully acclimatised by Garcilaso. While the octosyllabic *canción* settled down quite early into a restricted range of metrical possibilities (a range which was still further restricted towards the end of the fifteenth century—see below, p. 198), the octosyllabic *decir* retained great freedom in the number of stanzas and the rhyme-scheme.

Some *cancioneros*, for novelty of content or some other reason, deserve our special attention. These are *Baena* (see above, p. 130); the *cancioneros*, whose archetype (early 1460s?) is now lost, which incorporate mainly the poetry written at the Neapolitan Court of Alfonso V of Aragon (*Stúñiga*, with which *Roma* and *Marciana* are associated); *Herberay des Essarts* and *Palacio*, compiled in the 1460s; and the *Cancionero general* of Hernando del Castillo (1511), imitated by Garcia de Resende's Portuguese *Cancioneiro geral* (1516). Of these collections, *Baena*, the Neapolitan group, and the *General* contribute by far the greatest amount of new work. *Herberay* seems to represent the taste of the Navarrese Court soon after the mid-century, and *Palacio* that of the Castilian and Aragonese Courts in the same period. It may be noted in passing that *Palacio* confronts us with a difficult problem of interpretation, since the poems chosen are described by the modern editor—with abundant justification—as representing an aristocratic and idealised approach to love, yet the illuminated initials of this carefully-executed manuscript contain highly erotic scenes. Perhaps they point to sexual euphemisms in the apparently chaste and idealised vocabulary of the poems.[2]

II. 'CANCIONERO DE BAENA'

Juan Alfonso de Baena, probably a *converso*, presented his *Cancionero* to King Juan II, himself a minor poet. Some poems of Baena's are included but his real importance (apart from his pioneer editorial work) lies in his prologue, which deals with the nature of poetry and with problems of versification. His *Cancionero* covers the poetry of Castile from about 1370 onwards, and the poets represented divide into two main groups, those active in or just before the reign of Juan I (1379-90), and the poets of the very late fourteenth and early fifteenth centuries. Some important works of the period are omitted, such as the didactic *Edades del mundo* (1418), by Pablo de Santa María (1350-1435), Chief Rabbi of Burgos and subsequently bishop of the same city.

In the first group are Pero Ferrús, probably the oldest of the *Baena* poets except for López de Ayala (see above, pp. 122-4); Garci Ferrández de Jerena, who seems to have led a dissolute life, while writing poems of notable technical originality, to have abandoned Christianity for Islam and defected to the Moors, and to have come back to a lonely old age in Castile; Gonzalo Rodríguez, archdeacon of Toro, whose ebullient writing includes a verse testament in *arte mayor*; and Macías, whose love-poetry is attractive but is overshadowed by his legend. Macías is reputed to have been driven mad by a hopeless passion, which ultimately caused his death, so that for the poets of the fifteenth century and even later he became the archetype of the suffering lover. Most of these poets normally used Galician-Portuguese for their love-poetry and Castilian for other types; only gradually did some of them move towards a general use of Castilian.[3]

Alfonso Álvarez de Villasandino (died *c.* 1424) was part of the earliest *Baena* group, but his poetic career of continuous experiment stretched over more than fifty years. Following the linguistic fashion, he ended as an entirely Castilian poet (see above, p. 130). He shows great versatility: courtly love-poems, panegyrics, satires, and lyrics which seem to give candid glimpses of his personal life, but which may (as with François Villon) mean simply that he has thought himself into the part. He lived by his poetry, turning bitterly against niggardly patrons, and against the new, more intellectual generation of which Francisco Imperial was the leading member. Despite his facility, Villasandino was a careful craftsman, and this won him Baena's praise. One of his later contemporaries is Martín el Tañedor, a *juglar* who could sing in both Castilian and Catalan, is supposed to have been blind, and composed poems of his own.[4]

The new generation of poets was of diverse origins: Francisco Imperial was a Genoese who settled in Seville, Mahomat el Xartosse de Guardafaxara was a Moor, and several were *conversos*: Ferrán Manuel de Lando, Ferrán Sánchez Calavera, probably Baena himself, and perhaps Diego de Valencia. One poet of this generation, Santillana's father, Diego Hurtado de Mendoza, wrote a *serranilla* and a parallelistic lyric which deals symbolically with love. The other leading poets of the time seem to have been men of strongly intellectual interests. The poems of Villena are lost, but he, like Baena, wrote on the theory of poetry (see above, p. 148). Francisco Imperial was long credited with the authorship of an ambitious allegorical poem, the *Dezir a las siete virtudes*, but this may well be the work of an anonymous poet. The verse is undeniably clumsy, but the intellectual level is impressive, and the poet has learned much from Dante, and from the allegorical *decir* which Imperial had previously written on a royal birth.[5]

Imperial's contemporaries seem, with the exception of Baena and Villasandino, to have followed his lead in technical matters, but strong intellectual disagreements were a feature of this generation. The dispute about the nature of the poetic gift—is it a gift from God or a matter of learning?—is related to theological issues, in which the influence of the Franciscans may be seen. The Franciscan reformers emphasised that uneducated people could attain knowledge of God by grace, and opposed the scholastic tradition. Franciscan influence may have encouraged these poets to write social criticism, either in the course of poems on other subjects, or by itself (Martínez de Medina, *Decir que fue fecho sobre la justicia*...; Diego de Valencia, *Pregunta*... *por qué son los fidalgos*; Ruy Páez de Ribera's poems on poverty). Whether other radical movements within the Church, especially those from northern Europe such as the Devotio Moderna, were influential in fifteenth-century Spanish poetry is a still unresolved question. It is also possible that Jewish habits of mind affected the religious thinking of some *converso* poets (Ferrán Manuel de Lando, Ferrán Sánchez Calavera), and blended with the influence of radical Christian movements.

A general interest in moral and religious issues distinguishes the poets of this period: leading examples are Ferrán Sánchez Calavera's treatment of the problem of predestination, and Fernán Pérez de Guzmán's *Coplas de vicios y virtudes* and *Confesión rimada*.[6]

The youngest poets to be included in *Baena* do not form a clear group. The best are Álvaro de Luna and Juan Rodríguez del Padrón (courtly love-poems), and Suero de Ribera (a parodic *Misa de amores*).

Though the Galician-Portuguese *cantigas de amigo* leave hardly any trace in *Baena* or its successors, the themes of the *cantigas de amor* (see above, pp. 12-14) are continued, though with differences, in the courtly *canciones*, and the *cantigas d'escarnho* are renewed by Villasandino and several other poets. Galician-Portuguese techniques of versification are used to some extent by the *Baena* poets, though on the whole they prefer (even if writing in Galician-Portuguese) the types of verse infrequently used by their predecessors.[7]

Other influences are strong, even in the *canciones*, and in the *decires* they far outweigh that of Galicia. Villasandino may have been influenced by the Provençal poets in his concern for technique; he certainly quotes some Provençal lines. Moreover, Castilian poets were now beginning to look to Catalonia, whose poetry, strongly influenced by Provençal, was read by men like Villena and Santillana.

The main ancestors of the *decires* are the French *dits*, which had been brought to a high level of sophistication, both in form and content, in the fourteenth century. French poetry was important in another way for the generations represented in *Baena*: one of the most influential of medieval European poems, the *Roman de la Rose*, began to have an effect in Castile. French influence continued during the fifteenth century, and in a few respects increased, but it was gradually overtaken by that of Italy. Italian poets and commentators (Dante, Petrarch, Boccaccio, and the Dante commentators) began to be read, and then to be imitated. The change came first in Catalonia, and then spread to Castile, the first poets to be strongly affected being those who had connections with Italy (Imperial) or with Catalonia (Santillana). The Italian influence was felt most strongly in the development of allegory, where it joined with that of France; in a revival of interest in classical mythology and rediscovery of some Latin writers neglected in earlier centuries; in some stylistic devices such as the increased use of antithesis (Petrarch was the chief influence here); in experiments in versification; and in an increasing intellectual depth as the century wore on (in this respect, religious influences were also important).[8]

The youngest poets in *Baena*—Álvaro de Luna, Suero de Ribera, and Juan Rodríguez del Padrón—continued to be read throughout the century, and, unlike Villasandino or Imperial, are included in the *cancioneros* of the Aragonese Court at Naples, and in the *General*. So are their great contemporaries, Santillana and Mena; change is mingled with continuity in fifteenth-century poetic taste.

III. SANTILLANA

Íñigo López de Mendoza, marqués de Santillana (1398-1458), spent some of his formative years in Aragon, and thus established contact with Catalan writers. Throughout his life he kept in touch with other writers, being deeply influenced in his early stages by Villena and Imperial, and in his later years having friendly literary relations with his younger contemporary Juan de Mena (though they took opposite sides on the great political issue that split Castile in the 1440s and early 1450s, the policies of Álvaro de Luna) and with the still younger Pedro, constable of Portugal. Santillana wrote poems in praise of Villena and the Catalan Jordi de Sant Jordi, and there were exchanges of poems between him and Mena, and between Mena and Dom Pedro, while Santillana sent to Dom Pedro a collection of his poems with, as an introduction, the famous *Carta* or *Prohemio*. These relationships confirm the impression given by Imperial's generation, that there is now a consciously literary world (though a small one), in which poets are aware of each other, whereas in the fourteenth century vernacular poets seemed on the whole to write in isolation from each other, conscious only of being rooted in a European ecclesiastical tradition. Another aspect of Santillana's contact with other writers is his rich library: he collected both books to read and annotate, and specially valuable display items. He could not read Latin, even though he collected Latin manuscripts, but he read several vernaculars with fluency, and was aware of contemporary developments in European poetry.[9]

Santillana wrote *canciones*, and in other genres as well, but his main effort went into his *decires*. Nineteen *canciones* survive, probably from widely differing periods of his life; the earlier ones owe a strong debt to the Galician-Portuguese tradition (one of them is written in that language), but in others he develops an independent style. The earliest *decires*, such as the *Querella de amor*, are lyrical in tone, and the *Querella* incorporates lyric fragments. In these, the Galician-Portuguese influence is still strong, but is soon replaced by that of Imperial's *decires*, and the narrative element predominates over the lyrical. In the growing maturity of these *decires*, allegory plays an important part, though some years are needed before Santillana can make an independent and fully satisfactory use of allegory, integrating it firmly into the structure and theme of the poem. The *Planto de la reina Margarida* and the *Coronación de Mossén Jordi de Sant Jordi*, both composed *c.* 1430, use the familiar allegorical technique of a vision in order to praise the dead queen of Aragon and the living Catalan poet.

At about the same time as the *Planto* and *Coronación*, Santillana composed the *Triumphete de amor*, whose title, implying dependence on Petrarch's *Trionfo d'amore*, is an accurate indication both of content and of technique. This poem, using the device of an allegorical procession set within the familiar medieval story of an adventure encountered while hunting, tells of the poet's wounding by love. The view of love that is expressed is, however, much closer to the previous Hispanic tradition than to Petrarch's analytical approach.

Two other *decires*, somewhat later than the *Triumphete*, deal with Santillana's involvement in love. The *Sueño* again tells how he fell in love, and the *Infierno de los enamorados* is the story of the cure; these are a deliberately contrasted pair, with the *Triumphete* as an earlier attempt. In the *Sueño*, which borrows from Lucan's *Pharsalia* and Boccaccio's *Fiammetta* to set the scene, the struggle within the poet is depicted in two ways: a debate between Seso and Coraçón, and a battle between the army of Diana (goddess of chastity) and that of Venus and Cupid. The result is a victory for love, but the change of a *locus amoenus* into a landscape of desolation at the beginning of the poem makes clear the disastrous effects of love:

> En aquel sueño me vía
> dentro en día claro, lumbroso,
> en un vergel espacioso
> reposar con alegría;
> el qual jardín me cobría
> de solaz de olientes flores,
> do circundan rruyseñores
> la perfecta melodía. . . .

> E los árboles sonbrosos
> del vergel ya recontados
> en punto fueron mudados
> en troncos fieros, ñudosos,
> e los cantos melodiosos
> en clamores redundaron,
> e las aves se tornaron
> en áspios poçoñosos. (st. 8-12)

These effects are emphasised in the *Infierno*. The poet is guided through a Hell openly based on that of the *Divina Commedia*, and his observation of the sufferings of the famous lovers whom he finds there convinces him that love is to be avoided. The *decir* belongs to a favourite late medieval genre, the erotic hell: the Christian picture of Hell is used either as a symbol of the pains of love, or to show the punishment of those who have offended against love's laws.

The *Comedieta de Ponza* (1436), in *arte mayor*, marks the culmination of Santillana's allegorical *decires*. It has an ambitious, complex, and satisfying structure, into which the image-patterns are integrated, and the only weakness is an unresolved difficulty as to whether this is primarily a patriotic poem, in which the Aragonese are seen as champions of Spain as a whole in their Italian campaign, or a poem about Fortune. Fortune assumes an increasing role in Santillana's poetry, but after the *Comedieta*, direct statement is preferred to allegory. In 1448, Santillana's cousin was imprisoned on political grounds (Álvaro de Luna was partly responsible), and *Bías contra Fortuna* is an attempt at consolation. The intellectual and structural control in this poem is entirely successful, and the Greek philosopher who is the spokesman for Santillana's views achieves a memorable statement of the case against letting oneself be dominated by the accidents of Fortune. The earlier *Proverbios* (1437), which also tries to do without allegory, is far less successful.

The struggle against Álvaro de Luna is the main subject of several other poems. The *Favor de Hércules contra Fortuna*, addressed to Juan II, is a savage attack on Luna, other poems against him were written between his overthrow and execution (1453), and the *Doctrinal de privados*, composed after the execution, seeks to draw moral lessons from Luna's career and fall. The *Doctrinal* shows Santillana in an unattractive light, for he uses the theme of Fortune and the technique of confession to make his dead enemy denounce his own actions.

Between 1423 and 1440, Santillana, following a family tradition, composed eight *serranillas* and parts of two others (collaborative *serranillas* were fairly frequent at this time). These poems show a gradual evolution from a more boisterous type, distantly recalling the *cánticas de serrana* of the Archpriest of Hita (which Santillana knew), to refined *serranillas* that are much closer to the Galician-Portuguese *pastorelas*. Some of the *serranillas* are among Santillana's most successful and immediately attractive lyrics, thanks to their rhythm, use of landscape, and incorporation of personal details:

Moça tan fermosa
non vi en la frontera,
como una vaquera
de la Finojosa.

Faziendo la vía
del Calatraveño
a Santa María
vençido del sueño,
por tierra fragosa
perdí la carrera,
do vi la vaquera
de la Finojosa.

En un verde prado
de rosas e flores,
guardando ganado
con otros pastores,
la vi tan graçiosa
que apenas creyera
que fuese vaquera
de la Finojosa.

Non creo las rosas
de la primavera
sean tan fermosas
nin de tal manera,
fablando sin glosa,
si antes supiera
de aquella vaquera
de la Finojosa. . . .

The *serranillas*, although belonging to a cultured genre, have traces of a popular tone, but the forty-two sonnets that Santillana wrote during the last twenty years of his life are a very consciously cultured innovation. He shows a settled determination to acclimatise this Italian verse-form, with its eleven-syllable lines, in Spanish, but although some of the sonnets come close to success, the metrical innovation proved in the end to be a failure. The number of syllables is correct, but an Italian hendecasyllable has a range of characteristic rhythms which clash with those of the octosyllable and the *arte mayor*, and Santillana's head was full of these older rhythms. Too often his hendecasyllables are merely *arte mayor* lines with one syllable omitted, and even if a sonnet starts correctly it may lapse into *arte mayor*: the one beginning

Léxos de vós e cérca de cuydádo

has as its tenth line

Nín son bastántes a sátisfazér   (cf. above, p. 178).

There were a few other attempts in the fifteenth century to use the Italian hendecasyllable, but all failed, and the new metre was not successfully acclimatised until Garcilaso, some eighty years after Santillana's death, showed his fellow-countrymen how to solve the problem.[10]

Santillana's most interesting prose-work, if we exclude the collection of *Refranes que dizen las viejas tras el fuego* (about whose authorship some doubt remains), is to be found in prologues which he wrote for some poems (*Bías, Proverbios*) and in the *Carta* to Dom Pedro (1449). The *Carta* discusses the nature of poetry, and offers a brief critical history of European, and especially of Spanish, poetry. The only critical traditions recognised by medieval writers were the philosophical and the legislative: that is, they dealt with the nature of poetry, and with the rules that poets should follow, whether metrical or rhetorical. Baena's preface to his *Cancionero* is philosophical, and Villena's *Arte de trovar* is legislative, venturing on description only when it deals with language. The novelty of Santillana's *Carta* in a Spanish context is that it contains descriptive criticism. In an uncertain and rudimentary fashion, Santillana tries to give some account of the main qualities and defects of the poets whom he mentions. This has been the chief task of European critics since the eighteenth century, but in the Middle Ages it is virtually confined to chance remarks by authors and copyists. For his general ideas on poetry, Santillana was able to draw on classical and patristic writers, and especially on Boccaccio's *De genealogia deorum*, but in his descriptive criticism he had little to guide him.[11]

IV. JUAN DE MENA

The other great poet of this period is Juan de Mena (1411-56), sometimes thought, on dubious evidence, to be a *converso*. Mena, employed by Juan II as a civil servant, was recognised by his contemporaries as an outstanding poet. As with Dante, his most important poem was soon equipped with commentaries (*glosas*), and the early printers met the public demand for his works by many editions. His few *canciones* and his more numerous *decires* on love are strongly intellectual in tone.

The *Laberinto de Fortuna* was completed and presented to Juan II in 1444. Mena was an ambitious poet who believed that Spanish could attain the same dignity as Latin, and the *Laberinto* is the fullest expression of his ambition. The structure is, he tells us, based on three wheels of Fortune, representing past, present, and future, and on the seven spheres of the sun, moon, and planets. In fact, the spheres are a device for arranging the characters of the poem in a catalogue, and the wheel of Fortune serves its usual medieval purpose of representing in the most vivid way the reversals of fortune to which men and women are subject. The real structure of the poem is to be found elsewhere, and is linked to its purpose.

This is a political poem, aimed at winning support for Álvaro de Luna, and especially at making the king commit himself more firmly on Luna's side. Mena presents us with two opposing groups, one containing Fortune, the great nobles, civil war, sin, black magic, and other undesirable things, and the other made up of Divine Providence, Luna, the Reconquest, fame, Mena's poetry, and, it is hoped, Juan II. These groups are not openly announced, but Mena establishes them by linking one bad element with another, or one good element with another, and also by depicting opposing pairs. Within this structure there are impressive narratives and descriptions, drawing on recent history, which is described in terms of literary sources. (Lucan is especially valuable here, but Mena prefers to blend two or more sources.) The description of a storm at sea in the episode of the Conde de Niebla, the lament of Lorenzo Dávalos's mother after his death in battle, and the conjuration of a witch are justly famous set-pieces:

> E busca la maga ya fasta que falla
> un cuerpo tan malo, que por aventura
> le fuera negado aver sepultura
> por aver muerto en non justa batalla;
> e quando de noche la gente más calla,
> pónelo ésta en medio de un çerco,
> e desde allí dentro conjura al huerco
> e todas las furias ultrizes que falla.
>
> Ya comenzava la invocación
> con triste murmullo su díssono canto,
> fingiendo las bozes con aquel espanto
> que meten las fieras con su triste son,
> oras silvando bien como dragón,
> o como tigre faziendo estridores,
> oras aullidos formando mayores
> que forman los canes que sin dueño son.   (st. 245-6)

This is the most heavily Latinised of all Mena's poems, both in vocabulary and in syntax, and there is a good deal of obscurity, which may well be an attempt to exclude those considered unfit to appreciate cultured poetry. A problem immediately arises: the *Laberinto* is a political poem, and political poetry normally uses a simplified style so that it may communicate. The explanation for this apparent contradiction is that the *Laberinto* is aimed primarily at one man, who was himself a poet. Thus Mena could simultaneously fulfil his two aims of writing a complex poem that would rival Latin, and of writing propaganda on Luna's behalf.

A number of poems prepare the way for the *Laberinto*, in experimental style, in political concerns, or in both. The *Coronación* (1438) uses a tribute to Santillana in order to denounce the evils of the age; the style is elaborate, even though the poem is in octosyllables, which Mena elsewhere uses for simpler work. In two poems, the *Claro-oscuro* and the untitled 'Al hijo muy claro de Hyperión', *arte mayor* stanzas alternate with octosyllables, the *arte mayor* containing many classical allusions and an elaborate style, with the octosyllables in marked contrast. Mena's prose-works show the same tendencies as his poetry: a *Tratado del amor* (of disputed attribution), which deals with courtly love, has links with his early love-poetry; the commentary on the *Coronación* is Mena's own work, as are the careful and elaborate prefaces; and the *Omero romançado* (*c.* 1442), a translation of the *Ilias latina* (see above, p. 160), turns the dull Latin of the original into carefully-wrought Spanish prose.

Nine years after the *Laberinto* was completed, in 1453, Luna fell, and Juan II himself died in the following year. Mena's political and personal hopes lay in ruins, and his last poem is full of disillusionment and asceticism. In the *Coplas contra los pecados mortales*, he simplifies his style in an attempt to convey a religious and moral message to a large audience. This is still an allegory but of an older and simpler type: it personifies the two conflicting sides of human nature, and sets them in epic combat; the main structural influence is probably Prudentius's *Psychomachia*, and the content derives from the medieval moralistic tradition. When Mena died, the *Coplas* were left unfinished, and three poets, of whom Gómez Manrique was the best known, wrote endings for them.[12]

V. DEBATE-POEMS

As we have already seen (above, p. 182), poets in the fifteenth century were aware of each other's work in a way unknown in the fourteenth, and there was a good deal of rivalry. This rivalry played a decisive part in a genre found from Villasandino's time to the end of the fifteenth century, but especially frequent in the reign of Juan II: the *pregunta* and *respuesta*, which derive ultimately from Provençal models. A poet asks a question in verse, and the recipient has to reply in the same rhyme-scheme. These are essentially court poems, and many of them seem to have been composed for the amusement of Juan II, who is known to have judged between them and rewarded the victor on some occasions.[13]

From the end of the fourteenth century, interest in debate-poems seems to be renewed in Spain. There are several successors to the earliest extant Spanish debate, the *Alma y cuerpo* (see above, p. 73); they derive not from the Spanish poem but from the Latin *Visio Philiberti*. There is a Spanish prose debate which closely follows the *Visio*, and two versions of an *arte mayor* poem which is based on the *Visio* (but, unusually for a medieval Spanish work, often compresses it) and which also uses other Latin debates on the same subject. The two versions begin in the same way, with an introductory dream, a description of the corpse, and a much more fully-developed debate; the body gives a vigorous reply to the soul, and in the version entitled *Disputa del cuerpo e del ánima* (called MSS. *P1* and *P2* by the modern editor) a devil carries off the white bird which represents the soul, and the narrator faints with terror. The other version, *Revelación de un hermitaño* (MS. E), which shares some features with the *Danza de la Muerte*, recasts the ending to produce a happy outcome: an angel rescues the soul, who denounces the World.

The body-soul debate retained its popularity in Spain long after these poems were composed. A late fifteenth-century *Tractado del cuerpo e de la ánima* ends with an angel delivering a written judgment which condemns both body and soul. This version, like the others, is divided into long speeches. The quick exchanges between the adversaries which are an important technical advance in fifteenth-century debate-poems (Santillana's *Bías contra Fortuna* leads the way, and is followed by the debates between Love and an old man, discussed below) have no place here. Technical innovations do not necessarily displace old techniques, and things can go on as before for decades and even centuries, a point that is confirmed by the *pliego suelto* debates on this theme, which continue well into the seventeenth century.[14]

In the second half of the fifteenth century, Rodrigo Cota (a *converso*, living in Toledo; died after 1504) wrote a *Diálogo entre el Amor y un viejo*. The old man describes his ruined house and garden, symbols of his emotional life:

> Ya la casa se deshizo
> de sotil lavor estraña,
> y tornósse esta cabaña
> de cañuelas de carrizo.
> Delos frutos hize truecos,
> por escaparme de ti,
> por aquellos troncos secos,

carcomidos, todos huecos ·
que parescen cerca mí.   (st. 4)

He resolves to avoid Love and thereby escape further suffering. Love
appears, gradually wins the old man's confidence, and persuades him
to love a young girl; when the old man is irrevocably committed, Love
mocks him for his presumptuous folly. The chief merits of this poem
are the psychological development, the cut-and-thrust of argument, and
the skilful deployment of imagery. It differs from the debates we have
so far considered, since it ends with the decisive victory of one of the
contenders; the function of the debate is here not simply to state the
opposing cases, but to convince (as in the debate-sections of the *Libro
de Buen Amor* and some other works).

An anonymous and untitled poem, usually referred to as *Diálogo
entre el Amor, el viejo y la hermosa*, dates from the late fifteenth century and seems to be a reworking of Cota's poem: Cota's words are not
used, but the plot is essentially the same. The garden description is
omitted, and there is more hesitation on the old man's part than in Cota:
he half agrees, withdraws into a prudent isolation, is lured on again, and
finally, after several vacillations, surrenders, thus adding to the psychological realism of the debate. This poem contains several lines that
suggest it was to be staged, so that we are now on the frontier between
debate-poems and the drama.[15]

VI. 'DANÇA DE LA MUERTE'

An increasing concern with death and its physical consequences is a
feature of the late Middle Ages, and its most characteristic manifesta-
tion is the Dances of Death. In most countries, these poems accompany
a series of pictures (paintings in churches or on the walls of cemeteries,
woodcuts in block-books) which show skeletons seizing representatives
of the different ranks of society and dragging them into the dance;
worms and decomposing corpses are a frequent feature of the illustrations. The Spanish *Dança general de la Muerte*, composed in the late
fourteenth or fifteenth century, and the amplified version printed at
Seville, 1520, are unaccompanied by illustrations, and perhaps for this
reason they lay less emphasis on physical decay. Nevertheless, they
sometimes present a gruesome picture, and are consistently pessimistic.

The European Dances of Death seem to have begun in the fourteenth
century, and are connected with the general pessimism of the late
Middle Ages, which had a variety of causes, including the economic and
demographic collapse caused by the Black Death. The sermons in which
the travelling friars sought to urge men to repentance involved a concentration on death, and especially on its negative aspects. No satisfac-

tory literary source has been found for the Dances of Death, whose real origin is in the social and intellectual background. At the time when this genre arose, dancing-manias—a form of epidemic hysteria—were common in western Europe, and clearly associated involuntary participation in a dance with unpleasant and sometimes fatal consequences. The dance also played an important part in the medieval world-picture, especially in the motion of the spheres, and the hierarchical arrangement of death's victims corresponds to another central feature of the world-picture. A combination of dance and hierarchy was thus familiar to medieval men and women, and it is likely that this joined with the prevalence of dancing-mania to make them see the terrifying power of death in the form of an involuntarily dancing hierarchy controlled not by God but by a personified Death.

The French *Danse macabre* was probably the earliest of the Dances of Death, and the Spanish *Dança general de la Muerte* seems to derive from it, though the immediate ancestor of the *Dança* may have come from the eastern part of the Peninsula.

As in the great majority of such works, the victims in the *Dança* are arranged in two hierarchies, ecclesiastical and lay, and are chosen alternately from each: Pope, Emperor, Cardinal, King, and so on. At the end come specifically Spanish characters. The dance is set within a moralising framework, beginning with a friar's sermon and ending with the decision of those still alive to repent of their sins, but within the dance itself the gloomiest view is taken of man's nature and his ultimate fate.

The arrangement of the victims imposes a clear structure on most Dances of Death, but that of the *Dança* is more regular than most, and the structure is reinforced by two dominant images, those of the dance and of eating. The dance is, obviously, the basic image of all such poems, but it is repeated in the *Dança* in a variety of ways, so that we never lose sight of the irresistible yet ultimately pointless movement in which the victims are engaged; this makes an interesting contrast to Jorge Manrique's poem on death (see below, p. 193). The image of eating is used in a subtle way not only to bind the poem together, but also to express the social criticism which is so noticeable a feature. The rich and powerful receive the strongest condemnation, and the *Dança* thus conforms to the tendency of fifteenth-century Spanish poetry to criticise strongly, and often satirically, the condition of society (see above, p. 181 and below, p. 195). Satire is only a subsidiary technique in the *Dança*, but it occurs nevertheless in the grimly contemptuous words that Death addresses to his victims.

In the amplification of the *Dança* printed in 1520, we see, as with the body-soul debates, the continuity of literary taste and of the old techniques, and we see also the danger of trying to include too much material. The amplifier yielded to the temptation of giving a comprehensive survey of society, and greatly increased the number of social groups represented; the great majority of the additions are laymen, and a regular alternation becomes impossible.[16]

In earlier periods, even a public loss, such as the death of a king, was normally presented with a stress on its personal aspects, whether the loss was fictional (Charlemagne's lament for Roland in *Roncesvalles*) or real (the *endechas* for Fernando III and for Guillén Peraza—see above, p. 29, n. 37). In the fifteenth century, however, we usually find public and ceremonial acts of mourning even on personal occasions: these are sometimes affected by the stress on corruption of the body found in the Dances of Death, as in Ferrán Sánchez Calavera's *Deçir de las vanidades del mundo*, on the death of Ruy Díaz de Mendoza, and may be allegorical, as in the *Triunfo del Marqués*, written on Santillana's death by his secretary, Diego de Burgos, which consists of over 1,800 heavily classicised lines. Sometimes the poem is put into the mouth of the dead man, as in Fray Migir's work on the death of Enrique III (cf. the *Doctrinal de privados*, above, p. 184).

At the same time, there is a shift from the positive to the negative aspects of death. The concept of life in this world as a journey towards man's real home, which was dominant in medieval Christian thought, led naturally to the view of death as the gateway to Heaven, and therefore as something to be welcomed by saints and martyrs (this is frequent in Berceo, and occurs also in the *Vida de Santa María Egipciaca*); this attitude is feebly reflected in the hermit's reaction in the *Dança general,* and more strongly in the monk's words, but all the other victims react with fear and loathing, seeing death as a purely destructive force, as the end of life, with nothing beyond but Hell, and this view is common in the late Middle Ages.[17]

VII. JORGE MANRIQUE

Both of these tendencies—the move from private to public mourning, and from a positive to a negative attitude towards death—are incorporated in the *Dança de la Muerte*, but reversed in one of the most famous of Spanish poems, Jorge Manrique's *Coplas que fizo por la muerte de su padre.* Manrique (c. 1440-79) was in most ways a typical aristocratic poet of his time: he wrote in the intervals of an active life—he was a soldier, and died in battle—and his poems, of which about fifty survive, are mainly on love. He wrote *canciones* of high technical competence, and *decires* in which love is presented in some of the favourite metaphors of the period: a castle, a siege, a religious order; if Manrique had never written the *Coplas* he would still be recognised as one of the leading lyric poets of the reign of Enrique IV.

The poet's father, Rodrigo Manrique, died in 1476, but the *Coplas* were probably written just before Jorge's own death. They are in octosyllables with *pie quebrado*, and employ the doctrinal and rhetorical commonplaces of the Middle Ages in a way which lacks intellectual originality but has great emotional power. The poem begins with general reflections on life and death, surveys some of the great men now dead, and then comes to the most recently dead, Don Rodrigo, who is presented first in comparison with famous men of Roman history, sharing the best quality of each, and then in his own right. The ending is Death's respectful visit to Rodrigo, who welcomes his arrival as the crown of a good life. The poet tells us that such a life earns fame, but that eventually even fame perishes, leaving 'estotra vida tercera', the life of Heaven; Don Rodrigo has gained both fame and salvation, and the recollection of this consoles his family.

The dominant image of the *Coplas*, used in a variety of forms, is that of the journey (cf. above, p. 191). Within this framing image are set others, which make Manrique's attitude to death quite clear. He is deeply moved by the death of his father (and perhaps by premonitions of his own), he urgently needs to resolve the intellectual and emotional problems with which this confronts him, and he wins through to consolation in terms that would have been frequent enough in the earlier Middle Ages, but which are unusual in the harassed and morbid days of Enrique IV. He reverts to an earlier, more balanced medieval attitude, in reaction against the late medieval pessimism of the *Dança*. The only aspect of the *Coplas* that perhaps shows the influence of the Renaissance is the emphasis on fame as a reward for a good life, and even this is firmly subordinated to religious considerations of a familiar medieval type.[18]

VII. THE POETS OF THE NEAPOLITAN COURT

Discussion of Manrique's *Coplas* has taken us too far chronologically, and we must now go back to consider the *cancioneros* of the 1460s. Of these, the most important is the lost one which contained the poems written at the Aragonese Court in Naples, and from which three extant *cancioneros* descend (see above, p. 179). Alfonso V, the Magnanimous, entered Naples in triumph in 1443, after an earlier Aragonese campaign had ended in the defeat of Ponza (cf. above, p. 184), and ruled there until his death in 1458. He gathered round him Italian humanists (see above, p. 147) and Spanish poets. This was not the first time that Spanish poets had settled in Italy—there is the strange case of the minstrel Juan de Valladolid or Juan Poeta, who lived in Sicily earlier in the century—but it was the first coherent group of such poets. The leading figures are Juan de Andújar, Carvajal, Juan de Dueñas, Pedro de Santa Fe, and Juan de Tapia. There is no evidence that Lope de Estúñiga was ever in Naples, but he may have been associated with his contemporaries in this group, since one of the *cancioneros*, although not compiled by him, bears his name.

The poets of Alfonso V's Court (including those who served with him before 1443) reach a high level of sophistication, combined in some poems with a freshness of tone which makes very attractive reading. They are, however, chiefly remarkable for what they do not do. They adhere closely to the traditional Spanish forms: *canciones* of courtly love, in which the lover suffering without hope of reward makes a frequent appearance, and in which the only discernible foreign influence is French; love-*decires* of a similar type; panegyrics, usually fairly short; *serranillas*, especially by Carvajal, sometimes of a parodic type that recalls the *Libro de Buen Amor*, but more often idealised, as in the later *serranillas* of Santillana. The influence of Italian humanism is nowhere to be seen: either Alfonso wished to keep his Italian scholars and his Spanish poets in separate compartments, or isolation from the majority of Spanish poets and inability to achieve integration in an Italian literary community led to a highly-polished provincial conservatism. This did not mean bad poetry, but it did mean that any Italianate innovations, whether intellectual or metrical, had to begin not in Naples but in Spain.

Although Estúñiga and Dueñas wrote political verse, it is not represented in the court *cancioneros*. Of the very few allegories, two deserve special mention: the *Visión de amor* of Juan de Andújar, and the *Nao de amor* of Juan de Dueñas (who also composed a parodic *Misa de amores*). In a few cases, the poems arise directly out of the circumstances of their author's life—those written by Juan de Tapia while a prisoner-of-war after Ponza are the best examples—but our lack of biographical information obscures this question.[19]

IX. GÓMEZ MANRIQUE AND HIS CONTEMPORARIES

At roughly the same time as the Neapolitan poets were writing, a new generation, too young to be included in the *Cancionero de Baena*, emerged in Spain. The leading figure is Gómez Manrique (*c.* 1412-*c.* 1490), Jorge Manrique's uncle, whose most significant work is in the early drama (see below, pp. 210-12), but who had by the middle of the century established himself as one of the most careful craftsmen in versification, and who maintained much the same style and technique in his non-dramatic verse for the rest of his life. Others include the *converso* Antón de Montoro (1404?-80?), a burlesque and satirical poet; Suero de Quiñones, best known for the *Passo honroso* (see above, p. 152); Pero Guillén de Segovia (born 1413), the author not only of a defence of Álvaro de Luna and other poems but of a rhyming dictionary, whose title of *Gaya ciencia* reflects its Provençal inspiration; and Juan Agraz, an elegiac and moralising poet.[20]

X. SATIRICAL VERSE

The political and social life of Castile during the first three-quarters of the fifteenth century was a constant provocation to satire. Some social criticism is found in the *Cancionero de Baena* and in the *Dança de la Muerte*, and in the reign of Juan II the struggles between Luna and the great nobles are reflected not only in Santillana's poems but also in the first of the important anonymous satirical poems, *Coplas de ¡Ay panadera!* This poem, supposedly narrated by a camp-follower, gives an account of the battle of Olmedo (1445) between Luna's supporters and his enemies. The description concentrates on the cowardice of both sides, devoting one octosyllabic stanza to each of the leading combatants, and showing the ludicrous, and occasionally revolting, results of their cowardice. The poet is concerned not to take sides but to heap ridicule on an aristocracy which is too degenerate to fight; this poem is the converse of the chivalresque romances and the chronicles inspired by them, but is scarcely realistic. It is, like the romances, an abstraction from reality arranged in an artistic form.

The other two most significant satires are also anonymous poems in octosyllables, the *Coplas de Mingo Revulgo* and the *Coplas del Provincial*, and like the *Panadera* they were imitated by later poets. They refer not to the reign of Juan II, but to the desperate situation of Castile under Enrique IV. The *Provincial* represents Castile as a corrupt monastery, whose superior in the order is reporting on a visitation. It was probably composed *c.* 1474, at the end of Enrique's reign, and refers to events of the previous nine years. There is a strong anti-Jewish bias in this poem, but even stronger are the wholesale accusations of sexual corruption. Almost every kind of vice and perversion is included (some of the accusations were no doubt correct), and sexual vice is used as an image of a generally corrupt society. *Mingo Revulgo* is less concerned with scandal, but no more optimistic. Castile is a flock of sheep, and Enrique IV is their shepherd Candaulo who lets the wolves (the great nobles) devour them. The other shepherds who comment on this speak a form of *sayagués*, the stylised rustic speech to be used in drama. The apocalyptic vision of Castile is vividly and movingly presented : this is aesthetically the best of the three satires. A commentary on the poem was written by the chronicler and biographer Hernando del Pulgar.

XI. ÍÑIGO DE MENDOZA AND RELIGIOUS POETRY

Mingo Revulgo may well be the work of the Franciscan friar Íñigo de Mendoza (*c.* 1425-*c.* 1507). Fray Íñigo, of *converso* ancestry on his mother's side, wrote a few love-poems in his youth, some political, religious, and moral poems, and the *Coplas de Vita Christi*, nearly 4,000 lines of octosyllables. The first version was composed about 1467-68, a second followed soon afterwards, and in 1482 a third, or official, version was printed. The *Vita*, despite its length, covers only the period from the Incarnation to the Massacre of the Innocents, but it weaves into the main story a great diversity of elements. There is much moral and social comment (*Mingo Revulgo* may have been a first sketch for this); a dialogue on Christ's birth which is in *sayagués* and, though not a play, has dramatic features and may have contributed to the development of religious drama; and several hymns. The sources are primarily biblical and patristic, but Mendoza also makes use of secular material, including Spanish verse of the earlier fifteenth century.[21]

Some of Íñigo de Mendoza's political verse, composed after the accession of the Catholic Monarchs, takes the form not of satire but of straightforward advocacy of a political programme, and in this he coincides with several other poets, including Gómez Manrique, Antón de Montoro, and Juan Álvarez Gato. The reason is simple: Fernando and Isabel brought back order and a sense of purpose, in place of the vacillation, corruption, and anarchy of Enrique's reign. It has even been suggested that only their actions averted a peasant revolt. Poets had an additional reason for praising them, since they favoured learning and literature (see above, p. 147), and it may be for this reason, as well as the more obvious one of financial reward, that several poets address to Isabel, either openly or by implication, poems in which praise merges into sexual admiration, which in turn takes on the note of blasphemous hyperbole that distinguishes courtly love-poetry of the late fifteenth century.[22]

The *Vita Christi* is one of a group of poems which constitute an important innovation within Spanish religious poetry, though here again, Spain's cultural belatedness is evident. The lives of saints and the miracles of the Virgin Mary are almost the only subjects for religious narrative in Spanish in the thirteenth and fourteenth centuries. In the thirteenth century, however, the Franciscans in other countries began to concentrate the attention of the faithful on the life and Passion of Christ, with the *Meditationes vitae Christi* at one time attributed to St Bonaventure, which had a strong influence not only on verse and prose-works, but also on drama and the visual arts. By the fourteenth century, Lives of Christ, of Franciscan inspiration, were common in a number of countries, and by the end of that century had spread to Catalonia, but it was not until the 1470s that similar works were composed in Castilian.

The poems concerned are, apart from Íñigo de Mendoza's: Diego de San Pedro's *Passión trobada*; Ambrosio Montesino's *Coplas sobre diversas devociones y misterios*; and the Comendador Román's *Trovas de la gloriosa Pasión*. These were printed in the 1480s, and some appear to have been composed a decade or so earlier. The decisive influence was not, as has been claimed, the Devotio Moderna, but the Franciscans, and especially the sermons preached by the reformed branch of the order, to which both Mendoza and Montesino belonged. Mendoza's *Vita Christi*, whose diverse nature we have already noted, may be regarded as a series of versified sermons for the Annunciation, Nativity, and so on; certainly the techniques of satire, dramatic dialogue, and vivid comparison are those found in English popular sermons. The comparisons used for religious subjects cover a wide range, and many are drawn from things familiar to the audience. This integration of the most solemn moments of Christ's existence on earth with the trivia of everyday life can be shocking to modern sensibilities, and was not approved of by all ecclesiastics at the time, but there is no doubt that it had a strong appeal, which it retained well into the seventeenth century.

Inevitably, these poems draw much of their material from the Bible, but whereas Mendoza and San Pedro make direct use of the Gospels, Montesino does so far less, and Román scarcely at all, taking his biblical material from other sources. On the other hand, Román uses a good deal of material from the Apocrypha. One clear tendency deriving from the *Meditationes* is a concentration on the most horrific aspects of the Crucifixion: for instance, San Pedro's *Passión trobada* describes in detail what must have happened when Christ's clothes were stripped from His back after the wounds of the scourging had begun to heal. Descriptions of this sort are not peculiar to Spain: in Scotland, San Pedro's near-contemporary William Dunbar uses almost exactly the same technique, and similar developments occur elsewhere. The *Passión trobada*, like Mendoza's *Vita*, has strong popular appeal and dramatic qualities (it may even have been staged in the sixteenth century), and it retained its popularity long after more modern treatments of the subject had come and gone. In the first decade of the sixteenth century, Montesino (died 1513) translated Ludolph of Saxony's *Vita Christi* (of Devotio Moderna origin) into Spanish, and the *Retablo de la vida de Cristo* by Juan de Padilla (1468-1522?) clearly uses Ludolph. Like most poems of this type, the *Retablo* remained popular for a century or so, but the *Passión trobada* far outstripped the other poems, and *pliegos sueltos* were still being printed for sale to ordinary people well into the nineteenth century. It should be added that the printed version of the *Passión* seems to be an abridgement of the version recently discovered in manuscript in the *Cancionero de Oñate-Castañeda* (compiled *c.* 1480).[23]

XII. 'CANCIONERO GENERAL'

The *cancioneros* so far discussed—*Baena, Palacio, Herberay,* and the descendants of the lost Neapolitan anthology—represent the taste of one man or of a homogeneous group, but the last *cancionero* to be considered (it is also by far the largest) is inclusive rather than selective. This is the *General,* assembled and arranged by Hernando del Castillo. He began about 1490 to collect all the poems he could find from the time of Mena onwards, including a few earlier poets who had retained their popularity. In 1509 he signed a printing contract, and early in 1511 the volume, containing over a thousand poems, was placed on sale. It was an immediate success, and expanded editions followed. The series of *cancioneros* descended from the *General* belongs to the literary history of the Golden Age, but the contents of Castillo's volume need to be discussed here, since they represent the poetic production of the reigns of Enrique IV and, especially, the Catholic Monarchs.

The *Cancionero* includes a final section of *Obras de burlas pro-vocantes a risa,* most of which are, to a greater or lesser extent, obscene, and this led a strange twilight existence, being detached from subsequent editions and printed separately, and in modern times being largely ignored by critics and literary historians. As with the Galician-Portuguese *cantigas d'escarnho e de maldizer,* the *Obras de burlas* include poems by authors well known then and now for their religious poems and their idealised treatment of courtly love.

In some respects, such as the ready inclusion of ballads and *villancicos,* the *Cancionero general* marks an enlargement of cultured poetry, but in other respects there is a growing restriction. The most notable of these is the *canción,* where the already formalised practice becomes much more closely delimited, in the number of stanzas, the number of rhymes, and the arrangements of the rhyme-scheme. This restriction is a sign of ingenuity: to operate successfully within the very narrow limits allowed by the new convention is a supreme test of a poet's skill. That skill may be exercised in other ways too: one poem in the *General* splits its lines so that the first and second halves may be read as independent poems, each with a different meaning from that formed by the whole lines.

The skill and the restriction are conceptual as well as metrical: the riddle known as the *perqué* is much cultivated, and antithesis, paradox, and verbal juggling are at their height among the poets of the last quarter of the fifteenth century, and are exercised under increasingly stringent conditions: the vocabulary is remarkably limited both in quantity and in type (nearly all of the words are abstract). This, of course, makes it very difficult for the modern reader to concentrate on even a short poem like a *canción,* and it makes comprehension of the poems equally difficult. It is tempting to regard these late *canciones* as displays of ultimately pointless ingenuity, and this may prove to be the right answer—some cultures do take disastrously wrong turnings. It is, however, also possible that modern readers have somehow missed the point, that some of the often-repeated abstract words such as *gloria* and *muerte* (in the *canciones* and elsewhere) are sexual euphemisms, and that many of the poems celebrate a sensual and consummated love.

In some cases, we know only the surname of a *General* poet: this is true of Soria, Tapia (almost certainly not the same person as Juan de Tapia—above, p. 194), and Guevara. All wrote good poems, and Guevara, as well as writing within the strictest conventions of his time, was also prepared on occasion to write more openly: the heading (not necessarily the poet's own work) to one of his poems tells us that he wrote it while in bed with his mistress. We have a little more information about three other poets: documentary evidence sheds some light, though not with absolute certainty, on the biographies of Cartagena and Quirós, and the heading to a poem tells us that Pinar is the brother of Florencia Pinar. Both Quirós and Pinar wrote elaborate poems based on card-games. This kind of elaboration on a previously-established basis seems to have suited Pinar, since most of his work consists of *glosas* on other poems. Quirós's production is more varied. He is, perhaps, the most typical writer of *canciones*, in the sense that four of his *canciones* exactly fit the restricted rules that may be deduced from a survey of the *General* poems, and another three come close to fitting them. Other poems of his are of a very different type; one develops the siege metaphor for love in a way which almost compels the reader to pursue the meaning on three levels:

Es una muy linda torre
la Discreción y el Saber,
Razón la tiene en poder
y la socorre
quando se quiere perder
de manera
que si alguno está defuera
aunque todo el mundo junte
y se ayunte
no l'entrará la barrera.

Porque quanta fuerça falta
a los que entralla queremos,
tanto más en ella vemos
ser tan alta
que ganalla no sabemos,
y la puerta
vémosla contino abierta,
mas está tan torreada
que cerrada
la halla quien no la acierta.

and another shows a lover's misfortunes by an allegory in which wild
men and a tomb represent aspects of his sufferings.

Florencia Pinar is unusual not only in being a woman in the almost
exclusively masculine preserve of *cancionero* poets, but also in her
preference for concrete objects in her few *canciones*. In one *canción*,
she describes love as a worm, and in another, she compares herself with
captive partridges; this second poem has been interpreted as an innocent
love of nature, but it has (as reference to a bestiary will show) highly
sensual implications.[24]

Much more is known about Juan Álvarez Gato (born *c.* 1440-50,
died *c.* 1510), a *converso* who served for a time in the royal household
and was strongly influenced by Hernando de Talavera; Diego López
de Haro, who served in an embassy to Rome in 1493; and Garci
Sánchez de Badajoz, who wrote most of his paradoxical and tormented
poems after 1500. Of these, Álvarez Gato covers the widest range of
non-dramatic verse: politics, satire, morality, allegory, love are all
within his scope, and he also left prose-writings. His most significant
contribution to the development of Spanish poetry is, however, his
group of love-poems *a lo divino*. The *contrafactum*, or profane poem
reworked in a religious sense, has a long ancestry in European literature,
but there was no consistent tradition of such writing in Spanish until
Álvarez Gato led the way. He was quickly followed by (and he probably
influenced) the Franciscan friars Íñigo de Mendoza and Ambrosio
Montesino. The themes, the images, and the forms of profane love-
poetry are used in *a lo divino* writing; we find not only the courtly
verse-forms used for this purpose, but also ballads and *villancicos*
(there is an isolated example in a play by Gómez Manrique—see below,
p. 211). These works appear at the very end of medieval Spanish
poetry, and in small numbers; they are to become one of the main
currents of Golden Age literature.[25]

Many poets who appear in *cancioneros* later than the *General*, or
in separate editions or manuscripts, have unmistakably medieval aspects
in their work, and some are wholly medieval in attitude and technique;
the continued popularity of some fifteenth-century poets again emphasises that there is no break in continuity. The descendants of the
General, like the ballads, the chivalresque romances, and the *Visión
deleitable* of Alfonso de la Torre, retain their hold on the public long
after new forms have been introduced. Medieval attitudes and tastes
survive Garcilaso's scornful rejection of the old conventions.

NOTES

1. For lists of the *cancioneros* and their contents, see Simón Díaz, Bibliografía, III, i; Charles V. Aubrun, 'Inventaire des sources pour l'étude de la poésie castillane au XVe siècle', *EMP*, IV (Madrid, 1953), 297-330; A. Rodríguez-Moñino and María Brey Mariño, *Catálogo de los manuscritos poéticos castellanos (siglos XV, XVI y XVIII) de The Hispanic Society of America* (3 vols., New York, 1965-66).

2. Whinnom, *Spanish Literary Historiography*, p. 21.

3. H. A. Rennert, *Macías, o namorado. A Galician trobador* (Philadelphia, 1900); K. H. Vanderford, 'M. in Legend and Literature', *MP*, XXXI (1933-34), 35-64; Carlos Martínez-Barbeito, *M. el enamorado y Juan Rodríguez del Padrón. Estudio y antología* (Santiago de Compostela, 1951).

4. Ezio Levi, 'L'ultimo re dei giullari', *SM*, n.s., I (1928), 173-80; Ferruccio Blasi, 'La poesia di Villasandino', *Messana*, ed M. Catalano (Messina, 1950), pp. 89-102; Giovanni Caravaggi, 'V. et les derniers troubadours de Castille', *Mélanges Lejeune*, I, 395-421. Joaquín Gimeno Casalduero, 'Pero López de Ayala y el cambio poético de Castilla a comienzos del siglo XV', *HR*, XXXIII (1965), 1-14. Rafael Lapesa, 'La lengua de la poesía lírica desde Macías hasta Villasandino', *RPh*, VII (1953-54), 51-9.

5. Edwin B. Place, 'The Exaggerated Reputation of Francisco Imperial', *Sp*, XXI (1946), 457-73; Archer Woodford, 'F.I.'s Dantesque *Dezir de las syete virtudes*: a study of certain aspects of the poem', *Italica*, XXVII (1950), 88-100, 'More about the Identity of Miçer F.I.', *MLN*, LXVIII (1953), 386-8, and 'Edición crítica del *Dezir a las syete virtudes*, de F.I.', *NRFH*, VIII (1954), 268-94; Rafael Lapesa, 'Nota sobre Micer F.I.', *NRFH*, VII (1953), 337-51 (repr. in *De la Edad Media*, pp. 76-94); Edwin B. Place, 'Present Status of the Controversy over F.I.', *Sp*, XXXI (1956), 478-84; Dorothy C. Clarke, 'Dante: a medieval poet's ideal', *RoN*, II (1960-61), 49-53, 'Church Music and Ritual in the *Decir a las siete virtudes*', *HR*, XXIX (1961), 179-99, 'The passage on Sins in the *DSV*', *SP*, LIX (1962), 18-30, 'A Comparison of F.I.'s *Decir al nacimiento del rey don Juan* and the *DSV*', *S*, XVII (1963), 17-29, and 'F.I., Nascent Spanish Secular Drama and the Ideal Prince', *PQ*, XLII (1963), 1-13; J. Gimeno Casalduero, 'Fuentes y significado del *Decir al nacimiento de Juan II* de F.I.', *RLC*, XXXVIII (1964), 115-20; Giuseppe E. Sansone, 'Émendations métriques au *DSV* de F.I.', *BH*, LXIX (1967), 5-25. Jules Piccus, 'El *Dezir que fizo Juan Alfonso de Baena*', *NRFH*, XII (1958), 335-56.

6. Charles F. Fraker, *Studies*, 'The *dejados* and the *Cancionero de Baena*', *HR*, XXXIII (1965), 97-117, 'Gonçalo Martínez de Medina, the *Jerónimos*, and the *Devotio Moderna*', *HR*, XXXIV (1966), 197-217, and 'Prophecy in G.M. de M.', *BHS*, XLIII (1966), 81-97. N. W. Eddy, 'Dante and Ferrán Manuel de Lando', *HR*, IV (1936), 124-35. Demetrius Basdekis, 'Modernity in Ferrant Sanches Calavera', *HBalt*, XLVI (1963), 300-3. Edwin B. Place, 'More about Ruy Páez de Ribera', *HR*, XIV (1946), 22-37. Andrés Soria, 'La *Confesión rimada* de Fernán Pérez de Guzmán', *BRAE*, XL (1960), 191-263.

7. Otis H. Green, 'Courtly Love in the Spanish *Cancioneros*', *PMLA*, LXIV (1949), 247-301; Clarke, *Morphology*.

8. F. B. Luquiens, 'The *Roman de la Rose* and Medieval Castilian Literature', *RF*, XX (1907), 284-320; Post, *Med. Spanish Allegory*; Arturo Farinelli, *Italia e Spagna* (2 vols., Torino, 1929); Le Gentil, *La Poésie lyrique*, and review by Eugenio Asensio, *RFE*, XXXIV (1950), 286-304;

Margherita Morreale, 'Dante in Spain', *ACLLS*, VIII (1966), 5-21, and 'Apuntes bibliográficos para el estudio del tema "Dante en España hasta fines del s. XVII" ', ibid., 93-134. See also notes on individual poets.

9. Mario Schiff, *La Bibliothèque du Marquis de Santillane* (BÉHÉ 153, Paris, 1905); Lapesa, *Santillana*, Ch. 8.

10. For main editions and critical books, see Bibliography. Also: A. Vegue y Goldoni, *Los sonetos al itálico modo de don Íñigo López de Mendoza, Marqués de Santillana. Estudio crítico y nueva edición* (Madrid, 1911); J. Seronde, 'A Study of the Relations of Some Leading French Poets of the XIV and XV Centuries to the M. de S.', *RR*, VI (1915), 60-86, and 'Dante and the French Influence on the M. de S.', *RR*, VII (1916), 194-210; R. Menéndez Pidal, 'Poesías inéditas del M. de S.', *Poesía árabe*, pp. 109-18; Mario Penna, 'Notas sobre el endecasílabo en los sonetos del M. de S.', *EMP*, V (Madrid, 1954), 253-82; Rafael Lapesa, 'El endecasílabo en los sonetos de S.', *RPh*, X (1956-57), 180-5, and 'Los *Proverbios* de S.: contribución al estudio de sus fuentes', *HispI*, I (1957), 5-19 (reprinted in *De la Edad Media*, pp. 95-111); Jules Piccus, 'Rimas inéditas del M. de S., sacadas del *Cancionero de Gallardo* (o de San Román), Acad. de la Hist., Sig. 2-7-2, ms. 2', *HispI*, I (1957), 20-31; Manuel Durán, 'S. y el prerrenacimiento', *NRFH*, XV (1961), 343-63; Arnold G. Reichenberger, 'The M. de S. and the Classical Tradition', *IR*, I (1969), 5-34; A. J. Foreman, 'The Structure and Content of S.'s *Comedieta de Ponça*', *BHS* (in press).

11. George Saintsbury, *A History of Criticism and Literary Taste in Europe from the earliest texts to the present day*, I (Edinburgh, 1900); J. W. H. Atkins, *English Literary Criticism*, I (Cambridge, 1943); George Watson, *The Literary Critics: a study of English descriptive criticism* (Harmondsworth, Penguin, 1962). The *Carta* is included in the eds. of Amador de los Ríos and Trend, and is separately ed. by Antonio R. Pastor and Edgar Prestage, *Letter of the Marquis of S. to Don Peter, Constable of Portugal* (Oxford, 1927). See Florence Street, 'Some Reflexions on S.'s *Prohemio e carta*', *MLR*, LII (1957), 230-3.

12. R. Foulché-Delbosc, 'Étude sur le *Laberinto* de Juan de Mena', *RH*, IX (1902), 75-138; C. R. Post, 'The Sources of J. de M.', *RR*, III (1912), 223-79; Inez Macdonald, 'The *Coronación* of J. de M.: poem and commentary', *HR*, VII (1939), 125-44; Florence Street, 'La vida de J. de M.', *BH*, LV (1953), 149-73, and 'The Allegory of Fortune and the Imitation of Dante in the *Laberinto* and *Coronación* of J. de M.', *HR*, XXIII (1955), 1-11; Rafael Lapesa, 'El elemento moral en el *Lab.* de M.: su influjo en la disposición de la obra' *HR*, XXVII (1959), 257-66 (repr. in *De la Edad Media*, pp. 112-22); Joaquín Gimeno Casalduero, 'Notas sobre el *L. de F.*', *MLN*, LXXIX (1964), 125-39; Alberto Vàrvaro, 'Lo scambio di *coplas* fra J. de M. e l'infante D. Pedro', *AION*, *Sez. Rom.*, VIII (1966), 199-214; Philip O. Gericke, 'The Narrative Structure of the *L. de F.*', *RPh*, XXI (1967-68), 512-22. The belief that Mena was a *converso* has now been strongly challenged: Eugenio Asensio, 'La peculiaridad literaria de los conversos', *AEM*, IV (1967), 327-51. On the literary treatment of Fortune, see H. R. Patch, *The Goddess Fortuna in Mediaeval Literature* (Cambridge, Mass., 1927), and Italo Siciliano, *François Villon et les thèmes poétiques du Moyen Âge* (Paris, 1934, pp. 281-311).

13. Le Gentil, *Poésie lyrique*, I, 459-96; John G. Cummins, 'Methods and Conventions in the 15th-Century Poetic Debate', *HR*, XXXI (1963), 307-23, and 'The Survival in the Spanish *Canacioneros* of the Form and Themes of Provençal and Old French Poetic Debates', *BHS*, XLII (1965), 9-17.

14. J. M. Octavio de Toledo, 'Visión de Filiberto', *ZRP*, II (1878), 40-69 (includes ed. of prose debate); Cyril A. Jones, 'Algunas versiones más del *Debate entre el cuerpo y el alma*', *Miscellanea di Studi Ispanici* (Pisa, 1963), pp. 110-34; Pierre Groult, 'La *Disputa del alma y el cuerpo*: sources et originalité', *Literary and Linguistic Studies in Honor of Helmut A. Hatzfeld*, pp. 221-9; E. M. Wilson, *Some Aspects of Spanish Literary History*, p. 16 and note 28.

15. E. Cotarelo, 'Algunas noticias nuevas acerca de Rodrigo Cota', *BRAE*, XIII (1926), 11-17 and 140-3; Augusto Cortina, 'R.C.', *RBAM*, VI (1929), 151-65; C. H. Leighton, 'Sobre el texto del *Diálogo entre el amor y un viejo*', *NRFH*, XII (1958), 385-90; Richard F. Glenn, 'R.C.'s *Diálogo entre el amor y un viejo*: debate or drama?', *HBalt*, XLVIII (1965), 51-6. Alfonso Miola, 'Un testo drammatico spagnuolo del XV secolo', *Miscellanea di Filologia e Linguistica in memoria Napoleone Caix e Ugo Angelo Canello* (Firenze, 1886), pp. 175-89.

16. Florence Whyte, *The Dance of Death in Spain and Catalonia* (Baltimore, 1931); James M. Clark, *The Dance of Death in the Middle Ages and the Renaissance* (Glasgow, 1950); Hellmut Rosenfeld, *Der mittelalterliche Totentanz: Entstehung—Entwicklung—Bedeutung* (Münster and Köln, 1954); J. M. Solá-Solé, 'El rabí y el alfaquí en la *Dança general de la Muerte*', *RPh*, XVIII (1964-65), 272-83, and 'En torno a la *DGM*', *HR*, XXXVI (1968), 303-27; Deyermond, 'El ambiente social e intelectual de la *DM*', *Actas del III Congreso Internacional de Hispanistas* (México, 1970), 267-76; Roger M. Walker, ' "Potest aliquis gustare quod gustatum affert mortem?" An aspect of imagery and structure in the *DGM*', *MAe* (in press). The 1520 amplification is ed. J. Amador de los Ríos, *Historia crítica de la literatura española*, VII (Madrid, 1865), 501-40. See also J. Huizinga, *The Waning of the Middle Ages* (London, 1924), Ch. 11.

17. The poems cited are *Baena* nos. 38 (Migir) and 530 (Sánchez Calavera), and Foulché-Delbosc, *Cancionero castellano*, no. 951 (Diego de Burgos). Cf. above, p. 132, n.17.

18. Eustaquio Tomé, *Jorge Manrique. Con el texto integro de las Coplas. . .* (Montevideo, 1930); Leo Spitzer, 'Dos observaciones sintáctico-estilísticas a las *Coplas* de M.', *NRFH*, IV (1950), 1-24; Stephen Gilman, 'Tres retratos de la muerte en las *Coplas* de J.M.', *NRFH*, XIII (1959), 305-24; Lida de Malkiel, *La idea de la fama*, pp. 291-4, and 'Para la primera de las *Coplas . . .*', *RPh*, XVI (1962-63), 170-3; Gualtiero Cangiotti, *Le Coplas di M. tra Medioevo e Umanesimo* (Testi e Saggi di Letterature Moderne, Saggi 2, Bologna, 1964); Peter N. Dunn, 'Themes and Images in the *Coplas . .* of J.M.', *MAe*, XXXIII (1964), 169-83; Alberto del Monte, 'Chiosa alle *Coplas* di J.M.', *Studi di Lengua e Letteratura Spagnola*, ed. G. M. Bertini (Torino, 1965), 61-79; Joseph Vinci, 'The Petrarchan Source of J.M.'s *Las coplas*', *It*, XLV (1968), 314-28; Richard P. Kinkade, 'The Historical Date of the *Coplas* and the Death of J.M.', *Sp*, XLV (1970), 216-24.

19. Ezio Levi, 'Un juglar español en Sicilia (Juan de Valladolid)', *Homenaje a Menéndez Pidal*, III, 419-39. Francisca Vendrell Gallostra, 'La corte literaria de Alfonso V de Aragón y tres poetas de la misma', *BRAE*, XIX (1932), 85-100, 388-405, 468-84, 584-607, 733-47, and XX (1933), 69-92. Carvajal, *Poesie*, ed. Emma Scoles (Officina Romanica 9, Roma, 1967); cf. M. Morreale, *RFE*, LI (1968), 275-87. Francisca Vendrell, 'La posición del poeta Juan de Dueñas respecto a los judíos españoles de su época', *Sef*, XVIII (1958), 108-13; Antonio Alatorre, 'Algunas notas sobre la *Misa de amores*', *NRFH*, XIV (1960), 325-8; Jules Piccus, 'La *Misa de amores* de

Juan de Dueñas', ibid., 322-5, and 'El Marqués de Santillana y J. de D.', *HispI*, 10 (1961), 1-7; Eloy Benito Ruano, 'Lope de Stúñiga. Vida y cancionero', *RFE*, LI (1968), 17-109.

20. Gómez Manrique, *Cancionero*, ed. Antonio Paz y Melia (2 vols., Colección de Escritores Castellanos 36 and 39, Madrid, 1885). Antón de Montoro, *Cancionero*, ed. Emilio Cotarelo y Mori (Madrid, 1900); Rafael Ramírez de Arellano, 'Antón de Montoro y su testamento', *RABM*, IV (1900), 484-9, and 'Ilustraciones a la biografía de A. de M. El motín de 1473 y las Ordenanzas de los aljabibes', ibid., 932-5; Erasmo Buceta, 'A. de M. y el *Cancionero de obras de burlas*', *MP*, XVII (1919-20), 175-82; Charles V. Aubrun, 'Conversos del siglo XVI (a propósito de A. de M.)', *Fi*, XIII (1968-69), 59-63. Pero Guillén de Segovia, *La gaya ciencia*, ed. J. M. Casas Homs and O. J. Tuulio (2 vols., Madrid, CH, 1962); H. R. Lang, 'The So-Called *Cancionero de P.G. de S.*', *RH*, XIX (1908), 51-81; O. J. Tallgren, 'Passages de P.G. de S. remontant à Lucain', *NMi*, XXXII (1931), 55-60; Eloy Benito Ruano, 'Los *Hechos del arzobispo de Toledo D. Alonso Carrillo*, por P.G. de S.', *AEM*, V (1968), 517-30.

21. Julio Rodríguez Puértolas, 'Sobre el autor de las *Coplas de Mingo Revulgo*', *Homenaje a Rodríguez-Moñino*, II, 131-42, 'Eiximenis y Mendoza: literatura y sociedad en la baja Edad Media hispánica', *RVF*, VII (1963-66), 139-74, and 'Leyendas cristianas primitivas en las obras de Fray I. de M.', *HR*, XXXVIII (1970), 368-85; Keith Whinnom, 'Ms. Escurialense K-III-7; el llamado *Cancionero de Fray I. de M.*', *Fi*, VII (1961), 161-72, and 'The Printed Editions and the Text of the Works of Fray I de M.', *BHS*, XXXIX (1962), 137-52.

22. María Rosa Lida, 'La hipérbole sagrada en la poesía castellana del siglo XV', *RFH*, VIII (1946), 121-30; R. O. Jones, 'Isabel la Católica y el amor cortés', *RLit*, XXI (1962), 55-64.

23. Román's *Trovas* (in the amplified version, *Coplas de la Pasión con la Resurrección*) and Montesino's *Coplas* were both reprinted in facsimile, with introductions by Sir Henry Thomas (London, 1936); for San Pedro, see Bibliography. Marcel Bataillon, 'Chanson pieuse et poésie de dévotion. Fr. Ambrosio Montesino', *BH*, XXVII (1925), 228-38; Erna R. Berndt, 'Algunos aspectos de la obra poética de Fray A.M.', *Arch*, IX (1959), 56-71; Joaquín Gimeno, 'Sobre el Cartujano y sus críticos', *HR*, XXIX (1961), 1-14; Keith Whinnom, 'The Religious Poems of Diego de San Pedro: their relationship and their dating', *HR*, XXVIII (1960), 1-15, 'The Supposed Sources of Inspiration of Spanish Fifteenth-Century Narrative Religious Verse', *S*, XVII (1963), 268-91, and 'El origen de las comparaciones religiosas del siglo de oro: Mendoza, Montesino y Román', *RFE*, XLVI (1963), 263-85; Dorothy S. Vivian, '*La Passión trobada*, de Diego de San Pedro, y sus relaciones con el drama medieval de la Pasión', *AEM*, I (1964), 451-70; Dorothy S. Severin, 'The Earliest Version of D. de S.P.'s *La Pasión trobada*', *RF*, LXXXI (1969), 176-92. See also Owst, *Literature and Pulpit*, pp. 507-11; Woolf, *English Religious Lyric*, Ch. 2 and 6.

24. Keith Whinnom, 'Hacia una interpretación y apreciación de las canciones del *Cancionero general* de 1511', *Fi*, XIII (1968-69), 361-81; Ernest Grey, 'An Ingenious Portrayal of a Split Personality', *RoN*, IX (1967-68), 334-7; Le Gentil, *La Poésie lyrique*, II. Juan B. Avalle-Arce, 'Cartagena, poeta del *Cancionero general*', *BRAE*, XLVII (1967), 287-310; Francisco Cantera, 'El poeta Cartagena del *Cancionero general* y sus ascendientes los Franco', *Sef*, XXVIII (1968), 3-39. For Florencia Pinar, see Deyermond, *Traces of the Bestiary*. For Quirós, I draw also on a forthcoming study by A. J. Foreman.

25. Mario Ruffini, *Observaciones filológicas sobre la lengua poética de Alvarez Gato* (Sevilla, 1953). For the biography of López de Haro, see Erasmo Buceta's articles in *AHDE*, VI (1929), 145-96, *BRAE*, XVII (1930), 363-95, and *RH*, LXXXI, 1 (1933), 456-74. Nicholas G. Round, 'Garci Sánchez de Badajoz and the Revaluation of *Cancionero* Poetry', *FMLS*, VI (1970), 178-87.

Chapter 8

THE BEGINNINGS OF DRAMA

I. LITURGICAL DRAMA

MEDIEVAL SPAIN HAS A STRONG TRADITION of most kinds of poetry, prose fiction, chronicles, and didactic prose. When we turn to the drama, there is a marked contrast: a very few brief religious plays in Latin, a vernacular religious play of the late twelfth century, and then nothing until the reign of Enrique IV, when Gómez Manrique composes a Nativity play and a couple of very short secular pieces. From the 1490s onwards, there is a steady series of plays, beginning with the work of Juan del Encina and Lucas Fernández, who continue writing well into the sixteenth century, but the contrast between the wealth of drama in the Golden Age and the almost total absence of extant plays from the Middle Ages could scarcely be more acute. The situation becomes even more surprising when we compare it with that in Catalonia, where there are plentiful Latin, and at a later stage vernacular, texts. In these circumstances it is natural to conclude that many plays must have been lost, and to look for evidence in legislation, chronicles, and other sources; it is natural also to consider semi-dramatic forms such as debate-poems and popular entertainments to be fully-fledged drama. Such attempts are, however, mistaken. All the evidence suggests that the drama was extraordinarily weak in medieval Castile; it may be added that it was even weaker in Portugal.

Semi-dramatic forms, popular entertainments, and literary texts in dialogue abound in medieval Europe, but the earliest plays are short pieces associated with the liturgy for Easter. Plays for other occasions, such as Good Friday, Christmas, and Epiphany, developed later, and the plays as a whole are known, because of their origins, as liturgical drama. The accepted view was for a long time that the liturgical drama evolved by a steady process, simple forms gradually being transferred to the churchyards and then to the streets, with a consequent secularisation and use of the vernacular. However, it has now been shown that this theory was based less on the evidence of texts than on the nineteenth-century assumptions of inevitable Darwinian progress which had been prevalent in the youth of the scholars concerned. The real picture is much less neat: some simple forms are later than complex ones, some Latin plays may well borrow from vernacular traditions, and the drama was not constantly struggling to free itself from a hostile Church, but on the contrary was fostered by the Mass, which was (before the virtual exclusion of the laity from an active part in the service) essentially dramatic in conception.[1]

The first liturgical play to develop was the *Quem quaeritis?* (or *Visitatio sepulchri*) of Easter, which probably began as a ceremony connected with the Mass at the Easter Vigil. The earliest extant *Quem quaeritis?* texts are from the tenth century, and by A.D. 1000 the plays are found in most of western Europe. The first to survive from Castile are in late eleventh-century breviaries written at the Benedictine monastery of Santo Domingo de Silos; the fuller of the two plays reads:

> Interrogat Angelus et dicit ad Discipulos: Quem queritis in sepulcro hoc, Cristicole?
> Respondent Discipuli et dicant: Ihesum Nazarenum crucifixum, o colicole.
> Iterum respondet Angelus: Non est hic, surrexit sicut loquutus est; ite, nuntiate quia surrexit Dominus, alleluia.
> Antiphona: Surrexit. Te Deum laudamus.

The other important types of liturgical play are the *Officium pastorum*, or visit of the shepherds to the infant Christ (this, which took its structure from the *Quem quaeritis?*, was the earliest Christmas play); the *Ordo stellae*, an Epiphany play which deals with the visit of the Magi; and the *Ordo prophetarum*, in which a series of Old Testament prophets, and others including Virgil and the Sybil, foretell the birth of Christ. The *Depositio*, or placing of Christ's body in the tomb on Good Friday, is more of a ceremony than a play until a fairly late period. These types are well represented in Catalonia, but there are no extant texts from medieval Castile. Even if we extend the area of enquiry to Portugal, Galicia, and Aragon, we can add only a *Quem quaeritis?* from Compostela, an *Officium pastorum* from Coimbra, and a small amount of rudimentary material from Saragossa and Huesca. References in documents to material no longer extant add something, but not very much, and the main point of interest is an eighteenth-century manuscript which gives mixed Latin and vernacular texts of a Sybil play and an *Officium pastorum*, claiming that they date from the thirteenth century. Other evidence shows that these plays go back at least to *c.* 1500 and to the fourteenth century, respectively, but we cannot tell how much older they may be.

The great scarcity of texts outside Catalonia cannot be primarily due to loss of manuscripts. We do not need to look very far for an explanation of the strong Catalan development, since at the crucial period Catalonia was ecclesiastically and culturally in the French sphere of influence; the only plausible explanation for the scarcity of liturgical drama elsewhere is the influence of the Cluniac monks, who from the late eleventh century dominated the ecclesiastical, and to a large extent the political and cultural, life of Castile, so that at the time when (given Spain's cultural belatedness) the liturgical drama might have taken root, a monastic order apparently uninterested in the drama was in possession.

What little liturgical drama existed seems to have been mainly for Easter, which was, for medieval Christians, the central point of the Church's year, overshadowing Christmas and all other holy days; its primacy is reflected by the earlier development of *Quem quaeritis?*. It is surprising that the equally scarce vernacular religious drama concentrates on the Nativity; but when the numbers involved are so small we cannot expect statistical regularity.[2]

II. 'AUTO DE LOS REYES MAGOS'

The only vernacular play before the fifteenth century is that known as the *Auto de los reyes magos* (there is no title in the manuscript). The three Kings meet, discuss the new star, and decide to go to Bethlehem and discover by offering gifts as a test whether the newly-born child is God, earthly king, or ordinary man. They visit Herod, who is appalled at their news, and who calls together the wise men of his Court immediately after the departure of the Kings. The wise men, unable to solve the mystery of Christ's birth, quarrel, and the manuscript breaks off at this point. It has been plausibly suggested that the complete play ended with the visit to the manger, and the child's acceptance of all three gifts, since He was man, king, and God at once. The *Auto* is very short (only 147 lines survive), yet achieves both definition of character (the three Kings are differentiated) and dramatic tension. A political issue, the nature of sovereignty, is raised, but the point on which much of the meaning depends is the figural relationship between the Old and New Testaments (cf. above, p. 79, note 32). The rabbis are unable to enlighten Herod: because they reject the new dispensation of Christ, they can no longer understand their own sacred texts adequately, and are left helpless.

The *Auto* was probably composed in the late twelfth century, and is often regarded as the sole survivor of a flourishing tradition of vernacular religious drama, but it seems increasingly likely to be an exotic import from across the Pyrenees. Some elements, and in particular the motif of the gifts as a test, derive from French narrative poems on the infancy of Christ (the main outline of the narrative is from St Matthew's Gospel). The language of the play points in the same direction: words which are supposed to rhyme but do not do so in Castilian would rhyme in Gascon pronunciation, and it is probable that the author was a Gascon priest who settled in Toledo, like so many Frenchmen at that period, and wrote the *Auto* for the Epiphany services there. If the *Auto* was composed in Spanish by a Gascon, or was translated from Gascon, it can no longer be used as evidence for an early Spanish dramatic tradition.[3] This does not, of course, lessen the quality of the play; nor does it disprove the existence of early vernacular drama, but we are left with a supposed tradition that has no extant texts and no clear evidence from other sources. It is probably safe to conclude that if vernacular religious plays existed between the twelfth and fifteenth centuries, they were few.

III. POPULAR AND COURT ENTERTAINMENTS

During this period of nearly three hundred years, there are several references in legislation to religious drama and to popular entertainments. The Church had for many centuries condemned lewd performances and rituals, some of which were probably survivals of pagan fertility rites (cf. above, p. 20), while others were degenerate forms of the classical drama. *Mimi* and *histriones* were denounced, and in the early days of the Church an actor who became a Christian had to abandon his work. These condemnations, whose frequency implies ineffectiveness, are repeated in the period we are considering: the Councils of Valladolid (1228), Toledo (1324), and Aranda (1473) prohibit such things as dancing in church, and *ludi* at Christmas. In the *Siete partidas*, Alfonso X forbids clergy to take part in *juegos de escarnio*, which in any case may not take place in churches, and says that clergy may participate in a *representaçión* of the presentation of Christ to the shepherds (*Officium pastorum*), or the three kings (*Ordo stellae*), or in an Easter play (*Quem quaeritis?*), provided that this happens under the authority of a bishop. This is important but inconclusive: we do not know the meaning of *juegos de escarnio*, and we do not know the language in which the approved *representaçión* could be, or the frequency of such performances. The likelihood is, however, that the *juegos* were not an early form of secular drama, but the performances of travelling entertainers or burlesque ceremonies such as that of the Boy Bishop. As to the kinds of entertainment available, we are much better informed: the *juglares* recited, sang, played instruments, and performed tricks. Popular entertainments included puppet-shows and increasingly elaborate automata, the latter forming part of ecclesiastical celebrations also. All of these entertainments, and the burlesque ceremonies, provided devices and techniques which could be exploited by dramatists, but they do not themselves constitute either drama or evidence for the existence of drama at the time.

Automata were much used in the Corpus Christi procession. The feast was proclaimed in 1264, but the procession did not become widespread until the early fourteenth century. Catalonia was the first part of the Peninsula to adopt it, but it was later taken up in Castile. Its importance for the history of the drama is twofold: it provided auxiliary techniques in the same way as popular entertainments, and it eventually became a prolific source of plays, since these were presented when the procession stopped at fixed points on its route. This development, however, did not affect Castile until much later.

Court and aristocratic festivities, like popular entertainments and church ceremonies, are a source of dramatic techniques, and sometimes themselves have dramatic qualities. Tournaments increasingly take on the nature of elaborately prepared performances, until the participants come close to imitating knights, as in 1461, when Miguel Lucas de Iranzo (cf. above, p. 153) feigned the defence of a bridge in the manner of the *Passo honroso*, or in 1463 and 1465, when the constable and his guests staged mock battles between Christians and Moors. Banquets involved increasingly elaborate arrangements, and became associated with mumming, or *momos*, which typically consisted of the use of some startling device, a disguising, the recitation of a poem, and the presentation of a gift. References to *momos* become frequent from the middle of the fifteenth century, and a full description of the *momos* at the Portuguese Court at Christmas 1500 is given by the Spanish ambassador. The machinery used becomes more and more spectacular, exercising an important influence on the staging of religious drama in the Golden Age, and the structure of the *momos* was incorporated into a play by Gómez Manrique, as we shall see shortly. It should be added that there was no sharp division between aristocratic festivities and religious drama: in the early 1460s, in Jaén, Miguel Lucas de Iranzo arranged representations of suitable Gospel scenes for Christmas and Epiphany, and on one occasion an actual play was performed.[4]

IV. GÓMEZ MANRIQUE

It will have been noticed that the more elaborate festivities belong to the second half of the fifteenth century, and this is the period when we no longer have to speculate about the possible existence of vernacular plays, since texts survive. The major figure here is Gómez Manrique (see above, p. 194), who composed four works that were capable of being staged, one of them being for performance by the nuns at the convent of Calabazanos where his sister was abbess. Two of these works are *momos*, one being a celebration of the fourteenth birthday of Prince Alfonso in 1467, and the other for the birth of the poet's nephew. In the first of these, which has a prose prologue, the ladies of the Court come forward in turn to confer virtues and talents on the young prince;

in the latter, personifications of the four cardinal and three theological virtues perform the same service for the newly-born child. It is not certain that these *momos* were for performance rather than reading, and the same is true of a third short work, the *Lamentaciones hechas para Semana Santa*, an exchange of speeches between the Virgin Mary and St John, which is an amplified translation of the liturgical *Planctus Mariae*.

There can be no doubt that the *Representación del nacimiento de Nuestro Señor* is a real play, intended for performance, even though it is not the same kind of play as the *Auto de los reyes magos*. The main outline is taken from the *Officium pastorum* (the Nativity story according to St Luke's Gospel), but into this is fitted an opening scene of farce, in which a ludicrously suspicious Joseph is rebuked by an angel:

> ' ¡ O viejo desventurado !
> Negra dicha fue la mía
> en casarme con María,
> por quien fuesse desonrrado.
> Yo la veo bien preñada,
> no sé de quién, nin de quánto;
> dizen que d'Espíritu Santo,
> mas yo desto non sé nada' . . .

> ' ¡ O viejo de muchos días,
> en el seso de muy pocos,
> el prinçipal delos locos !
> ¿Tú no sabes que Ysaýas
> dixo: "Virgen parirá",
> lo qual escrivió por esta
> donzella gentil, onesta,
> cuyo par nunca será ? '

(There is a medieval tradition of Joseph as a comic figure, since the Marian cult made it emotionally necessary to minimise the role of Mary's husband). Then come a meditation by Mary on her new-born child, in which she foresees the Crucifixion; a conversation between the shepherds (not in *sayagués*); *momos*, in which symbols of the Passion are presented to the infant Christ; and a lullaby in the form of a *villancico* without an *estribillo*, which closes the play. The scenes which fill out the Gospel narrative are thus amplifications of elements within that narrative (perhaps achieved by using the Franciscan technique of meditation—see above, pp. 196-7), or, in the case of the last two, secular forms turned *a lo divino*.

The *Representación* is often compared unfavourably with the *Auto* on the grounds that it is less dramatic, but this is a misunderstanding of the nature of the works. They are plays of different types, the *Auto* having the strict dramatic causality which was the almost universal characteristic of a good play from the late sixteenth to the mid-twentieth century, whereas the *Representación* seeks to make a point by a series of scenes that are almost tableaux. In the *Auto*, each scene follows inevitably from the preceding one, and hardly any could be omitted or moved without destroying the play; in the *Representación*, scenes with different techniques are harmoniously arranged so as to illuminate a central point of doctrine. Manrique has been careful in the construction of the play, but he could have arranged most of his scenes in a different order had he wished. There is, therefore, not a failure of technique but a new kind of play. Manrique could not have known the *Auto*, but he must have known some liturgical plays, and he has blended the liturgical drama with the *momos* to excellent effect. It is useful at this point to recall the controversy over the origins of liturgical drama: the misunderstanding that led to an undervaluation of the *Representación* by most critics was based on the assumption that in the history of drama there is steady development along a single line.

The doctrinal content of the *Representación* remains to be considered. Manrique is reminding his audience that Nativity and Crucifixion are indissolubly linked; he is giving dramatic form to the familiar doctrine that Christ was made man in order to die on the Cross.[5]

Manrique's dramatic activity in the reign of Enrique IV seems to stand alone. It reveals the poet's knowledge of some form of liturgical or semi-liturgical Christmas play, but it is not evidence of a continuous dramatic tradition from the time of the *Auto de los reyes magos*. The verdict for vernacular drama before the middle of the fifteenth century must be the same as for Latin liturgical drama outside Catalonia: the scarcity of texts rules out any possibility of a flourishing and continuous tradition. There were plays, but they were few and isolated. Only in the second half of the fifteenth century does anything like a vernacular tradition in the drama begin to emerge.

V. SEMI-DRAMATIC FORMS IN LITERARY TEXTS

We have seen dramatic features in popular and courtly entertainments, but they are not confined to these: they occur also in literary texts. Scholars have pointed to dramatic qualities in Francisco Imperial's *decir* on the birth of Juan II and, with more confidence, Íñigo de Mendoza's *Vita Christi*. Diego de San Pedro shows awareness, in his *Passión trobada*, of the dramatic tradition (not necessarily a Spanish vernacular tradition) of the Crucifixion, and, although he shows no signs of intending the *Passión* to be staged, staging was possible, and seems to have happened once in the sixteenth century. Among the debate-poems, dramatic qualities are to be expected, but in one case things seem to have gone further: as we have already seen, the anonymous *Diálogo entre el Amor, el viejo y la hermosa* may well have been intended for staging (above, p. 190).[6]

One final group of texts must be considered: Latin plays that were read but not performed. Terence was, because of his stylistic merits, used as a medieval school text, though there seems to be no Spanish equivalent of the tenth-century German nun Hrotsvitha who wrote a series of neo-Terentian Latin plays, apparently as a literary exercise and for her own satisfaction. Plautus and Seneca were read intermittently, and in the fifteenth century Seneca's plays were translated, as were other works by him or wrongly attributed to him. We have no evidence that any Classical Latin plays were performed in Spain before the early sixteenth century, and the likelihood is that there were no performances. The same is probably true of the elegiac and humanistic comedies. All these groups of Latin plays had a literary influence, and it was sometimes a very powerful influence—the elegiac comedy on the *Libro de Buen Amor*, the humanistic comedy on *La Celestina*—but they had no effect on the growth of Spanish drama until the Golden Age.[7] The few Spanish plays before the 1490s grew not from the inheritance of classical, medieval, and humanistic Latin drama, but from the Church and from the semi-dramatic entertainments of medieval society. All these tentative and sporadic experiments with dramatic and semi-dramatic forms in the Spanish Middle Ages prepared the way for the plays of Juan del Encina and Lucas Fernández in the last decade of the fifteenth century and the opening decades of the sixteenth. In them and in Gil Vicente, the medieval Spanish drama at last finds full expression, and the drama of the Golden Age is born.

NOTES

1. Hardison, *Christian Rite*. For earlier views, see E. K. Chambers, *The Mediaeval Stage* (2 vols., Oxford, 1903); Karl Young, *The Drama of the Medieval Church* (2 vols., Oxford, 1933).

2. Alexander A. Parker, 'Notes on the Religious Drama in Mediaeval Spain and the Origins of the *Auto sacramental*', *MLR*, XXX (1935), 170-82; Joseph E. Gillet, 'The *Memorias* of Felipe Fernández Vallejo and the History of the Early Spanish Drama', *Essays and Studies in Honor of Carleton Brown* (New York, 1940), pp. 264-80; Georges Cirot, 'Pour combler les lacunes de l'histoire du drame religieux en Espagne avant Gómez Manrique', *BH*, XLV (1943), 55-62.

3. Rafael Lapesa, 'Sobre el *Auto de los reyes magos*: sus rimas anómalas y el posible origen de su autor', *De la Edad Media*, pp. 37-47 (but see J. Corominas, *NRFH*, XII, 1958, 75n); Wardroper, 'The Dramatic Texture of the *ARM*', *MLN*, LXX (1955), 46-50; Guillermo Díaz-Plaja, 'El *ARM*', *EstE*, 4 (1959), 99-126; David W. Foster, 'Figural Interpretation and the *ARM*', *RR*, LVIII (1967), 3-11.

4. R. Menéndez Pidal, *Poesía juglaresca*; J. P. W. Crawford, *Spanish Drama before Lope de Vega* (2nd ed., Philadelphia, 1967); I. S. Révah, 'Gil Vicente a-t-il été le fondateur du théâtre portugais?', *Bulletin d'Histoire du Théâtre Portugais*, I (1950), 153-85, and 'Manifestations théâtrales prévicentines: les *momos* de 1500', ibid., III (1952), 91-105; Millett Henshaw, 'The Attitude of the Church towards the Stage to the End of the Middle Ages', *MH*, VII (1952), 3-17; J. E. Varey, *Historia de los títeres en España desde sus orígenes hasta mediados del siglo XVIII* (Madrid, 1957); Luciana Stegagno Picchio, *Ricerche sul teatro portoghese* (Officina Romanica 14, Roma, 1969), 39-62; Francis G. Very, *The Spanish Corpus Christi Procession: a literary and folkloric study* (Valencia, 1962). The relevant passage of the *Siete partidas* is I vi 34; not all of this is necessarily a reflection of Spanish conditions, since much of Alfonso's code is translated from foreign ecclesiastical legislation.

5. Harry Sieber, 'Dramatic Symmetry in Gómez Manrique's *La representación del nacimiento de Nuestro Señor*', *HR*, XXXIII (1965), 118-35.

6. Dorothy C. Clarke, 'Francisco Imperial, Nascent Spanish Secular Drama and the Ideal Prince', *PQ*, XLII (1963), 1-13; Dorothy S. Vivian, '*La Passión trobada*, de Diego de San Pedro'; Charlotte Stern, 'Fray Íñigo de Mendoza and Medieval Dramatic Ritual', *HR*, XXXIII (1965), 197-245.

7. R. L. Grismer, *The influence of Plautus in Spain before Lope de Vega* (New York, 1944); Justo García Soriano, *El teatro universitario y humanístico en España. Estudios sobre el origen de nuestro arte dramático* (Toledo, 1945); Edwin J. Webber, 'The Literary Reputation of Terence and Plautus in Medieval and Pre-Renaissance Spain', *HR*, XXIV (1956), 191-206, and 'Manuscripts and Early Printed Editions of Terence and Plautus in Spain', *RPh*, XI (1957-58), 29-39; Nicholas G. Round, 'Las versiones medievales catalanas y castellanas de las tragedias de Séneca', *AEM* (in press).

BIBLIOGRAPHY

GENERAL WORKS

Antti Aarne and Stith Thompson, *The Types of the Folktale. A classification and bibliography* (3rd ed., Folklore Fellows Communications 184, Helsinki, 1961)

Juan L. Alborg, *Historia de la literatura española*, I (2nd ed., Madrid, 1970)

José Amador de los Ríos, *Historia crítica de la literatura española* (7 vols., Madrid, 1861-65)

Dorothy Bethurum, ed., *Critical Approaches to Medieval Literature* (New York, 1960)

Américo Castro, *España en su historia. Cristianos, moros y judíos* (Buenos Aires, 1948); revised as *La realidad histórica de España* (México, 1954, again revised México, 1962)

H. J. Chaytor, *From Script to Print* (Cambridge, 1945)

Ernst R. Curtius, *European Literature and the Latin Middle Ages* (London, 1953)

Manuel C. Díaz y Díaz, *Index scriptorum latinorum medii aevi hispanorum* (Madrid, 1959)

Joan Evans, ed., *The Flowering of the Middle Ages* (London, 1966)

Bartolomé J. Gallardo, *Ensayo de una biblioteca española de libros raros y curiosos* (4 ols., Madrid, 1863-89)

Pascual de Gayangos, ed., *Escritores en prosa anteriores al siglo XV* (BAE, LI)

Sister Francis Gormly, *The Use of the Bible in Representative Works of Medieval Spanish Literature 1250-1300* (Washington 1962)

Otis H. Green, *Spain and the Western Tradition. The Castilian mind in literature from El Cid to Calderón* (4 vols., Madison and Milwaukee, 1963-66)

Denys Hay, ed., *The Age of the Renaissance* (London, 1967)

Friedrich Heer, *The Medieval World. Europe from 1100 to 1350* (London, 1962)

Pedro Henríquez Ureña, *Estudios de versificación española* (Buenos Aires, 1961)

Vincent F. Hopper, *Medieval Number Symbolism. Its sources, meaning, and influence on thought and expression* (Columbia University Studies in English and Comparative Literature 132, New York, 1938)

Johan Huizinga, *The Waning of the Middle Ages* (London, 1924)

Florencio Janer, ed., *Poetas castellanos anteriores al siglo XV* (BAE, LVII)

Henry Kraus, *The Living Theatre of Medieval Art* (London, 1967)

Pierre Le Gentil, *La Poésie lyrique espagnole et portugaise à la fin du Moyen Age* (2 vols., Rennes, 1949-53)

C. S. Lewis, *The Discarded Image. An introduction to medieval and Renaissance literature* (Cambridge, 1964)

María Rosa Lida de Malkiel, *La idea de la fama en la Edad Media castellana* (México and Buenos Aires, 1952)

Francisco López Estrada, *Introducción a la literatura medieval española* (3rd ed., Madrid, BRH, 1966)

Susan I, McMullan, 'The World Picture in Medieval Spanish Literature', *AION, Sez. Rom.*, XIII (1971), 27-105

William Matthews, ed., *Medieval Secular Literature. Four essays* (Berkeley and Los Angeles, 1965)

Marcelino Menéndez y Pelayo, *Antología de poetas líricos castellanos* (Edición Nacional, 10 vols., Madrid, 1944-45)

——, *Orígenes de la novela* (4 vols., NBAE, Madrid, 1905-15)

Ramón Menéndez Pidal, *Crestomatía del español medieval* (2 vols., Madrid, 1965-66)

G. R. Owst, *Literature and Pulpit in Medieval England* (2nd ed., Oxford, 1961)

Howard R. Patch, *The Goddess Fortuna in Mediaeval Literature* (Cambridge, Mass., 1927)

——, *The Other World according to Descriptions in Medieval Literature* (Cambridge, Mass., 1950); Spanish translation (México and Buenos Aires, 1956) with appendix by María Rosa Lida de Malkiel

Chandler R. Post, *Mediaeval Spanish Allegory* (HSCL 4, Cambridge, Mass., 1915)

Robert Pring-Mill, *El microcosmos lul·lià* (Palma de Mallorca and Oxford, 1961)

F. J. E. Raby, *A History of Christian-Latin Poetry* (2nd ed., Oxford, 1953)

——, *A History of Secular Latin Poetry in the Middle Ages* (2nd ed., 2 vols., Oxford, 1957)

David Talbot Rice, ed., *The Dark Ages* (London, 1965)

Claudio Sánchez-Albornoz, *España, un enigma histórico* (2 vols., Buenos Aires, 1956)

B. Sánchez Alonso, *Historia de la historiografía española*, I (Madrid, 1941)

Homero Serís, *Nuevo ensayo de una biblioteca española de libros raros y curiosos* (2 vols., New York, 1964-69)

José Simón Díaz, *Bibliografía de la literatura hispánica*, III (2nd ed., 2 vols., Madrid, 1963-65)

R. W. Southern, *Western Society and the Church in the Middle Ages* (Harmondsworth, Penguin, 1970)

A. C. Spearing, *Criticism and Medieval Poetry* (London, 1964)

Stith Thompson, *The Folktale* (New York, 1946)

——, *Motif-Index of Folk-Literature* (2nd ed., 6 vols., Copenhagen and Bloomington, Ind., 1955-58)

Lynn Thorndike, *A History of Magic and Experimental Science* (New York, 1923-41)

E. M. W. Tillyard, *The Elizabethan World Picture* (London, 1943)

Alberto Vàrvaro, *Manuale di filologia spagnola medievale.* II, *Letteratura* (Napoli, 1969)

J. Vicens Vives, *Aproximación a la historia de España* (2nd ed., Barcelona, 1960)

——, ed., *Historia social y económica de España y América*, I-II (Barcelona, 1957)

Keith Whinnom, *Spanish Literary Historiography: three forms of distortion* (Exeter, 1967)

Rosemary Woolf, *The English Religious Lyric in the Middle Ages* (Oxford, 1968)

BIBLIOGRAPHY TO PARTICULAR CHAPTERS

Chapter 1

Margit Frenk Alatorre, ed., *Lírica hispánica de tipo popular* (México, 1966)

José María Alín, ed., *El cancionero español de tipo tradicional* (Madrid, 1968)

Dámaso Alonso and J. M. Blecua, ed., *Antología de la poesía española: poesía de tipo tradicional* (Madrid, BRH, 1956)

Manuel Alvar, ed., *Poesía tradicional de los judíos españoles* (México, 1966)

Eugenio Asensio, *Poética y realidad en el cancionero peninsular de la Edad Media* (2nd ed., Madrid, BRH, 1970)

Francisco Luis Bernárdez, ed., *Florilegio del Cancionero Vaticano. Poesía amorosa galaicoportuguesa de la Edad Media* [with Spanish translations] (Buenos Aires, 1952)

C. M. Bowra, *Primitive Song* (London, 1962)

Peter Dronke, *Medieval Latin and the Rise of European Love-Lyric* (2nd ed., 2 vols., Oxford, 1968)

——, *The Medieval Lyric* (London, 1968)

Emilio García Gómez, *Poesía arábigoandaluza. Breve síntesis histórica* (Madrid, 1952)

Emilio García Gómez, ed., *Las jarchas romances de la serie árabe en su marco* (Madrid, 1965)

M. Rodrigues Lapa, *Lições de literatura portuguesa. Época medieval* (6th ed., Coimbra, 1966)

——, ed., *Cantigas d'escarnho e de mal dizer dos cancioneiros medievais galego-portugueses* (Vigo, 1965)

Pierre Le Gentil, *Le Virelai et le villancico. Le problème des origines arabes* (Paris, 1954)

E. P. and J. P. Machado, ed., *Cancioneiro da Biblioteca Nacional (antigo Colocci-Brancuti)* (8 vols., Lisboa, 1949-64)

Carolina Michaëlis de Vasconcellos, ed., *Cancioneiro da Ajuda* (2 vols., Halle, 1904)

J. M. Millás Vallicrosa, *Literatura hebraicoespañola* (Barcelona, 1967)

E. Monaci, ed., *Il Canzoniere portoghese della Bibliotheca Vaticana* (Halle, 1875)

J. J. Nunes, ed., *Cantigas d'amigo dos trovadores galego-portugueses* (3 vols., Coimbra, 1928)*

——, *Cantigas d'amor dos trovadores galego-portugueses* (2 vols., Coimbra, 1932)

Stephen Reckert, *Lyra Minima. Structure and symbol in Iberian traditional verse* (London, 1970)

Antonio Sánchez Romeralo, *El villancico (Estudios sobre la lírica popular en los siglos XV y XVI)* (Madrid, BRH, 1969)

S. M. Stern, ed., *Les Chansons mozarabes* (Palermo, 1953)

Giuseppe Tavani, *Repertorio metrico della lirica galego-portoghese* (Officina Romanica 7, Roma, 1967)

E. M. Torner, *Lírica hispánica. Relaciones entre lo popular y lo culto* (Madrid, 1966)

Chapter 2

C. M. Bowra, *Heroic Poetry* (London, 1952)

Rosa Castillo, ed., *Leyendas épicas españolas* (Valencia, Odres Nuevos, 1956)

Albert B. Lord, *The Singer of Tales* (HSCL 24, Cambridge, Mass., 1960)

Ramón Menéndez Pidal, *La epopeya castellana a través de la literatura española* (Buenos Aires and México, 1945; first publ. 1910, in French)

——, *Historia y epopeya* (Madrid, 1934)

——, *Poesía juglaresca y orígenes de las literaturas románicas. Problemas de historia literaria y cultural* (6th ed. [of *Poesía juglaresca y juglares*], Madrid, 1957)

——, ed., *Primera crónica general* (2nd ed., 2 vols., Madrid, 1955)

——, ed., *Reliquias de la poesía épica española* (Madrid, 1951)

——, Diego Catalán, *et al.*, ed., *Romancero tradicional*, I-II (Madrid, 1957-63)

El rey Rodrigo

R. Menéndez Pidal, ed., *Floresta de leyendas heroicas españolas: Rodrigo, el último godo*. I, *La Edad Media* (Madrid, CC, 1925)

Roncesvalles

Jules Horrent, *Roncesvalles. Étude sur le fragment de cantar de gesta conservé à l'Archivo de Navarra (Pampelune)* (BFPLUL, CXXII, Paris, 1951)

R. Menéndez Pidal, '*Roncesvalles*. Un nuevo cantar de gesta español del siglo XIII', *RFE*, IV (1917), 105-204 (abridged in *Tres poetas primitivos* [Buenos Aires, Austral, 1948])

Poema de Fernán González

ed. C. Carroll Marden (Baltimore and Madrid, 1904)
ed. R. Menéndez Pidal, *Reliquias*
ed. Alonso Zamora Vicente (2nd ed., Madrid, CC, 1954)*

Siete Infantes de Lara

R. Menéndez Pidal, *La leyenda de los infantes de Lara* (2nd ed., Madrid, 1934)

Cantar de Mio Cid

Edmund de Chasca, *El arte juglaresco en el CMC* (2nd ed. [of *Estructura y forma en el PMC*], Madrid, BRH, 1967)
——, *Registro de fórmulas verbales en el CMC* (Iowa City, 1968)
R. Menéndez Pidal, ed., *CMC* (3rd ed., 3 vols., Madrid, 1954-56)*
——, ed., *PMC* (3rd ed., Madrid, CC, 1929)
——, *En torno al Poema del Cid* (Barcelona and Buenos Aires, 1963)
——, *La España del Cid* (5th ed., 2 vols., Madrid, 1956)
Facsimile of manuscript (Madrid, 1961)

Cantar de Sancho II

Carola Reig, *El cantar de Sancho II y cerco de Zamora* (*RFE* anejo XXXVII, Madrid, 1947)

Mocedades de Rodrigo

ed. R. Menéndez Pidal, *Reliquias*
A. D. Deyermond, *Epic Poetry and the Clergy: studies on the Mocedades de Rodrigo* (London, Tamesis, 1969)
Facsimile of manuscript (New York, 1904)

Chapter 3

Christopher Brooke, *The Twelfth Century Renaissance* (London, 1969)
Marshall Clagett, *et al.*, ed., *Twelfth-Century Europe and the Foundations of Modern Society* (Madison, 1961)
Charles H. Haskins, *The Renaissance of the Twelfth Century* (Cambridge, Mass., 1927)
Friedrich Heer, *The Medieval World: Europe from 1100 to 1350* (London, 1962)

Cuaderna vía

P. L. Barcia, *El mester de clerecía* (Enciclopedia Literaria 9, Buenos Aires, 1967)

Berceo

Alfonso Andrés, ed., *Vida de Santo Domingo de Silos* (Madrid, 1958)
Joaquín Artiles, *Los recursos literarios de Berceo* (Madrid, BRH, 1964)
Clemente Canales Toro, ed., *Signos del Juicio Final* (Santiago de Chile, 1955)
Brian Dutton, *La vida de San Millán de la Cogolla, de G. de B. Estudio y edición crítica* (London, Tamesis, 1967)*
——, ed., *Los milagros de Nuestra Señora* (London, Tamesis, 1971)
John D. Fitz-Gerald, ed., *La vida de Santo Domingo de Silos* (BÉHÉ, CXLIX, Paris, 1904)
Carmelo Gariano, *Análisis estilístico de los Milagros de Nuestra Señora, de B.* (Madrid, BRH, 1965)
Gerhard Koberstein, ed., *Estoria de San Millán* (Münster, 1964)
C. Carroll Marden, ed., *Cuatro poemas de B.* (*RFE* anejo IX, Madrid, 1928) [*Santa Oria**, *San Millán*, and two *Milagros*]
——, ed., *Veintitrés Milagros* (*RFE* anejo X, Madrid, 1929)
——, ed., '*B.'s Martirio de San Lorenzo*', *PMLA*, XLV (1930), 501-15
Germán Orduna, ed., *Vida de Santo Domingo de Silos* (Salamanca, Anaya, 1968)*
T. Anthony Perry, *Art and Meaning in B.'s Vida de Santa Oria* (Yale Romanic Studies, 2nd series, XIX, New Haven and London, 1968)
A. G. Solalinde, ed., *Milagros de Nuestra Señora* (Madrid, CC, 1922)*
——, ed., *El sacrificio de la Misa* (Madrid, 1913)
BAE, LVII (for works not separately edited)

Libro de Alexandre

E. Alarcos Llorach, *Investigaciones sobre el L. de A.* (*RFE* anejo XLV, Madrid, 1948)
Ian Michael, *The Treatment of Classical Material in the L. de A.* (Manchester, 1970)

Raymond S. Willis, *The Relationship of the Spanish L. de A. to the Alexandreis of Gautier de Châtillon* (EMRLL, 31, Princeton and Paris, 1934)

——, *The Debt of the Spanish L. de A. to the French Roman d'Alexandre* (EMRLL, 33, Princeton and Paris, 1935)

——, ed., *El libro de A.* (EMRLL, 32, Princeton and Paris, 1934)

Libro de Apolonio

C. Carroll Marden, ed., *L. de A.* (2 vols., EMRLL, 6, Baltimore and Paris, 1917, and 11-12, Princeton and Paris, 1922)

Vida de Santa María Egipciaca

Manuel Alvar, ed., *Poemas hagiográficos de carácter juglaresco* (Madrid, 1967)

María S. de Andrés Castellanos, ed., *La VSME (BRAE* anejo XI, Madrid, 1964)*

Libre dels tres reys d'Orient

Manuel Alvar, ed., *Libro de la infancia y muerte de Jesús (Libre dels TRO)* (Madrid, CH, 1965)

——, ed., *Poemas hagiográficos . . .*

Facsimile of manuscript (New York, 1904)

¡Ay Jherusalem!

María del Carmen Pescador del Hoyo, ed., 'Tres nuevos poemas medievales', *NRFH*, XIV (1960), 242-7

Disputa del alma y el cuerpo

Ramón Menéndez Pidal, ed., '*Disputa . . .*', *RABM*, IV (1900), 449-53

Razón de amor

Mario Di Pinto, *Due contrasti d'amore nella Spagna medievale (Razón de amor e Elena y María)* (Pisa, 1959)

G. H. London, ed., 'The *Razón . . .* and the *Denuestos . .* New readings and interpretations', *RPh*, XIX (1965-66), 28-47

Ramón Menéndez Pidal, ed., '*Razón de amor*, con los *Denuestos del agua y el vino*', *RH*, XIII (1905), 602-18*

Elena y María

Mario Di Pinto, *Due contrasti . . .*

Ramón Menéndez Pidal, ed., '*Elena y María* (Disputa del clérigo y el caballero). Poesía leonesa inédita del siglo XIII', *RFE*, I (1914), 52-96 (revised version in *Tres poetas primitivos* [Buenos Aires, Austral, 1948])

Chapter 4

J. M. Millás Vallicrosa, *Estudios sobre historia de la ciencia española* (Barcelona, 1949)

——, *Nuevos estudios sobre historia de la ciencia española* (Barcelona, 1960)

——, *Las traducciones orientales en los manuscritos de la Biblioteca Catedral de Toledo* (Madrid, 1942)

Earliest Prose

Almerich, Arcidiano de Antiochia, *La fazienda de Ultra Mar. Biblia romanceada et itinéraire biblique en prose castillane du XIIe siècle*, ed. Moshé Lazar (Salamanca, 1965)

Corónicas navarras, ed. A. Ubieto Arteta (Textos Medievales 14, Valencia, 1964)

Liber regum, ed. Louis Cooper (*AFA* anejo 5, Zaragoza, 1960)*

——, ed. M. Serrano y Sanz, '*Cronicón Villarense . . .*', *BRAE*, VI (1919), 192-220, and VIII (1921), 367-82

Semeiança del mundo. A medieval description of the world, ed. William E. Bull and Harry F. Williams (UCPMP, LI, Berkeley and Los Angeles, 1959)

Alfonso X

Antología de Alfonso X el Sabio, ed. Antonio G. Solalinde (4th ed., Madrid, Austral, 1960)

Cantigas de Santa Maria, ed. W. Mettmann (3 vols., Coimbra, 1959-64)

General estoria, I, ed. A. G. Solalinde (Madrid, 1930)

——, II, ed. Solalinde, Lloyd A. Kasten, and Victor R. B. Oelschläger (2 vols., Madrid, 1957-61)

Primera crónica general, ed. R. Menéndez Pidal (2nd ed., 2 vols., Madrid, 1955)

Antonio Ballesteros-Beretta, *Alfonso X, el sabio* (Barcelona and Madrid, 1963)

Diego Catalán Menéndez-Pidal, *De Alfonso X al Conde de Barcelos. Cuatro estudios sobre el nacimiento de la historiografía romance en Castilla y Portugal* (Madrid, 1962)

Evelyn S. Procter, *Alfonso X of Castile, Patron of Literature and Learning* (Oxford, 1951)

Exemplum and Wisdom Literature

Castigos e documentos para bien vivir ordenados por el rey don Sancho IV, ed. Agapito Rey (IUHS 24, Bloomington, 1952)

La historia de la donzella Teodor, ed. Walter Mettmann (Mainz, 1962)

El libro de Calila e Digna, ed. John E. Keller and Robert W. Linker (Madrid, CH, 1967)

El libro de los engaños, ed. John E. Keller (UNCSRLL 20, Chapel Hill, 1959; also Valencia, 1959)

Los lucidarios españoles, ed. Richard P. Kinkade (Madrid, 1968)

Pedro Alfonso, *Disciplina clericalis*, ed. Ángel González Palencia (Madrid and Granada, 1948)

John E. Keller, *Motif-Index of Mediaeval Spanish Exempla* (Knoxville, 1949)

Chapter 5

Libro de miseria de omne, ed. Miguel Artigas, 'Un nuevo poema por la cuaderna vía', *BBMP*, I (1919) and II (1920)

Pero López de Ayala, *Poesías*, ed. Albert F. Kuersteiner (2 vols., New York, 1920)

Proverbios de Salamón, ed. C. E. Kany, *Homenaje a Menéndez Pidal* (Madrid, 1925), I, 269-85

Santob de Carrión, *Proverbios morales*, ed. I. González Llubera (Cambridge, 1947)

Pedro de Veragüe, *Tractado de la doctrina*, BAE, LVII

Raúl A. del Piero, *Dos escritores de la baja Edad Media castellana (Pedro de Veragüe y el arcipreste de Talavera, cronista real)* (Madrid, 1970)

Vida de San Ildefonso, BAE, LVII

Rodrigo Yáñez, *Poema de Alfonso XI*, ed. Yo ten Cate (2 vols., Amsterdam, 1942; Madrid, 1956)

Diego Catalán Menéndez-Pidal, *Poema de Alfonso XI. Fuentes, dialecto, estilo* (Madrid, BRH, 1953)

Coplas de Yoçef. A medieval Spanish poem in Hebrew characters, ed. I. González Llubera (Cambridge, 1935)

Poema de Yúçuf, ed. R. Menéndez Pidal (Colección Filológica 1, Granada, 1952)

——, BAE, LVII

Libro de Buen Amor

ed. Giorgio Chiarini (Documenti di Filologia 8, Milano and Napoli, 1964)

ed. Joan Corominas (Madrid, BRH, 1967)

ed. Manuel Criado de Val and E. W. Naylor (Madrid, CH, 1965)*

ed. Jean Ducamin (Toulouse, 1901)

Félix Lecoy, *Recherches sur le LBA de Juan Ruiz, Archiprêtre de Hita* (Paris, 1938)

LBA Studies, ed. G. B. Gybbon-Monypenny (London, Tamesis, 1970)

María Rosa Lida de Malkiel, *Two Spanish Masterpieces: the Book of Good Love and the Celestina* (Illinois Studies in Language and Literature 49, Urbana, 1961)

Anthony N. Zahareas, *The Art of Juan Ruiz, Archpriest of Hita* (Madrid, 1965)

Ballads

Paul Bénichou, ed., *Romancero judeo-español de Marruecos* (Madrid, 1968)

Agustín Durán, ed *Romancedo general, o colección de romances castellanos anteriores al siglo XVIII* (BAE, X and XVI)

Ángel González Palencia, ed., *Romancero general* (2 vols., Madrid, 1947)

R. Menéndez Pidal, Diego Catalán, *et al.*, ed., *Romancero tradicional* (Madrid, 1957-   )

C. Colin Smith, ed., *Spanish Ballads* (Oxford, 1964)

F. J. Wolf and C. Hofmann, ed., *Primavera y flor de romances* (Berlin, 1856) (repr. with additions, Menéndez y Pelayo, *Antología*, VIII-IX)

Paul Bénichou, *Creación poética en el romancero tradicional* (Madrid, BRH, 1968)

Diego Catalán, *Por campos del romancero. Estudios sobre la tradición oral moderna* (Madrid, BRH, 1970)

——, *Siete siglos de romancero (historia y poesía)* (Madrid, BRH, 1969)

W. J. Entwistle, *European Balladry* (Oxford, 1939)

Ramón Menéndez Pidal, *Romancero hispánico (hispano-portugués, americano y sefardí). Teoría e historia* (2 vols., Madrid, 1953)

——, *Los romances de América y otros estudios* (Buenos Aires, Austral, 1939)

——, Diego Catalán and Álvaro Galmés, *Cómo vive un romance: dos ensayos sobre tradicionalidad* (*RFE* anejo LX, Madrid, 1954)

E. M. Wilson, *Tragic Themes in Spanish Ballads* (Diamante VIII, London, 1958)

Chapter 6

Juan Marichal, *Voluntad de estilo* (Barcelona, 1957)

Franco Meregalli, *Cronisti e viaggiatori castigliani del quattrocento* (Milano and Varese, 1957)

Prosistas castellanos del siglo XV, I, ed. Mario Penna (BAE, CXVI, 1959); II, ed. F. Rubio (BAE, CLXXI, 1964)

Juan Manuel

Obras, ed. J. M. Castro y Calvo and Martín de Riquer, I (Barcelona, CH, 1955) (*Prólogo, Cavallero et escudero, Armas*)

Conde Lucanor, ed. José M. Blecua (Madrid, Clásicos Castalia, 1969)

Libro infinido y Tractado de la Asunçión, ed. José M. Blecua (Colección Filológica II, Granada, 1952)

Libro de los estados, ed. J. M. Castro y Calvo (Madrid, 1968)
Pedro L. Barcia, *Análisis de El Conde Lucanor* (Enciclopedia Literaria 27, Buenos Aires, 1968)
Andrés Giménez Soler, *Don J. M., biografía y estudio crítico* (Zaragoza, 1932)

Martínez de Toledo
Arçipreste de Talavera, ed. Mario Penna (Torino, n.d.)*
——, ed. J. González Muela and Mario Penna (Madrid, Clásicos Castalia, 1970)
Christine J. Whitbourn, *The Arcipreste de Talavera and the Literature of Love* (Occasional Papers in Modern Languages 7, Hull, 1970)
Raúl A. del Piero, *Dos escritores de la baja Edad Media castellana* (*Pedro de Veragüe y el arcipreste de Talavera, cronista real* (Madrid, 1970)

Exemplum-Collections
El libro de los gatos, ed. John E. Keller (Madrid, CH, 1958)
Clemente Sánchez de Vercial, *Libro de los exenplos por A.B.C.*, ed. John E. Keller (Madrid, CH, 1961)
John E. Keller, *Motif-Index of Mediaeval Spanish Exempla* (Knoxville, 1949)

Miscellaneous Didactic Works
Juan de Lucena, *Libro de vida beata*, ed. A. Paz y Melia, *Opúsculos literarios de los siglos XIV a XVI* (SBE, IX, Madrid, 1892), 105-217
Alfonso de Madrigal, *Tractado cómo al ome es nescesario amar*, ed. A. Paz y Melia, ibid., 221-44
Alfonso de la Torre, *Visión deleitable*, BAE, XXXVI
Enrique de Villena, *Los doze trabajos de Hércules*, ed. Margherita Morreale (Biblioteca Selecta de Clásicos Españoles, n.s., 20, Madrid, 1958)
Emilio Cotarelo y Mori, *Don Enrique de Villena. Su vida y obras* (Madrid, 1896)

Chronicles
Crónica de don Álvaro de Luna, ed. Juan de Mata Carriazo (Colección de Crónicas Españolas 2, Madrid, 1940)
Robert B. Tate, *Ensayos sobre la historiografía peninsular del siglo XV* (Madrid, BRH, 1970)

Biographies
Gutierre Diez de Games, *El Victorial. Crónica de don Pero Niño*, ed. Juan de Mata Carriazo (Col. de Cr. Esp., 1, Madrid, 1940)

Leonor López de Córdoba, *Memorias*, CODOIN, LXXXI (Madrid, 1883), 33-44
——, [excerpts], ed. Menéndez Pidal, *Crestomatía*, II, 522-25*
Fernán Pérez de Guzmán, *Generaciones y semblanzas*, ed. R. B. Tate (London, Tamesis, 1965)*
——, ed. J. Domínguez Bordona (Madrid, CC, 1924)
Hernando del Pulgar, *Claros varones de Castilla*, ed. R. B. Tate (Oxford, 1971)
——, ed. J. Domínguez Bordona (Madrid, CC, 1923)

Travel
Ruy González de Clavijo, *Embajada a Tamorlán*, ed. Francisco López Estrada (Nueva Colección de Libros Raros o Curiosos 1, Madrid, 1943)
Pero Tafur, *Andanças e viajes*, ed. M. Jiménez de la Espada (Colección de Libros Españoles Raros o Curiosos 8, 2 vols., Madrid, 1874)
——, ed. José M. Ramos (Madrid, 1934)

Romances
Adolfo Bonilla y San Martín, ed., *Libros de caballerías* (NBAE, VI and XI, Madrid, 1907-08)
Martín de Riquer, *Caballeros andantes españoles* (Madrid, Austral, 1967)
Justina Ruiz de Conde, *El amor y el matrimonio secreto en los libros de caballerías* (Madrid, 1948)
Henry Thomas, *Spanish and Portuguese Romances of Chivalry* (Cambridge, 1920; Spanish transl., with amplified bibliography, *RLit* anejo 10, Madrid, 1952)
Pedro Bohigas Balaguer, *Los textos españoles y gallego-portugueses de la demanda del Santo Grial* (*RFE* anejo VII, Madrid, 1925)
——, ed., *El baladro del sabio Merlín* (3 vols., Selecciones Bibliófilas, n.s. 2, 14, 15, Barcelona, 1957-62)
W. J. Entwistle, *The Arthurian Legend in the Literatures of the Spanish Peninsula* (London, 1925)
G. T. Northup, ed., *El cuento de Tristán de Leonís* (Chicago, 1928)
Karl Pietsch, ed., *Spanish Grail Fragments: El libro de Josep ab Arimatia, La estoria de Merlin, Lançarote* (2 vols., Chicago, 1924)
El libro del cauallero Zifar (El libro del cauallero de Dios), ed. Charles P. Wagner (Ann Arbor, 1929)
——, ed. Martín de Riquer (2 vols., Selecciones Bibliófilas, n.s., Barcelona, 1951)
Gran conquista de Ultramar, BAE, XLIV
La leyenda del cauallero del çisne, ed. E. Mazorriaga (Madrid, 1914)
Amadís de Gaula, ed. Edwin B. Place (4 vols., Madrid, 1959-69)

Historia troyana en prosa y verso, ed. R. Menéndez Pidal and E. Varón Vallejo (*RFE* anejo XVIII, Madrid, 1934) (abridged in *Tres poetas primitivos* [Buenos Aires, Austral, 1948])

Agapito Rey and Antonio García Solalinde, *Ensayo de una bibliografía de las leyendas troyanas en la literatura española* (IUHS 6, Bloomington, 1942)

Barbara Matulka, *The Novels of Juan de Flores and their European Diffusion* (New York, 1931)

Juan Rodríguez del Padrón, *Obras*, ed. Antonio Paz y Melia (SBE, XXII, Madrid, 1884)

Diego de San Pedro, *Obras*, ed. Samuel Gili y Gaya (Madrid, CC, 1950)

——, ed. Keith Whinnom and Dorothy S. Severin (3 vols., Madrid, Clásicos Castalia, 1971-)

La Celestina

ed. Julio Cejador y Frauca (2 vols., Madrid, CC, 1910)
ed. Manuel Criado de Val and G. D. Trotter (Madrid, CH, 2nd ed., 1965)
ed. Dorothy S. Severin (Madrid, 1969)*

J. M. Aguirre, *Calisto y Melibea, amantes cortesanos* (Zaragoza, 1962)
Marcel Bataillon, *La Célestine selon Fernando de Rojas* (Paris, 1961)
Erna R. Berndt, *Amor, muerte y fortuna en La C.* (Madrid, BRH, 1963)
Américo Castro, *La C. como contienda literaria (castas y casticismos)* (Madrid, 1965)
F. Castro Guisasola, *Observaciones sobre las fuentes literarias de la C.* (*RFE* anejo V, Madrid, 1924)
A. D. Deyermond, *The Petrarchan Sources of La C.* (Oxford, 1961)
Fernando Garrido Pallardó, *Los problemas de Calisto y Melibea y el conflicto de su autor* (Figueras, 1957)
Stephen Gilman, *The Art of La C.* (Madison, 1956)
María Rosa Lida de Malkiel, *La originalidad artística de la C.* (Buenos Aires, 1962)
——, *Two Spanish Masterpieces: the Book of Good Love and the C.* (Illinois Studies in Language and Literature 49, Urbana, 1961)
José A. Maravall, *El mundo social de la C.* (Madrid, BRH, 1964)
June H. Martin, *Love's Fools: Aucassin, Troilus, Calisto and the parody of the courtly lover* (London, Tamesis, in press)
Marcelino Menéndez y Pelayo, *Orígenes de la novela*, Ch. 10 (separately published, Buenos Aires, Austral, 1947, as *La C.*)
Carmelo Samonà, *Aspetti del retoricismo nella C.* (Roma, 1954)
Dorothy S. Severin, *Memory in La C.* (London, Tamesis, 1970)

Chapter 7

Eduardo Camacho Guizado, *La elegía funeral en la poesía española* (Madrid, BRH, 1969)

Dorothy C. Clarke, *Morphology of Fifteenth Century Castilian Verse* (Pittsburgh and Louvain, 1964)

Michel Darbord, *La Poésie religieuse espagnole des Rois Catholiques à Philippe II* (Paris, 1965)

Antonio Rodríguez-Moñino, *Poesía y cancioneros (siglo XVI)* (Madrid, 1968)

Julio Rodríguez-Puértolas, *Poesía de protesta en la Edad Media castellana. Historia y antología* (Madrid, BRH, 1968)

Bruce W. Wardropper, *Historia de la poesía lírica a lo divino en la Cristiandad occidental* (Madrid, 1958)

——, ed., *Poesía elegíaca española* (Salamanca, Anaya, 1968)

R. Foulché-Delbosc, ed., *Cancionero castellano del siglo XV* (NBAE, XIX and XXII, Madrid, 1912-15)

Cancioneros

Cancionero de Baena, ed. José M. Azáceta (3 vols., Madrid, CH, 1966)

Charles F. Fraker, *Studies on the Cancionero de Baena* (UNCSRLL 61, Chapel Hill, 1966)

Cancionero de Lope de Stúñiga, ed. Marqués de la Fuensanta del Valle and J. Sancho Rayón (Colección de Libros Españoles Raros o Curiosos 4, Madrid, 1872)

El cancionero de Roma, ed. M. Canal Gómez (Biblioteca Hispano-Italiana 2 and 3, Florencia, 1935)

Le Chansonnier espagnol d'Herberay des Essarts, ed. Charles V. Aubrun (BÉHÉ Hispanique 25, Bordeaux, 1951)

El cancionero de Palacio, ed. Francisca Vendrell de Millás (Barcelona, 1945)

Cancionero general [facsimile of 1511 edition], ed. Antonio Rodríguez-Moñino (Madrid, 1958)

Suplemento al Cancionero general, ed. Antonio Rodríguez-Moñino (Valencia, 1959)

Santillana

Obras, ed. José Amador de los Ríos (Madrid, 1852)

Canciones y decires, ed. Vicente García de Diego (Madrid, CC, 1913)*

Prose and Verse, ed. J. B. Trend (London, 1940)

Josefina Delgado, *El Marqués de Santillana* (Enciclopedia Literaria 41, Buenos Aires, 1968)

Rafael Lapesa, *Los decires narrativos del M. de S.* (Madrid, 1954)

——, *La obra literaria del M. de S.* (Madrid, 1957)

Mena

Laberinto de Fortuna, ed. J. M. Blecua (Madrid, CC, 1943)*
——, ed. John G. Cummins (Salamanca, Anaya, 1968)
María Rosa Lida de Malkiel, *Juan de Mena, poeta del prerrenacimiento español* (México, 1950)
Alberto Vàrvaro, *Premesse ad un'edizione critica delle poesie minori di J. de M.* (Napoli, 1964)

Debates

Dos versiones castellanas de la disputa del alma y el cuerpo del siglo XIV, ed. E. von Kraemer (Helsinki, 1956)
Rodrigo Cota, *Diáloga entre el Amor y un viejo*, ed, Elisa Aragone (Firenze, 1961) [also contains the anonymous sequel]
Francisco Cantera Burgos, *El poeta Ruy Sánchez Cota (Rodrigo Cota) y su familia de judíos conversos* (Madrid, 1970)

Jorge Manrique

Cancionero, ed. Augusto Cortina (Madrid, CC, 1929)
Poesía, ed. J. M. Alda-Tesán (Salamanca, Anaya, 1965)
Anna Krause, *Jorge Manrique and the Cult of Death in the Cuatrocientos* (Publications of the University of California at Los Angeles in Languages and Literatures I, 3, Berkeley, 1937)
Pedro Salinas, *J. M., o tradición y originalidad* (Buenos Aires, 1947)
Antonio Serrano de Haro, *Personalidad y destino de J. M.* (Madrid, BRH, 1966)

Other Poets

Juan Álvarez Gato, *Obras completas*, ed. Jenaro Artiles Rodríguez (Los Clásicos Olvidados IV, Madrid, 1928)
Francisco Márquez Villanueva, *Investigaciones sobre Juan Álvarez Gato. Contribución al conocimiento de la literatura castellana del siglo XV* (BRAE anejo IV, Madrid, 1960)
Danza general de la Muerte, ed. Haydée Bermejo Hurtado and Dinko Cvitanovic (Bahía Blanca, 1966)
——, ed. Margherita Morreale, *ACLLS*, VI (1963)
Patrick Gallagher, *The Life and Works of Garci Sánchez de Badajoz* (London, Tamesis, 1968)
Íñigo de Mendoza, *Cancionero*, ed. Julio Rodríguez-Puértolas (Madrid, CC, 1968)
Julio Rodríguez-Puértolas, *Fray Íñigo de Mendoza y sus Coplas de Vita Christi* (Madrid, BRH, 1968)

Chapter 8

Auto de los reyes magos, ed. R. Menéndez Pidal, *RABM*, IV (1900), 453-62

——, ed. Sebastião Pestana (Lisboa, 1965-66)

Gómez Manrique, *Cancionero*, ed. Antonio Paz y Melia (2 vols., Colección de Escritores Castellanos 36 and 39, Madrid, 1885) (also in Foulché-Delbosc, *Cancionero castellano del siglo XV*, II)

Richard B. Donovan, *The Liturgical Drama in Medieval Spain* (Pontifical Institute of Medieval Studies, Studies and Texts 4, Toronto, 1958)

O. B. Hardison, *Christian Rite and Christian Drama in the Middle Ages. Essays in the origin and early history of modern drama* (Baltimore, 1965)

A. M. Kinghorn, *Mediaeval Drama* (London, 1968)

Fernando Lázaro Carreter, *Teatro medieval* (2nd ed., Madrid, Odres Nuevos, 1965), pp. 9-94

Humberto López Morales, *Tradición y creación en los orígenes del teatro castellano* (Madrid, 1968)

António J. Saraiva, *Gil Vicente e o fim do teatro medieval* (2nd ed., Estudos e Documentos 34, Lisboa, 1965)

N. D. Shergold, *A History of the Spanish Stage from medieval times until the end of the seventeenth century* (Oxford, 1967)

Winifred Sturdevant, *The Misterio de los reyes magos: its position in the development of the mediaeval legend of the three kings* (Johns Hopkins Studies in Romance Literatures and Languages X, Baltimore and Paris, 1927)

INDEX

The English, not the Spanish, alphabetical order is used. Literary works are indexed under the form of the title used in the text (thus Libro del cavallero Zifar *under* Libro, *not* Zifar*); modern scholars are included only where there is discussion (rather than mere citation) of their work, and place-names only where they are significant for the narrative. Monarchs of Castile, or of the unified kingdom of Castile and León, are indexed by name only; in all other cases the name of the country is given.*

Printed in Great Britain by
The Garden City Press Limited, Letchworth, Hertfordshire, SG6 1JS